Microsoft® Office System
Plain & Simple
2003 Edition

Jerry Joyce and Marianne Moon

PUBLISHED BY
Microsoft Press
A Division of Microsoft Corporation
One Microsoft Way
Redmond, Washington 98052-6399

Library of Congress Cataloging-in-Publication Data
Joyce, Jerry, 1950-
   Microsoft Office System Plain & Simple--2003 ed. / Jerry Joyce, Marianne Moon.
       p. cm.
   Includes index.
   ISBN 0-7356-1982-4
     1. Microsoft Office.   2. Business--Computer programs.   I. Title: Microsoft Office system
plain and simple.   II. Moon, Marianne.   III. Title.

HF5548.4.M525J69   2003
005.369--dc22   2003058834

Printed and bound in the United States of America.

5 6 7 8 9   QWT   8 7 6 5

Distributed in Canada by H.B. Fenn and Company Ltd.

A CIP catalogue record for this book is available from the British Library.

Microsoft Press books are available through booksellers and distributors worldwide. For further information about international editions, contact your local Microsoft Corporation office or contact Microsoft Press International directly at fax (425) 936-7329. Visit our Web site at www.microsoft.com/ mspress. Send comments to *mspinput@microsoft.com*.

Acquisitions Editor: Alex Blanton   **Interior Graphic Artist:** Kari Fera
Project Editor: Laura Sackerman   **Typographer:** Kari Fera
Manuscript Editor: Marianne Moon   **Proofreader/Copyeditor:** Alice Copp Smith
Technical Editor: Jerry Joyce   **Indexer:** Jan Wright (Wright Information Indexing Services)

Body Part No. X10-08379

Contents

4 Creating Different Types of Documents — 45

5 Enhancing a Document — 65

6 Working in Excel — 87

7 Analyzing Your Data — 113

8 Presenting Your Data — 135

9 Communicating Using Outlook — 149

10 Managing with Outlook 163

11 Working with a Database 183

12 Creating a PowerPoint Presentation 203

13 Creating a Publication in Publisher 223

14 Creating Web Pages and Web Sites   243

18 Working with Graphics and Objects 305

19 Alternative Ways to Add Content 321

Acknowledgments

This book is the result of the combined efforts of a team of people whose work we trust and admire and whose friendship we have enjoyed for many years. Kari Fera, our typographer, did the work of two people and did it superbly; she not only produced and refined the interior graphics but also laid out the complex design. The quality of her work is such that she makes it look *so* easy (but Kari, we know it's not!). Our dear friend Alice Copp Smith has helped us improve every one of the 11 books we've written. Alice does so much more than proofread and copyedit: Her gentle and witty chiding on countless yellow sticky notes makes us laugh as well as moan and groan, but she teaches us to write better because she's *always* right! And we are fortunate indeed to be able to work with indexer *par excellence* Jan Wright, whose insights reveal in microcosm the soul of any book she puts under her indexing microscope. We thank this dedicated and hardworking trio for their exceptional work and their unwavering good humor in the face of many an impossible deadline.

At Microsoft Press we thank Alex Blanton for asking us to write this book, and Laura Sackerman for her valuable insight and helpful suggestions. Many thanks also to Gregory Beckelhymer and Jim Kramer.

On the home front, as always, Roberta Moon-Krause, Rick Krause, and Zuzu Abeni Krause provided love, laughter, and inspiration, while faithful puppies Baiser and Pierre provided fun with pine cones and champagne corks.

This book is dedicated to the people of The Smile Train. A portion of the authors' proceeds from the sales of this book will be donated to The Smile Train (www.smiletrain.org), an organization that provides free surgery to repair the cleft lips and palates of poor children who would otherwise live their lives in shame and isolation, unable to eat or speak properly, go to school, or smile. The Smile Train provides services and programs in more than 51 countries, including the United States, and gives free training to local surgeons in developing countries so that they can perform the surgeries themselves.

1 About This Book

If you want to get the most from your computer and your software with the least amount of time and effort—and who doesn't?—this book is for you. You'll find *Microsoft Office System Plain & Simple— 2003 Edition* to be a straightforward, easy-to-read reference tool. With the premise that your computer should work for you, not you for it, this book's purpose is to help you get your work done quickly and efficiently so that you can get away from the computer and live your life.

No Computerese!

Let's face it—when there's a task you don't know how to do but you need to get it done in a hurry, or when you're stuck in the middle of a task and can't figure out what to do next, there's nothing more frustrating than having to read page after page of technical background material. You want the information you need—nothing more, nothing less—and you want it now! *And* it should be easy to find and understand.

That's what this book is all about. It's written in plain English— no technical jargon and no computerese. No single task in the book takes more than two pages. Just look up the task in the index or the table of contents, turn to the page, and there's the information you need, laid out in an illustrated step-by-step format. You don't get bogged down by the whys and wherefores: Just follow the steps and get your work done with a minimum of hassle. Occasionally you might have to turn to another page if the procedure you're working on is accompanied by a *See Also*. That's because there's a lot of overlap among tasks, and we didn't want to keep repeating ourselves. We've scattered some useful *Tips* here and there, and thrown in a *Try This* or a *Caution* once in a while. (Every so often, when there's a technical concept we think you might want to know more about, we've written a descriptive sidebar—but you don't have to read it if technical stuff makes you squirm.) By and large, we've tried to remain true to the heart and soul of the book, which is that the information you need should be available to you at a glance, with plain and simple instructions.

Useful Tasks...

Whether you use the programs in the Microsoft Office System on one home computer, on several computers that are part of a home network, in a home office or small-business environment, or in a large corporation, we've tried to pack this book with procedures for everything we could think of that you might want to do, from the simplest tasks to some of the more esoteric ones.

...And the Easiest Way to Do Them

Another thing we've tried to do in this book is find and document the easiest way to accomplish a task. The Office programs often provide a multitude of methods to achieve a single end result, and the variety of choices can be daunting or delightful, depending on the way you like to work. If you tend to stick with one favorite and familiar approach, we think the methods described in this book are the way to go. If you like trying out alternative techniques, go ahead! The intuitiveness of Office invites exploration, and you're likely to discover ways of doing things that you think are easier or that you like better than ours. If you do, that's great! It's exactly what the developers of Office had in mind when they provided so many alternatives.

A Quick Overview

Your new computer might have come with Office preinstalled; otherwise, if you'll be installing it yourself, the Setup Wizard makes installation so simple that you won't need our help anyway. So, unlike many computer books, this one doesn't start with installation instructions and a list of system requirements.

Next, you don't have to read this book in any particular order. It's designed so that you can jump in, get the information you need, and then close the book and keep it near your computer. But that doesn't mean we scattered the information about with wild abandon. We've organized the book into some sections that deal with the individual programs in Office, and some that show you how to use the programs together. If you're new to Office, we recommend that you first read section 2, "Office Basics," for an introduction to the ways in which the programs look and work alike. Try out the step-by-step procedures that are common to most of the programs: creating and working with files, using menus and toolbars, working with task panes and smart tags, formatting text, moving and copying content, printing documents, getting help, and so on. Regardless of which program you're working in, you'll find that the tasks you want to accomplish are always arranged in two levels. The overall type of task you're looking for is under a main heading such as "Using Menus and Toolbars" or "Formatting Your Text." Then, under each of those headings, the smaller tasks within the main task are arranged in a loose progression from the simplest to the more complex.

Sections 3, 4, and 5 are dedicated to Microsoft Office Word, and they take you step by step through the basics to some of the more complex tasks you can accomplish in Word: working with styles, creating bulleted and numbered lists, finding and replacing text, using templates and wizards, creating letters and envelopes, doing a mail merge, working with tables, creating chapters and tables of contents, wrapping text around a picture, adding footnotes, and generally enhancing your documents.

Sections 6, 7, and 8 are about Microsoft Office Excel. Again, we start with the basics: using worksheets and workbooks; entering, editing, copying, and moving data; formatting cells, numbers, and worksheets; and working with multiple workbooks. After the basics, we advance through analyzing data; using cell references, formulas, and functions; troubleshooting formulas; sorting and filtering data; creating charts and PivotTables; working with trendlines and error bars; and a whole lot more.

Sections 9 and 10 focus on Microsoft Office Outlook. Section 9 deals with e-mail: setting up one or more e-mail accounts; sending, receiving, and reading e-mail; replying to and forwarding messages; sending attachments with your e-mail; using Word as your e-mail editor; and sending faxes. Section 10 explores Outlook's ability to manage your Contacts list and your daily, weekly, or monthly schedule. Outlook also enables you to view your workgroup's schedule, which is enormously helpful when you need to get a bunch of busy people together for a meeting.

Section 11 concentrates on Microsoft Office Access—a relational database program. If you need to understand and work with a database, this is a good place to start. You'll find basic information about databases, tables, and forms; and you'll learn how to add data to tables, add tables to a database, extract information from your database, analyze the data with a PivotChart, and define relationships among tables.

Sections 12, 13, and 14 walk you through the creation of a slide-show presentation in Microsoft Office PowerPoint, a well-designed publication in Microsoft Office Publisher, and a Web page or Web site in Microsoft Office FrontPage. PowerPoint makes it easy to create an informative slide show, whether you use a pre-designed presentation or create your own design. You can easily achieve professional looking results with the program's text animation and transition effects, and you can create notes for yourself or a presenter, and printed handouts for your audience. If you're creating a newsletter, menu, brochure, catalog, or any of the myriad other publication types Publisher offers, you'll be inspired! Use a predesigned publication, or create an original design from scratch—no matter which way you go, you'll be surprised at the relative ease with which you can produce a great looking publication. If your goal is to produce a Web page or Web site, you'll find an able assistant in Microsoft Office FrontPage—you'll learn how to customize your page or site, create hyperlinks and hotspots, use tables for laying out your page design, and even learn a bit about HTML code (but only if you want to!). We'll also clue you in on some other, simpler ways to create a Web site.

Sections 15 through 19 describe a mixed bag of tricks. Section 15 is about creating and filling out forms with Microsoft Office InfoPath. If you don't work with forms, you can skip this section; if you do use forms, you'll find good information here about designing forms, using schemas, working with XML code, and so on. Section 16 introduces Microsoft Office OneNote— a useful little program that works like a notebook in which you might jot down notes at a meeting or doodle in the margin, working in a nonlinear way that's alien to most computer programs. Section 17 focuses on the way the Office programs work together. Why use more than one program at a time? Because the powerful features in one program often complement those of another program; drawing on the major strengths of each gives you the best possible result with the least expenditure of time and effort. Section 18 covers everything you ever wanted to know about working with graphics and other objects, including transforming text into art; working with and formatting clip art, drawings, diagrams, and shapes; and wrapping text around pictures. Section 19 offers some intriguing ways to add content to your files—scanning text, using the speech-recognition feature to enter text without all that laborious typing, or using the the Handwriting program to insert hand-written text.

Section 20 is about collaborating with your coworkers. There's a lot of information here about using a SharePoint Web site as a central information hub from which you and your colleagues can access and work simultaneously on your Office files, using the convenience of a shared workspace. You can send out files for review, discuss files on line, and painlessly merge all reviews and comments into a cohesive and well-documented whole. And, when your files are final, go to section 21 for information about fine-tuning your work so that it will look beautiful and won't contain any embarrassing errors. Section 22 shows you how you can customize your Office programs so that they work exactly as you want them to. You can add or remove any Office components (or parts thereof), customize and/or rearrange your toolbars, toolbar buttons, and menus; create your own commands; control your services; and get rid of that Office Assistant if you can't stand it! Section 23, the final section, is dedicated to a topic that's of great concern to computer users worldwide: security for your computer, your files, and your e-mail, and for safe surfing on the Internet.

What's New in Office 2003?

Office has some new features that are immediately obvious: new programs such as InfoPath and OneNote, substantial changes to the look and feel of Outlook, and the introduction of Reading view—a new view you can use in Word and Outlook. Support for the XML format provides smooth interoperability among programs, gives you the ability to extract information from files, and makes for increased productivity with the use of built-in and custom smart tags and Actions buttons. Collaboration with coworkers is much improved, thanks to the tight integration of the Office programs and Microsoft Windows SharePoint Services—a Web service and Web site from which your team can coordinate your activities, store your shared files, and work simultaneously on files in a shared workspace. Security has been enhanced—you can protect portions of a file from changes by coworkers while allowing other sections to be modified by those who have permission to do so. Information Rights Management is another powerful tool that protects your files from changes and even from being viewed by those to whom you or an administrator haven't granted permission.

Other new, but less obvious, features can ease your work substantially. The new Research task pane is a handy way to find information: alternative wording, translations, definitions, and so on. If you use an ink device such as a Tablet PC, you'll find greatly improved support in Office, including the ability to jot down your notes and comments right in the program and have your handwriting saved with the file. You'll find nice little enhancements scattered throughout the Office programs: the ability to compare revised files side by side in Word and Excel; the new Package For CD tool in PowerPoint, which ensures that everything you need for your presentation is copied onto a CD; the advanced commercial printing tools in Publisher that simplify the creation of color separations; the ability to export an Access table to a list in a SharePoint site for your workgroup to view; the side-by-side display of multiple calendars in Outlook; and so much more. Take a stroll through this book and through your Office programs—you'll find all sorts of new features that will help make your work easier and more efficient than ever.

A Few Assumptions

We had to make a few educated guesses about you, our audience, when we started writing this book. Perhaps your computer is solely for personal use—e-mail, the Internet, and so on. Or you might run a small business or work for a giant corporation. After taking these quite varied possibilities into account, we assumed that you're familiar with computer basics—the keyboard, your little friend the mouse, and so on—and that you're connected to the Internet and/or a company intranet. We also assumed that you're familiar with the basics of whichever Windows operating system you're using. If not, we recommend a couple of other books we've written that you'll find helpful: *Microsoft Windows 2000 At a Glance* and *Microsoft Windows XP Plain & Simple.*

A Final Word (or Two)

We had three goals as we wrote this book:

- Whatever you want to do, we want the book to help you get it done.

- We want the book to help you discover how to do things you *didn't* know you wanted to do.

- And, finally, if we've achieved the first two goals, we'll be well on the way to the third, which is for our book to help you *enjoy* using Office. We think that's the best gift we could give you to thank you for buying our book.

We hope you'll have as much fun using *Microsoft Office System Plain & Simple—2003 Edition* as we've had writing it. The best way to learn is by *doing,* and that's how we hope you'll use this book.

Jump right in!

2 Office Basics

The Microsoft Office System is a group of tools, or programs, that you can use individually or in combination with each other. The programs have all been designed to look and work as much like each other as possible, the philosophy being that once you've seen one, you've seen 'em all! Of course, it's not quite that simple because each program has a different purpose, so you'll discover features that are specific to the tasks you'll be working on in certain programs. However, by and large, the look of each program's interface and the way you use its tools—the menus, buttons, dialog boxes, fonts, check boxes, and so on—are basically the same.

So, although this book isn't meant to be read in any particular order, we suggest that you read and try out some of the procedures in this section first. Once you've mastered the basic skills outlined here, you'll have a good working knowledge of the way all the Office programs work. There's a brief description of each program's purpose on the next two pages, followed by step-by-step procedures that are common among most of the programs—creating and working with files; using menus, toolbars, task panes, and smart tags; moving, copying, and formatting text; doing research; making sure your spelling is correct; printing your files; and getting help if you run into problems. You can feel confident knowing that these things all work the same way in all the Office programs.

Once you're armed with the basics—and with this book as your guide—encountering some of the elements that are unique to individual programs won't seem quite so much like sailing into unknown waters.

What's Where in Office?

Here's a listing of all the programs in Microsoft Office, with a brief description of each program's purpose. All the programs share one basic design, although some individual programs have additional features and design elements. As you become familiar with that basic design, you'll find that it's easy to understand the way the programs work as you switch from one to another. Take a look at the windows of a few of the Office programs and note the similar design elements.

Microsoft Office Programs

- Microsoft Office Word: a powerful word processing program for doing everything from writing a letter to writing a novel to Web publishing.

- Microsoft Office Excel: a spreadsheet program for organizing, analyzing, and graphing data.

- Microsoft Office Outlook: an e-mail program as well as a way to manage your contacts, tasks, and schedules.

- Microsoft Office Access: a relational database program for storing, retrieving, and analyzing data.

- Microsoft Office PowerPoint: a program for developing and presenting electronic slide shows with accompanying lecture notes and supporting printed handouts, to be shown on a computer screen or on the Web.

- Microsoft Office Publisher: a desktop publishing program for intricate placement of text and graphics on a printed page or on the Web.

- Microsoft Office FrontPage: a development tool for creating and managing sophisticated and powerful Web sites and Web pages.

- Microsoft Office InfoPath: a program for creating and using forms. The information gathered in the forms is designed to be easily used in other programs.

- Microsoft Office OneNote: a program for taking and using electronic notes via handwriting, typing, or speech, or for copying content from other programs.

- Microsoft Windows SharePoint Services: a program that provides intranet- or Internet-based services for collaboration and communication—for example, file sharing, using message boards, and creating group Web sites.

- Microsoft Office Tools: programs that you can use in conjunction with the main Office programs and that provide resources for such tasks as working in different languages, scanning files, organizing pictures, and transferring your personal Office settings to a different computer.

Title bars

Toolbars

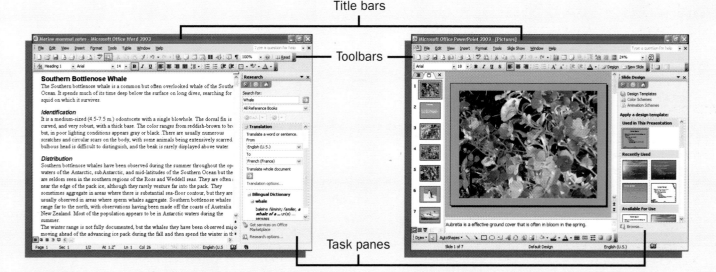

Task panes

Menu bars

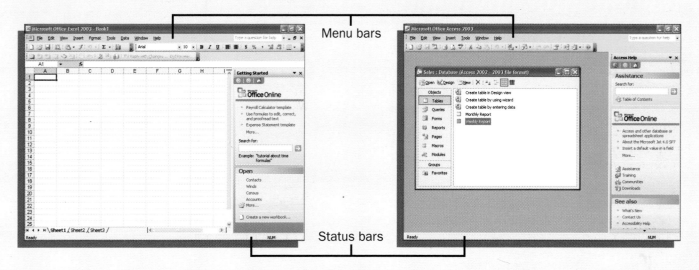

Status bars

Creating a New File

When you want to create a new file—a Word document, an Excel workbook, or an Access database, for example—how do you begin? It's easy—you just start the program. There are several different ways to start, depending on how Office was installed, but the tried-and-true method is to choose the program you want from the Windows Start menu. When the program starts, you're all set to create a new file.

Start an Office Program

(1) Start an Office program from the Windows Start menu.

In Word, Excel, PowerPoint, or FrontPage, click the Close button on the Getting Started task pane, and then start working on the blank file that appears.

(2) Add some content to your file.

In Access, click Create A New File. In the New File task pane that appears, click Blank Database, name and save the database, and then add content to your new database.

In Publisher, click Blank Print Publication, and then start working on the blank publication.

In InfoPath, click Design A Form, and then click New Blank Form on the Design A Form task pane that appears.

Save the File

(1) Click the Save button on the Standard toolbar.

! TIP: After you've named your file, click the Save button or press Ctrl+S periodically as you work. Your program will save the file and all your changes under that file's name, and the Save As dialog box won't keep popping up. It's quick and easy, and you'll never have to worry about losing your work if the computer is accidentally shut off or if there's a power failure.

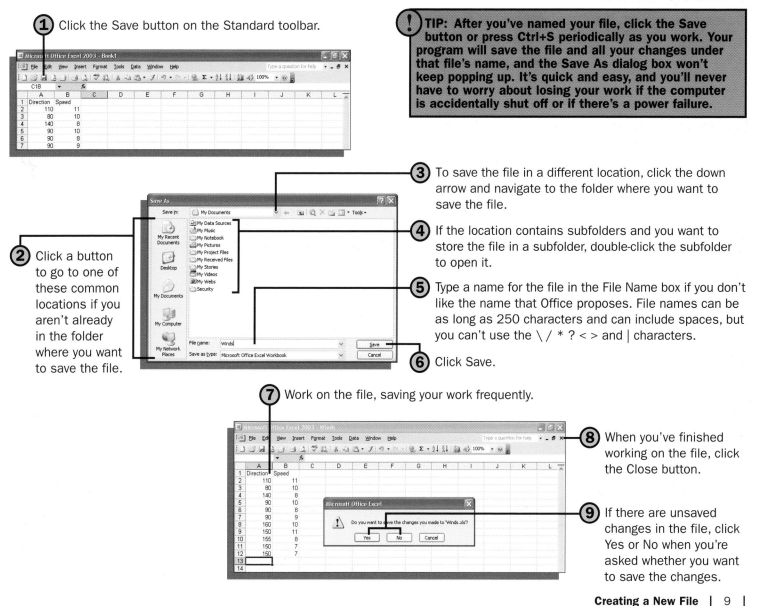

(3) To save the file in a different location, click the down arrow and navigate to the folder where you want to save the file.

(4) If the location contains subfolders and you want to store the file in a subfolder, double-click the subfolder to open it.

(2) Click a button to go to one of these common locations if you aren't already in the folder where you want to save the file.

(5) Type a name for the file in the File Name box if you don't like the name that Office proposes. File names can be as long as 250 characters and can include spaces, but you can't use the \ / * ? < > and | characters.

(6) Click Save.

(7) Work on the file, saving your work frequently.

(8) When you've finished working on the file, click the Close button.

(9) If there are unsaved changes in the file, click Yes or No when you're asked whether you want to save the changes.

Working with an Existing File

Unless you always work on really short projects—a letter, a small spreadsheet, a slide show with just a few slides, for example—you'll often need to continue working on a file that you started but didn't complete in an earlier session. You simply open the saved file, add more content, and then save and close the file again.

! TIP: If the task pane isn't open, and if the file you want to open is one you used recently, it might be listed at the bottom of the File menu. If so, click the file's name to open it. Otherwise, choose Open from the File menu or click the Open button on the Standard toolbar.

Open a File

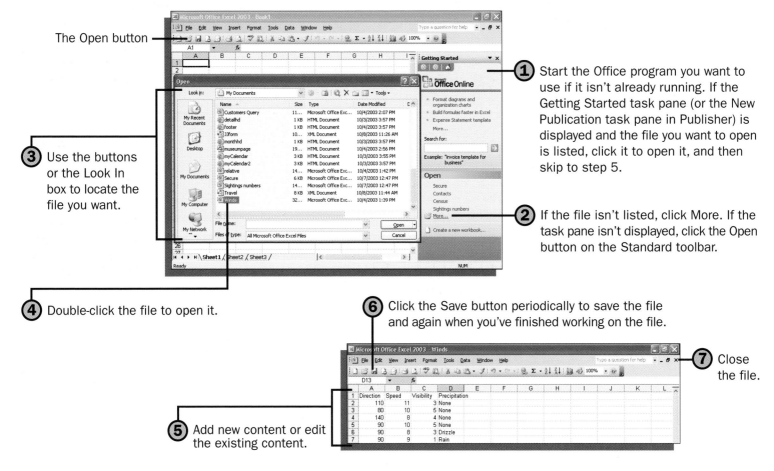

The Open button

1 Start the Office program you want to use if it isn't already running. If the Getting Started task pane (or the New Publication task pane in Publisher) is displayed and the file you want to open is listed, click it to open it, and then skip to step 5.

3 Use the buttons or the Look In box to locate the file you want.

2 If the file isn't listed, click More. If the task pane isn't displayed, click the Open button on the Standard toolbar.

4 Double-click the file to open it.

6 Click the Save button periodically to save the file and again when you've finished working on the file.

7 Close the file.

5 Add new content or edit the existing content.

Finding a File

If you need to work on an existing file but you don't know its name or where it's stored, you can ask your Office program to search for the file, based on any text in the file or on any of the file's properties (date, author, and so on).

TIP: The File Search feature isn't available in InfoPath, Outlook, or OneNote. In Outlook, however, you can use the Find command on the Tools menu to search for messages, contacts, and so on.

Search for a File

(1) Choose File Search from the File menu to display the Basic File Search task pane.

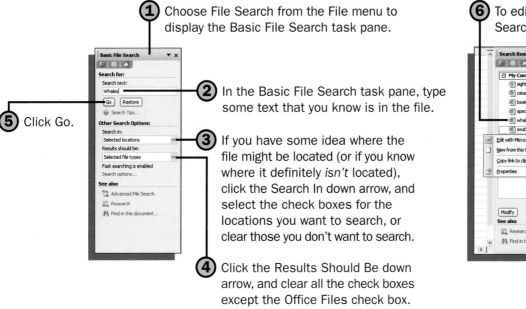

(2) In the Basic File Search task pane, type some text that you know is in the file.

(5) Click Go.

(3) If you have some idea where the file might be located (or if you know where it definitely *isn't* located), click the Search In down arrow, and select the check boxes for the locations you want to search, or clear those you don't want to search.

(4) Click the Results Should Be down arrow, and clear all the check boxes except the Office Files check box.

(6) To edit the file, click its name in the Search Results task pane to open it.

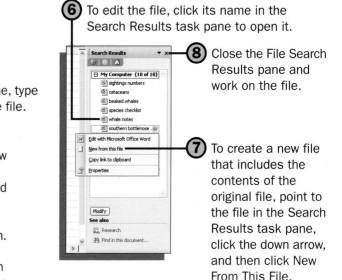

(8) Close the File Search Results pane and work on the file.

(7) To create a new file that includes the contents of the original file, point to the file in the Search Results task pane, click the down arrow, and then click New From This File.

TIP: To search quickly for a file whose name you know, choose Search from the Windows Start menu.

Using Menus and Toolbars

If menus are the gateways to the power of your programs, toolbars are shortcuts to the most frequently used features you can access from the menus. Stored within the menus are *keyboard shortcuts* that speed up your work. And there are even special context-sensitive *shortcut menus* that pop up right in the middle

of your work when you right-click the mouse button. To make your work quick and easy regardless of which Office program you're using, the menus and toolbars all use the same basic structure, with customizations for each program.

> **TIP:** To open a menu without using the mouse, press and release the Alt key and then press the underlined letter in the menu name. Then, to execute a command, press the underlined letter of the command.

Explore the Menus

1 In any Office program, click to open the File menu.

2 Click a right-pointing arrow to see the contents of the submenu.

A submenu

3 If there are two down-pointing arrows at the bottom of the menu, click to display the entire menu.

4 Click to open the Edit menu, and take a look at the items listed. The icon at the left of a menu item is the toolbar button you can use to execute that command. The text at the right of the command is the keyboard shortcut for the command.

5 Continue exploring the different menus in this and other Office programs.

6 To execute any command, click it.

7 To close a menu without executing a command, click outside the menu.

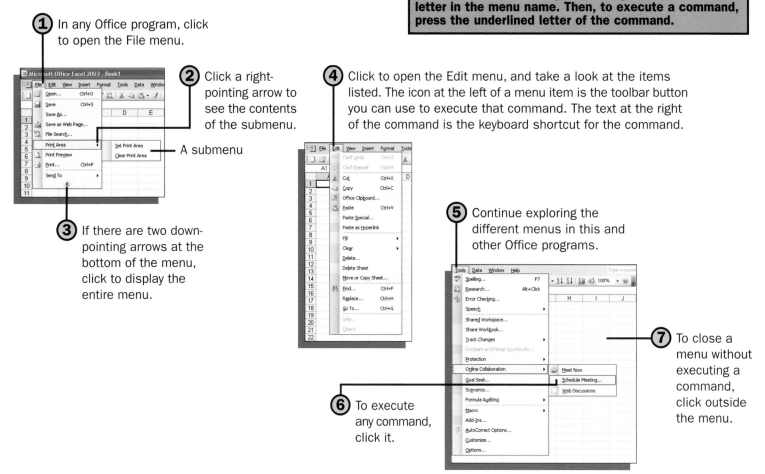

Use Toolbars

① Point to a button on the toolbar and wait for a *ScreenTip*, showing the button's name, to appear. Click the button to execute that action.

② If a button looks "pressed," click it again if you want to turn off that feature.

③ If the toolbar shares a single line with another toolbar and is truncated—that is, part of it isn't visible—click the right-pointing arrows to display the hidden buttons.

Use Shortcut Menus

① Click or select the part of your file where you want to execute an action.

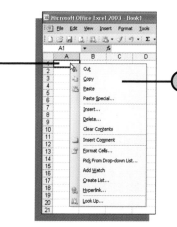

② Right-click the mouse button, and choose the action you want from the context-sensitive shortcut menu that appears.

> **! TIP:** Items that are grayed on the menus or toolbars are items that aren't available at the moment. For example, if you haven't copied anything, the Paste button is grayed because there's nothing to paste.

> **✓ SEE ALSO:** For information about managing and customizing your toolbars and menus, see "Managing Toolbars and Menus" on page 376, "Rearranging Toolbars" on page 377, and "Customizing Toolbars and Menus" on page 380.

Working with Task Panes

Office programs use *task panes* that help you get your work done. Each task pane has a specific purpose—creating a new file, searching for information, using ClipArt, and so on. In most cases, the task pane you need appears almost magically, but you can display a task pane manually and can change which task pane is displayed.

View the Task Panes

1 If no task pane is displayed, choose Task Pane from the View menu to display a task pane.

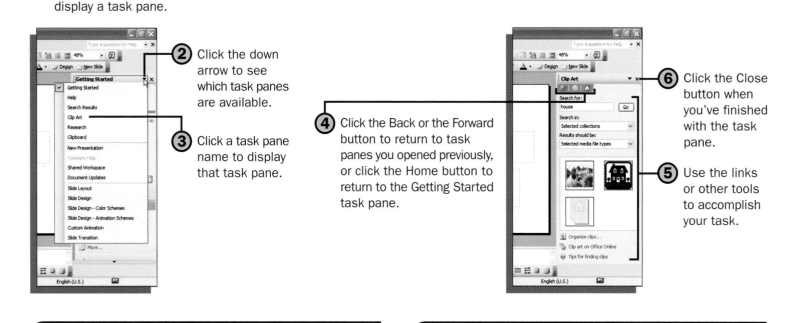

2 Click the down arrow to see which task panes are available.

3 Click a task pane name to display that task pane.

4 Click the Back or the Forward button to return to task panes you opened previously, or click the Home button to return to the Getting Started task pane.

6 Click the Close button when you've finished with the task pane.

5 Use the links or other tools to accomplish your task.

Using Smart Tags

Word, Excel, PowerPoint, and Outlook (when you're using Word as your e-mail editor) provide many different types of *smart tags,* and you can add new and custom-designed smart tags. Despite some differences, smart tags have a common structure, so you can easily figure out how to manage and use them. Basically, the program you're using searches your file for certain recognizable text elements (names, phone numbers, stock symbols, and so on) and, when it finds one of them, attaches a smart tag to it. You use the smart tag to obtain additional information about an item or to perform some type of action.

Manage the Tags

(1) Choose AutoCorrect Options from the Tools menu, and, on the Smart Tags tab of the AutoCorrect dialog box, select this check box to use smart tags.

(2) Select or clear the check boxes to choose which smart tags you want to use.

(3) In Excel, select this option to display both indicator and button. In Word, select the Show Smart Tag Actions Buttons check box, if it isn't already selected.

(4) In Excel or PowerPoint, select this option to have the tags embedded and saved with the file.

(5) Click OK.

Use the Tags

(1) Point to a smart tag indicator in your file.

(2) Click the Actions button that appears.

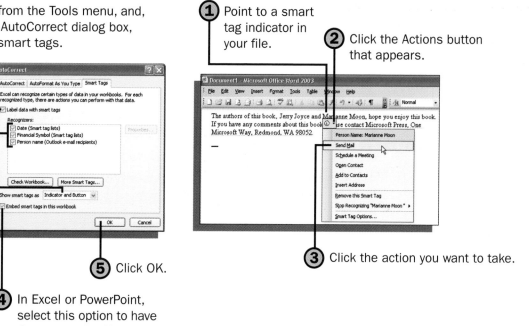

(3) Click the action you want to take.

! TIP: Smart tag indicators are purplish-red dotted lines in Word and PowerPoint, and purplish-red triangles in Excel.

SEE ALSO: For information about using Word as your e-mail editor, see "Using Word for E-Mail Messages" on page 158.

Formatting Your Text

Sometimes, as creativity flows from your brain to the computer, you'll want to create a special look for certain characters or words. You might want to change the size of the characters or use an especially distinctive font. You might want a few words—in a heading, for example—to be bolder than the rest of the text to emphasize their importance. Not all items can be formatted, of course—you can't apply bold or italic formatting to a picture, for example.

Change the Font or Font Size

(1) Select the text you want to format. If the text is contained in cells in an Excel worksheet, select the cells.

(2) Click the down arrow at the right of the Font list on the Formatting toolbar.

(!) TIP: In most cases, you'll want to use a font that displays the TrueType symbol (a double "T") at the left of its name. TrueType fonts look the same on the screen as when they're printed, so you can see an accurate representation of what your printed file will look like.

(3) Scroll through the list to find the font you want to use. Click the font.

(4) Click the down arrow at the right of the Font Size list on the Formatting toolbar. Click the font size you want to use. If the size isn't listed, type the size you want in the box.

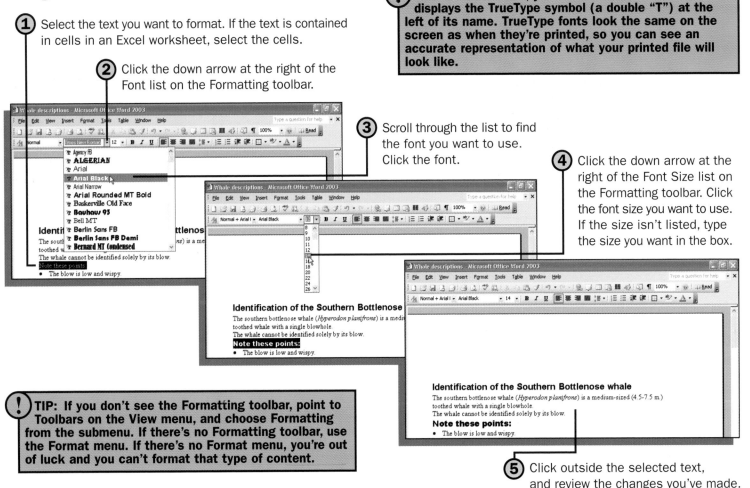

(!) TIP: If you don't see the Formatting toolbar, point to Toolbars on the View menu, and choose Formatting from the submenu. If there's no Formatting toolbar, use the Format menu. If there's no Format menu, you're out of luck and you can't format that type of content.

(5) Click outside the selected text, and review the changes you've made.

Apply Emphasis

 1 Select the text you want to format.

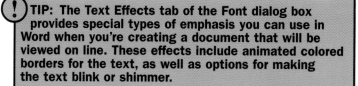

2 Click an emphasis button on the Formatting toolbar. To apply more than one characteristic (for example, both bold and italic), click the second emphasis button.

3 If you don't see the emphasis you want, choose Font from the Format menu.

4 On the Font tab of the Font dialog box, select as many check boxes as necessary to apply the emphasis or the effect you want.

5 Click OK.

6 Click outside the selected text, and review your formatting changes.

> ⚠ **TIP: The Text Effects tab of the Font dialog box provides special types of emphasis you can use in Word when you're creating a document that will be viewed on line. These effects include animated colored borders for the text, as well as options for making the text blink or shimmer.**

Moving and Copying Content

Office programs use a tool called the *Clipboard* as a temporary holding area for text and other content that you want to move (cut) or copy to another part of your file, to another file in the same program, or to a file in another Office program. You simply park your text on the Clipboard and then, when you're ready, you retrieve it and "paste" it into its new location. The Office programs use two different Clipboards: the Windows Clipboard, which stores the single item that was most recently cut or copied; and the Office Clipboard, which can store as many as 24 different items, including the most recently cut or copied item. You'll probably use the Paste button when you're pasting the last item you cut or copied, and the Office Clipboard when you want to move several different pieces of text from one place to another.

Cut or Copy Content

① Select the content to be cut or copied.

② Do either of the following:

- Click the Cut button to delete the selected content and store it on the Clipboard.
- Click the Copy button to keep the selected content where it is and place a copy on the Clipboard.

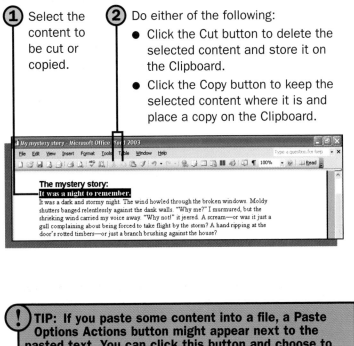

> **!** **TIP:** If you paste some content into a file, a Paste Options Actions button might appear next to the pasted text. You can click this button and choose to have the inserted text match either the formatting of its source or the formatting of its new location. The Paste Options Actions button appears only in files that contain extensive formatting, including those created in Word, Excel, Publisher, PowerPoint, and OneNote.

Paste the Cut or Copied Content

① Click in your file where you want to insert the content.

② Click the Paste button.

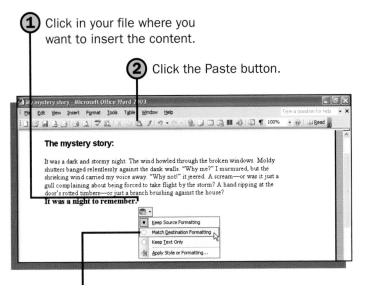

③ If the Paste Options Actions button appears, click it, and specify how you want the content inserted.

> **!** **TIP:** You can use both the Windows Clipboard and the Office Clipboard to store different types of items, including text, pictures, tables, data from worksheets, and even whole charts.

Copy and Paste Multiple Items

① If the Office Clipboard task pane isn't displayed, choose Office Clipboard from the View menu.

② In this file, or in any Office file, select and then cut or copy the items you want. If necessary, switch to the file into which you want to paste some or all of the items you cut or copied.

③ Click where you want to insert one of the items.

⑤ To paste all the items you copied into one location, click Paste All.

⑥ Click Clear All when you no longer need any of the copied items and want an empty Clipboard to collect and store new items.

④ Click the item you're inserting. Continue inserting, cutting, and copying text as necessary.

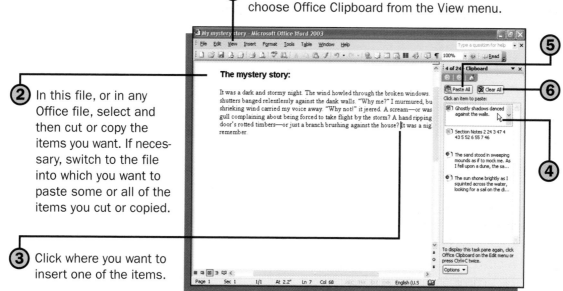

!TIP: Click the Options button at the bottom of the Clipboard task pane to customize the Clipboard for the way you like to work.

!TIP: Although the Windows Clipboard is limited to storing only one item at a time, you can use it to transfer information among many different programs, including non-Office programs. The Office Clipboard works only with Office programs.

SEE ALSO: For information about using OneNote to store information from different sources and then to insert the information into different files, see "Transferring Information" on page 289.

Researching a Subject

Wouldn't it be great if you could look up the definition of a word or even translate it into another language just by clicking the word? Or get information about a place simply by clicking its name? Well, we have good news for you! You can do just that with the research feature that's built into most Office programs.

Do Some Research

(1) Point to a word (or select a group of words) that you want information about, hold down the Alt key, and click the left mouse button.

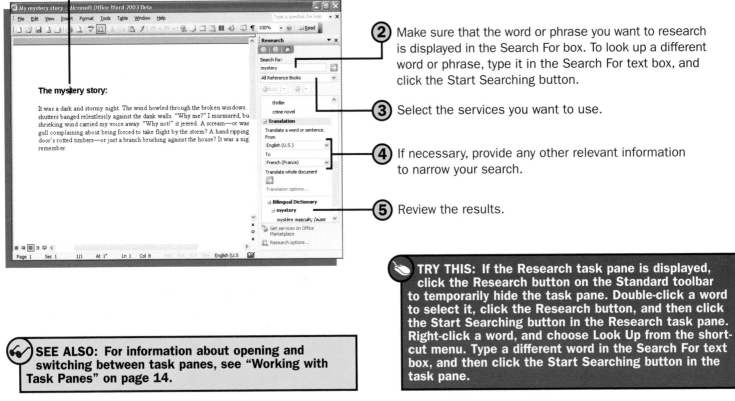

The mystery story:

(✓) SEE ALSO: For information about using Word as your e-mail editor, see "Using Word for E-Mail Messages" on page 158.

(✋) CAUTION: A currency symbol next to a result means there's a fee for retrieving the information.

(2) Make sure that the word or phrase you want to research is displayed in the Search For box. To look up a different word or phrase, type it in the Search For text box, and click the Start Searching button.

(3) Select the services you want to use.

(4) If necessary, provide any other relevant information to narrow your search.

(5) Review the results.

(✎) TRY THIS: If the Research task pane is displayed, click the Research button on the Standard toolbar to temporarily hide the task pane. Double-click a word to select it, click the Research button, and then click the Start Searching button in the Research task pane. Right-click a word, and choose Look Up from the short-cut menu. Type a different word in the Search For text box, and then click the Start Searching button in the task pane.

(✓) SEE ALSO: For information about opening and switching between task panes, see "Working with Task Panes" on page 14.

Getting Help

Nothing can replace this book, of course, but Office does provide you with other resources to help solve any problems you might encounter. Office's Help system has several different ways to render assistance.

Interrogate Office

(1) Click in the Type A Question For Help box, and type a word or phrase that describes a specific problem or an area in which you're having a problem. Press Enter.

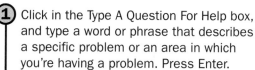

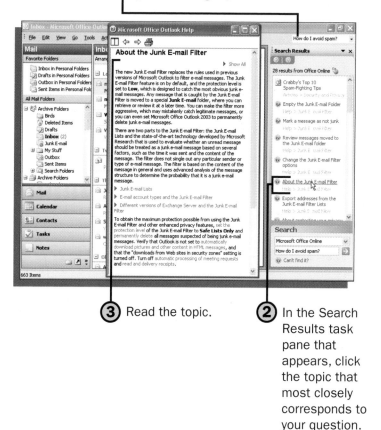

(3) Read the topic.

(2) In the Search Results task pane that appears, click the topic that most closely corresponds to your question.

Get More Help

(1) Press the F1 key (or choose Microsoft Help from the Help menu) to display the Help task pane.

(2) Click the Table Of Contents link if you want to browse the Help files on your computer by topic.

(3) Click to view featured topics on Microsoft Office Online.

(4) Click to get additional online information, training, and help.

> **(!) TIP:** If you're familiar with the Office Assistant and you miss it, you can make it appear by choosing Show The Office Assistant from the Help menu. To hide the Office Assistant again, right-click it, and choose Hide from the shortcut menu.

> **(!) TIP:** If your computer is connected to the Internet, Office's Help system will search the Office Online Web site. If you're not connected, only the Help files that are installed on your computer will be searched.

Printing

Printing a file is a similar process in most Office programs, although some programs might have a few more options than others do. The basics: Designate the printer you're going to use, preview your file to make sure it's going to turn out the way you want it, select what gets printed, and then send the file to the printer.

Select a Printer

1 Choose Print from the File menu to display the Print dialog box.

2 If the printer you want to use isn't listed, select it in the list of printers.

3 Click Properties (if available) to specify options such as color and print quality for the selected printer.

4 Click the Close button (or the Cancel button if you made no changes to the printer).

Preview the Printing

1 When your file looks just the way you want, choose Print Preview from the File menu to open the preview window.

2 Use the buttons at the top of the preview window to adjust what you're viewing and how you view it. Each program has its own set of buttons, depending on the settings needed to properly view its file.

3 Click the Close button when you've finished.

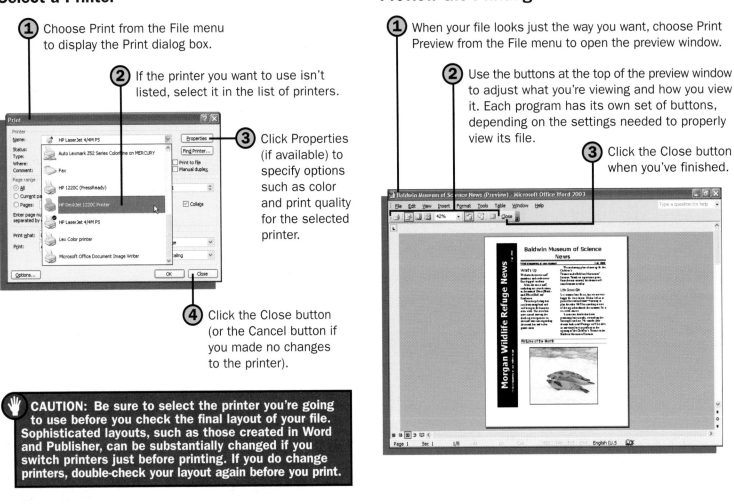

CAUTION: Be sure to select the printer you're going to use before you check the final layout of your file. Sophisticated layouts, such as those created in Word and Publisher, can be substantially changed if you switch printers just before printing. If you do change printers, double-check your layout again before you print.

Print a File

① After you've made any necessary corrections to your file and previewed it again to make sure the layout is correct, choose Print from the File menu to display the Print dialog box.

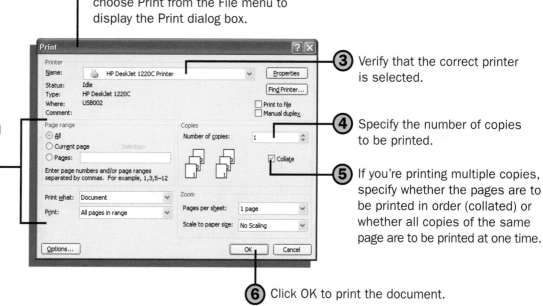

② Specify whether you want to print the entire document, a single page, some selected text, or a range of pages.

③ Verify that the correct printer is selected.

④ Specify the number of copies to be printed.

⑤ If you're printing multiple copies, specify whether the pages are to be printed in order (collated) or whether all copies of the same page are to be printed at one time.

⑥ Click OK to print the document.

SEE ALSO: For information about printing from a specific program, see "Printing a Word Document" on page 64, "Printing a Worksheet" on page 110, and "Printing Your Publication" on page 242.

TIP: The Selection option in the Page Range section of the Print dialog box is available only if you've selected some content in your file prior to choosing the Print command.

TIP: If you want to print additional files and don't need to change any settings in the Print dialog box, you can quickly print a file by clicking the Print button on the Standard or the Print Preview toolbar (or on the Database toolbar in Access).

TRY THIS: Choose Print from the File menu of several different Office programs. You'll notice that although the Print dialog boxes are similar, each has been adapted to the features and abilities of the individual program.

Correcting Your Spelling

You can avoid the embarrassment of distributing a file full of misspellings even if you don't have a proofreader or an editor at your disposal. Office comes to the rescue by discreetly pointing out your spelling errors. When you see one of those helpful little squiggles under a word in Word, PowerPoint, Publisher, and OneNote, you can choose what you want to do to correct the mistake—if it really is a mistake.

Correct a Spelling Error

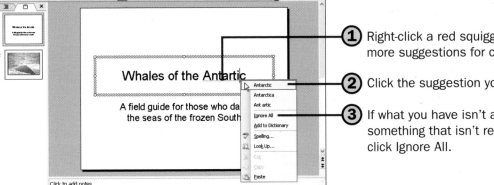

TIP: If your file isn't being automatically checked for spelling errors, press the F7 key, or choose Spelling from the Tools menu. In Excel, Access, and FrontPage, the Spelling dialog box appears whenever you run a spelling check. Use this dialog box to find and correct any errors.

TIP: If Office didn't offer any suggestions when you right-clicked a squiggle, return to your file and try to correct the error yourself. If the squiggle remains, right-click it, and see if there are any suggestions now.

(1) Right-click a red squiggle to see one or more suggestions for correcting the error.

(2) Click the suggestion you want to use.

(3) If what you have isn't an error but merely something that isn't recognized by Office, click Ignore All.

SEE ALSO: For information about checking your spelling in different languages, see "Proofreading in Another Language" on page 362.

For information about checking grammar problems, see "Reviewing Your Grammar in Word" on page 366.

TIP: If you see either a blue or a green squiggle while you're correcting your spelling errors in Word, don't despair. A green squiggle means there's a problem with your grammar, and a blue squiggle indicates formatting inconsistencies, which you can correct now or at another time.

3 Working in Word

After getting used to a new gizmo or gadget, invention or innovation, haven't you said to yourself, "What did I *do* before this came along?" Plastic wrap, sticky notes, microwave ovens, the Internet…the list is endless. If you're familiar with Microsoft Office Word, you've probably asked yourself that very question. And we'll bet that if you haven't used Word before, you'll soon hear yourself saying those eight little words!

This section of the book introduces you to Word 2003. Look through the visual glossary on the next two pages to see the multitude of tools and features Word offers. It's a good idea to jump right in and go exploring—opening menus and drop-down lists, clicking buttons, selecting check boxes, and turning options on and off to see what happens. You'll learn a lot about Word and the way it works by simply trying to accomplish a task. Once you realize how intuitive Word is, you'll find it easy and rewarding to explore and try things out—in other words, you'll learn by doing. If you get stuck when you try one of the more advanced tasks, you'll find the answers to most of your questions in other sections of this book, or in Word's Help system.

In the pages that follow we've covered many of the skills you'll use every day—editing and formatting text, creating lists, finding and replacing text, setting up the page so that it looks the way you want when it's printed, and so on. You'll find information about the different ways you can view your Word documents and why you'd choose one view over another. You'll also find out why there are so many different ways to accomplish routine tasks such as selecting text prior to moving or copying it. What did you ever do before Word came along?

What's Where in Word?

Microsoft Word has many faces and can be customized in countless ways. The pictures on these two pages show many of the common features you'll see when you're working with Word, and they also introduce just a few of the customizations you can use. We've identified many of the screen elements for you, but it's a good idea to explore Word's interface while you're looking at these two pages. For example, open each of the menus and get to know the names of the commands. If you're not sure what the buttons on the toolbars are used for, point to one of them. In a moment or two, you'll see a ScreenTip that tells you the button's name and usually gives you a pretty good idea of the tool's function.

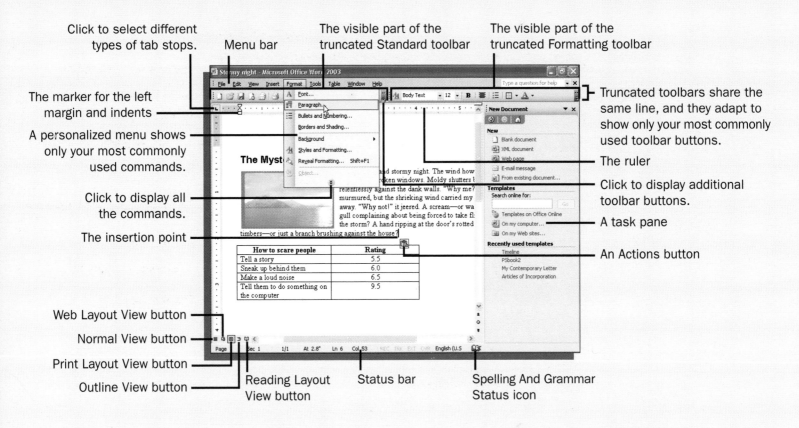

Click to select different types of tab stops.

Menu bar

The visible part of the truncated Standard toolbar

The visible part of the truncated Formatting toolbar

The marker for the left margin and indents

A personalized menu shows only your most commonly used commands.

Click to display all the commands.

The insertion point

Truncated toolbars share the same line, and they adapt to show only your most commonly used toolbar buttons.

The ruler

Click to display additional toolbar buttons.

A task pane

An Actions button

Web Layout View button

Normal View button

Print Layout View button

Outline View button

Reading Layout View button

Status bar

Spelling And Grammar Status icon

The picture below shows the Word interface with just a few changes. As you use Word and experiment with its multitude of options, you'll realize that the customizations shown here illustrate only some of the *many* ways you can view Word's interface. You can see more toolbars, including a floating toolbar, and many toolbar buttons that were hidden, in the picture on this page.

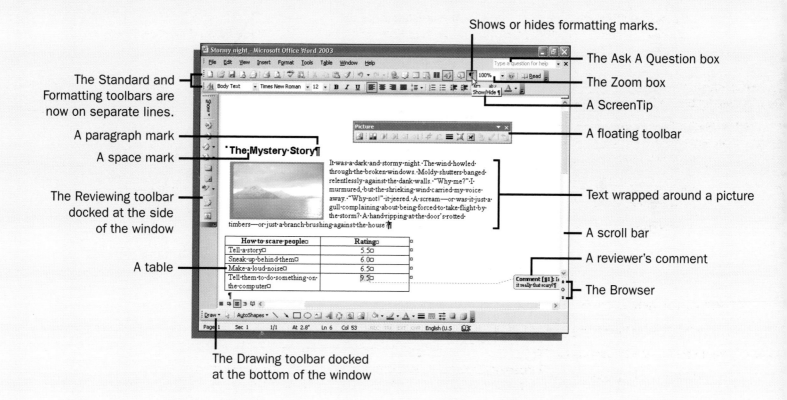

Shows or hides formatting marks.

The Ask A Question box

The Standard and Formatting toolbars are now on separate lines.

The Zoom box

A ScreenTip

A paragraph mark

A space mark

A floating toolbar

The Reviewing toolbar docked at the side of the window

Text wrapped around a picture

A scroll bar

A table

A reviewer's comment

The Browser

The Drawing toolbar docked at the bottom of the window

Editing Text

Whether you're creating a business letter, a financial report, or the Great American Novel, it's a sure bet that you're going to need to go back into your document to do some editing. Word provides a great variety of ways to edit. To edit existing content, you simply select it and make your changes.

Select and Modify Text

TIP: If you delete text by accident, immediately click the Undo button on the Standard toolbar to restore the deleted text.

SEE ALSO: For information about starting a new document, see "Creating a New File" on page 8.

For more information about different ways to select text, see "So Many Ways to Do It" on pages 40–41.

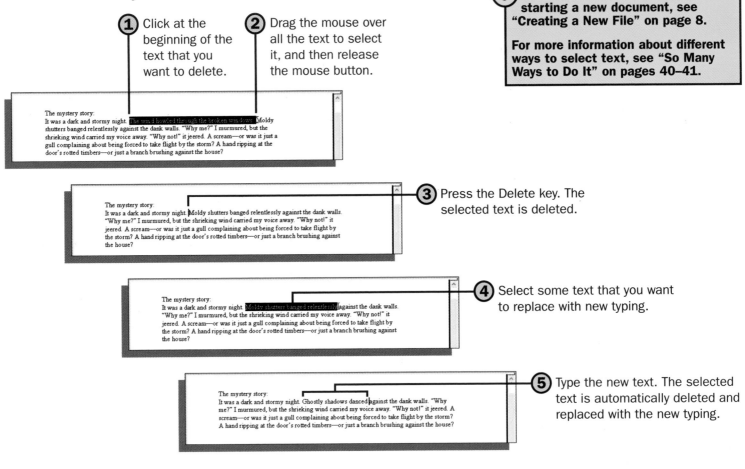

1 Click at the beginning of the text that you want to delete.

2 Drag the mouse over all the text to select it, and then release the mouse button.

3 Press the Delete key. The selected text is deleted.

4 Select some text that you want to replace with new typing.

5 Type the new text. The selected text is automatically deleted and replaced with the new typing.

Formatting Text

Rarely, except possibly in an e-mail message, is a document composed of just plain text, with all the paragraphs in the same font and font size and with the same indents and line spacing. Word provides many predefined paragraph styles that you can use to give your documents that professional look.

> **TIP:** If you don't see a style that appeals to you or that's appropriate for your document, click All Styles in the Show list at the bottom of the Styles And Formatting task pane.

Apply a Style

(1) Type your text without worrying about the formatting, and then click in the paragraph that you want to format.

(2) Click the Styles And Formatting button on the Formatting toolbar.

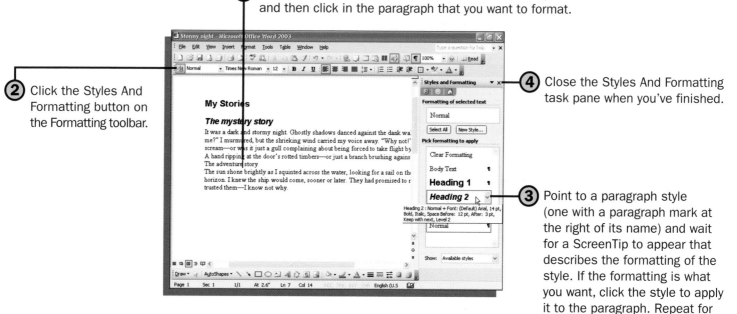

(4) Close the Styles And Formatting task pane when you've finished.

(3) Point to a paragraph style (one with a paragraph mark at the right of its name) and wait for a ScreenTip to appear that describes the formatting of the style. If the formatting is what you want, click the style to apply it to the paragraph. Repeat for any other paragraphs you want to format.

> **SEE ALSO:** For information about styles and different ways of formatting text and other content, see "Templates, Styles, Wizards, and Direct Formatting" on pages 48–49.
>
> For information about arranging each toolbar on a separate line, see "Customizing Toolbars and Menus" on page 380.

Formatting Your Document

Word offers you many ways to format the content of your document. However, we think the easiest way to turn out a good-looking document is to create the content of the document first, without worrying about any formatting, and then go back through the document using styles to apply the formatting you want.

Apply Preset Formatting

(1) After you've created your document based on the appropriate template, click the Styles And Formatting button.

A heading paragraph style

A phrase formatted with a character style

Paragraphs formatted with a list style

A table formatted with a table style

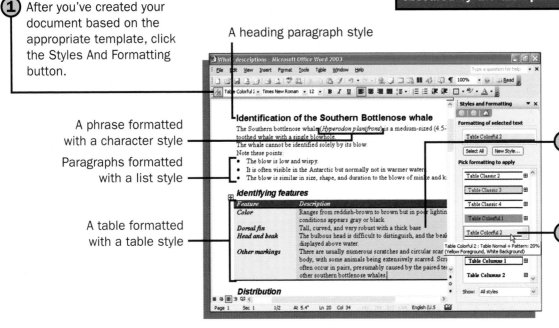

TRY THIS: If the Styles And Formatting task pane (or any other task pane, for that matter) hides some of your text, you can set the view so that all the text is visible. To do this, click the Normal View button at the bottom left of the Word window (if you aren't already in Normal view). Choose Options from the Tools menu, and, on the View tab, select the Wrap To Window check box. Click OK. Now your text won't be obscured by the task pane.

(2) In your document, click in a paragraph or a table; or select a series of characters, a word, or a group of words that you want to format.

(3) In the Styles And Formatting task pane, click the style you want to apply. If the style you want isn't listed, click All Styles in the Show list to see a long list of all the styles available from your template. Then locate and click the style or the formatting you want to use. Continue applying styles until you're happy with the look of the document.

TIP: If you're accustomed to applying styles using the Style drop-down list on the Formatting toolbar, don't despair! You can still use the Style list, but give the Styles And Formatting task pane a try—you might find it easier and more powerful than the Style list.

Reapply Custom Formatting

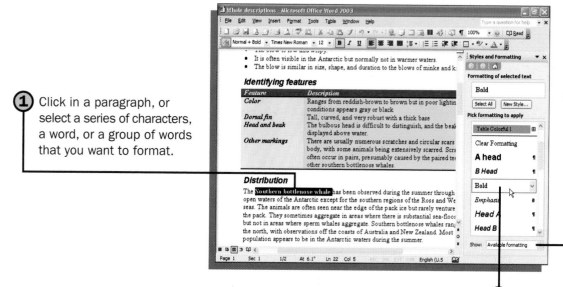

(1) Click in a paragraph, or select a series of characters, a word, or a group of words that you want to format.

(2) In the Styles And Formatting task pane, click Available Formatting in the Show list to see any custom formatting that has already been used, any styles that have already been used, and your custom styles and the common heading styles available in the template.

(3) Click the formatting you want to apply.

(!) **TIP:** Any direct formatting you apply will be displayed only if you've set Word to track the formatting. To do so, choose Options from the Tools menu, select the Keep Track Of Formatting check box on the Edit tab, and click OK.

TRY THIS: You can "steal" font formatting from a paragraph style without applying the style to the entire paragraph. Type some text in a document, and then select a word in a sentence. Display the Styles And Formatting task pane, and click the Heading 1 style. Select another word in the document, and click the Heading 2 style. Continue experimenting with different styles. Finally, select the entire paragraph, and click Clear Formatting in the Styles And Formatting task pane to restore the paragraph to its original state.

SEE ALSO: For information about applying formatting that isn't part of an existing style, see "Formatting Your Text" on page 16 and "Custom-Formatting a Paragraph" on page 32.

For information about using templates, see "Templates, Styles, Wizards, and Direct Formatting" on pages 48–49, "Customizing a Template" on page 56, and "Designing a Template" on page 58.

Custom-Formatting a Paragraph

When none of the existing paragraph styles is exactly right, you can create a custom style to achieve the look you want. However, if this is the only instance of the paragraph you'll ever need, you can design the formatting for that one-time-only paragraph.

TIP: If you're not sure which screen elements are which, point to each item and wait for the ScreenTip to tell you the item's name. If a ScreenTip doesn't appear, choose Options from the Tools menu. On the View tab, select the ScreenTips check box, and click OK.

TIP: If the ruler isn't displayed, choose Ruler from the View menu.

Modify a Paragraph

1. Select the entire paragraph you want to format.

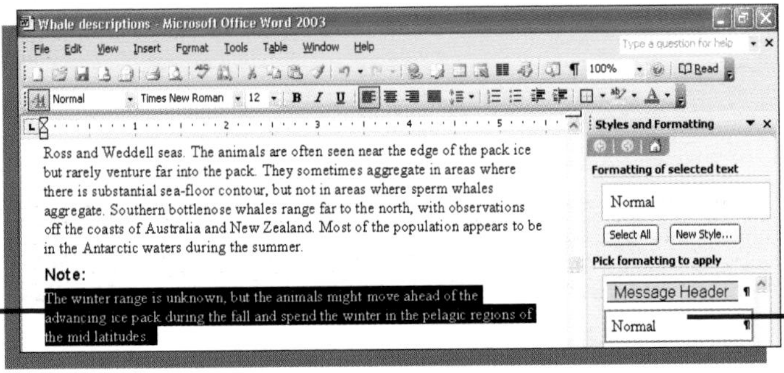

2. Use the Styles And Formatting task pane to apply a style that's as close as possible to the way you want the paragraph to look. Close the Styles And Formatting task pane.

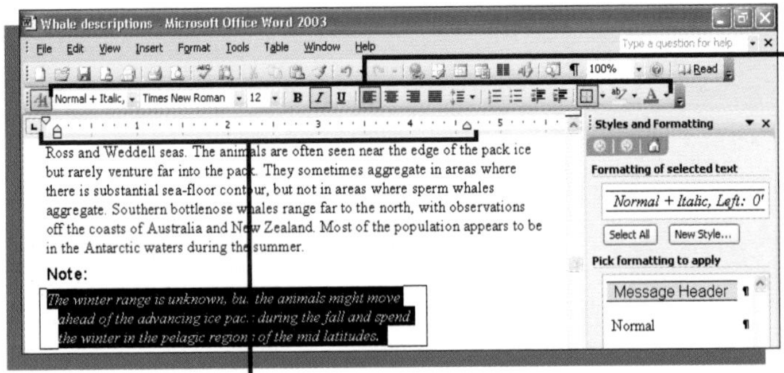

3. Use the buttons and lists on the Formatting toolbar to change any or all of the following characteristics of the paragraph:
   - Font, font size, font color
   - Character emphasis
   - Paragraph alignment
   - Line spacing
   - List style (numbered or bulleted)
   - Borders

4. Drag the Left Indent, First-Line Indent, and Right Indent markers to set the indents for the paragraph. Click outside the paragraph, and review your formatting.

Creating a Bulleted or Numbered List

A great way to present information briefly yet clearly is to put it into a numbered or bulleted list. Not only does Word add numbers or bullets to your list, with consistent spacing between the number or bullet and the text, but it keeps track of the items in a numbered list so that if you move one of them, Word will renumber the list to keep the items in the correct order.

Create a List

> **TIP:** Sometimes, between the items in a numbered list, you might want to insert unnumbered paragraphs that aren't part of the list. You can control whether the numbering of the items in the part of the list that follows the unnumbered paragraphs should continue the numbering from the previous item or restart the numbering. To do so, right-click the paragraph following the unnumbered paragraph, and click either Restart Numbering or Continue Numbering.

> **SEE ALSO:** For information about using AutoFormat to create a bulleted or numbered list, see "Set the Automatic Changes" on page 39.

> **TRY THIS:** Create a list. When you've entered the last item, press Enter twice.

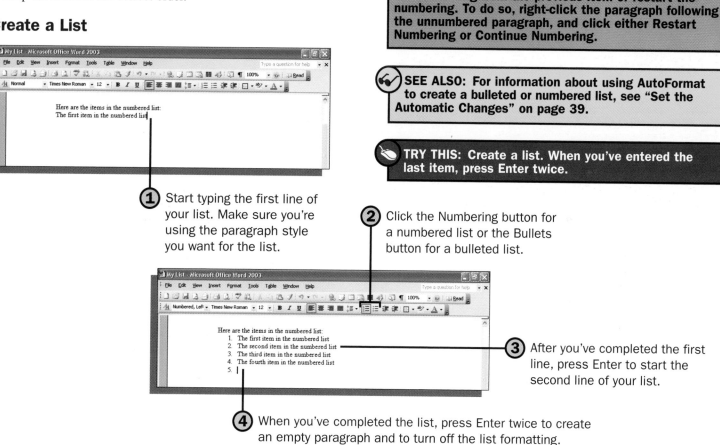

1. Start typing the first line of your list. Make sure you're using the paragraph style you want for the list.

2. Click the Numbering button for a numbered list or the Bullets button for a bulleted list.

3. After you've completed the first line, press Enter to start the second line of your list.

4. When you've completed the list, press Enter twice to create an empty paragraph and to turn off the list formatting.

So Many Ways to View It

Word gives you several ways to view your document as you work on it, and you'll find that your efficiency increases and your work becomes easier when you use the correct view for the task at hand. You can use the View menu or the five view buttons at the bottom left of the window to change your view.

Normal View

Normal view is designed for speed of entry and editing. It's based on the commercial publishing technique of creating *galleys*. You place the text and other elements in one long, continuous column that flows from one page to the next, and you deal with the placement of elements after you've ironed out any content problems.

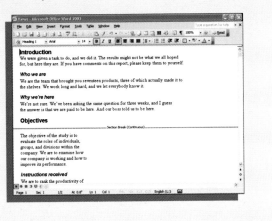

Web Layout View

Web Layout view is exclusively for working with online documents just as though they're Web pages. All the elements are displayed, but font size, line length, and page length all adjust to fit the window—just like a Web page.

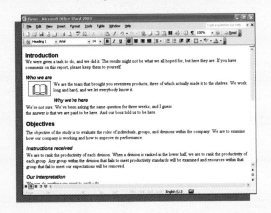

Print Layout View

The standard working view for print documents, Print Layout view shows you how your document will look when it's

printed—the placement of pictures, the arrangement of columns, the distance of the text from the edge of the page, and so on.

Outline View

Outline view displays your document as an outline, with the paragraph formatting defining the levels of the outline. By default, Word's standard heading styles have corresponding outline levels—Heading 1 is level one, Heading 2 is level two, and so on—and other paragraph styles, such as Normal, are treated as regular text. You can use Outline view to organize your topics before you start writing, or you can use it to reorganize an existing document.

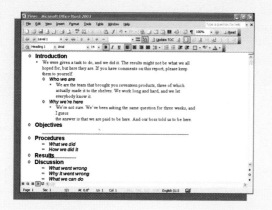

Reading Layout View

Reading Layout view is designed to make it easy to read documents on your screen. The text is laid out in long vertical pages (or screens) like those you see in most books. If you increase the size of the text for better readability, the content simply flows from one screen to the next. To maximize the area of the screen that's available for the document's content, the elements you normally see in the other views—the Standard toolbar and the status bar, for example—are no longer visible. You can also display thumbnail pictures of all the pages or use the Document Map to jump to specific pages or topics.

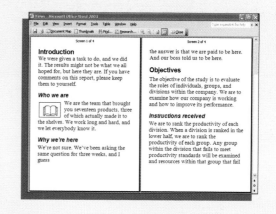

Although these five views are the ones you'll probably use most often, there are other views and options that are useful in various circumstances: Print Preview, Web Page Preview, Full Screen View, Document Map, draft font, picture placeholders, and more. You'll find information about these items in the discussions of the tasks and procedures where their use is the most relevant.

Setting Up the Page

When you create a document that's going to be printed, you need to tell Word how you want the page to be set up—what size paper you're using, whether the page will be printed in landscape or portrait orientation, the size of the margins, and so on. If the document will be printed on both sides of the paper or is going to be bound, you can tell Word to accommodate those design elements. A good template will set up the specifics for you, but you might need to readjust the settings to get everything exactly right.

Set Up a Standard Page

① Choose Page Setup from the File menu to display the Page Setup dialog box.

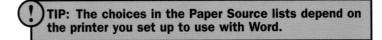

TIP: The choices in the Paper Source lists depend on the printer you set up to use with Word.

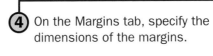

② On the Paper tab, verify that the correct paper size is selected. If it isn't, specify the size of the paper you're using. If the paper size isn't listed, click Custom Size in the Paper Size list, and specify the dimensions of the paper.

③ If you're using a printer that has multiple paper trays, specify the tray for the first page (for example, the tray that contains the letterhead paper) and the tray for all subsequent pages.

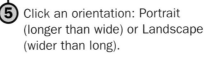

④ On the Margins tab, specify the dimensions of the margins.

⑤ Click an orientation: Portrait (longer than wide) or Landscape (wider than long).

TIP: The gutter is the extra space you add to the margin where the document is to be bound so that the text won't disappear into the binding.

⑥ Click OK.

Set Up for a Two-Sided Document

(1) Choose Page Setup from the File menu to display the Page Setup dialog box.

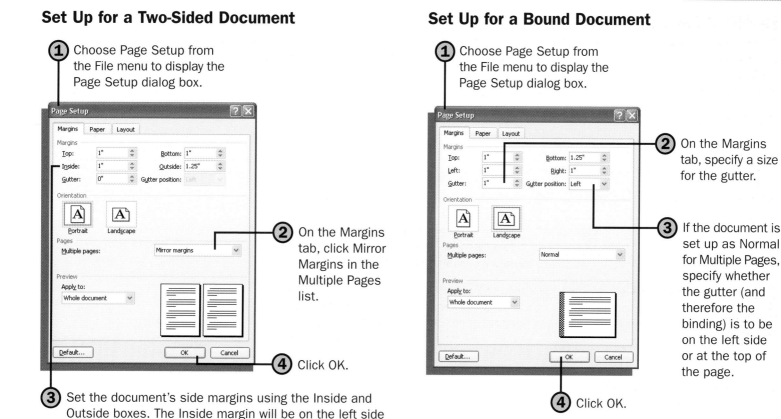

(2) On the Margins tab, click Mirror Margins in the Multiple Pages list.

(4) Click OK.

(3) Set the document's side margins using the Inside and Outside boxes. The Inside margin will be on the left side of odd-numbered (right-hand, or *recto*) pages and on the right side of even-numbered (left-hand, or *verso*) pages.

Set Up for a Bound Document

(1) Choose Page Setup from the File menu to display the Page Setup dialog box.

(2) On the Margins tab, specify a size for the gutter.

(3) If the document is set up as Normal for Multiple Pages, specify whether the gutter (and therefore the binding) is to be on the left side or at the top of the page.

(4) Click OK.

(!) TIP: You can apply a gutter to any document layout. However, you can specify the gutter location (left or top) only if you're printing a single page on a sheet of paper (that is, Normal is specified in the Multiple Pages list). In all other cases, Word uses the default location for the gutter for the type of layout you've chosen. Use the preview to see the placement of the gutter.

Formatting as You Compose

Some people like to create the content of a document first and then go back and format it. Others prefer to do the formatting while they're creating the content. When you're typing, the easiest way to apply styles or direct character formatting is to use special keyboard shortcuts so that you don't need to take your hands off the keyboard. Word can give you extra help by automatically formatting some text for you, provided you've told it to do so.

Format Your Text

1 Start typing the content of your document. Make sure that nothing is selected and that the insertion point is in the paragraph you want to format. Press the keyboard shortcut for the style you want, or use the Styles And Formatting task pane to specify a style.

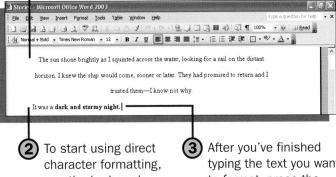

2 To start using direct character formatting, use the keyboard shortcut to turn on the formatting you want, or click a tool on the Formatting toolbar. Then type your text.

3 After you've finished typing the text you want to format, press the same keyboard shortcut or click the same formatting tool to turn off the formatting.

Common Formatting Keyboard Shortcuts

Formatting	Keyboard shortcut
Bold	Ctrl+B
Italic	Ctrl+I
Underline a single letter	Ctrl+U
Underline a whole word	Ctrl+Shift+W
Small capital letters	Ctrl+Shift+K
Superscript	Ctrl+Shift++ (plus sign)
Subscript	Ctrl+= (equal sign)
Single line spacing	Ctrl+1
Line-and-a-half spacing	Ctrl+5
Double line spacing	Ctrl+2
Blank line before a paragraph	Ctrl+0 (zero)
Center a paragraph	Ctrl+E
Left-align a paragraph	Ctrl+L
Right-align a paragraph	Ctrl+R
Justify a paragraph	Ctrl+J
Heading 1 style	Ctrl+Alt+1
Heading 2 style	Ctrl+Alt+2
Heading 3 style	Ctrl+Alt+3
Normal style	Ctrl+Shift+N
List style	Ctrl+Shift+L

> **!** **TIP: Word provides many more keyboard shortcuts than those listed here. Type** keyboard shortcuts **in the Type A Question For Help box, and press Enter. You can also define your own keyboard shortcut for a style when you create or modify a style.**

> **!** **TIP: You can use keyboard shortcuts to format existing text. To do so, select the text, and then use the keyboard shortcuts instead of the tools on the Formatting toolbar or the commands on the Format menu.**

Set the Automatic Changes

(1) Choose AutoCorrect Options from the Tools menu to display the AutoCorrect dialog box.

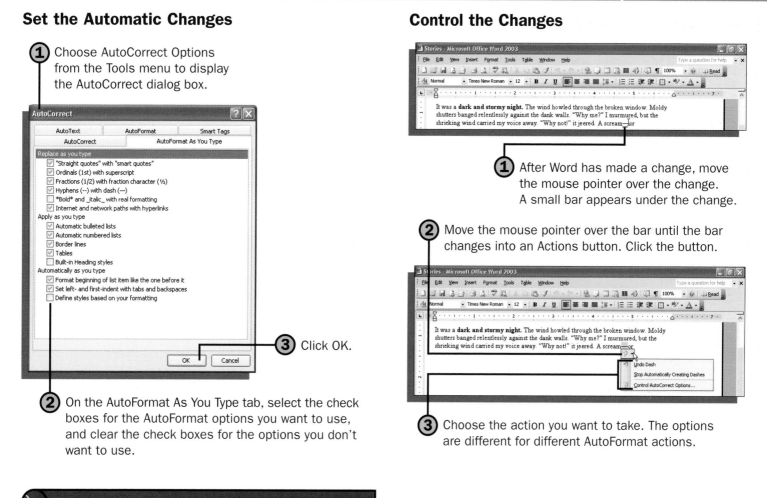

(3) Click OK.

(2) On the AutoFormat As You Type tab, select the check boxes for the AutoFormat options you want to use, and clear the check boxes for the options you don't want to use.

TRY THIS: Make sure that all the options on the AutoFormat As You Type tab are turned on. Type *Fruit. Apples and Oranges.* **Press Enter, and type** Grain. Wheat and Rye. **Press Enter, turn off the Bullets button on the Formatting toolbar, type ---- and press Enter. Then type +----+----+ and press Enter. Now try to figure out which AutoFormat As You Type feature caused which effect!**

Control the Changes

(1) After Word has made a change, move the mouse pointer over the change. A small bar appears under the change.

(2) Move the mouse pointer over the bar until the bar changes into an Actions button. Click the button.

(3) Choose the action you want to take. The options are different for different AutoFormat actions.

So Many Ways to Do It

Microsoft Word offers you a variety of ways to do most things. You might, for example, be able to use a button, a menu item, a key combination, a task pane, or a mouse-click to accomplish the same result. Why are there so many choices? Well, one reason is that we all work differently. Given several choices, we usually do some experimenting, find the way that works best for us and that we're most comfortable with, and then stick with it. Another reason is that certain methods work best in certain situations.

Two procedures that you'll be using frequently—selecting text and moving or copying text—can be accomplished with quite a few different methods, some of which might cause you a bit of difficulty if you use them in the wrong situation. The tips we offer here will help you choose which method to use in which circumstances.

Try these common methods of selecting text and see which works best for you. Of course, there are other ways to select text, and, depending on whether and how you've customized Word, some selection methods might work a bit differently from those described here. For information about customizing Office, see section 22, "Customizing Office," starting on page 373.

Text-Selection Methods

To select	Use this method
Characters in a word	Drag the mouse over the characters.
A word	Double-click the word.
Several words	Drag the mouse over the words.
A sentence	Hold down the Ctrl key and click anywhere in the sentence.
A line of text	Move the pointer to the far left of the window, and click when you see a right-pointing arrow.
A paragraph	Move the pointer to the far left of the window, and double-click when you see a right-pointing arrow.
A long passage	Click at the beginning of the passage, and then hold down the Shift key and click at the end of the passage.
Nonadjacent blocks of text	Drag the mouse to select the first block. Hold down the Ctrl key and drag the mouse to select the second block.
A vertical block of text	Click at the top-left corner of the text block. Hold down the Alt key and drag the mouse over the text block.
The entire document	Choose Select All from the Edit menu, or press Ctrl+A.

After you've selected the text, your next step might be to move it or copy it. Again, some methods are better than others, depending on the situation. The process of moving or copying contents uses different tools, depending on what you want to do. When you use the F2 key or the Shift+F2 key combination, the selected material is stored in Word's short-term memory, where it's remembered only until you paste it into another location or execute any other Office activity.

The Cut and Copy buttons on the Standard toolbar store the selected material on the very single-minded Windows Clipboard, from where you can retrieve the information once or numerous times. The information you've stored on the Windows Clipboard stays there until you replace it with another item or until you shut down Windows. The Windows Clipboard is more than just a holding area, though—it's also a pathway through which you can transfer your cut or copied information to other documents or programs. Although the *Windows* Clipboard stores only one item at a time, the *Office* Clipboard stores up to 24 items, which you can retrieve one at a time or all at once. For more information about the Office Clipboard, see "Moving and Copying Content" on page 18.

If you're feeling overwhelmed by the number of ways in which you can accomplish the same tasks, hold onto your hat—there are more! If you really want to explore all the different ways to do these tasks, take a stroll through Word's Help files and try out some of the other methods.

Moving and Copying Methods

To do this	Use this method
Move a short distance	Drag the selection to the new location.
Copy a short distance	Hold down the Ctrl key, drag the selection to the new location, and release the Ctrl key.
Move a long distance or to a different document or program	Click the Cut button, click at the new location, and click the Paste button. OR press Ctrl+X, click at the new location, and press Ctrl+V.
Copy a long distance or to a different document or program	Click the Copy button, click at the new location, and click the Paste button. OR press Ctrl+C, click at the new location, and press Ctrl+V.
Copy several items and insert all of them in one place	Choose Office Clipboard from the Edit menu, click the Copy button, select the next item, click the Copy button again, and repeat to copy up to 24 items. OR hold down the Ctrl key, select multiple items, and then click the Copy button. Click at the new location, and then click the Paste All button in the Clipboard task pane.
Move a long or short distance	Press the F2 key, click at the new location, and press Enter.
Copy a long or short distance	Press Shift+F2, click at the new location, and press Enter.

Finding Text

If you're not sure where to find some text in your document, Word can locate it for you. You can broaden the search so that Word finds similar words, or you can narrow the search to a designated part of the document or to text that uses specific formatting.

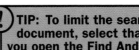
TIP: To limit the search to only a specific part of a document, select that part of the document before you open the Find And Replace dialog box.

Find Text One Instance at a Time

(1) Choose Find from the Edit menu to display the Find And Replace dialog box.

(2) Type the text you want to find.

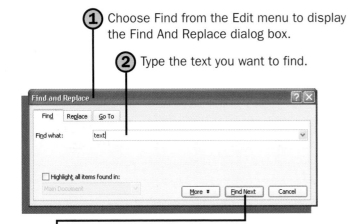

(3) Click Find Next. Continue clicking Find Next to move through the document, finding each instance of the text.

Find All Instances of Text

(1) Select this check box to find and select (that is, to highlight) every instance of the text.

(2) Specify Main Document to search the entire document.

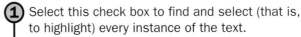

(3) Click Find All to view every instance of the selected text.

TRY THIS: If you choose to select all instances of certain text but then you edit only one instance, all the other instances of the text will no longer be selected. To edit each instance of the text, search for the first instance, make your edit, and then click Find Next to go to the next instance of the text to edit it.

TIP: When you use the Find Next command, the Select Browse Object button at the bottom of the vertical scroll bar automatically uses the information you entered in the Find And Replace dialog box. To find text again after you've closed the dialog box, click the Next Find/GoTo button below the Select Browse Object button.

Modify the Search

 1 Click the More button, if it's displayed, to show the full dialog box.

3 Select the check box or check boxes you need in order to customize the search:

- Match Case to find only text that exactly matches the capitalization of the text in the Find What box

- Find Whole Words Only to find text only if the matching text consists of whole words, not parts of words

- Use Wildcards to use certain characters as wildcard characters

- Sounds Like to find words that sound the same but are spelled differently (*their* and *there*, for example)

- Find All Word Forms to find all words that are forms of the word (its plural or its past tense, for example) in the Find What box

 2 Select Up, Down, or All to specify whether you want to search all or part of the document. (This option is available only if the Highlight All Items Found In check box is *not* selected.)

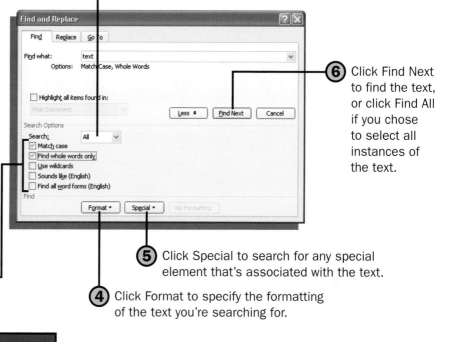

6 Click Find Next to find the text, or click Find All if you chose to select all instances of the text.

5 Click Special to search for any special element that's associated with the text.

4 Click Format to specify the formatting of the text you're searching for.

TRY THIS: In your document, type To be or not to be is asked too often. **In the Find What box, type** o?t **and select the Use Wildcards check box. Click Find Next until the entire selection has been searched. Then change the Find What text to** o*t **and repeat the search. Then use** to **as the search text, select the Sounds Like check box, and search the document. Finally, use** is **as the search text, select the Find All Word Forms check box, and search the document. Note the different results.**

TIP: "Wildcard" characters are used to represent other characters. The most commonly used wildcards are ? (question mark) and * (asterisk). The ? wildcard represents any single character, and the * wildcard represents any number of characters. For a complete list of wildcards, select the Use Wildcards check box, and click the Special button.

Replacing Text

When you need to replace a word or phrase with a different word or phrase in several places in your document, let Word do it for you. It's a great way to use Word's speed and power to make quick work of those tedious document-wide changes.

! TIP: If you used the Replace All button and the results aren't what you expected, click the Undo button on the Standard toolbar. You can then try the replacement again, this time with more specific search parameters.

Replace Text

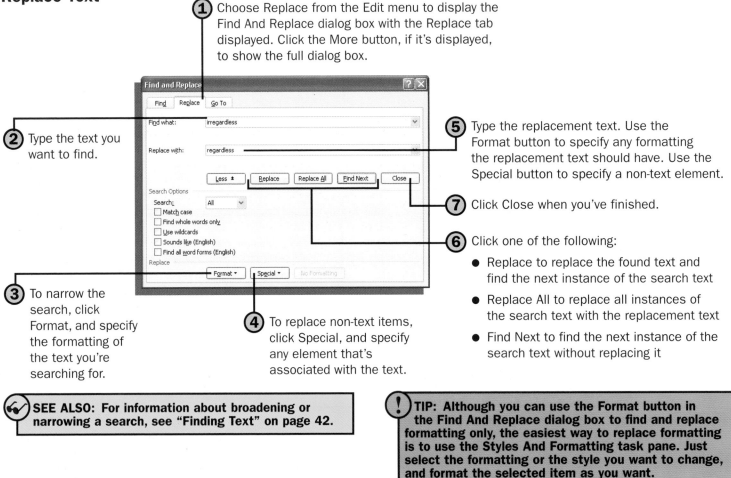

1 Choose Replace from the Edit menu to display the Find And Replace dialog box with the Replace tab displayed. Click the More button, if it's displayed, to show the full dialog box.

2 Type the text you want to find.

3 To narrow the search, click Format, and specify the formatting of the text you're searching for.

4 To replace non-text items, click Special, and specify any element that's associated with the text.

5 Type the replacement text. Use the Format button to specify any formatting the replacement text should have. Use the Special button to specify a non-text element.

7 Click Close when you've finished.

6 Click one of the following:

- Replace to replace the found text and find the next instance of the search text
- Replace All to replace all instances of the search text with the replacement text
- Find Next to find the next instance of the search text without replacing it

SEE ALSO: For information about broadening or narrowing a search, see "Finding Text" on page 42.

! TIP: Although you can use the Format button in the Find And Replace dialog box to find and replace formatting only, the easiest way to replace formatting is to use the Styles And Formatting task pane. Just select the formatting or the style you want to change, and format the selected item as you want.

4 Creating Different Types of Documents

Even if you don't have the time, the inclination, or the experience to design the documents you use every day, you can still produce professional-looking, well-designed letters and envelopes, memos, faxes, reports, brochures, and even a thesis or two. You do this by using templates, styles, and wizards—the principal tools Microsoft Office Word 2003 provides for creating, designing, and maintaining consistency throughout the documents you work with every day. Depending on your desired end result and how little or how much involvement you want in the design, you can use the predesigned elements, or you can create your own styles and templates or modify existing ones so that they're tailored more precisely to your needs. Whether you're creating a long, detailed report or business proposal or simply changing the design of your company's letter template, you'll wonder how you ever managed to get your work done on time without templates, styles, and wizards.

"Okay," you ask, "you say it's easy enough to create a letter and an envelope, but I have to send letters out to a bunch of people. How do I do that?" You use the marvelous mail merge feature—an incredible time-saver when you need to send the same information to a few individuals or to a large group of people. You provide a main document and a data source (names and addresses, for example), and Word combines, or *merges*, the information into a new, personalized document. You can create form letters, envelopes, mailing labels, and so on, as well as incorporate data from Microsoft Office Excel and Microsoft Office Access into mail-merged documents. And last but not least, in this section you'll find the details about printing your Word documents.

Using Word's Templates

Word comes loaded with useful templates that you can use to quickly create your documents. When you start a new document based on a template, the document contains its own design elements, and the template's predefined styles ensure that all your paragraphs work together.

Start the Document

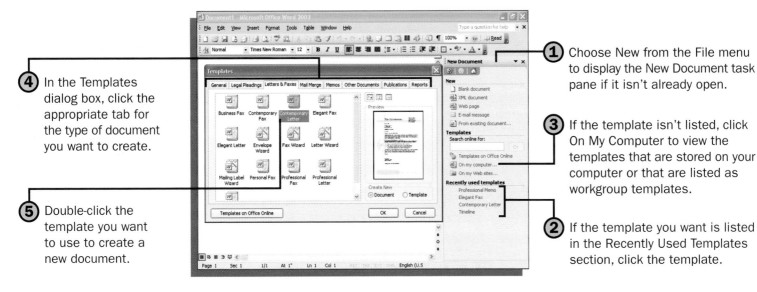

TIP: The New Document task pane works as a control center. You can use it to edit an existing document, create a new blank document, create a new document based on an existing document, or create a new document based on a template.

(4) In the Templates dialog box, click the appropriate tab for the type of document you want to create.

(5) Double-click the template you want to use to create a new document.

(1) Choose New from the File menu to display the New Document task pane if it isn't already open.

(3) If the template isn't listed, click On My Computer to view the templates that are stored on your computer or that are listed as workgroup templates.

(2) If the template you want is listed in the Recently Used Templates section, click the template.

TIP: If you or someone in your company set up your templates to be stored either on your personal Web site or on a Microsoft SharePoint Web site, click On My Web Sites to access those templates. To access additional templates prepared by Microsoft that weren't included with Word, click Templates On Office Online in the New Documents task pane.

TIP: Some items in the Templates dialog box are listed as "wizards." These are special tools that step you through a series of dialog boxes to help you create your document. In most cases, the wizards also provide the opportunity to select a specific template.

Complete the Document

(3) Save the document with the file name you want, in the location you want.

(4) If the Show/Hide ¶ button on the Standard toolbar isn't already turned on, click it so that you can see all the elements in the template.

(2) Read the placeholder text, if any, that tells you how to complete the template.

Document2 - Microsoft Office Word 2003

File Edit View Insert Format Tools Table Window Help

Type a question for help

Company Name ▾ Times New Roman ▾ 30 ▾ B I U

[Click here and type return address]¶

Company·Name·Here¶

October 2, 2003¶

[Click here and type recipient's address]¶

Dear Sir or Madam: ¶

Type your letter here. For more details on modifying this letter template, double-click this icon: ✉ . To return to this letter, use the Window menu ¶

Sincerely, ¶

[Click here and type your name]¶
[Click here and type job title]¶

Page 1   Sec 1   1/1   At 1.2"   Ln 2   Col 18   English (U.S.

(5) Replace any placeholder text with your own text.

(6) If Word automatically inserts information such as the date, don't modify the information—it was inserted using a Word field that's automatically updated and formatted.

(7) If there are paragraphs that tell you to "Click here...", do so, and then insert the appropriate text.

(1) If you aren't already in Print Layout view, click the Print Layout View button.

(8) Don't delete any of the special design elements—doing so could ruin the layout of the document. Complete the document, and then save, print, and distribute it.

CAUTION: Don't delete any paragraph marks—they contain your paragraph formatting. If you delete a paragraph mark, you'll lose any special formatting that was designed for that specific paragraph.

SEE ALSO: For information about modifying templates, see "Customizing a Template" on page 56.

For information about creating your own templates, see "Designing a Template" on page 58.

Templates, Styles, Wizards, and Direct Formatting

Templates and styles are invaluable. They're quick ways of applying formatting and layouts, and they help you maintain consistency throughout a document and throughout all documents of the same type.

Wizards are interactive programs within Word that help you easily use styles and templates to create specialized documents. If a style doesn't supply exactly what you want, you can change the look by directly modifying the formatting.

Templates

A template is both a blueprint for your document and a container that holds the specialized tools you need to work on the document: styles, AutoText, toolbars, macros, page-layout specifications, and view settings. A template can also contain text, graphics, and any other elements that will always be included in the documents you create using that template. You can use a template as is, modify it to fit your needs, or create your own template.

Word always uses the Normal template, which contains Word's predefined styles and default content. When you make changes to this global template, the changes are available to all your documents. You can also use a specialized template that contains information specific to a certain type of document. In this case, the contents of the Normal template *and* the contents of the specialized template are available to your document. If there's a conflict (if the two have different formatting for a Heading 1 style, for example), the contents of the specialized template take precedence over those of the Normal template. For example, when you choose Blank Document from the New Document task pane,

Word uses only the Normal template; when you choose a different type of document, Word uses the specialized template for that document *and* the Normal template.

Your templates can be located in a variety of places. The Normal template and the other templates that came with Word are usually stored on your computer, in the same folder as your personal settings. That way, each user of your computer has his or her own templates. Another set of templates, the Workgroup templates, might be stored in a network location so that everyone on that network has access to the same templates. That way, only one copy of a template needs to be customized, and everyone in the workgroup can use the same template. Microsoft also posts a large collection of templates on its Web site, and you can store templates on your own Web site.

Don't neglect your templates—along with the styles they include, templates are your key to producing professional looking documents with an absolute minimum of effort.

Styles

A style is a definition of the way a specific item is formatted. Word comes with an abundance of predefined styles. To view them, open a new blank document, and click the Styles And Formatting button on the Formatting toolbar. In the Styles And Formatting task pane, choose All Styles from the Show list, and scroll through the list. A paragraph mark at the right of the style name denotes a paragraph style, an underlined "a" denotes a character style, a grid denotes a table style, and a blank area denotes a list style. You can use a style as is, redefine its formatting, or create your own style.

By using a style, you can apply consistent—and, if necessary, complex—formatting with a quick click! Word provides four different types of styles:

- A *paragraph style* is the blueprint for the look of a paragraph—the font and its size; the line spacing; the way the text is indented from the margins by using left, right, or first-line indents; the types of tab stops and their positions; the borders; and even the paragraph's position on the page. The formatting you apply with a paragraph style applies to the entire paragraph.

- A *character style* defines the look of one or more characters (letters or numbers), and it applies only to the characters to which you assign that style.

- A *table style* defines the look of a table—its borders, shading, and character fonts. If you apply a table style to standard text, the table style creates a table and places the text in the table. If you apply a table style to an existing table, the formatting of the table changes to that style. Using a table style is similar to using the Table AutoFormat command on the Table menu, except that you can customize a table style and apply it to only part of the table if you want.

- A *list style* defines the type of bullets or the numbering scheme used in a list. You can add a list style to an existing paragraph style or table style so that the layout and formatting remain consistent in your document.

Wizards

Wizards really live up to their name! They use the templates and styles you have, but they hide from your view the macros, fields, and whatever other tools they need, and simply step you painlessly through the creation of a document. You make choices and provide information, and Word's wizards work their magic behind the scenes, quietly taking care of all the details and allowing you to concentrate on the content.

You can't create your own wizards or modify existing wizards, and sometimes you might even find it easiest to complete your work without using a wizard. However, if you're working your way through a complex procedure or doing something you've never done before, and if there's a wizard available, *use it!* You'll find that a wizard reduces a difficult task to a few simple steps.

Direct Formatting

Although it makes sense to use styles whenever you can, sometimes it's quicker and easier to apply direct formatting to your document. Direct formatting means that you select what you want to format and then use the tools on the Formatting toolbar or those on the Format menu to apply the formatting you want to the selection. The main disadvantage of using direct formatting is that you're likely to introduce formatting inconsistencies into your document. Fortunately, Word provides several tools to help you inspect and modify any inconsistencies. These tools include a feature that automatically detects and marks formatting inconsistencies; a task pane that compares the formatting of selected texts; and the Styles And Formatting task pane, in which you can quickly modify your formatting if necessary.

Creating a Letter

When you want to write a letter, you can decide which of three different methods you prefer. You can format each line as you write it; you can use a letter template; or you can use Word's Letter Wizard. In most cases, we think the Letter Wizard is the easiest way to go. You make a few choices and fill in a few blanks, and Word creates a letter format that's ready and waiting for you to insert your message.

Start the Letter

① Start a new document. Point to Letters And Mailings on the Tools menu, and choose Letter Wizard from the submenu.

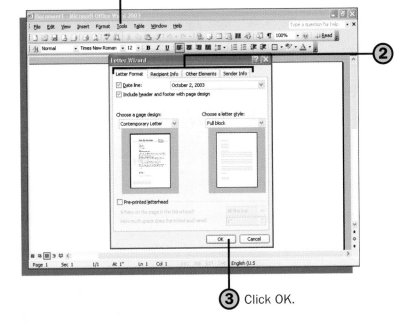

③ Click OK.

> **! TIP:** Although the Letter Wizard is undeniably handy, there are times when it's just easier to insert the information directly into the letter. To create a letter without using the Letter Wizard, simply start a document based on a letter template.

> **SEE ALSO:** For information about starting a document based on a specific template, see "Using Word's Templates" on page 46.

> **! TIP:** If the template you want to use isn't shown in the Page Design list (for example, if it's located on a Web site), start a document based on the template before you start the Letter Wizard.

② Complete the following items on each tab of the wizard:

- On the Letter Format tab, define the basic layout by choosing a page design (the template) and a letter style. The Page Design list should contain all your letter templates except for any that are stored in a remote location such as a Web site.

- On the Recipient Info tab, specify the recipient's name and address and an appropriate salutation style.

- On the Other Elements tab, select the check boxes for any additional elements you want to include, and enter the required specific information for each element.

- On the Sender Info tab, verify your return address, and specify the letter's closing elements.

> **✋ CAUTION:** If you're going to print the letter on paper that has a letterhead, be sure to select the Pre-Printed Letterhead check box in the Letter Wizard dialog box, and specify the position and size of the letterhead. Otherwise, part of your letter might print right on top of the letterhead.

Complete the Letter

(1) Replace the placeholder text with your own text.

(3) To make several changes to items that were completed by the wizard, rerun the wizard from the Tools menu and make your changes. The changes you make in the wizard will appear in your document.

(2) Review any items that were completed by the wizard. To make a change to an item, right-click it, and choose an alternative from the shortcut menu.

(4) Save the letter.

> **!** TIP: Not every item completed by the wizard displays a list when right-clicked. If there's no list, edit the item in the usual manner.

> **!** TIP: Many of the items inserted by the wizard are *fields*. A field is a bit of code that's used to insert some information or to execute a task automatically. A field usually becomes shaded when you click inside it, letting you know that it acts differently from your normal text.

> **⌕** TRY THIS: Create a watermark for your letter. Point to Background on the Format menu, and choose Printed Watermark from the submenu. In the Printed Watermark dialog box, either specify a picture or enter and format the text you want to use. Click OK.

Printing an Envelope

When you've taken the time and trouble to create a professional looking letter or other document, you don't want to ruin the good impression with a handwritten envelope! Word makes it easy for you to create crisp, businesslike printed envelopes. You can easily include your return address, and, in the United States, you can add electronic postage and a postal bar code. If you already have the mailing address in your letter, Word usually detects it and copies it to the Envelopes And Labels dialog box. You can also type the address directly in the dialog box.

Add the Address

(1) Point to Letters And Mailings on the Tools menu, and choose Envelopes And Labels from the submenu to display the Envelopes And Labels dialog box.

(2) If a delivery address is displayed on the Envelopes tab, verify that it's correct.

(3) If no delivery address is shown, or if you want to use a different address, type the address. If the address is in your Microsoft Outlook Contacts list, click the Insert Address button.

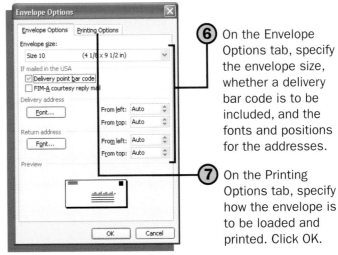

(6) On the Envelope Options tab, specify the envelope size, whether a delivery bar code is to be included, and the fonts and positions for the addresses.

(7) On the Printing Options tab, specify how the envelope is to be loaded and printed. Click OK.

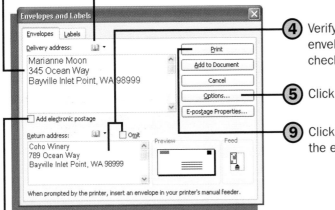

(4) Verify that the return address is correct. If you're using an envelope with a preprinted return address, select the Omit check box so that the return address won't be printed.

(5) Click Options.

(9) Click to print the envelope.

> **TIP:** Your return address is based on the user information Word has stored for you. To review this information, choose Options from the Tools menu, click the User Information tab, and make any changes you want. To change only the return address, edit it in the Envelopes And Labels dialog box, and Word will make the change for you in the user information.

(8) If you have Electronic Postage (E-Postage) software installed, select this check box to use electronic postage. Click the E-Postage Properties button to make changes to your e-postage setup.

Printing a Mailing Label

Whether you need to print a single mailing label or a full page of mailing labels, Word has a tool that takes care of most of the details for you. All you need to do is specify the type of label you're using, the address, and how you want the labels printed. Word does the rest for you.

SEE ALSO: For everything you always wanted to know about mail merge, see "Mail Merge: The Power and the Pain" on pages 60–61 and "Creating a Form Letter" on pages 62–63.

Print a Label

(1) Make a note of the manufacturer and design number of the labels you'll be using. If you're going to print only one label, figure out which label on the sheet you're going to use; later you'll need to specify the label by row (the horizontal line of labels) and by column (the vertical line of labels). Insert the sheet of labels into your printer (usually into the manual feed tray, if there is one).

(6) Select this check box to add a delivery bar code to the address. Not all labels have room for a bar code, so this option might not be available.

(5) Click the appropriate option to print a whole page of identical labels or only one label on the sheet of labels. If you want to print only one label, specify the label by row and column.

(2) Point to Letters And Mailings on the Tools menu, and choose Envelopes And Labels from the submenu to display the Envelopes And Labels dialog box. Click the Labels tab.

(3) Use the proposed address, type a new one, or click the Insert Address button to insert an address from your Outlook Contacts list. To insert your return address, select the Use Return Address check box.

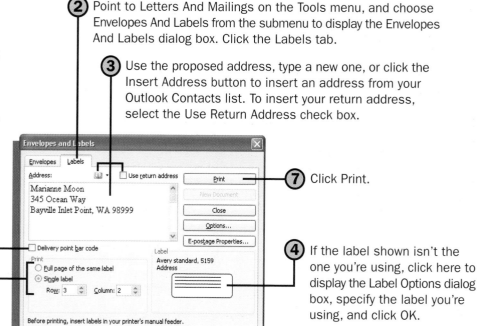

(7) Click Print.

(4) If the label shown isn't the one you're using, click here to display the Label Options dialog box, specify the label you're using, and click OK.

TIP: If you need to print many different mailing labels, consider using the mail merge feature.

Creating Your Own Styles

Whether you're creating or modifying a template or just working on a document, you might find that none of the existing styles is right for your purposes. If that's the case, you can create your own style and define all its elements in a few quick steps. If one style almost works, and you don't want to go through the effort of creating an entirely new style, you can modify that style.

Create a Style

(3) Select Paragraph to create a paragraph style, or select Character to create a character style.

(4) Select the style from which this style will be cloned.

(5) For a paragraph style, select the style that will automatically be applied to the paragraph that follows a paragraph with this style.

(6) Use the formatting tools to specify how this style differs from the style on which it's based.

(2) Type a name for the style you're going to create.

(1) Click the Styles And Formatting button on the Formatting toolbar to display the Styles And Formatting task pane if it isn't already open. Click New Style.

(9) Click OK.

(8) Select this check box to add the style to the document's template, or leave the check box cleared to create the style in the current document only.

(7) Click to apply additional formatting to the style. For example, you can include additional font specifications, add another language, or designate a keyboard shortcut to apply the style. For a paragraph style, you can specify the paragraph design in greater detail: set tabs; add borders; or use absolute positioning (frame), heading numbering, and so on.

> **! TIP:** You can also use the procedure on this page to create new table and list styles by choosing Table or List from the Style Type list.

Modify a Style in a Document

① Create a paragraph, or type some text based on the style you want to modify. Select the entire paragraph to modify a paragraph style, or select the text to modify a character style. Format the paragraph or text to look the way you want, using the direct formatting tools on the Formatting toolbar or those on the Format menu.

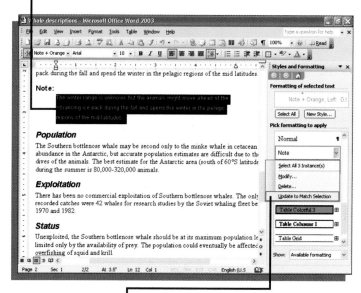

② Point to the style in the Styles And Formatting task pane. Click the down arrow that appears, and click Update To Match Selection.

Specify Style Changes

① Point to the style in the Styles And Formatting task pane, click the down arrow that appears, and click Modify to display the Modify Style dialog box.

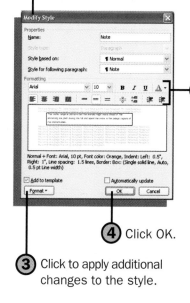

② Use the settings in the dialog box to make changes to the style. (You can't change the nature of the style—that is, a paragraph style can't become a character style, and vice versa.) Be sure to select the Add To Template check box if you want to add the change to the document's template.

④ Click OK.

③ Click to apply additional changes to the style.

CAUTION: When you modify a style based on a selection, the style is changed only in the document, not in the template. The next document based on the template will use the original style settings. To save the style changes, point to the style in the task pane, click the down arrow to open the menu, and click Modify. Don't modify any of the settings except to select the check box to add the style to the template. Click OK, and when you close the document, you'll be able to save the style change to the template.

Customizing a Template

Word provides templates that are useful for many different purposes. However, they're generic templates that might not include every element you need. If you use a template frequently, you can create a more personalized document—and save lots of time—by creating a new, customized template from the existing template.

! **TIP:** To research the dates the template was created and/or modified, as well as who has permission to use and modify it, right-click the template in the Templates dialog box, and choose Properties from the shortcut menu.

Open the Template

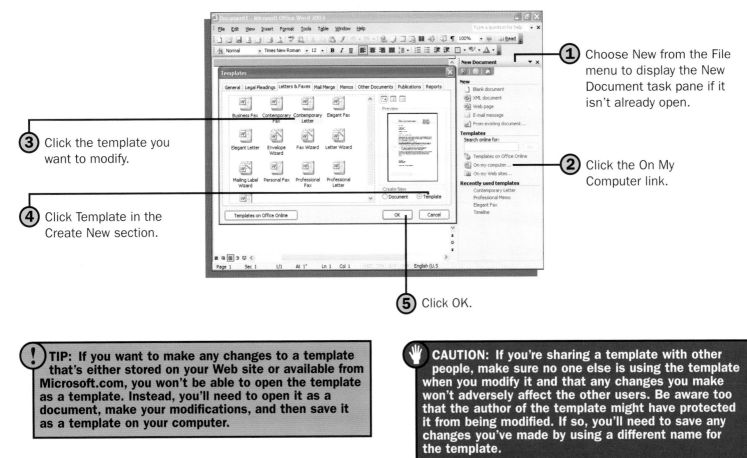

① Choose New from the File menu to display the New Document task pane if it isn't already open.

③ Click the template you want to modify.

④ Click Template in the Create New section.

② Click the On My Computer link.

⑤ Click OK.

! **TIP:** If you want to make any changes to a template that's either stored on your Web site or available from Microsoft.com, you won't be able to open the template as a template. Instead, you'll need to open it as a document, make your modifications, and then save it as a template on your computer.

✋ **CAUTION:** If you're sharing a template with other people, make sure no one else is using the template when you modify it and that any changes you make won't adversely affect the other users. Be aware too that the author of the template might have protected it from being modified. If so, you'll need to save any changes you've made by using a different name for the template.

Modify the Template

(1) Click the Save button on the Standard toolbar, type a unique and descriptive file name for your new template, and click Save. The template will be saved in your personal Templates folder and will appear on the General tab of the Templates dialog box.

(!) TIP: Most paragraph styles are based on the Normal style, so when you make changes to the Normal style, those changes will also take place in the other styles.

Template1 - Microsoft Office Word 2003

File Edit View Insert Format Tools Table Window Help   Type a question for help

Normal   Times New Roman   10   B I U

c/o Microsoft Press¶
one Microsoft Way¶
Redmond, WA 98052¶

Moon·Joyce·Resources¶

October 2, 2003¶

[Click **here** and type recipient's address]¶

Dear Sir or Madam:¶

¶

Sincerely,¶

Read·our·books!¶

Jerry·Joyce¶
Boss¶

Draw ▾   AutoShapes ▾

Page 1   Sec 1   1/1   At 3.1"   Ln 8   Col 1   English (U.S

(2) Click the Show/Hide ¶ button on the Standard toolbar if it isn't already turned on.

(3) Replace the placeholder text with any text that will be common to all documents based on this new template.

(4) Add any new text or other page elements.

(5) Redefine or create your own paragraph styles and character styles.

(6) Save and close the template. Create a document based on the new template to confirm that the template is correct. (In the Templates dialog box, be sure to specify that you're creating a document and not a new template.)

(!) TIP: When you save a template, it's normally stored in the Templates folder (which is the default user templates folder), and any templates in that folder will appear on the General tab of the Templates dialog box. To store the templates in a different location and to have them appear on a different tab in the Templates dialog box, create a new folder, and, in Word, choose Options from the Tools menu. Click the File Locations tab, double-click the User Templates item, and enter the path to the new folder. Any templates that you store in this folder will be listed in the Templates dialog box on a new tab, using the name of the new folder.

(✓) SEE ALSO: For information about starting a document based on a template, see "Using Word's Templates" on page 46.

Designing a Template

Sometimes an existing template just doesn't do the job for you, no matter how much you modify it. If that's the case, you'll want to create a template from scratch. The easiest way to do this is to use an existing document and set it up as a template. If you don't have an existing document that incorporates all the special elements you need, create one, and then save it. Review the entire document to determine whether the design really works, and then close it. You'll be using a copy of the document as the basis for your template's design, so if you don't like the resulting template, you can simply delete it and then revise it, using the same document.

Create the Design

(1) Choose New from the File menu to display the New Document task pane if it isn't already open.

(2) Click From Existing Document, use the New From Existing Document dialog box to locate the document you want to use, and create a new document based on it.

(3) Choose Save As from the File menu.

(4) Type a unique and descriptive file name.

(5) Click Document Template in the Save As Type list. Word then switches to your Templates folder. If you want to store the template in a subfolder or work-group folder, navigate to that folder.

(6) Save the template.

Customize the Content

① Click the Show/Hide ¶ button on the Standard toolbar if it isn't already turned on.

⑤ Click the Save button on the Standard toolbar.

⑥ Close the template when you've finished. Create a document based on the new template to confirm that the template is correct.

④ Use AutoText in running headers or footers to insert information that will be updated automatically.

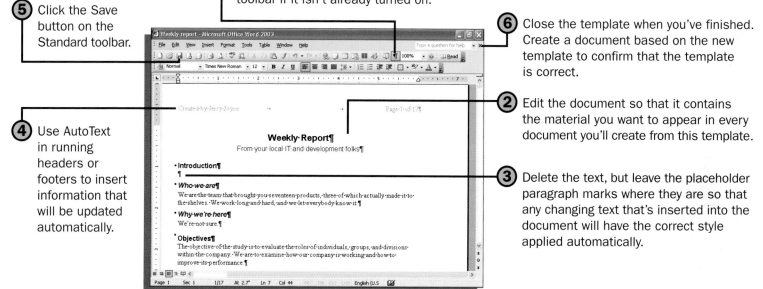

② Edit the document so that it contains the material you want to appear in every document you'll create from this template.

③ Delete the text, but leave the placeholder paragraph marks where they are so that any changing text that's inserted into the document will have the correct style applied automatically.

TIP: To include the date and time and have them updated each time you create a new document, choose Date And Time from the Insert menu, click the format you want to use, select the Update Automatically check box, and click OK.

CAUTION: A date or time that's set to update automatically is useful in a template but can sometimes cause problems in a completed document by updating when you don't want it to. To stop it from ever updating again, click the date or time, and press Ctrl+Shift+F9.

SEE ALSO: For information about using AutoText, see "Inserting Frequently Used Information" on pages 72–73.

For information about working with headers and footers, see "Numbering Pages and Creating Running Heads" on page 77.

Mail Merge: The Power and the Pain

Mail merge is a tool that combines two different parts into a sleek and well-crafted whole: a series of identical printed documents (form letters, for example) with the appropriate information (individual names and addresses) inserted automatically into each document. The two parts are a *master document* and a *data source.* The master document is the template (although not a template in the Word-document sense) that lays out your document and contains text or other items that never change. The master document also contains instructions to insert data from a data source into each document. The data source is a uniform collection of information from one of a number of sources.

Mail merge is an almost unbelievable time-saver once you've set it up, and its power can be awesome. But—and here's the rub—you have to be willing to deal with the complexities of *fields* and *conditional expressions.* The good news is that the mail merge feature is extremely *scalable*— that is, it's easy to do a simple, basic mail merge, but the process becomes increasingly demanding as your mail merge becomes more complex. If, for example, you simply want to address a stack of envelopes to people whose addresses are contained in a Word table, an Excel worksheet, or your Outlook Contacts list, you can just jump in and do it with little preparation and a great likelihood of success.

If you want to go beyond the basics—for example, printing letters and envelopes that are grouped by a specific city or postal code—you'll need to venture into a bit of data management and selective merging. And if you want to get even more deeply involved—using conditional content, for example, whereby certain text is included only when some data value meets or exceeds a certain threshold—you'll find yourself wandering around Word's fields. Once you get involved in complex mail merges, you'll need to exercise caution by testing your setup. You'll want to make sure

there's no major error that will cause you to toss out all those printed letters or envelopes or, even worse, send them out only to discover too late that the merge made a horrible mess of your intentions.

Managing the Data

In many types of mail merge there's no need for you to manipulate the data—you simply specify the data source and create the merged documents from the existing data. In other situations, however, you'll want to either sort the data according to a certain parameter (ZIP code or other postal code, for example) or exclude data that doesn't meet specific criteria (someone who didn't contribute enough money).

Word can use data from many different sources. For some types of data, it's often easiest to modify the data in its original program and then do a simple mail merge in Word without worrying about data manipulation. For example, if you're using a list of addresses in Excel and you want to print envelopes grouped by city, you can sort the data by city in Excel. Or if you want to send a message to only the top contributors, and all your data is in an Access database, you can run a query in Access and use the results of the query for your mail merge.

However, Word provides data-manipulation tools, and these are especially useful for data from sources that you can't manipulate. When you specify a data source in the Mail Merge Wizard, you can decide (in Word, rather than in the source program) which data fields are to be used, and, by sorting the data by one or more of the data fields, you can also decide how the data records are to be grouped. For example, you might want to sort all the data first by city and then by ZIP code or other postal code so that the final documents will already be sorted for you when you print them. Another way to manipulate the data is to *filter* them—

that is, to specify criteria that must be met in order for the data to be included. For example, you could set the criteria to send a letter only to contributors who live in a specific city and whose contributions exceed a certain amount of money. If you're using data from an Outlook Contacts list or from a large database used for many purposes, you'll find these features particularly useful.

Setting Conditional Content

One of the real powers of mail merge is the ability it gives you to tailor the content of a document based on some data stored in your mailing list. For example, you might offer a tour of your company to individuals who have invested a large amount of money in the company, and offer only a free brochure to the small investors. If you have an entry in your data file for the level of investment, you can use that data to control the content of your document.

You control conditional content by using the IF Word field. To use this field, you place it in your document where you want the conditional text to appear by clicking the Insert Word Field button on the Mail Merge toolbar and then clicking If…Then…Else in the list that appears. In the Insert Word Field: IF dialog box, you specify the data field that lists the value to be tested (for example, amount of investment), the comparison (Greater Than Or Equal To), and the value (5000). Then you insert the text to be used if the comparison is true ("Please call to arrange a tour.") or untrue ("Please call to receive your full-color brochure.").

It's More than Letters

The mail merge feature can do more than create form letters and address envelopes. By using the buttons on the Mail Merge toolbar, you can send your merged documents by e-mail or as faxes. You can create almost any type of document by using a specific template or creating a design from scratch. All Word needs is a data document with some data fields in it. You can create mailing labels and address books, awards, parts lists, different versions of exams, and catalogs designed for specific geographical areas or demographic populations. The uses for mail merge are limited only by your imagination, your willingness to experiment with different data fields and Word fields, and your decision as to whether mail merge would be faster than manually creating individual documents.

The Pain of Mail Merge

Mail merge is undeniably powerful, but it's also a bit tricky. The Mail Merge task pane and the specially designed tasks it contains—creating letters or envelopes, for example—simplify the process. However, any inconsistencies or errors in the data and any typographic or layout errors in the master document can produce some surprising results. Fortunately, the Mail Merge Wizard and the tools on the Mail Merge toolbar let you preview the results of your mail merge on the screen; conduct a simulated merge, which reports any errors in the merge; or print a sampling of your documents for a visual check of the finished product.

If you do find a problem in a merge, carefully track down the source of the problem—is it a problem in the data source, in the master document, or in the way you sorted or filtered the data? Once you've determined the source of the problem, correct it, and then test the merge again. Don't assume, however, that the merge will have no further problems. Your fix might not have completely fixed the problem or might have caused a different problem. Don't despair! Just be aware that setting up a mail merge that works perfectly might take a while. Once you've perfected it, though, you'll be amazed by the speed with which you can accomplish your mailings.

Creating a Form Letter

"Mail merge"—a dreaded phrase in the world of word processing! Not only does it conjure up an image of piles of junk mail, but associated words such as "fields" and "conditional statements" add to the intimidation factor. However, with just a little effort—and a lot of help from Word—when you need to send nearly identical letters to numerous people, you can create your own mail-merged documents and personalized form letters.

Set Up Your Letter

1 Create your letter as you would any other letter, leaving blank any parts of the letter you want to be completed with data from your mailing list. Save the letter.

2 Point to Letters And Mailings on the Tools menu, and choose Mail Merge from the submenu to open the Mail Merge task pane.

3 Complete the first two steps of the wizard, clicking Next to move to each new step. Make sure that Letters is selected as the document type and that you're using the current document as your starting document.

4 Specify the type of data you want to use for your mailing list:

- Data that exists in a file Word can read. Click Browse to locate and specify the file. To see what type of data sources you can use, open the Files Of Type list in the Select Data Source dialog box, and review the list.

- Data from your Outlook Contacts list. Click Choose Contacts Folder to specify the folder, and review the data in that folder.

- Data that you enter to create a new list. Click Create to start entering data.

5 Sort the order of the items in the Mail Merge Recipients dialog box, or select those recipients you don't want to be included in the mail merge. Click OK when you've finished, and then click Next to continue.

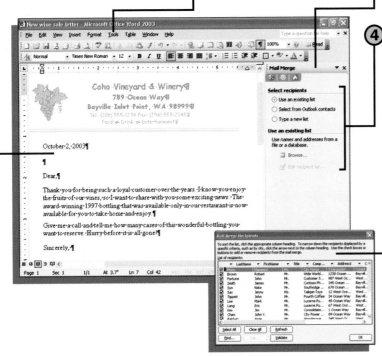

Specify the Data to Be Merged

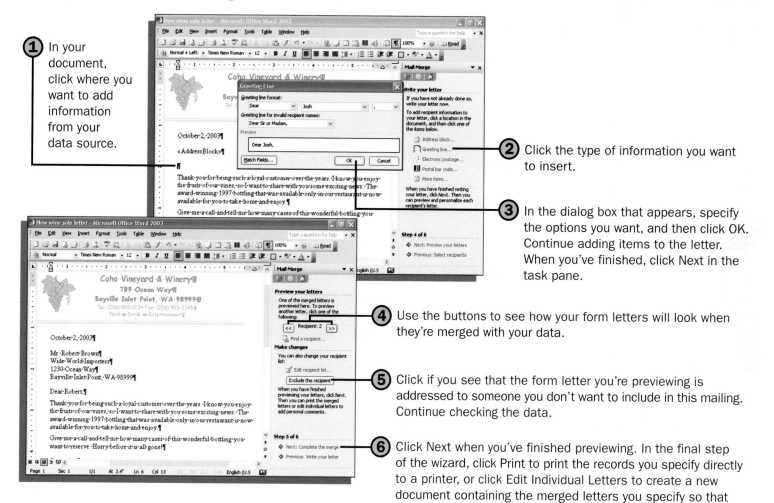

① In your document, click where you want to add information from your data source.

② Click the type of information you want to insert.

③ In the dialog box that appears, specify the options you want, and then click OK. Continue adding items to the letter. When you've finished, click Next in the task pane.

④ Use the buttons to see how your form letters will look when they're merged with your data.

⑤ Click if you see that the form letter you're previewing is addressed to someone you don't want to include in this mailing. Continue checking the data.

⑥ Click Next when you've finished previewing. In the final step of the wizard, click Print to print the records you specify directly to a printer, or click Edit Individual Letters to create a new document containing the merged letters you specify so that you can review and edit each letter before you print it.

Printing a Word Document

E-mail, shared documents, and Web documents are oh-so-slowly bringing the paperless office a bit closer to reality, but the most common way to distribute a finished document is still to print it.

Word gives you precise control of the content you want to print and how it's printed.

Print a Document

① Look over your document to make sure it's complete and free of errors. Then choose Print from the File menu to display the Print dialog box.

③ Designate the printer you're going to use. Click the Properties button if you need to change settings for the printer.

④ Click to send the print job to an electronic file instead of to the printer. This lets you transfer your document to another computer and printer for printing.

⑤ Click to print only on one side of the paper. You'll be prompted to reload the paper so that you can then print on the other side.

② Specify whether you want to print

- The entire document, a single page, some selected text, or a range of pages.

- Only the document itself, or other content—for example, the document properties (author, date, and so on), any markup, or a list of styles.

- Only odd- or even-numbered pages, or all the pages.

- Special content, such as only the data in forms, field codes, or hidden text.

⑧ Click OK to print the document.

⑥ Specify the number of copies to be printed and, if you're printing multiple copies, whether the pages are to be printed in order (collated) or whether all copies of the same page are to be printed at one time.

⑦ Specify how many pages are to be printed on one sheet. Specify the scaling size if you want to print on paper that's a different size from the paper the document was originally set up for.

TRY THIS: Complete your document, and click the Print Preview button on the Standard toolbar. Inspect the document to make sure it's laid out correctly. Click the Close button. Choose Print from the File menu, click the Options button, and note all the different ways you can print. Click OK, and print your document.

TIP: If you don't need to change any settings in the Print dialog box, you can quickly print a document just by clicking the Print button on the Standard toolbar.

5

Enhancing a Document

Microsoft Office Word 2003 can help you lift your documents out of the realm of the mediocre and make them interesting, well-organized, and polished—and, at the same time, can make your work faster and more enjoyable than you ever dreamed it could be. Do you have a ton of information that would be best presented and understood in the form of a table? Let Word create a generic table for you; then, after you add your information, Word can format the table, using a pre-designed table style that you choose or one that you design yourself.

If you work with long, complex documents, Word is a lifesaver. Let's say, for example, that you type the same word or phrase repeatedly—maybe it's a technical term or a long, complicated name. Save it as AutoText by giving it a short nickname, and then, when you type the nickname, Word's AutoComplete tool magically inserts the whole name or phrase for you. Does your paper or report need footnotes or endnotes? Choose the symbols or numbers you want to mark your footnotes, and Word inserts them for you *and* saves you the headache of figuring out the required amount of space at the end of the page.

As you work through this section, you'll see how Word really shines. Word can make it easy for you to insert and position drawings to illustrate and liven up your work; to organize a long document with paragraph styles that assign an outline level to every paragraph, and then, if you want, to reorganize the document using this outline structure; to number the headings in a document so that it's easy to find and refer to a particular section that's under review; and to number pages and create running heads, chapters, and a table of contents.

Creating a Table

If you think of tables merely as containers for numbers, think again. Tables are a superb way to organize almost any kind of information, and Word makes it so easy. You can draw your table with a little onscreen pencil if you want, but it's easier and faster to let Word do the work for you. Just specify the number of rows and columns you want in your table, and Word will create them for you. Then you can put your content into the cells, adding more rows and columns if you need to, or changing their sizes to make everything fit.

Create a Table

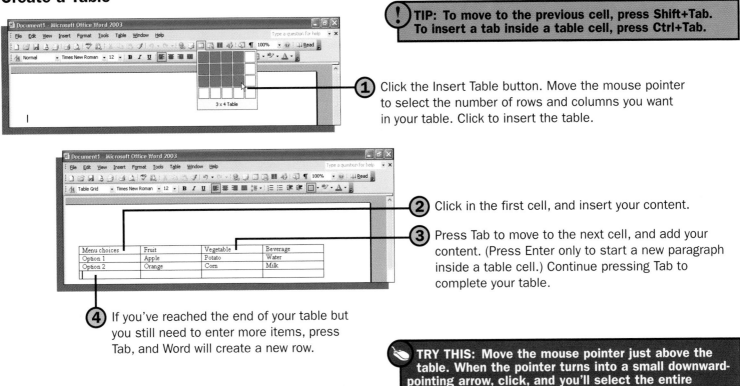

TIP: To move to the previous cell, press Shift+Tab. To insert a tab inside a table cell, press Ctrl+Tab.

1 Click the Insert Table button. Move the mouse pointer to select the number of rows and columns you want in your table. Click to insert the table.

2 Click in the first cell, and insert your content.

3 Press Tab to move to the next cell, and add your content. (Press Enter only to start a new paragraph inside a table cell.) Continue pressing Tab to complete your table.

4 If you've reached the end of your table but you still need to enter more items, press Tab, and Word will create a new row.

TIP: To convert existing text into a table, select the text, point to Convert on the Table menu, and choose Text To Table from the submenu. Use the options in the Convert Text To Table dialog box to create the table you want.

TRY THIS: Move the mouse pointer just above the table. When the pointer turns into a small downward-pointing arrow, click, and you'll select the entire column. Move the mouse pointer over another column, hold down the Ctrl key, and click to select a second column. Move the mouse pointer to the left of the table, and click to select an entire row. With columns or rows selected, you can delete all the text, or change the formatting of all the selected cells, at one time.

Add to the Table

① Click in the table next to where you want to add a row or column.

② Point to Insert on the Table menu, and, from the submenu, choose what you want to add.

Delete from the Table

① Click in a table cell that's in the row or column you want to delete.

② Point to Delete on the Table menu, and, from the submenu, choose what you want to delete.

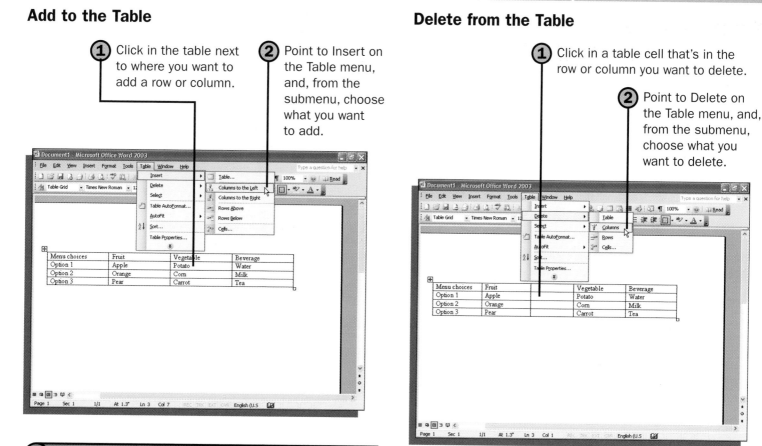

⚠ TIP: To insert a single cell instead of a row or column, right-click in a cell, and choose Split Cells from the shortcut menu. To combine one or more cells into a single cell, select the cells, right-click, and choose Merge Cells from the shortcut menu.

⚠ TIP: To delete the content of a row or column without deleting the row or column itself, select the row or column, and press the Delete key.

✋ CAUTION: If you want to delete content from a row or column without deleting the row or column, make sure your selection doesn't extend outside the table. If it does, you'll delete whatever part of the table is selected, as well as its content.

Formatting a Table

You can manually add individual formatting elements to a table—enhance it with a nice border, shade some cells, use a different font for the headings—but why take the time to do all that work manually when Word can do it for you automatically? And if you don't find a format you like among those that Word provides, simply create your own table style so that you can use it over and over again.

Apply Table Formatting

1 Click anywhere inside the table.

2 Choose Table AutoFormat from the Table menu to display the Table AutoFormat dialog box.

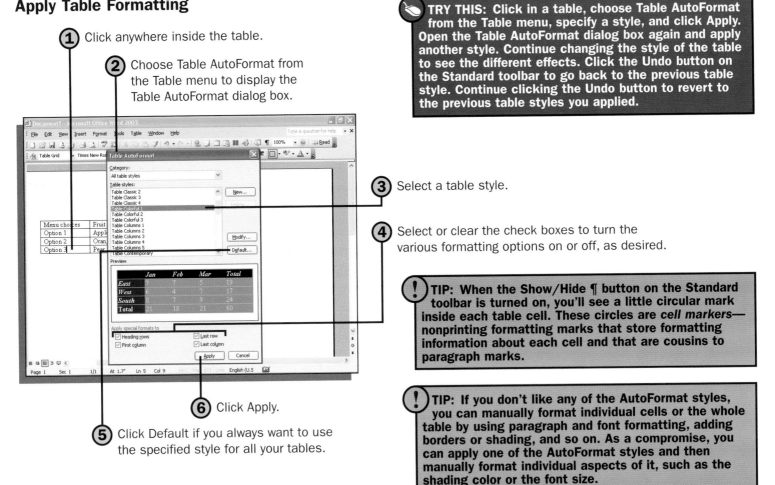

3 Select a table style.

4 Select or clear the check boxes to turn the various formatting options on or off, as desired.

6 Click Apply.

5 Click Default if you always want to use the specified style for all your tables.

> **TRY THIS:** Click in a table, choose Table AutoFormat from the Table menu, specify a style, and click Apply. Open the Table AutoFormat dialog box again and apply another style. Continue changing the style of the table to see the different effects. Click the Undo button on the Standard toolbar to go back to the previous table style. Continue clicking the Undo button to revert to the previous table styles you applied.

> **TIP:** When the Show/Hide ¶ button on the Standard toolbar is turned on, you'll see a little circular mark inside each table cell. These circles are *cell markers*—nonprinting formatting marks that store formatting information about each cell and that are cousins to paragraph marks.

> **TIP:** If you don't like any of the AutoFormat styles, you can manually format individual cells or the whole table by using paragraph and font formatting, adding borders or shading, and so on. As a compromise, you can apply one of the AutoFormat styles and then manually format individual aspects of it, such as the shading color or the font size.

Customize the Formatting

(1) With the insertion point in the table, choose Table AutoFormat from the Table menu. Review the existing table styles, noting the name of the style that's most like the one you want to use.

(!) TIP: To make small or quick changes to a table, click the Tables And Borders button on the Standard toolbar, and use the various buttons and list boxes on the Tables And Borders toolbar to merge or split cells, change the border, add color to the cells, or align the content in the cells. To change the dimensions of a row or column, just drag a border of that row or column.

(2) Click New to display the New Style dialog box.

Table AutoFormat

Category:
All table styles

Table styles:
Table 3D effects 3
Table Classic 1
Table Classic 2
Table Classic 3
Table Classic 4
Table Colorful 1
Table Colorful 2
Table Colorful 3
Table Columns 1
Table Columns 2
Table Columns 3
Table Columns 4

New...
Delete...
Modify...
Default...

Preview

	Jan	Feb	Mar	Total
East	7	7	5	19
West	6	4	7	17
South	8	7	9	24
Total	21	18	21	60

Apply special formats to
☑ Heading rows   ☑ Last row
☑ First column   ☑ Last column

Apply   Cancel

New Style

Properties
Name: My table style
Style type: Table
Style based on: ⊞ Table Columns 1

Formatting
Apply formatting to: Whole table
Arial   12   **B** *I* U A ▾

½ pt   ▾ ▾ ⊞ ▾ ▾ ▤ ▾

	Jan	Feb	Mar	Total
East	7	7	5	19
West	6	4	7	17
South	8	7	9	24
Total	21	18	21	60

Table Columns 1 + Font: Arial, 12 pt, Centered, Center

☑ Add to template   ☐ Automatically update
Format ▾   OK   Cancel

(3) Type a name for your style.

(4) Click the style name that you noted in step 1.

(5) Click Whole Table, and use the formatting tools or click the Format button to specify any formatting that will be common to all the elements of the table—the font, for example. Click a different element in the list, and use the formatting tools or click the Format button to redefine the formatting for that element. Continue clicking different elements and changing their formatting as necessary.

(7) Click OK.

(8) Click Apply to format the table.

(6) Select this check box if you want to use this style in other documents based on the current template.

The Anatomy of a Table

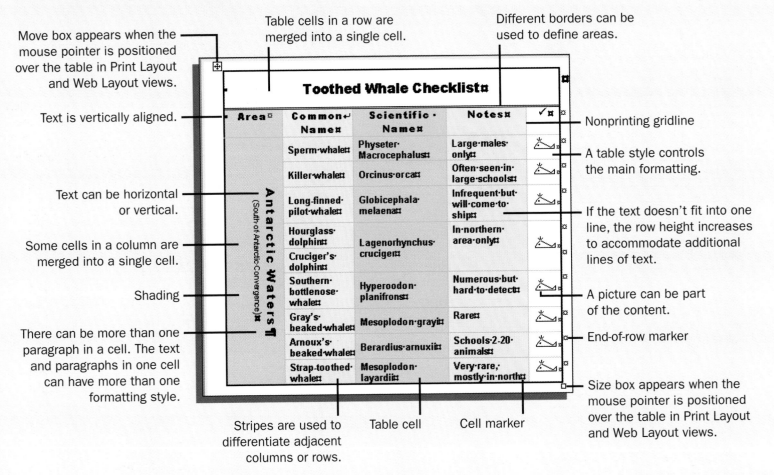

Move box appears when the mouse pointer is positioned over the table in Print Layout and Web Layout views.

Table cells in a row are merged into a single cell.

Different borders can be used to define areas.

Text is vertically aligned.

Nonprinting gridline

A table style controls the main formatting.

Text can be horizontal or vertical.

Some cells in a column are merged into a single cell.

If the text doesn't fit into one line, the row height increases to accommodate additional lines of text.

Shading

A picture can be part of the content.

There can be more than one paragraph in a cell. The text and paragraphs in one cell can have more than one formatting style.

End-of-row marker

Size box appears when the mouse pointer is positioned over the table in Print Layout and Web Layout views.

Stripes are used to differentiate adjacent columns or rows.

Table cell

Cell marker

Toothed Whale Checklist¤

Area¤	Common↵ Name¤	Scientific · Name¤	Notes¤	✓ ¤	¤
Antarctic Waters¶ (South of Antarctic Convergence)¤	Sperm·whale¤	Physeter· Macrocephalus¤	Large·males· only¤		¤
	Killer·whale¤	Orcinus·orca¤	Often·seen·in· large·schools¤		¤
	Long-finned· pilot·whale¤	Globicephala· melaena¤	Infrequent·but· will·come·to· ship¤		¤
	Hourglass· dolphin¤ Cruciger's· dolphin¤	Lagenorhynchus· cruciger¤	In·northern· area·only¤		¤
	Southern· bottlenose· whale¤	Hyperoodon· planifrons¤	Numerous·but· hard·to·detect¤		¤
	Gray's· beaked·whale¤	Mesoplodon·grayi¤	Rare¤		¤
	Arnoux's· beaked·whale¤	Berardius·arnuxii¤	Schools·2-20· animals¤		¤
	Strap-toothed· whale¤	Mesoplodon· layardii¤	Very·rare,· mostly·in·north¤		¤

Organizing Your Information

Tables and lists are invaluable tools for presenting information briefly and clearly, and you can make them even more useful by organizing them as efficiently as possible. If you have a table or a list that you want to rearrange so that it's presented in alphabetic or numeric order, all you need to do is tell Word to sort it for you.

Sort a Table

(1) With the insertion point anywhere in the table, choose Sort from the Table menu to display the Sort dialog box.

(3) Specify the title of the column you want to use to sort the table, the type of content in the column, and whether you want the information to be sorted in ascending or in descending order.

Sort a List

(2) Choose Sort from the Table menu to display the Sort Text dialog box.

(3) Specify whether to sort by paragraphs, the type of information that's in the list, and whether you want the information to be sorted in ascending or in descending order.

(1) Select the entire list.

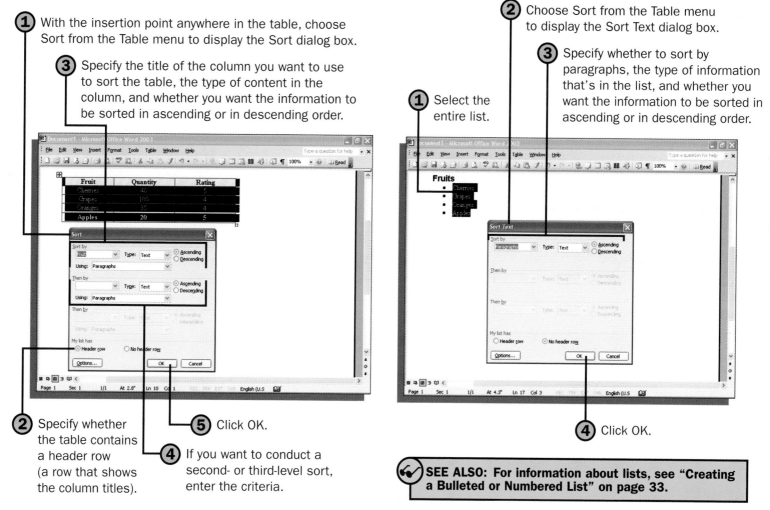

(2) Specify whether the table contains a header row (a row that shows the column titles).

(5) Click OK.

(4) If you want to conduct a second- or third-level sort, enter the criteria.

(4) Click OK.

SEE ALSO: For information about lists, see "Creating a Bulleted or Numbered List" on page 33.

Inserting Frequently Used Information

If you type the same words or phrases repeatedly, you can save yourself a lot of time (especially if you use long technical terms or difficult names) by saving those words or phrases as AutoText. You assign the AutoText a short name—a nickname of sorts, with at least four letters—and when you type the nickname, or just the first few letters of it, Word's AutoComplete feature inserts the word or phrase into your document. AutoText isn't limited to text; the information can be anything you can put into a document—pictures, tables, even fields. Word comes already equipped with numerous AutoText entries for some of the most common types of information.

Store the Information

1 In your document, select all the information you want to include in the AutoText entry.

2 Point to AutoText on the Insert menu, and choose New from the submenu.

3 Accept the suggested name, or type a new name for the entry, and click OK. (The name must contain at least four characters for the AutoComplete feature to work.)

> **! TIP: If the AutoComplete tip never appears, choose AutoCorrect Options from the Tools menu. On the AutoText tab, select the Show AutoComplete Suggestions check box, and click OK.**

Insert the Information

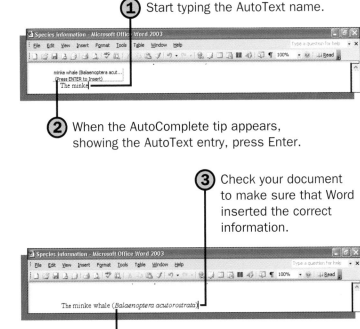

1 Start typing the AutoText name.

2 When the AutoComplete tip appears, showing the AutoText entry, press Enter.

3 Check your document to make sure that Word inserted the correct information.

Word inserts the complete AutoText entry.

Find and Insert an AutoText Entry

(1) Point to AutoText on the Insert menu.

(2) Point to the appropriate category on the submenu.

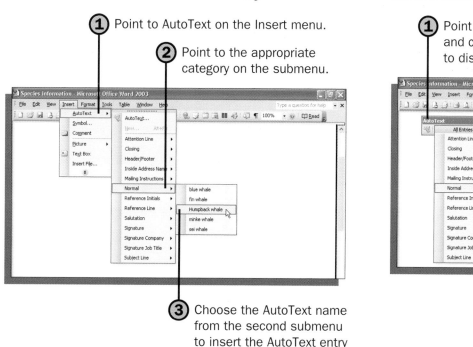

(3) Choose the AutoText name from the second submenu to insert the AutoText entry into your document.

Insert Multiple Entries

(1) Point to Toolbars on the View menu, and choose AutoText from the submenu to display the AutoText toolbar.

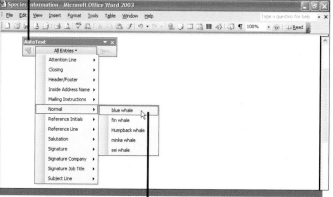

(2) Click the All Entries button, and choose an AutoText entry from the submenu of one of the categories listed. Continue inserting AutoText entries from the toolbar as needed.

> **TIP:** To store an AutoText entry in an open template other than the Normal template, point to AutoText on the Insert menu, and choose AutoText from the submenu to display the AutoCorrect Options dialog box. On the AutoText tab, specify the template, type a name for the AutoText entry, and click Add. You can also use the AutoCorrect dialog box to delete AutoText entries you no longer need. Click OK when you've finished.

> **TRY THIS:** Type sund and press Enter to insert the AutoComplete suggestion "Sunday." This is just one example from Word's long list of built-in AutoText entries that frequently show up as AutoComplete entries.

Organizing with Styles

Paragraph styles do more than quickly apply formatting to your paragraphs; they also assign an outline level to each paragraph in a document. Word uses these outline levels to understand how you're organizing the document—which paragraphs are headings, which are subheadings, and which are text. You can use Word's defined outline hierarchy, or you can create your own structure by defining the outline levels for your styles. When your document is organized with headings, you can use Word's Document Map, the Outline View buttons, and the Table of Contents feature to navigate through your document.

TIP: To see all your text when the Styles and Formatting task pane is open, choose Options from the Tools menu. On the View tab of the Options dialog box, select the Wrap To Window check box, and click OK.

SEE ALSO: For information about creating styles, see "Creating Your Own Styles" on page 54.

For information about using Outline view to look at your heading hierarchy, see "Reorganizing a Document" on page 82.

Create a Heading Hierarchy

(1) Start Word, and open your document if it isn't already open. Switch to Normal view.

(2) Click the Styles And Formatting button to display the Styles And Formatting task pane if it isn't already open.

(3) Click in a paragraph.

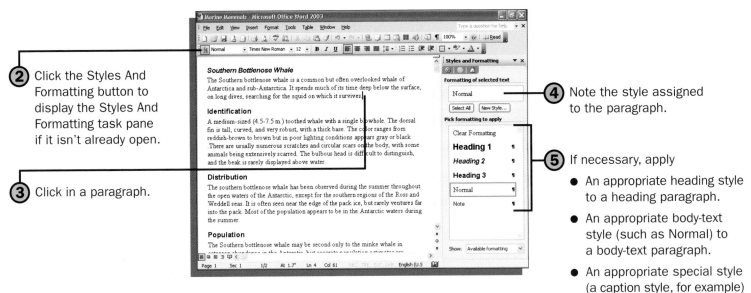

(4) Note the style assigned to the paragraph.

(5) If necessary, apply

- An appropriate heading style to a heading paragraph.

- An appropriate body-text style (such as Normal) to a body-text paragraph.

- An appropriate special style (a caption style, for example) to a special paragraph.

Define a Style as a Heading

(1) Click in a paragraph whose style you want to define as a heading in an outline.

(2) Point to the style, click the down arrow, and choose Modify from the menu that appears.

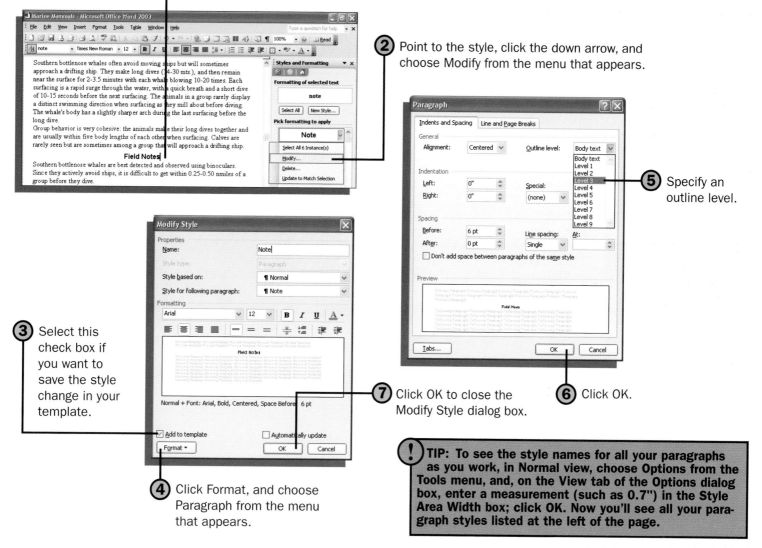

(5) Specify an outline level.

(3) Select this check box if you want to save the style change in your template.

(7) Click OK to close the Modify Style dialog box.

(6) Click OK.

(4) Click Format, and choose Paragraph from the menu that appears.

(!) TIP: To see the style names for all your paragraphs as you work, in Normal view, choose Options from the Tools menu, and, on the View tab of the Options dialog box, enter a measurement (such as 0.7") in the Style Area Width box; click OK. Now you'll see all your paragraph styles listed at the left of the page.

Numbering Headings

It's a commonly accepted practice to number each heading level in certain long documents so that when the document is being reviewed or is under discussion at a meeting, it's easy to refer to the relevant sections. Word uses the outline-level setting for each style as the basis for the numbering hierarchy.

SEE ALSO: For information about setting outline levels, see "Organizing with Styles" on pages 74–75.

TIP: To number all the lines in a document, choose Page Layout from the File menu, and click the Line Numbers button on the Layout tab.

Number the Headings

③ Choose Bullets And Numbering from the Format menu.

② Click in the first heading paragraph.

① Verify that all the headings have the correct heading styles applied.

④ Click the Outline Numbered tab.

⑤ Click one of the numbering schemes shown in the bottom row.

⑥ Click OK.

⑦ Verify that your document headings are numbered correctly. If you don't like the numbering scheme, click the Undo button on the Standard toolbar.

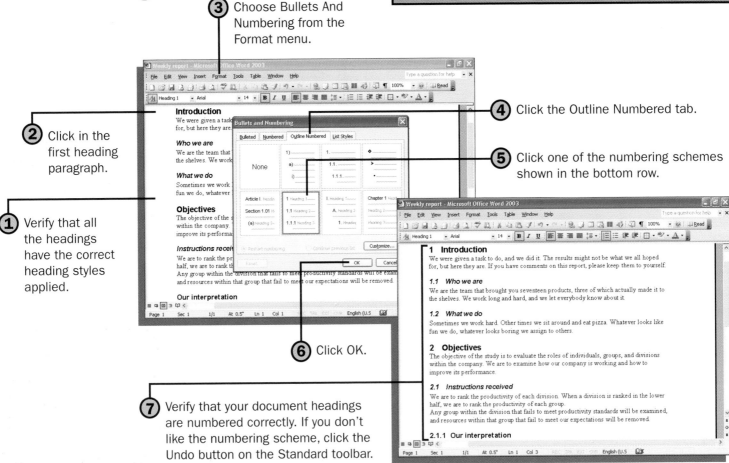

Numbering Pages and Creating Running Heads

In addition to page numbers, a long document usually has some type of identifying text—called a *running head*—at the top or bottom of each page of the document. All you do is create the running head once, and Word places it on the pages you designate. For the sake of consistency, we're using the term *running head*

for the heading itself, and the terms *header* and *footer* to describe the running head's position on the page. Note that on the screen you can see the headers and footers on your page only in Print Layout view or in Print Preview.

Create a Header

(1) Choose Header And Footer from the View menu.

(2) Type the text you want for the header in the Header area. Use tabs, paragraph spacing and alignment, and font settings to customize the layout.

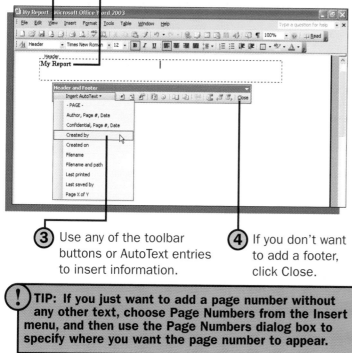

(3) Use any of the toolbar buttons or AutoText entries to insert information.

(4) If you don't want to add a footer, click Close.

> **TIP:** If you just want to add a page number without any other text, choose Page Numbers from the Insert menu, and then use the Page Numbers dialog box to specify where you want the page number to appear.

Create a Footer

(1) Click the Switch Between Header And Footer button.

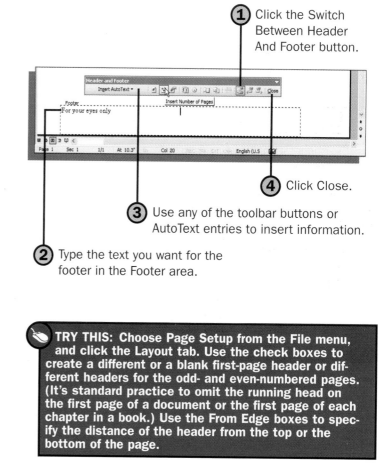

(4) Click Close.

(3) Use any of the toolbar buttons or AutoText entries to insert information.

(2) Type the text you want for the footer in the Footer area.

> **TRY THIS:** Choose Page Setup from the File menu, and click the Layout tab. Use the check boxes to create a different or a blank first-page header or different headers for the odd- and even-numbered pages. (It's standard practice to omit the running head on the first page of a document or the first page of each chapter in a book.) Use the From Edge boxes to specify the distance of the header from the top or the bottom of the page.

Creating Chapters

A long document is usually divided into chapters or sections, each of which should begin on an odd-numbered (right-hand, or recto) page. Word will start your chapters or sections on odd-numbered pages, and will create running heads to your specifications.

SEE ALSO: For information about running heads, see "Numbering Pages and Creating Running Heads" on page 77.

Start a New Chapter

1 In the document you want to divide into different chapters, place the insertion point at the beginning of the paragraph that starts a new chapter or section.

2 Choose Break from the Insert menu to display the Break dialog box.

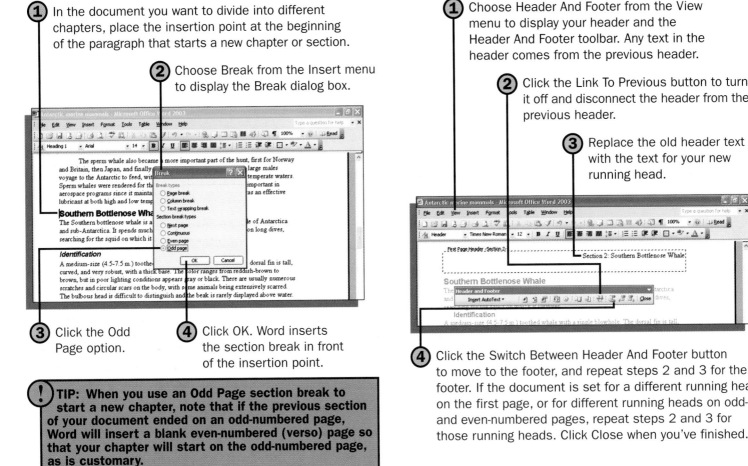

3 Click the Odd Page option.

4 Click OK. Word inserts the section break in front of the insertion point.

! TIP: When you use an Odd Page section break to start a new chapter, note that if the previous section of your document ended on an odd-numbered page, Word will insert a blank even-numbered (verso) page so that your chapter will start on the odd-numbered page, as is customary.

Change the Running Heads

1 Choose Header And Footer from the View menu to display your header and the Header And Footer toolbar. Any text in the header comes from the previous header.

2 Click the Link To Previous button to turn it off and disconnect the header from the previous header.

3 Replace the old header text with the text for your new running head.

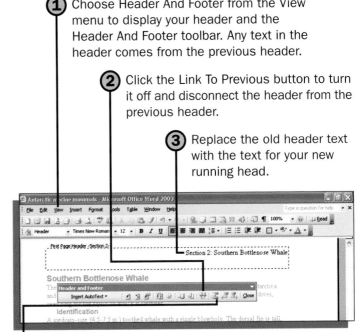

4 Click the Switch Between Header And Footer button to move to the footer, and repeat steps 2 and 3 for the footer. If the document is set for a different running head on the first page, or for different running heads on odd- and even-numbered pages, repeat steps 2 and 3 for those running heads. Click Close when you've finished.

Creating a Table of Contents

Provided your document is organized by styles, it's a snap to have Word create a well-organized table of contents for you. You design your table of contents by selecting a format and designating which levels are assigned to the headings. Word can adjust the appearance of the table of contents depending on how you're viewing it. In Web Layout view, for example, the table can consist of links, but in Print Layout view or Print Preview it looks like a table of contents you'd see in a book. Either way, when your document is viewed on line, the table of contents is active, so if you click it (or press Ctrl+click, depending on your settings), you'll jump right to that part of your document.

Create and Format Your TOC

(1) With the insertion point located in your document where you want the table of contents to appear, point to Reference on the Insert menu, and choose Index And Tables from the submenu to display the Index And Tables dialog box. Click the Table Of Contents tab.

(2) Select a check box to display the page numbers either next to corresponding entries in the table of contents or aligned at the right side of the page. If you want the page numbers right-aligned, specify a style for the tab leader that's placed between the entry and the page number.

(4) Select this check box to display links in Web Layout view, or clear the check box if page numbers are to be displayed.

(5) Specify the lowest outline level to be included in the table of contents. Paragraphs whose style has been assigned an outline level that's included within this range will appear in the table.

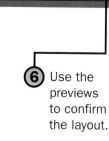

(3) Specify the style of the table of contents. (Some styles will cause some of the layout options to be unavailable.)

(8) Click Modify if you want to change the formatting of the styles used in the table of contents. (You can modify only the styles that come from the template.)

(9) Click OK to create the table of contents.

(6) Use the previews to confirm the layout.

(7) Click Options if you want to specify which styles are included instead of relying on outline levels.

 TIP: To update the table of contents after you've made changes to your document, click the Update TOC button on the Outlining toolbar.

SEE ALSO: For information about assigning outline levels to styles, see "Organizing with Styles" on pages 74–75.

Creating a Drawing

For those of us who aren't great artists, Word's drawing tools provide a quick and easy way to create a variety of professional looking drawings directly on the page. For an extremely complex drawing, you'll probably want to use a drawing program and then insert the picture, but try using Word's tools first. As artistically challenged individuals, we were really astonished at some of the lively effects we created.

Draw a Shape

> ⚠️ **TIP:** You can work on all the different elements of a drawing on the Drawing Canvas. When you've completed your drawing, all the elements stay together, and you can scale or move them as a unit. You can also format the Drawing Canvas to provide a backdrop for your drawing. If the Drawing Canvas doesn't appear when you insert an AutoShape, choose Options from the Tools menu, and, on the General tab, select the Automatically Create Drawing Canvas When Inserting AutoShapes check box.

① Click the Drawing button on the Standard toolbar to display the Drawing toolbar if it isn't already displayed.

③ On the Drawing Canvas that appears, drag the mouse to create the shape in the dimensions you want. Hold down the Shift key while dragging to draw the shape without distortion.

② Click AutoShapes, point to a type of AutoShape, and click the shape you want.

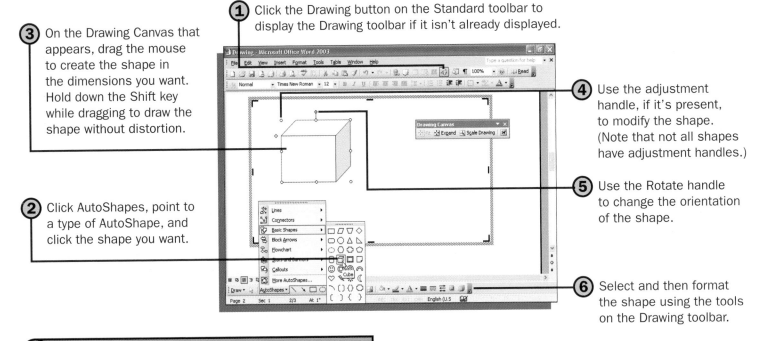

④ Use the adjustment handle, if it's present, to modify the shape. (Note that not all shapes have adjustment handles.)

⑤ Use the Rotate handle to change the orientation of the shape.

⑥ Select and then format the shape using the tools on the Drawing toolbar.

> ⚠️ **TIP:** If you have a drawing tablet attached to your computer, or if you can draw really well with the mouse, you can use the Drawing Pad to create and insert a drawing. The Drawing Pad is one of the Handwriting tools, which must be installed to enable you to use this feature.

> **SEE ALSO:** For information about the Handwriting tools, see "Writing Text by Hand" on page 332.

Combine Drawings

⑥ Drag the drawing to the location you want.

⑦ Click outside the Drawing Canvas to return to your normal text.

> **SEE ALSO:** For information about formatting a drawing, see "Drawing on a Canvas" on page 309, "Drawing AutoShapes" on pages 310–11, and "Formatting an Object" on page 319.

① Create and format any additional AutoShapes you want. Drag the objects (the drawings) to arrange them. Right-click an object, choose Order from the shortcut menu, and change the *stacking order* of the objects. Continue rearranging the objects until they're in the desired form.

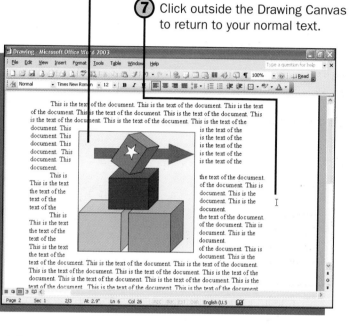

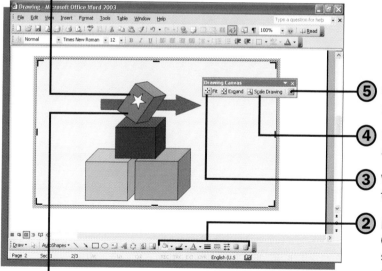

⑤ Click Text Wrapping, and specify how you want the drawing positioned in relationship to the text.

④ If you want to scale the entire drawing, click Scale Drawing, and drag the sizing handles on the canvas to scale it.

③ When all the elements are arranged to your liking, click Fit to shrink the Drawing Canvas to fit the drawing.

② If you want to format the background or the border of the Drawing Canvas, click inside the canvas so that no drawing element is selected, and then use the tools on the Drawing toolbar to add a color fill, a line border, or a shadow or 3-D effect.

The stacking order of the objects is set so that the star is on top of the box, and the box is on top of the arrow.

Reorganizing a Document

Outline view provides a powerful way for you to view the structure of your document and to rearrange the order of presentation of the topics in the document. The outline structure assumes that you've used specific styles to organize your document into a hierarchy of topics and subtopics.

> **TRY THIS:** Drag a topic's plus or minus sign to the left to quickly promote the topic's outline level, to the right to demote it, or to the far right to turn it into body text. Changing the outline level also changes the style that's assigned to that paragraph.

View a Document's Outline

(1) Start Word, and open your document if it isn't already open. Switch to Outline view.

(2) Specify which levels of headings are to be displayed.

(4) Click to change the outline level of a heading by promoting it one level, demoting it one level, or specifying the outline level.

(5) Click to expand or collapse the content under the heading.

(3) Click in a heading.

A minus sign indicates that there's no content under the heading.

A plus sign indicates that there's some content under the heading.

A squiggle indicates that the content under the heading is collapsed and not shown.

> **TIP:** To quickly expand or collapse a section, double-click the plus sign next to the heading.

Move a Paragraph

① Expand the outline so that the paragraph you want to move and the area into which you want to move it are both displayed.

② Click in the paragraph that you want to move.

③ Click to move the paragraph up or down in the document.

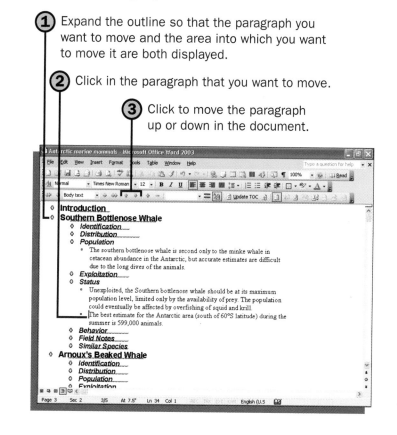

Move a Section

① Click the plus sign to select the entire section.

② Click to move the topic up or down in the document.

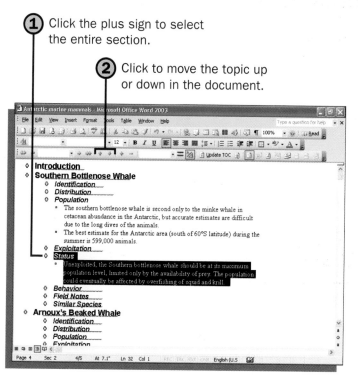

> **TIP:** When you select and move a section, all the paragraphs in that section are moved, including those that haven't been expanded and displayed.

> **TIP:** To quickly move a section, click the plus sign next to the heading, and then drag the heading up or down in the document.

> **CAUTION:** Be very careful about editing text in Outline view. For example, if the text of a section is collapsed under its heading, you might think that you're deleting only the heading, but you're actually deleting all the text in that section.

Positioning a Picture

When you position a picture within a paragraph of text, you usually place the picture in line with the text so that the picture aligns just like a single text character—albeit a very large one. By changing the text wrapping, you can change the way the picture is positioned in the document.

TRY THIS: Choose Options from the Tools menu, and, in the Insert/Paste Pictures As list on the Edit tab, specify the type of text wrapping you'll want to use for most of the pictures you'll be inserting. Click OK. Now you won't need to change the text-wrapping option each time you insert a picture.

Set the Text Wrapping

(1) Click the picture to select it and to display the Picture toolbar if it isn't already displayed.

(2) Click the Text Wrapping button, and specify the text-wrapping option you want.

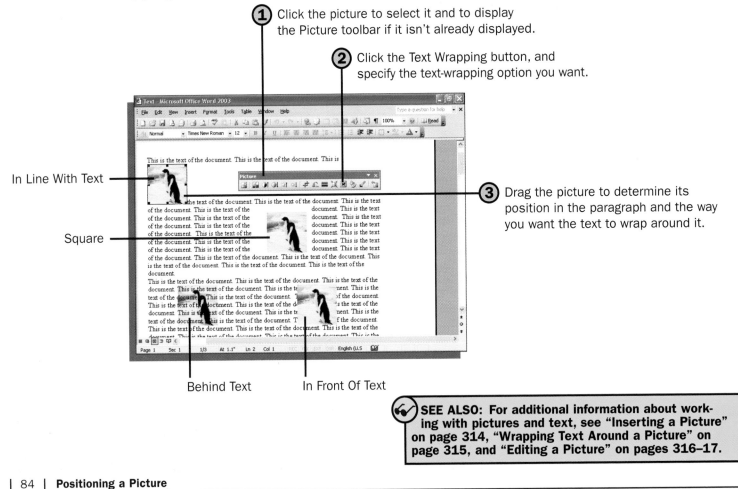

In Line With Text

Square

Behind Text

In Front Of Text

(3) Drag the picture to determine its position in the paragraph and the way you want the text to wrap around it.

SEE ALSO: For additional information about working with pictures and text, see "Inserting a Picture" on page 314, "Wrapping Text Around a Picture" on page 315, and "Editing a Picture" on pages 316–17.

Rotate the Picture

(1) Click the picture to select it and to display the Picture toolbar if it isn't already displayed.

(2) Click the Rotate Left button to rotate the picture 90 degrees. Continue clicking the button to rotate the picture at 90-degree increments.

(!) **TIP:** If you've made numerous changes to a picture and then decide that you don't like the results, you can easily revert to the original picture and start over. To do so, click the picture to select it, and then click the Reset Picture button on the Picture toolbar. Be aware, however, that this removes all your changes, including those you've made to the dimensions, color, text wrapping, and rotation.

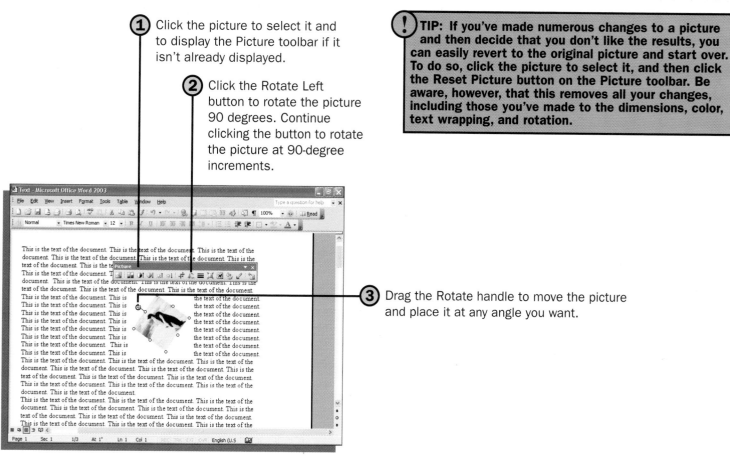

(3) Drag the Rotate handle to move the picture and place it at any angle you want.

(!) **TIP:** You can't rotate a picture with the Rotate handle until Word has changed the picture into an object. Word does this automatically when you set the picture for text wrapping or when you click the Rotate Left button on the Picture toolbar.

TRY THIS: Rotate the picture using the Rotate handle. Click the Format Picture button on the Picture toolbar, and, on the Size tab of the Format Picture dialog box, set the rotation to a specific angle. Click OK.

Creating Footnotes

Word makes it so easy to add footnotes to a document! Word can mark the footnoted material for you with an automatic series of numbers or symbols, or you can insert your own choice of symbols. When you leave it to Word to insert the footnote number, it updates the number whenever you add or delete a footnote. Word also figures out how much space is required at the bottom of the page for the footnote, and when a footnote is too long for the page, Word automatically continues it on the next page. How clever!

Insert a Footnote

(1) With the insertion point located where you want the footnote to appear, point to Reference on the Insert menu, and choose Footnote from the submenu to display the Footnote And Endnote dialog box.

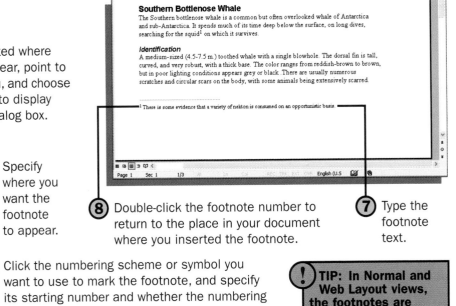

(2) Click the Footnotes option.

(6) Click to insert the footnote.

(3) Specify where you want the footnote to appear.

(4) Click the numbering scheme or symbol you want to use to mark the footnote, and specify its starting number and whether the numbering scheme is continuous throughout the document or restarts at a specific location—each page or each section, for example.

(5) Specify whether the changes apply to the whole document or to a specific part of it.

(8) Double-click the footnote number to return to the place in your document where you inserted the footnote.

(7) Type the footnote text.

> **! TIP: In Normal and Web Layout views, the footnotes are entered in a special Footnote pane that appears at the bottom of the window.**

> **! TIP: Endnotes are just like footnotes, except that endnotes appear all together at the end of a document (or the end of a section) instead of at the foot of each page. Use the Convert button to change footnotes into endnotes, and vice versa.**

> **TRY THIS: Insert a footnote. Type the footnote, and double-click the footnote number. Select the footnote reference number in the document, and cut it (press Ctrl+X). The footnote is gone. Click elsewhere in your document, and paste the footnote reference number (press Ctrl+V) to restore the footnote. Double-click the footnote reference number, and edit the footnote.**

6 Working in Excel

If you've never used it before, open up Microsoft Office Excel 2003 and take a look at it. You'll see a worksheet that contains a seemingly endless grid of columns and rows—256 columns and 65,536 rows, to be exact. The space at the intersection of each column and row is a cell, and it doesn't take a mathematical genius to realize that you're looking at *millions* of cells! You'll probably never need them all, but there they are, ready to hold your data, whether those data are words (students' names, for example); numbers (individual test scores); or formulas for calculating prices, discounts, and totals for your store's merchandise. And speaking of mathematical geniuses, you don't have to be one to work easily and efficiently in Excel.

You can work with a single worksheet if that's all you need, or you can use multiple worksheets for large projects. You can organize several worksheets that all pertain to one set of data into their own *workbook*. If you work on several large projects, you can give each project its own workbook. When you start a new workbook, you'll see that it contains three worksheets, but you can add more if you need them.

In this section of the book, you'll see how to add visual appeal and clarity to your worksheets by formatting them with fonts, colors, borders, and so on. You can create your own "look" or use templates that quickly apply predefined styles to your worksheets or workbooks. You'll learn how to format numbers in various ways—as currency, percentages, decimals, and so on—for readability. We'll also show you how to update, change, move, or copy your data, and how to print your worksheets.

What's Where in Excel?

Excel has several faces, each with the same purpose—to help you get the most out of your data. The face you see below is a simple worksheet, in which you create your columns and rows of data. Starting a new workbook in which to keep your worksheets and charts is simple: Just choose New from Excel's File menu, and choose Blank Workbook in the New Workbook task pane.

Standard toolbar   Workbook

Formatting toolbar

Column headers

Formula bar

Worksheet

Row headers

Selected cell G10

Gridlines

Status bar

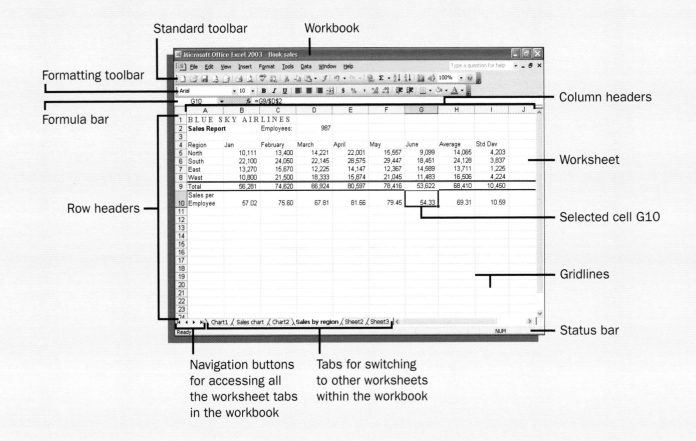

Navigation buttons for accessing all the worksheet tabs in the workbook

Tabs for switching to other worksheets within the workbook

The face you see on this page is a chart, in which you create a visual representation of your data. You can create and customize many types of charts. In addition to adjusting the scale of the axes and changing their color, you can create an additional X and/or Y axis, each with a different scale from that of the primary X and/or Y axis. You can also create a three-dimensional image by adding a Z axis. In addition to

these views, Excel has several other faces, in which you can create a PivotTable or a PivotChart to examine parts of your data, to create personal views, or to display only certain parts of a list that meet your criteria. For information about PivotTables and PivotCharts, see "Summarizing Data with a PivotTable" on pages 130–131.

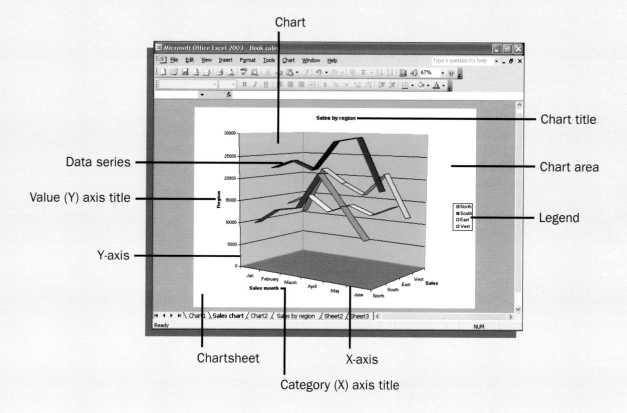

Chart

Chart title

Data series

Value (Y) axis title

Chart area

Legend

Y-axis

Chartsheet

X-axis

Category (X) axis title

Entering Data

Because Excel is all about working with data, whether the items are numbers or names, you'll need to enter the data before Excel can start working its magic. To enter your data, place one data item in each cell, arranged in the way that works best for you.

TIP: To move backward in a row, press Shift+Tab. You can also use your keyboard's arrow keys or the mouse to move to any cell.

Enter Your Data

(1) Start a new workbook if you don't already have a blank worksheet open. Save the workbook with a new file name.

(2) Type the header (the title) of the first column, press Tab, and type the header of the next column. Continue across the top row until all your columns have headers. Press Enter after you've typed the last item.

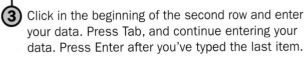

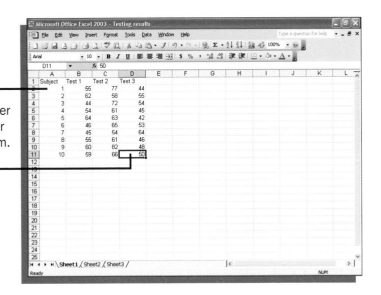

(3) Click in the beginning of the second row and enter your data. Press Tab, and continue entering your data. Press Enter after you've typed the last item.

(4) Continue entering your data row by row, and be sure to save the file periodically.

SEE ALSO: For information about changing and correcting your data, see "Editing the Data" on page 96.

Using a Predefined Workbook

Wouldn't it be great to have a workbook all set up and formatted for you so that all you'd have to do would be enter your information? Well, dream no more! When you use one of Excel's existing templates, you don't have to worry about structure and formatting—they're already taken care of for you. Not only that, but many templates have an extensive array of formulas and relationships already built into them that provide some powerful data analysis.

Open and Use a Template

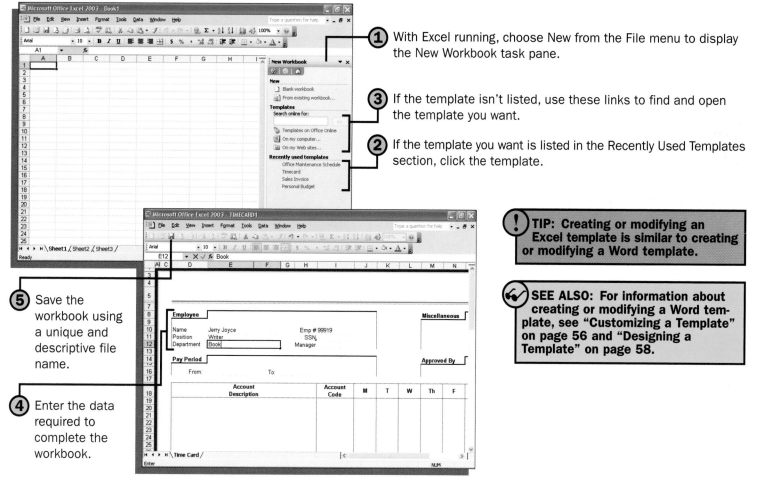

1. With Excel running, choose New from the File menu to display the New Workbook task pane.

3. If the template isn't listed, use these links to find and open the template you want.

2. If the template you want is listed in the Recently Used Templates section, click the template.

TIP: Creating or modifying an Excel template is similar to creating or modifying a Word template.

SEE ALSO: For information about creating or modifying a Word template, see "Customizing a Template" on page 56 and "Designing a Template" on page 58.

5. Save the workbook using a unique and descriptive file name.

4. Enter the data required to complete the workbook.

Excel's Eccentricities

If you're familiar with the way a program such as Microsoft Office Word works, your first reaction to Excel's idiosyncratic behavior might be "Huh?" or "What happened?" To be comfortable with Excel, you need to understand that it's a completely different creature from Word. It behaves differently because it's designed for the organization and analysis of data.

Excel is made up of vertical columns and horizontal rows. At the intersection of a column and a row is a cell. This grid structure is designed to help you organize your data. Look at the worksheet below. All the data in column A are related—that is, each cell contains the name of a student. Similarly, all the data in columns B, C, and D are related—they represent scores for different exams. The data in rows are related too. All the items in row 2 are related to each other—that is, each is about John A.'s exam scores. So, at the intersection of a column and a row is a single piece of data—a *data point*. At the intersection of column C and row 2 is the data point indicating that in Exam 2 (column C), John A. (row 2) scored 77. In Excel's cell notation—its shorthand language—this data point is located in cell C2.

Keep in mind that Excel is all about data. Unlike Word, it cares little about presentation. You can, with a little work, make a fine-looking presentation in Excel, but Excel might occasionally stymie you because its priority is to preserve the integrity of the data when the data are being edited. This means that if you click in a cell and start typing, you'll be replacing the existing data rather than adding to it. Why? Because, to Excel, each cell contains that single piece of data. When you click in a cell that contains data, Excel thinks that you want to either update or correct the data. This can definitely throw you off when you're used to the normal Office protocol of selecting something before you change it! You'll see the same thing when you copy or move columns, rows, or cells. Unlike Word, for example, Excel doesn't automatically add columns or rows to a table to compensate for your actions—you have to manage the columns, rows, or cells yourself.

It might take you a little while to get used to Excel's differences, but, as you start crunching your data, you'll find that what seems like Excel's quirky behavior actually helps you get accurate results very efficiently. Of course, Excel does have many other complexities, such as using *relative* or *absolute* references to cells, and building complex formulas that contain sophisticated functions. However, these features really are designed to make your work with data as precise and accurate as possible. We'll go into detail about cell references, formulas, and functions in "Cell References, Formulas, and Functions" on pages 116–117.

	A	B	C	D
1	Student	Exam 1	Exam 2	Exam 3
2	John A.	55	77	44
3	James	62	58	55
4	Roberta	44	72	54
5	Marianne	54	61	45
6	Jenny	64	63	42
7	Jim	46	65	53
8	John Z.	45	54	64
9	Robert	55	61	46
10	Beth	60	82	48
11	Rick	59	66	50

Formatting Cells

Reviewing or working with the data in your worksheets might not be high on the list of tasks you do with great enthusiasm, but you can make your work in Excel visually interesting by formatting the cells in your worksheets. You can use your favorite fonts, adding emphasis such as italics or bold type if you want; you can add borders and color to the cells; and you can align your data for the greatest clarity.

> **TIP:** To select a large range of cells, select the first (top-left) cell of the selection, scroll down and/or over, hold down the Shift key, and then click the last (bottom-right) cell of the selection.

> **SEE ALSO:** For information on automatically formatting a large selection or an entire worksheet, see "Formatting a Worksheet" on page 104.

Format Some Cells

2 Use the buttons on the Formatting toolbar to format the cells with fonts, emphasis, alignment, borders, and colors.

Click to select the entire worksheet.

Click a row header to select a row.

1 Select the cells you want to format.

3 Choose Cells from the Format menu, and click the Alignment tab in the Format Cells dialog box.

Click a column header to select a column.

Hold down the Ctrl key, and click or drag to select nonadjacent areas.

Drag the mouse over the cells to select them.

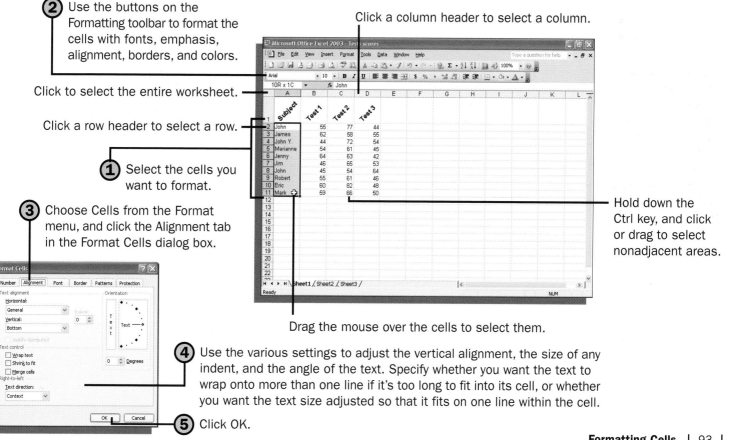

4 Use the various settings to adjust the vertical alignment, the size of any indent, and the angle of the text. Specify whether you want the text to wrap onto more than one line if it's too long to fit into its cell, or whether you want the text size adjusted so that it fits on one line within the cell.

5 Click OK.

Formatting Numbers

When you look at columns and rows stacked full of numbers, it isn't always immediately clear what those numbers represent. Do they indicate currency? Are they percentages of something?

You can improve the readability of your workbook by using standard numeric formatting to make everything as clear as possible.

Format Some Numbers

1 Select the cells, rows, or columns that contain numbers that are all going to be formatted in the same way.

Percent Style button ── Comma Style button

Currency Style button ── Increase Decimal button

Decrease Decimal button

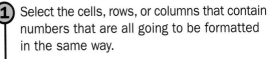

2 Use the buttons on the Formatting toolbar to set the numeric formatting.

Select a Formatting Style

1 Select the cells you want to format.

2 Choose Cells from the Format menu, and click the Number tab in the Format Cells dialog box.

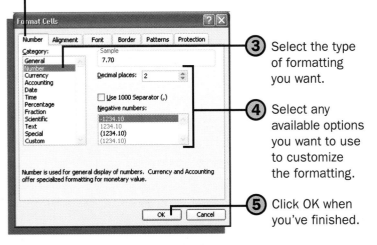

3 Select the type of formatting you want.

4 Select any available options you want to use to customize the formatting.

5 Click OK when you've finished.

> **TRY THIS: Create a custom format. In the Format Cells dialog box, click the Number tab, and choose Custom from the Category list. Select 0.00 in the list, and in the Type text box, change the code so that it reads #.000, and then click OK. In the formatted cell, type 0.1, and press Enter. Return to the cell, type 1.001, and press Enter. Note that in the formatting code, the # symbol is an optional placeholder, so if the value is zero, nothing appears in that place, whereas the 0 in the code is a mandatory digit, so that digit will always appear, even if its value is zero.**

Adding and Viewing Comments

Isn't it unnerving to look at some work you did a month or a week ago (or even something you slaved over yesterday) and to think, "Now why did I do *that?*" Adding a note with an explanatory comment to an item in a worksheet can help keep you sane by keeping track of what you're doing now and what you've done previously, not to mention clarifying what you did and why for a coworker who'll be using or reviewing that worksheet.

Create a Comment

1 Right-click the cell to which you want to attach your comment, and choose Insert Comment from the shortcut menu to create the note.

2 Type your comment. Press Enter only if you need to start a new paragraph in the note. Click outside the note when you've finished it.

Read a Comment

2 If you can't find a comment, or if you want to review several comments, use one of the Comments buttons to find and review comments or to display all the comments at one time. If the Reviewing toolbar isn't displayed, right-click any toolbar, and choose Reviewing from the shortcut menu.

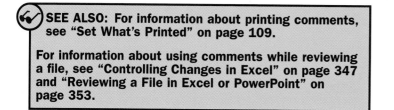

The Reviewing toolbar

1 Move the mouse pointer over a cell that contains a red triangle in the top-right corner. Read the comment that appears.

SEE ALSO: For information about printing comments, see "Set What's Printed" on page 109.

For information about using comments while reviewing a file, see "Controlling Changes in Excel" on page 347 and "Reviewing a File in Excel or PowerPoint" on page 353.

TIP: To change the user name that's displayed in a comment, choose Options from the Tools menu, and, on the General tab, change the name in the User Name text box. To always display all the comments in the workbook, select the Comments & Indicator option on the View tab of the Options dialog box.

Editing the Data

Sometimes you need to go back into a worksheet and make changes to your data. Perhaps something needs to be updated (a price has changed, for example, or one item has been replaced with another), or you've discovered an error (you've misspelled someone's name). You can correct the data quickly and easily, either by replacing the contents of an entire cell or by editing the existing content.

Replace the Data

① Click in the cell whose data you want to replace.

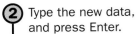

② Type the new data, and press Enter.

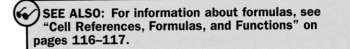

CAUTION: Before you edit the data in a cell, make sure that the cell doesn't contain an equal sign (=). The equal sign means that the cell contains a formula rather than data. If you accidentally edit a formula, you can press the Esc key to cancel the editing.

SEE ALSO: For information about formulas, see "Cell References, Formulas, and Functions" on pages 116–117.

Edit the Existing Data

(1) Double-click the cell to activate it for editing.

(2) Click where you want to edit.

(3) Use the Backspace or Delete key to remove whatever you don't want, and type the new information. Press Enter when you've finished.

TIP: If you double-click a cell but nothing seems to happen, choose Options from the Tools menu, select the Edit Directly In Cell check box on the Edit tab, and click OK.

TRY THIS: You can do some easy editing without using the mouse. Click in the first cell of a row in which you want to edit several items. Press the F2 key to activate editing, edit the cell contents, and then press the Tab key to go to the next cell. Press the F2 key again, make your edits, and press the Tab key again.

TIP: You can also use the Formula bar to edit or replace the text of a selected cell if you prefer. The changes you make in the Formula bar will appear in the selected cell.

Moving and Copying Data

As in most Office programs, you can move the existing information around by copying or cutting it. However, when you copy data in Excel, you'll need to have a blank area ready to receive the data, or else Excel will overwrite any existing data. You can also tell Excel to copy the contents of a cell to a group of adjacent cells.

Move Some Content

(1) Select all the cells you want to move.

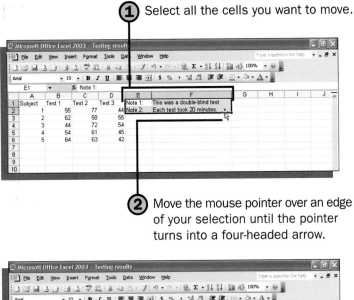

(2) Move the mouse pointer over an edge of your selection until the pointer turns into a four-headed arrow.

(3) Drag the selection to a blank location.

Copy or Cut Some Content

(1) Select all the cells you want to copy or cut.

(2) Click either the Copy or the Cut button.

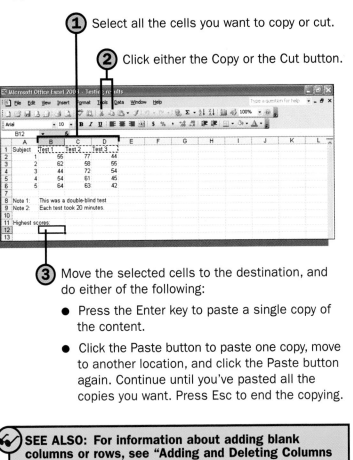

(3) Move the selected cells to the destination, and do either of the following:

- Press the Enter key to paste a single copy of the content.

- Click the Paste button to paste one copy, move to another location, and click the Paste button again. Continue until you've pasted all the copies you want. Press Esc to end the copying.

✅ **SEE ALSO:** For information about adding blank columns or rows, see "Adding and Deleting Columns and Rows" on page 100.

Copy Content to Adjacent Cells

(1) Select the cell whose content you want to copy.

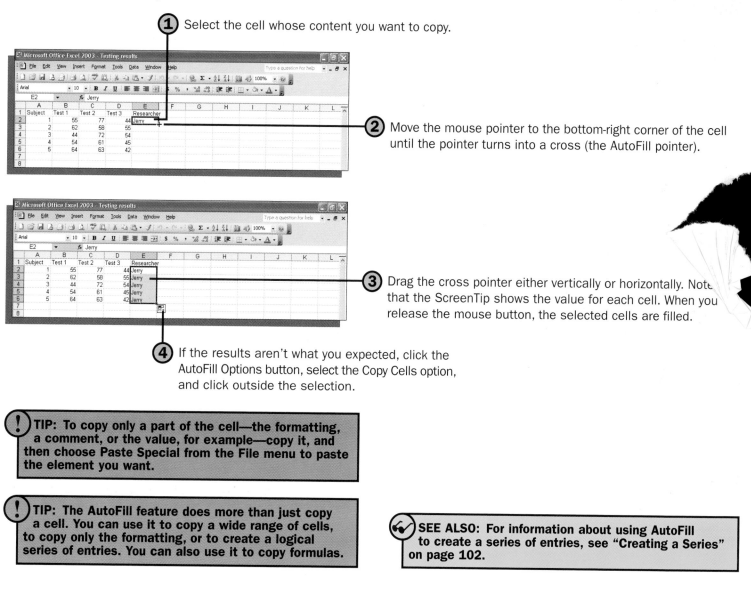

(2) Move the mouse pointer to the bottom-right corner of the cell until the pointer turns into a cross (the AutoFill pointer).

(3) Drag the cross pointer either vertically or horizontally. Note that the ScreenTip shows the value for each cell. When you release the mouse button, the selected cells are filled.

(4) If the results aren't what you expected, click the AutoFill Options button, select the Copy Cells option, and click outside the selection.

> **TIP:** To copy only a part of the cell—the formatting, a comment, or the value, for example—copy it, and then choose Paste Special from the File menu to paste the element you want.

> **TIP:** The AutoFill feature does more than just copy a cell. You can use it to copy a wide range of cells, to copy only the formatting, or to create a logical series of entries. You can also use it to copy formulas.

> **SEE ALSO:** For information about using AutoFill to create a series of entries, see "Creating a Series" on page 102.

Adding and Deleting Columns and Rows

It might take a little time to get your worksheet laid out perfectly, but getting it exactly right is simple enough and very satisfying. You'll probably need to rearrange some rows or columns, delete empty or useless rows or columns, or add new ones. You might need to make room for some data that you want to move. If you find that you need an existing row or column but that its current content is useless, you can simply delete the content but leave the empty row or column intact.

Add a Column

(1) Right-click the column header at the right of where you want the new column.

Excel will create a new column C.

(2) Choose Insert from the shortcut menu.

Add a Row

(1) Right-click the row header below where you want the new row.

(2) Choose Insert from the shortcut menu.

Excel will create a new row 5.

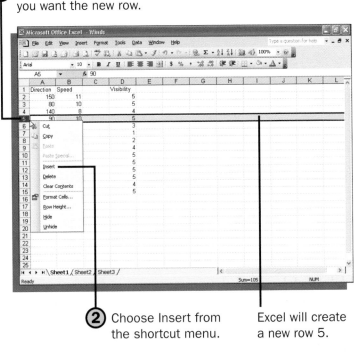

> **! TIP:** To add or delete several rows or columns at one time, or to clear the contents of multiple rows or columns at one time, select multiple column or row headers before you right-click. To select nonadjacent rows or columns, hold down the Ctrl key as you click each row or column header.

Delete a Column or a Row

(1) Right-click the column header or row header.

(2) Choose Delete from the shortcut menu.

Delete the Contents of a Column or a Row

(1) Click the column header or row header.

(2) Point to Clear on the Edit menu, and choose what you want to delete from the submenu.

SEE ALSO: For information about hiding columns or rows without deleting them, see "Hiding Columns and Rows" on page 103.

TRY THIS: In a cell, type a number or some text, and then click the Bold button on the Formatting toolbar. In the next cell in the same row, type another number or some text, and then click the Italic button on the Formatting toolbar. Select the row, and press the Delete key to delete the contents of the row. Now type some numbers or text in the two cells you just formatted, and note that the formatting remains. Select the row again, point to Clear on the Edit menu, and choose Formats from the submenu. Note the changes.

Creating a Series

When you're working with a series—that is, a particular set of data such as a series of dates or a list of consecutive numbers—numbering or labeling all the items in the series can be quite time-consuming. Why not put your time to better use by letting Excel do the work for you? All you need to do is make sure that Excel recognizes the data as a series.

Create a Series

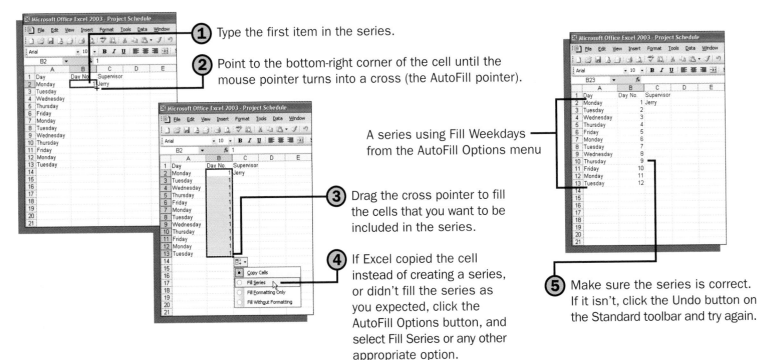

(1) Type the first item in the series.

(2) Point to the bottom-right corner of the cell until the mouse pointer turns into a cross (the AutoFill pointer).

A series using Fill Weekdays from the AutoFill Options menu

(3) Drag the cross pointer to fill the cells that you want to be included in the series.

(4) If Excel copied the cell instead of creating a series, or didn't fill the series as you expected, click the AutoFill Options button, and select Fill Series or any other appropriate option.

(5) Make sure the series is correct. If it isn't, click the Undo button on the Standard toolbar and try again.

> **TIP:** To define a numeric or date series that is non-linear, that doesn't use a single-step value, or that is very long, point to Fill on the Edit menu, choose Series from the submenu, and use the Series dialog box to set the parameters for your series.

> **TIP:** If the Fill Series option isn't listed on the Auto-Fill Options shortcut menu, Excel doesn't recognize the data as a series. You can define your own series by choosing Options from the Tools menu and, on the Custom Lists tab, defining your list. Sometimes the AutoFill Options shortcut menu provides additional choices for creating specific types of series.

Hiding Columns and Rows

When you create a worksheet, it sometimes contains columns and rows of data that aren't relevant for every review or use of the worksheet, even though they're important in various analyses.

You can hide these columns and rows from view when they're not needed and reveal them again when you or someone else wants to review or work with them.

Hide Columns or Rows

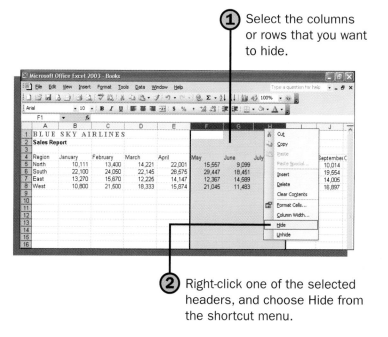

1 Select the columns or rows that you want to hide.

2 Right-click one of the selected headers, and choose Hide from the shortcut menu.

Reveal Hidden Columns or Rows

1 Select the columns or rows that are adjacent to the hidden rows or columns.

2 Right-click one of the selected headers, and choose Unhide from the shortcut menu.

> **TIP:** You don't have to do much detective work to know where columns or rows are hidden—just look for header titles that aren't consecutive.

> **TRY THIS:** Choose Custom Views from the View menu, and, in the Custom Views dialog box, click Add. Type Unhidden, and click OK. Hide some columns and/or rows, and then use the Custom Views dialog box to name them Hidden. Choose Custom Views from the View menu, select the Unhidden name, and click Show. You can add multiple custom views so that you can view the worksheet exactly the way you want.

Formatting a Worksheet

You've already seen how much you can improve the appearance of your worksheets by formatting the cells, so you'll be glad to know that you can use those same elements—fonts, colors, borders, and so on—to format all or part of the worksheet to add clarity and visual appeal to your data. Excel provides a multitude of formats that you can apply automatically; the only difficulty might be deciding which one to choose!

Format a Table

(1) Select the cells that you want to format as a table.

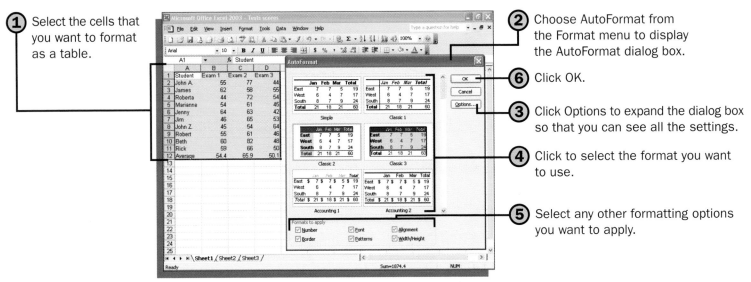

(2) Choose AutoFormat from the Format menu to display the AutoFormat dialog box.

(6) Click OK.

(3) Click Options to expand the dialog box so that you can see all the settings.

(4) Click to select the format you want to use.

(5) Select any other formatting options you want to apply.

> **! TIP:** To select the entire worksheet, click the blank header between the "1" row header and the "A" column header. If the cells in the area you want to format are contiguous—that is, all the cells are adjacent to one another—just click in any one of the cells before you choose AutoFormat, and Excel will figure out the area to be formatted.

> **TRY THIS:** Point to Sheet on the Format menu, and choose Background from the submenu. Find a picture that you like or that's relevant to your data, and click Insert. Format your data so that it's easily readable on top of your picture. Now that's adding some *real* interest to your formatting!

Set the Column Width

(1) Select the columns whose widths you want to change.

(2) Right-click one of the selected column headers, and choose Column Width from the shortcut menu to display the Column Width dialog box.

Set the Row Height

(1) Select the rows whose heights you want to change.

(2) Right-click one of the selected row headers, and choose Row Height from the shortcut menu to display the Row Height dialog box.

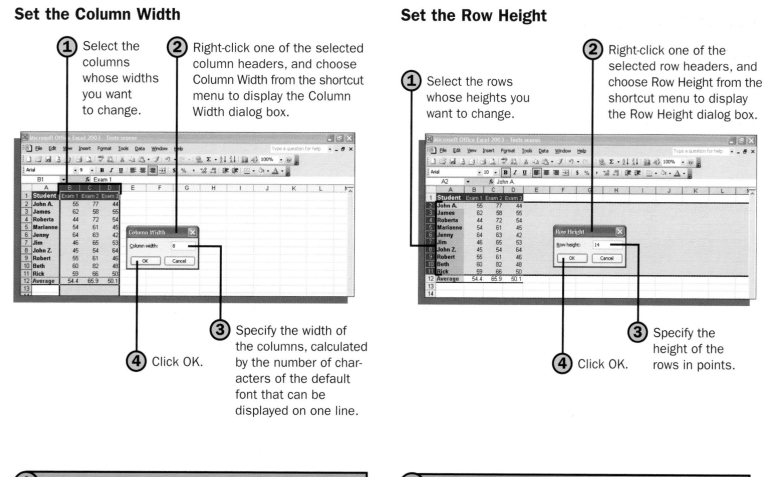

(4) Click OK.

(3) Specify the width of the columns, calculated by the number of characters of the default font that can be displayed on one line.

(4) Click OK.

(3) Specify the height of the rows in points.

! **TIP:** To adjust the height of a single row, drag the boundary of the row header up or down. To adjust the width of a single column, drag the column header right or left. To manually adjust the height of several rows or the width of several columns so that they're the same height or width as each other, select the rows or columns, and then drag the boundary of one of the selected row headers or column headers to the height or width you want.

! **TIP:** To set a standard width of columns for the entire worksheet, point to Columns on the Format menu, choose Standard Width from the submenu, and enter the desired width in the Standard Width dialog box.

Organizing Your Worksheets

When you're working on a big project, you can spend so much time deep in your Excel workbook that it becomes an alternate universe. You can do a lot to make that workbook universe a comfortable place in which to work. Give your worksheets descriptive names—rather than Sheet 1, Sheet 2—to make them easy to recognize; reorganize them into a logical order; add new worksheets if you need to, or delete unused ones to get rid of any unnecessary clutter.

Name the Worksheets

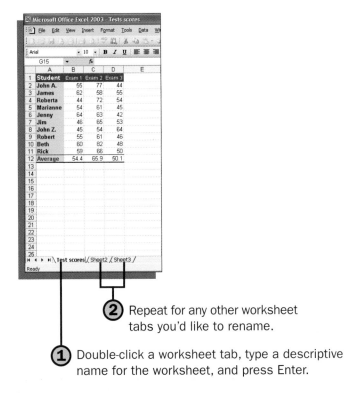

(2) Repeat for any other worksheet tabs you'd like to rename.

(1) Double-click a worksheet tab, type a descriptive name for the worksheet, and press Enter.

Change Their Order

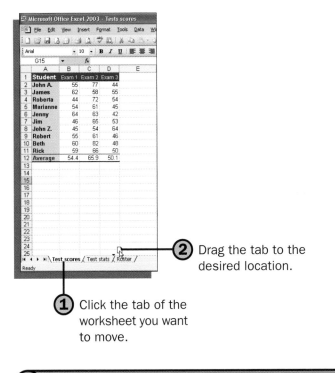

(2) Drag the tab to the desired location.

(1) Click the tab of the worksheet you want to move.

> **!** TIP: To change the color of a worksheet tab, right-click the tab, choose Tab Color from the shortcut menu, and select a color in the Format Tab Color dialog box.

Insert a Worksheet

Delete a Worksheet

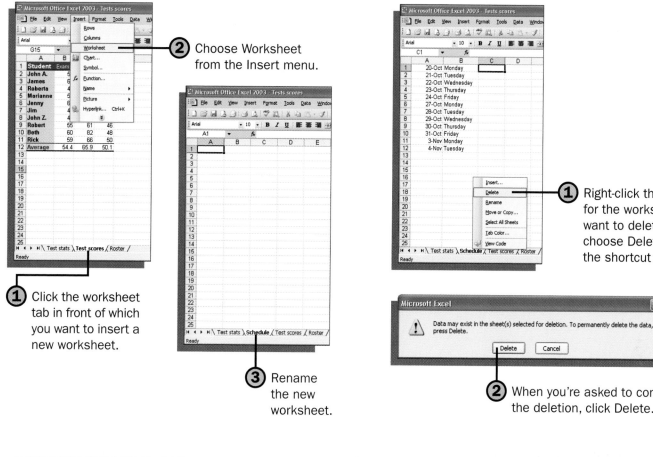

(2) Choose Worksheet from the Insert menu.

(1) Click the worksheet tab in front of which you want to insert a new worksheet.

(3) Rename the new worksheet.

(1) Right-click the tab for the worksheet you want to delete, and choose Delete from the shortcut menu.

(2) When you're asked to confirm the deletion, click Delete.

! TIP: To hide a worksheet from view instead of deleting it, click the tab to select the sheet, point to Sheet on the Format menu, and choose Hide from the submenu.

TRY THIS: Right-click a worksheet tab, and choose Insert from the shortcut menu. On the Spreadsheet Solutions tab, double-click one of the worksheet templates, and note that you have now added a new worksheet, based on an existing template, to your existing workbook.

Setting Up the Page

You don't really need to worry about page setup in Excel until you're ready to print your worksheet, but at that point it's crucial that you attend to several details so that you get the results you want.

CAUTION: Your computer must have a printer (either a local or a network printer) set up and available for use in order for you to make settings in the Page Setup dialog box.

Set the Dimensions

(1) Choose Page Setup from the File menu to display the Page Setup dialog box.

TIP: If you're going to print more than one worksheet, use the Page Setup dialog box to make the settings for each worksheet.

(2) On the Page tab, select either the Portrait (longer than wide) or the Landscape (wider than long) printing orientation.

(3) Specify the scaling to change the size of the printed worksheet or to force the worksheet to fit onto a set number of pages.

(4) Specify the printing information.

(6) Click the Margins tab, and specify the margins you want for the page.

(5) Change if you'll be numbering the pages and you want the first page to start on a number other than 1.

(7) Specify whether you want the worksheet to be centered horizontally or vertically if its contents don't fill the whole page.

Set the Header and Footer

Set What's Printed

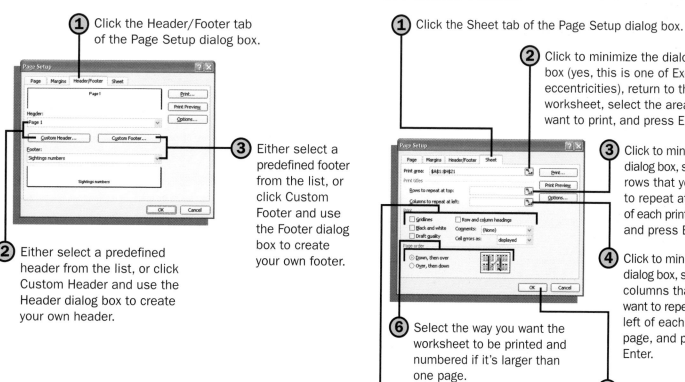

1 Click the Header/Footer tab of the Page Setup dialog box.

1 Click the Sheet tab of the Page Setup dialog box.

2 Click to minimize the dialog box (yes, this is one of Excel's eccentricities), return to the worksheet, select the area you want to print, and press Enter.

3 Either select a predefined footer from the list, or click Custom Footer and use the Footer dialog box to create your own footer.

3 Click to minimize the dialog box, select any rows that you want to repeat at the top of each printed page, and press Enter.

2 Either select a predefined header from the list, or click Custom Header and use the Header dialog box to create your own header.

4 Click to minimize the dialog box, select any columns that you want to repeat at the left of each printed page, and press Enter.

6 Select the way you want the worksheet to be printed and numbered if it's larger than one page.

7 Click OK.

5 Select the items that you want to print.

! **TIP:** If the data area of your worksheet is made up of contiguous cells, Excel will automatically print only the part of the worksheet that contains your data. If you want to print only a section of the worksheet, however, you'll need to set the print area manually.

! **TIP:** You can also set the print area of the worksheet by selecting the area, pointing to Print Area on the File menu, and choosing Set Print Area from the submenu.

Printing a Worksheet

If you don't set it up exactly right, printing an Excel worksheet can be a trip down a rocky road, as well as a waste of paper. To avoid such calamities, you'll need to preview the page before you print it, make a few adjustments, and then preview it again and again—as many times as you need to until you're satisfied that the final product will live up to your expectations.

Check the Layout

1 After you've completed and saved your worksheet, click the Print Preview button on the Standard toolbar, and scrutinize your work.

2 If the page breaks aren't where you want them, click the Page Break Preview button.

4 Click the Print Preview button again to make sure the pages are correctly laid out.

3 Drag a page break to a new position, and adjust other page breaks if necessary.

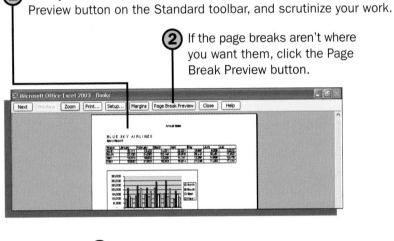

5 If everything looks good, click Print, and use the Print dialog box to print the worksheet or workbook.

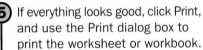

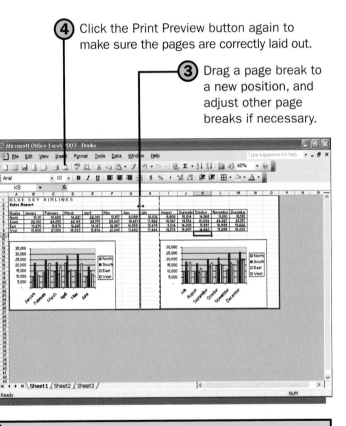

> **SEE ALSO:** For information about using the Print dialog box to specify what you want to print, see "Printing" on page 22.
>
> For information about making basic page settings—margins, orientation, scaling, and so on—see "Setting Up the Page" on pages 108–109.

Reviewing Your Data

Worksheets can quickly become huge and unwieldy. When you need to review your data, you can "freeze" certain parts of the worksheet—the column and/or row titles, for example—so that they'll remain in view while you scroll through other parts of the worksheet. You can also review several workbooks simultaneously.

Freeze It

1 Click in a single cell that's at the right of the columns and/or below the rows to freeze the columns and/or the rows.

2 Choose Freeze Panes from the Window menu.

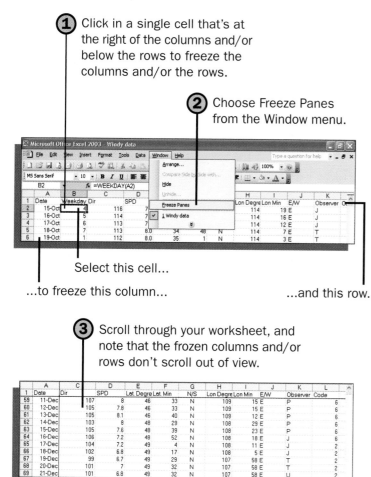

Select this cell...

...to freeze this column...   ...and this row.

3 Scroll through your worksheet, and note that the frozen columns and/or rows don't scroll out of view.

View Multiple Workbooks

1 Open all the workbooks you want to review.

2 Choose Arrange from the Window menu to display the Arrange Windows dialog box.

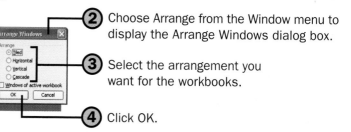

3 Select the arrangement you want for the workbooks.

4 Click OK.

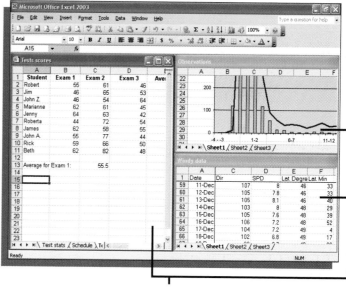

Tiling the windows gives you access to all your open workbooks.

Working with Multiple Workbooks

When you're working on a project in which you need to use several different workbooks at the same time, you can save a list of those workbooks, along with their arrangement on the screen, their print areas, and so on. That way, whenever you have to stop and then resume your work, all you have to do is open the list (Excel calls it your *workspace*), and presto! All the workbooks in the workspace are open and in their preassigned locations.

Create a Workspace

1 Open all the workbooks you need for the project, and arrange them on the screen exactly as you want them.

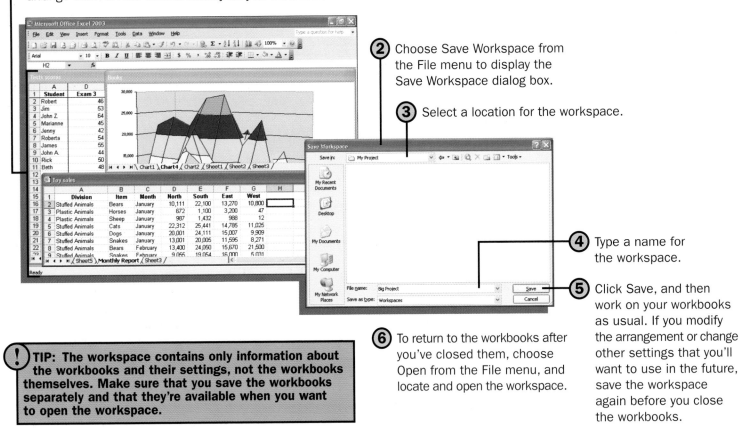

2 Choose Save Workspace from the File menu to display the Save Workspace dialog box.

3 Select a location for the workspace.

4 Type a name for the workspace.

5 Click Save, and then work on your workbooks as usual. If you modify the arrangement or change other settings that you'll want to use in the future, save the workspace again before you close the workbooks.

6 To return to the workbooks after you've closed them, choose Open from the File menu, and locate and open the workspace.

> **! TIP: The workspace contains only information about the workbooks and their settings, not the workbooks themselves. Make sure that you save the workbooks separately and that they're available when you want to open the workspace.**

7 Analyzing Your Data

There's a lot more to working with your data than organizing the information on worksheets and making it look pretty. That's just the first step. Your goal is to analyze all that information and figure out what it means! And this is where you'll unleash the real power of Microsoft Office Excel 2003: its ability to make calculations, from simple ones, such as adding two numbers, to complex statistical, financial, and mathematical computations. Most of these calculations are really quite easy to do, but, of course, it's ultimately your responsibility to know the meaning and significance of the results of those calculations.

In this section, we'll examine the method by which Excel references individual cells and ranges of cells in your worksheets—called *cell notation*. Then we'll move on to the way you use cell notation to create the formulas that make the calculations for you. Cell notation comes in two varieties—relative and absolute—and you'll find examples of both in the procedures and graphics in this section. Then we'll talk about *functions*—ready-made little bits of programming code—that make calculations even simpler by doing the math for you.

There's some fairly advanced stuff in this section: creating a PivotTable that lets you look at relationships among your data, filtering the data so that you can display only the rows in your worksheet that meet the criteria you specify, playing around with arithmetic operators, troubleshooting formulas, using the AutoFill feature to create a series of calculations, importing data from a Web page or a Web service…and more. Take your time as you work your way through this section, and you'll soon feel like that mathematical genius we mentioned earlier.

Making Lists

It's true that Excel is all about data, but data can include more than just numbers. Excel's column-and-row format lends itself smoothly to creating and reviewing lists. Excel provides special features that make short work of sorting your list by specific criteria; filtering it—that is, viewing only part of the list; or summarizing the data in the list.

Create a List

(1) In a worksheet, enter the data for your list, saving the file as you work.

(2) Select the entire list.

(3) Point to List on the Data menu, and choose Create List from the submenu to display the Create List dialog box.

(4) Select this check box if your list has headers (titles) for the columns in the first row, or clear the check box to have Excel provide generic headers (column1, column2, and so on) for the columns.

(5) Click OK to confirm the dimensions of your list.

SEE ALSO: For information about the notation Excel uses to describe ranges of cells, see "Excel's Eccentricities" on page 92 and "Cell References, Formulas, and Functions" on pages 116–117.

SEE ALSO: For information about other ways to view and to extract information from your data, see "Sorting Your Data" on page 126, "Filtering Your Data" on page 127, and "Summarizing Data with a Pivot-Table" on pages 130–131.

Use the List

1 Click in the list, and then click the down arrow at the top of the column that you want to use to sort or filter the list; then select the action you want to take. Repeat for any other column whose data you want to sort or filter.

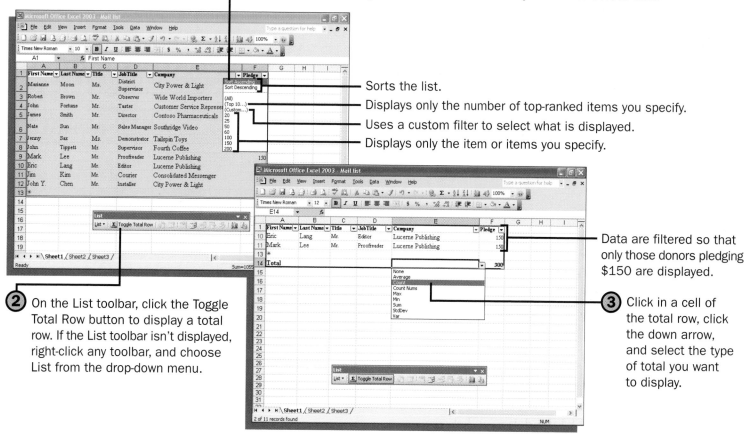

Sorts the list.

Displays only the number of top-ranked items you specify.

Uses a custom filter to select what is displayed.

Displays only the item or items you specify.

Data are filtered so that only those donors pledging $150 are displayed.

2 On the List toolbar, click the Toggle Total Row button to display a total row. If the List toolbar isn't displayed, right-click any toolbar, and choose List from the drop-down menu.

3 Click in a cell of the total row, click the down arrow, and select the type of total you want to display.

! TIP: To add more data to the list, enter the data in the row that contains the asterisk. Excel automatically creates a new row for your data above the bottom row.

! TIP: To convert a list back to standard data in your worksheet, click in the list, point to List on the Data menu, and then choose Convert To Range from the submenu.

Cell References, Formulas, and Functions

Every cell in an Excel worksheet has its own label, or address. For example, if you go to the third column (column C) and work your way down to the fourth row, that cell's label, or address, is C4 (column C, row 4). To quickly determine a *cell reference*, click in the cell, and look in the Name Box at the left of the Formula bar.

A selected range of cells is listed from the top-left cell to the bottom-right cell, so if you select cells from the aforementioned C4 to the sixth column (column F) and the ninth row, the selection goes from cell C4 to cell F9 and, in Excel's cell notation method, is designated as C4:F9. Excel also uses this notation to designate when whole rows or columns are selected. Select row 12 and Excel calls it 12:12; select columns G and H, and their designation is G:H.

Before we go further in this discussion about ranges, there are three special situations you need to be aware of. Occasionally, to make working in Excel more user-friendly, someone will give a cell or a range of cells a name, and will use the name instead of the cell reference. So, if you click in a cell and see a name in the Name Box instead of a cell reference, you'll know why. However, you can ignore the name and use the cell reference if you prefer—just pretend the name doesn't exist. For more information about naming a cell or a range of cells, see "Naming Cells and Ranges" on page 129.

The second situation you might encounter is a style of cell referencing that you're not familiar with. If you look at your workbook and notice that the columns use numbers instead of letters as their titles, or headers, the workbook has been set up to use the R1C1 reference style. This is an old style of cell referencing that some people prefer, but it isn't Excel's default style. In this style, what was cell C4 is referred to as cell R4C3. If you want to switch back to Excel's default reference style, choose Options from the Tools menu,

and, on the General tab, clear the R1C1 Reference Style check box, and then click OK.

The third situation is pretty simple and logical. Because your workbook typically contains more than one worksheet, cell references often include the name of the worksheet as well as the cell references on that worksheet. When your references are exclusively within one worksheet, you can simply omit the worksheet reference. However, if you're including data from more than one worksheet, you need to reference each worksheet so that Excel can understand which cells you're referencing. For example, the cell in reference Sheet1!C4 is a different cell from the one in reference Sheet2!C4. Fortunately, in most cases, Excel adds the sheet reference for you when necessary.

You'll use cell references frequently in Excel—when you designate the area of a worksheet you want to print, for example. One of the most important uses of cell references, however, is in formulas. A formula is what you use to put Excel to work by making calculations for you. A formula can be just a little arithmetic (=4.201*12.8), or it can use values already in the worksheet (=C4/B3). Note that all formulas begin with an equal sign (=). The * (asterisk) symbol indicates multiplication; the / (forward slash) symbol indicates division. The complexity of your formulas is limited only by your mathematical and logical abilities, and by the way you need to manipulate the data.

Another component of a formula can be a function. A function is a bit of computer programming code that does the math for you. What you have to do is insert the correct function and provide the necessary data for the function. For example, if you want to know the total for cells C4 through C20, instead of creating a formula of =C4+C5+C6, and so on, all the way up to +C20, you can simply use the Sum function and create the formula =Sum(C4:C20).

Of course, now that you've got this all figured out, Excel makes it a bit more complicated! There are actually a couple of additional ways to reference cells. You probably won't need to deal with them too often, and, when you do, they'll make more sense to you and can often solve some problems for you. The cell reference we just described is called a relative reference. The other method is called an absolute reference. An absolute reference always references a particular cell, and it's useful when you always want to reference the same constant value. A relative reference is useful when you're working on a series and want to reference a relative position. So, for example, when you reference cell C4 from cell D6, and you're using the absolute reference, you're actually saying, "I don't care what you copy or move or how you fill other cells with this reference; this reference is always to the value in cell C4." When you use the relative reference, you're saying, "I want the value from the cell that's up two rows and over one column; so, from cell D6, I'm referencing cell C4." However, if you copy this relative reference or use it to fill other cells, the cell you'll be referencing is not cell C4 but whatever cell is two rows up and one column over. Got it? Good!

Take a look at the two views of the worksheet below; it uses both relative and absolute references. The first view shows the first three rows of a standard invoice, with the sales tax listed in cell B1, making it easy to modify if the tax rate goes up or (however unlikely!) down. The second view

shows the formulas in this part of the invoice. Note that all the references are relative except for the one in cell E3.

If we use Excel's AutoFill feature to fill row 4 with formulas, as shown in the worksheet below, the formulas relate to items in row 4 and not to those in row 3, except for the absolute reference. That's because when you create the series, AutoFill sees the formula in column D as being the value of the cell two cells to the left plus the value of the cell one cell to the left. If all the references were absolute, each row would have the same values in columns D, E, and F. However, if cell E3 used a relative reference for the tax, the formula in cell E4 would be D4*B2—a meaningless value.

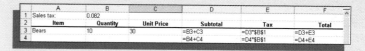

Now that the formulas have the correct references and the cells are filled with the correct formulas, Excel will generate a correct invoice, as shown in the worksheet below.

	A	B	C	D	E	F	G	H	I	J	K	L
1	Sales tax:	8.20%										
2	Item	Quantity	Unit Price	Subtotal	Tax	Total						
3	Bears	10	$ 30.00	$ 40.00	$ 3.28	$ 43.28						
4	Lions	5	$ 10.00	$ 15.00	$ 1.23	16.23						
5	Tigers	3	$ 15.00	$ 18.00	$ 1.48	19.48						
6	Monkeys	12	$ 22.50	$ 34.50	$ 2.83	37.33						
7	Birds	36	$ 12.50	$ 48.50	$ 3.98	52.48						
8			$ -	$ -	$ -							
9			$ -	$ -	$ -							
10	Total			$ 156.00	$ 12.79	$ 168.79						

For more information about creating formulas with AutoFill, and about using absolute references, see "Creating a Series of Calculations" on page 121. For information about calculating totals, see "Summing the Data" on page 120. For information about displaying formulas, see "Troubleshooting Formulas" on pages 124–125.

	A	B	C	D	E	F	G	H	I	J	K	L
1	Sales tax:	8.20%										
2	Item	Quantity	Unit Price	Subtotal	Tax	Total						
3	Bears	10	$ 30.00	$ 40.00	$ 3.28	$ 43.28						
4												

	A	B	C	D	E	F
1	Sales tax:	0.082				
2	Item	Quantity	Unit Price	Subtotal	Tax	Total
3	Bears	10	30	=B3+C3	=D3*B1	=D3+E3
4						

Doing the Arithmetic

Working with math in Excel is similar to working on paper, except that you actually do less work! All you have to do is type the values and arithmetic operators and then leave it to Excel to do all the calculations. You can easily change the values you've entered if necessary, or make the values equal to a value in another cell or series of cells.

Calculate a Value

┌ The formula is also displayed
  in the Formula bar.

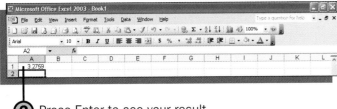

(1) In the cell in which you want the result of the calculation to be displayed, type an equal sign and then the numbers and operators for your calculation.

(2) Press Enter to see your result.

TIP: Excel makes its calculations based on the standard order of precedence for arithmetic operations—that is, negation, percentage, exponentiation, multiplication and division, and addition and subtraction. If two operators have the same precedence, Excel makes the calculation from left to right. To change the order of calculation, you use parentheses to group portions of the formula.

Arithmetic Operators

Action	Operator
Addition	+ (plus sign)
Subtraction	- (minus sign)
Negation	- (minus sign)
Multiplication	* (asterisk)
Division	/ (forward slash)
Percentage	% (percent sign)
Exponentiation	^ (caret)
Set order of actions	( ) (opening and closing parentheses)

TRY THIS: In an empty cell, type =10+5*30+6/3 and press Enter. Copy the formula to a new cell, and then press the F2 key to activate editing of the cell. Add a pair of parentheses to the formula so that it's now (10+5)*30+6/3 and press Enter. Note that using the parentheses changed the order of the operations and thus the result. Continue adding, moving, or deleting pairs of parentheses in the formula to see the effects on the final result.

Calculate the Value of Cells

 In the cell where you want the result to be displayed, type an equal sign.

TIP: You can mix cell references and numeric values in a cell—for example, a formula might be =C1+C3+10. You can also reference cells in other worksheets or in other workbooks.

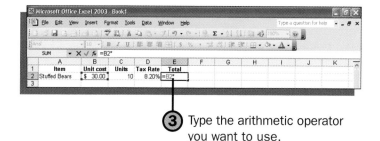

② Click in the cell whose value you want to use.

③ Type the arithmetic operator you want to use.

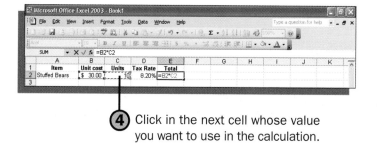

④ Click in the next cell whose value you want to use in the calculation.

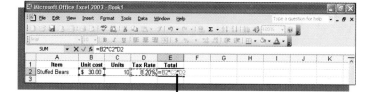

⑤ Continue typing in the operators and clicking in cells until you've completed the formula, and then press Enter.

CAUTION: Don't assume that a formula contains an error just because it uses different operators from those you're familiar with. Some formulas are logical tests that return a true or false value, while others are used to manipulate text. For example, a formula of =C3=10 would display TRUE if the value in cell C3 was equal to 10, and would display FALSE otherwise.

Summing the Data

It's probable that one of the most frequent calculations you'll make in Excel is to sum, or add up, a series of numbers. Luckily, summing is also one of the easiest calculations, with the AutoSum feature just a click away.

! TIP: To adjust the range of cells you're summing, double-click the cell containing the total to activate it for editing, and then modify the selection rectangle that appears.

Sum the Numbers

② Click the AutoSum button.

① Click in a cell below or at the right of the series of cells you want to sum.

③ Make sure the selection rectangle encloses all the cells you want to sum. If you've accidentally included any unwanted cells or omitted any desired cells, move the mouse pointer over a corner of the selection until a two-headed arrow appears, and then drag the selection rectangle to resize it so that it includes all the correct cells. You can also move the entire selection rectangle by pointing to a side of the rectangle and dragging it to a new location.

④ Press Enter to sum the cells and see the result.

TRY THIS: Click in a cell below a series of numbers, click the down arrow at the right of the AutoSum button, choose a different function, and press Enter.

Creating a Series of Calculations

When you reference cells in a formula and then use the AutoFill feature, Excel modifies the reference to cells relative to the new filled cells. That way, you can create a whole series of calculations simply by creating a single calculation and then filling cells with the formula. And if you need to use a single constant value in all the calculations, you can use an absolute reference to a cell instead of a relative reference.

> **TRY THIS: Click in a cell containing a formula with a relative cell reference. Press the F4 key, and note that the reference changes to an absolute reference. Continue pressing the F4 key and noting how the reference changes.**

Create a Series

① Create the first formula, referencing the cells.

② Drag the AutoFill box to fill adjacent cells.

④ Verify that the formula is correct.

③ Click in a filled cell.

Include a Constant

① Start creating the first formula, and click in the cell that contains the value for the constant. Press the F4 key to convert the cell reference from relative to absolute. Complete the formula.

② Drag the AutoFill box to fill the adjacent cells, and then click in a filled cell to verify that the formula is correct.

Making Calculations with Functions

Excel is jam-packed with functions that can make you look like a financial wizard or a mathematical genius (if you aren't either or both of those already, of course!). Do you want to know the standard deviation of a series of numbers? What about the sum of the squares? How about calculating the number and amount of the payments needed to retire a loan over a certain period? If you're a real stickler for precision, you can even use a function that returns the value of pi, accurate to 15 digits.

> ✋ **CAUTION: Make sure that you understand the purpose of a function and the meaning of the result. Although the functions enable you to do complex analyses, the result can be meaningless or misleading if you apply the wrong function. Fortunately, the Excel Help files provide extensive support that explains the purpose and use of each function.**

Find a Function

(2) Click the Insert Function button. If the Formula bar isn't displayed, choose Function from the Insert menu.

(3) In the Insert Function dialog box, type the name of the function or a description of the action you want to take, and press Enter.

(1) Click in the cell in which you want the results of the function to be displayed.

(4) Select the function you want from the list.

(5) If the function isn't listed, choose a different category, and then select the function from the list.

(6) Verify that the function will do what you want it to do.

(7) Click OK.

> ❗ **TIP: To use a function that you used recently, click the down arrow at the right of the Functions box (at the left of the Formula bar), and choose the function from the list.**

Add Your Arguments

(1) In the Function Arguments dialog box that appears, type any values that you want to enter directly, or type the cell references.

(2) To select cell ranges, click to minimize the dialog box and return to the worksheet.

(3) Select the cell or range of cells you want to use as an *argument*, or parameter, for the function.

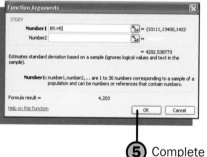

(4) Click to return to the Function Arguments dialog box.

(5) Complete any other arguments that are required for the function, and then click OK.

! TIP: A function requires specific types of data, delivered in a specific order; these are the arguments for the function. Some functions don't have any arguments—for example, NOW( ); some have a single argument—SQRT(*number*); and some have multiple arguments—NPER(*rate,pmt,pv,fv,type*). For information about the arguments for a function, select the function in the Insert Function dialog box, and click Help On This Function.

! TIP: You can integrate more than one function into a formula, or you can include other elements—for example, standard arithmetic operations such as adding or multiplying by a number or a value in another cell.

! TIP: Numerous functions don't return a value but are logical tests instead. The powerful IF function, for example, returns one value you've set if the logical test is true and a second value if the logical test is false. Many other functions, such as ISBLANK, return true or false values only.

Troubleshooting Formulas

Formulas are extremely powerful tools, especially when they include functions, and constructing valid formulas can be a bit tricky. Fortunately, Excel provides a group of formula-auditing tools that can help you find and fix errors such as circular references, incorrect syntax in a formula, or a referenced cell that has been deleted.

Review the Errors

(1) Point to Formula Auditing on the Tools menu, and choose Formula Auditing Mode from the submenu to display all the formulas in the worksheet.

(3) Review your formulas and correct any that are obviously wrong.

(2) Point to Formula Auditing on the Tools menu again, and choose Show Formula Auditing Toolbar from the submenu to display the Formula Auditing toolbar.

(4) Click the Error Checking button.

(5) In the Error Checking dialog box, use the Next and Previous buttons to find and review the errors in your worksheet.

(6) Click the Edit In Formula Bar button if you see the mistake and want to correct the formula.

> **TIP:** To fix a single error, click in a cell that displays an error such as #REF!, #NAME!, or #VALUE. Click the Actions button that appears, and choose an appropriate command from the menu to fix the error. If an Actions button doesn't appear, choose Options from the Tools menu, and, on the Error Checking tab, select the Enable Background Error Checking check box, and click OK.

> **TIP:** When the error is a reference error (#REF!), the Show Calculation Steps button is replaced by the Trace Error button. Click this to map out the references and see where the error occurs.

Evaluate a Formula

(1) If you can't figure out the error, click the Show Calculation Steps button in the Error Checking dialog box to display the Evaluate Formula dialog box.

(2) Note the formula and the underlined item.

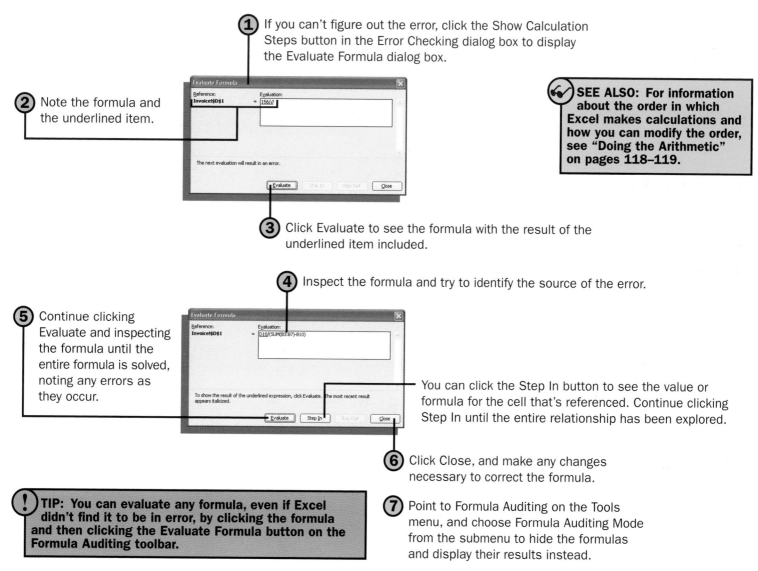

SEE ALSO: For information about the order in which Excel makes calculations and how you can modify the order, see "Doing the Arithmetic" on pages 118–119.

(3) Click Evaluate to see the formula with the result of the underlined item included.

(4) Inspect the formula and try to identify the source of the error.

(5) Continue clicking Evaluate and inspecting the formula until the entire formula is solved, noting any errors as they occur.

You can click the Step In button to see the value or formula for the cell that's referenced. Continue clicking Step In until the entire relationship has been explored.

(6) Click Close, and make any changes necessary to correct the formula.

TIP: You can evaluate any formula, even if Excel didn't find it to be in error, by clicking the formula and then clicking the Evaluate Formula button on the Formula Auditing toolbar.

(7) Point to Formula Auditing on the Tools menu, and choose Formula Auditing Mode from the submenu to hide the formulas and display their results instead.

Sorting Your Data

One of the easiest ways to organize or evaluate your data is to use Excel's Sort feature. There are a couple of ways to control the sort—you can do a simple ascending or descending sort, or you can specify which data you want to sort and the type of sort you want to conduct.

Specify the Sort

CAUTION: If the data in each row are related—for example, if the first cell is a student's name and the second cell is the student's score—make sure you select all the columns in that row that contain information about that student or that you need to keep together, or the data will become meaningless. If you mistakenly mix up your data when you're doing a sort, click the Undo button on the Standard toolbar.

(1) Select the columns or portions of columns whose contents you want to sort.

(2) Choose Sort from the Data menu to display the Sort dialog box.

(4) Specify which column you want to sort by.

(5) Specify whether the sort is to be ascending or descending.

(6) If you want to refine the sort by also sorting by a second column, specify the column and then the sort order.

(7) Choose the column and sort order if you want the sort to be further refined by a third-level sort.

(3) Specify whether or not the columns have header names.

(8) Click if you want to change the type of sort, conduct a case-sensitive sort for text, or sort by rows instead of by columns.

(9) Click OK to sort the data.

When the first sort was done by the Average column and then by the Student column, people who had the same score were sorted by the alphabetic order of their names.

TIP: To do a simple sort based on the first column selected, select the data, and then click the Sort Ascending or Sort Descending button on the Standard toolbar.

Filtering Your Data

Filtering is a quick and easy way to find and work with a subset of data so that you can display only the rows in your worksheet that meet the criteria you specify—for example, rows that contain specific text, or numbers that are greater than or less than a specific number. Filtering temporarily hides the rows that don't meet your criteria so that you see only the data you're interested in. Excel simplifies the power of filtering, or querying, your data without your having to use a separate database. All you do is set up the filtering and select the items you want to display.

Filter the Data

(1) Select the data you want to filter.

(2) Point to Filter on the Data menu, and choose AutoFilter from the submenu.

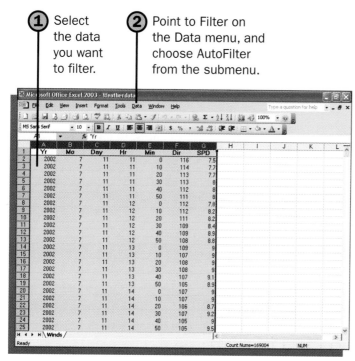

(3) Click the down arrow for the column you want to use as the filter, and select the item you want to use as the filter.

The data have been filtered for a Direction value (Dir) of 123, and are about to be filtered to include only data from the 7th month (Mo).

(4) To filter by another column, click the down arrow for that column, and select the item you want to use as the filter.

(5) When you've finished with the filtered data, either

- Click the down arrow for the column, and choose All from the list to remove the column from filtering.

- Point to Filter on the Data menu, and choose Show All from the submenu to remove all filtering based on all columns.

- Point to Filter on the Data menu, and choose AutoFilter from the submenu to completely remove the filtering.

> **(!) TIP: It's easy to see which items have filtering applied—they display blue down arrows instead of black down arrows.**

Creating Worksheet Subtotals

When you've accumulated a mass of data, you can leave it to Excel to calculate the subtotals in your worksheets—how many boxes of crayons you sold in January, for example, or the number of different songbirds you've seen in your back yard. All you need to do is gather the items together and tell Excel to *outline*—that is, to classify and prioritize—your data, and to calculate the subtotals.

Create Subtotals

(1) Select and sort the data by the columns for which you want to create the subtotals.

(2) Choose Subtotals from the Data menu to display the Subtotal dialog box.

(!) **TIP:** To remove all the subtotals, select the cells with the data and the subtotals, choose Subtotals from the Data menu, and, in the Subtotal dialog box, click the Remove All button.

(!) **TIP:** For the subtotals to work, you need to group the data by the items to be subtotaled. To do this, you sort the data before you tell Excel to create the subtotals.

(◉) **SEE ALSO:** For information about sorting data by columns, see "Sorting Your Data" on page 126.

(3) Select the columns that you want to be subtotaled.

(4) Select the function to be used to calculate the subtotal.

(5) Select the column or columns in which you want the results to be displayed.

(6) Select any other options you want.

(8) Review the results, hiding or displaying details.

(7) Click OK.

Click the outline-level symbols to display or hide details.

Click a minus button to hide the details, or click a plus button to display them.

Naming Cells and Ranges

If you find Excel's cell-referencing notation difficult to use and understand, you'll be glad to know that there's a friendlier option available that works just as well. You can name a cell, a column, a row, or a range of cells, and then you can reference the cell or cells just by using the name. What a great idea!

Define and Use a Name

TRY THIS: Name part of a column (for example, Exam1), and then name part of a row that intersects the named part of the column (for example, Robert). Now get the value for the cell where the two named ranges intersect by using both names, separated by a space (for example, =Robert Exam1).

(1) Select the cell or range of cells you want to name.

(2) Type the name in the Name Box, and press Enter.

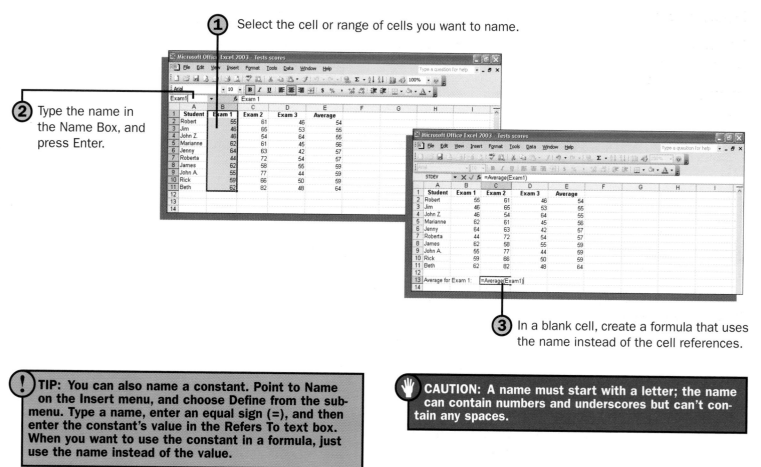

(3) In a blank cell, create a formula that uses the name instead of the cell references.

TIP: You can also name a constant. Point to Name on the Insert menu, and choose Define from the submenu. Type a name, enter an equal sign (=), and then enter the constant's value in the Refers To text box. When you want to use the constant in a formula, just use the name instead of the value.

CAUTION: A name must start with a letter; the name can contain numbers and underscores but can't contain any spaces.

Summarizing Data with a PivotTable

A PivotTable is a dynamic and powerful analysis tool that lets you look at relationships among your data and enables you to extract only the portions of the data that are of interest to you. It can sometimes be a bit difficult to figure out the proper arrangement of the data fields, but once you've created the PivotTable, you'll find it easy to work with and very useful.

Create a PivotTable

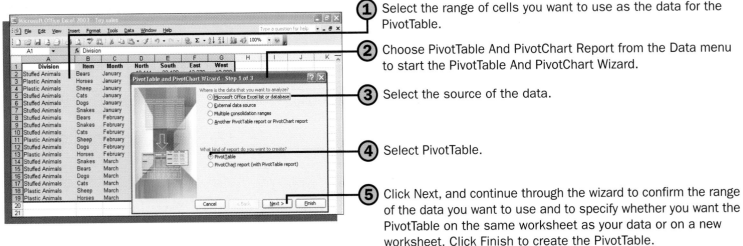

(1) Select the range of cells you want to use as the data for the PivotTable.

(2) Choose PivotTable And PivotChart Report from the Data menu to start the PivotTable And PivotChart Wizard.

(3) Select the source of the data.

(4) Select PivotTable.

(5) Click Next, and continue through the wizard to confirm the range of the data you want to use and to specify whether you want the PivotTable on the same worksheet as your data or on a new worksheet. Click Finish to create the PivotTable.

(6) Drag the data fields from the PivotTable Field List into the appropriate portions of the PivotTable.

Use a major classification to separate the data into logical pages.

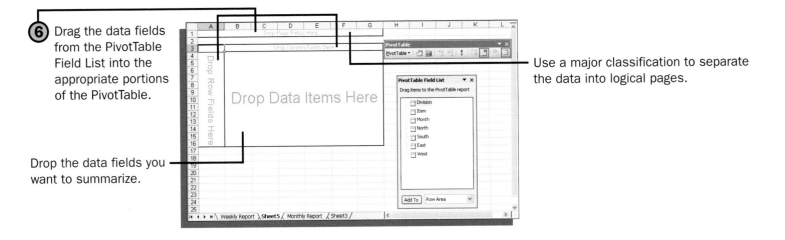

Drop the data fields you want to summarize.

Use the PivotTable

(1) Click the down arrow in the Page field, select the item you want to be displayed, and click OK.

TIP: By default, Excel sums the data. To change the way Excel summarizes the data and/or to change the text of the field label, click in the data field, and then click the Field Settings button on the PivotTable toolbar. You can also change the formatting for the number that's displayed in the PivotTable Field dialog box.

SEE ALSO: For information about creating a PivotChart in Microsoft Office Access, see "Create a PivotChart" on page 200.

(4) Continue selecting the items you want to be displayed in the other fields.

(2) Click in a Column or Row field, and clear the Show All check box.

(3) Select the items you want to be displayed, and click OK.

TIP: A PivotChart works just like a PivotTable, except that the data are displayed as a chart instead of as numbers. You might find it easiest to create a PivotTable, modify it, and then use it as the source for a chart. The chart will be a PivotChart in which you can change the data that are displayed.

Automatically Highlighting Certain Data

When you use conditional formatting, you can tell Excel to highlight—that is, apply specific formatting to—any cells that meet the specific criteria you set. For example, you can tell Excel to format a cell whenever the number of sales falls below a certain minimum or whenever the cost rises above a certain figure. Excel will apply the cell formatting only when the conditions you set are found to be true.

> **! TIP: Base the conditional formatting on a formula if you want to base the formatting on the value in one or more cells other than the selected cell.**

Set the Conditional Formatting

① Select the cells, columns, or rows to which the formatting will apply.

② Choose Conditional Formatting from the Format menu to display the Conditional Formatting dialog box.

③ Specify whether the condition is based on a cell value or on a formula.

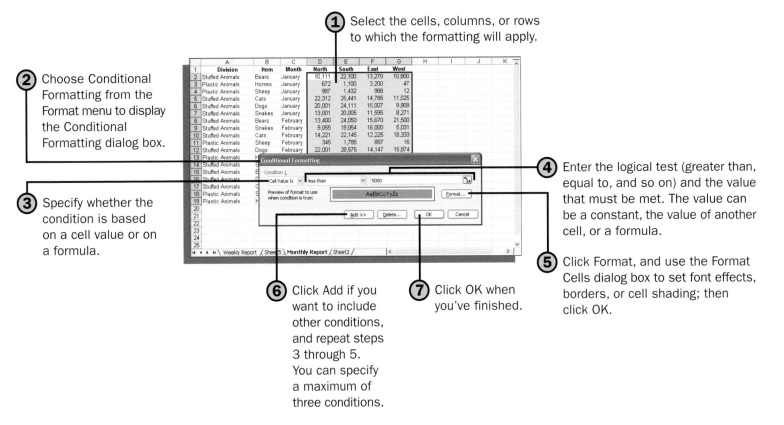

④ Enter the logical test (greater than, equal to, and so on) and the value that must be met. The value can be a constant, the value of another cell, or a formula.

⑤ Click Format, and use the Format Cells dialog box to set font effects, borders, or cell shading; then click OK.

⑥ Click Add if you want to include other conditions, and repeat steps 3 through 5. You can specify a maximum of three conditions.

⑦ Click OK when you've finished.

Importing Data from a Web Page

If you've ever reviewed data from a Web page, you know how frustrating it is to try to do any further analysis of the data. You might be able to select the data and copy it into Excel or Word, or open up the Web page for editing in Excel, but chances are that you'll have to waste a lot of your time deleting parts of the Web page that you don't need and then reformatting everything. Excel to the rescue! Excel uses the underlying code in the Web page to identify tables, and lets you select, copy, and modify only the data from the selected table.

Import the Web Data

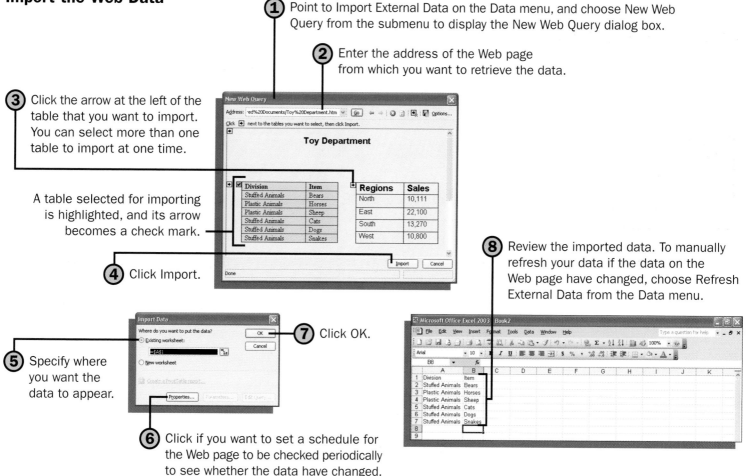

(1) Point to Import External Data on the Data menu, and choose New Web Query from the submenu to display the New Web Query dialog box.

(2) Enter the address of the Web page from which you want to retrieve the data.

(3) Click the arrow at the left of the table that you want to import. You can select more than one table to import at one time.

A table selected for importing is highlighted, and its arrow becomes a check mark.

(4) Click Import.

(5) Specify where you want the data to appear.

(6) Click if you want to set a schedule for the Web page to be checked periodically to see whether the data have changed.

(7) Click OK.

(8) Review the imported data. To manually refresh your data if the data on the Web page have changed, choose Refresh External Data from the Data menu.

Importing Data from a Service

Excel has some powerful built-in queries, so it's a simple matter to connect to a Web service and automatically obtain the data you want. Because you're sending a query to an active Web page whose data are updated frequently, your information is always up to date.

Import the Data

 1 Click the location in your worksheet where you want the data to appear.

2 Point to Import External Data on the Data menu, and choose Import Data from the submenu to display the Select Data Source dialog box.

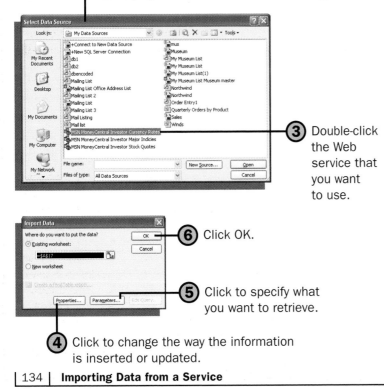

3 Double-click the Web service that you want to use.

6 Click OK.

5 Click to specify what you want to retrieve.

4 Click to change the way the information is inserted or updated.

7 Wait for the data to be retrieved, and then review it.

8 Presenting Your Data

You've created the worksheets and analyzed the data, and, depending on the nature of your work, that might be all you need to do. However, if you have to present your data—at a company meeting, for example, where you might show the data in a slide presentation; as part of an annual financial report; or in a newspaper or magazine article—the most effective way to do so is to use a chart. The visual appeal of a chart will hold your audience's interest more closely than will the lackluster columns and rows of the worksheet on which the chart is based, even though both represent the same information.

So how do you turn that worksheet into an impressive chart? You let the behind-the-scenes magic of Microsoft Office Excel 2003's Chart Wizard do most of the work for you. The Chart Wizard offers an abundance of different chart types and subtypes that, with just a few quick steps, can transform your data into a chart. If you're not satisfied with the type of chart you've chosen, you can experiment with different chart types until you're pleased with the results. If you want to customize your chart—change the colors, add or delete borders or shadows, add patterns or three-dimensional effects, or even use a combination of chart types—you can do that too. Excel does more than just make your chart look attractive, though. You can plot trendlines to show your audience how your sales figures have improved over time or how your company's bottom line is on a downward trend. If you're statistically inclined, you can add error bars that test the accuracy of the data. And if you've spent a lot of time customizing the design of your chart, you can save it and use the same design for another set of data.

Charting Your Data

One of the best ways to present your data in a clear and understandable form is to use a well-designed chart. A chart provides a visual impact that makes your data come alive in such a way that difficult concepts and comparisons become immediately clear. You'll need to decide what you want to include, where to put everything, and the type of chart you want to use.

Choose a Chart

① Select the data you want to use in the chart.

② Click the Chart Wizard button on the Standard toolbar.

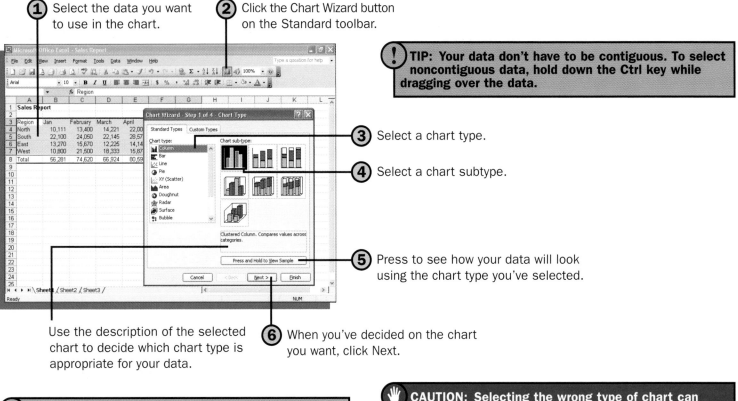

! TIP: Your data don't have to be contiguous. To select noncontiguous data, hold down the Ctrl key while dragging over the data.

③ Select a chart type.

④ Select a chart subtype.

⑤ Press to see how your data will look using the chart type you've selected.

Use the description of the selected chart to decide which chart type is appropriate for your data.

⑥ When you've decided on the chart you want, click Next.

! TIP: The Custom Types tab of the Chart Wizard offers additional types of charts that can create dramatic presentations and/or can simplify the construction of complex chart types.

✋ CAUTION: Selecting the wrong type of chart can render your data misleading or even meaningless. Be sure to use the appropriate kind of chart, or to change the chart type if the one you're using doesn't present the data properly.

Complete the Chart

(2) Use the Series tab to modify the range for the individual data series and/or to change which data series are included. Click Next when you've finished.

(3) Use the different tabs to add elements to the chart. For example:

- Text for the chart title, the X-axis, and the Y-axis
- The inclusion and type of the X-axis and the Y-axis
- Whether gridlines appear
- Whether the legend is displayed and, if so, where
- Whether the data series have labels in the chart
- Whether a table of the data is included on the chartsheet with the chart

(1) Confirm the data you're going to use on the Data Range tab of the wizard.

(4) Click Next.

(5) Specify whether you want the chart to be created on a new chartsheet or included in an existing worksheet.

(6) Click Finish to create the chart.

> **! TIP:** The numbers or the text on the chart's axes are based on the worksheet data you're using. To make changes to these elements, you'll need to make the changes in your worksheet.

Formatting a Chart

You can customize your chart as you're creating it with the Chart Wizard, but, after you've finished it, you'll probably want to improve its appearance by changing the formatting of some of the elements (or you might want to change it just because it's so simple and quick to see the different results).

Format an Element

1 Display the Chart toolbar if it isn't already displayed.

3 Click the Format button. (Note that this button's name changes depending on the element you're formatting.)

2 Select the chart element you want to format.

4 Use the different tabs of the Format dialog box to make your modifications.

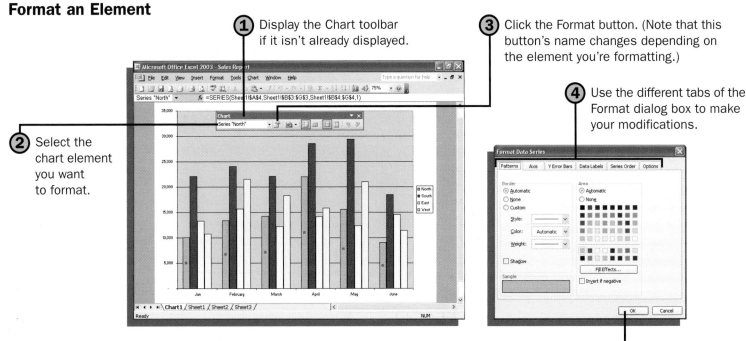

5 Click OK when you've finished.

> **TRY THIS:** If the data labels on one axis are so close together that they're difficult to read, you can change either the interval between them or the number of zeros that are displayed for large numbers. Right-click the Y-axis, and choose Format Axis from the shortcut menu. On the Scale tab, change the values for the major unit. In the Display Units list box, select a unit for your numbers, and then click OK.

Change the Chart Type

① Select Chart Area on the Chart toolbar.

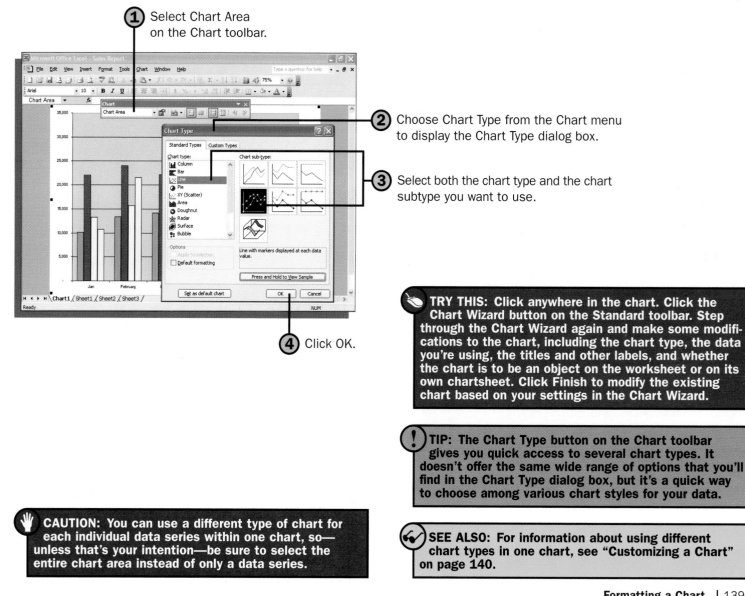

② Choose Chart Type from the Chart menu to display the Chart Type dialog box.

③ Select both the chart type and the chart subtype you want to use.

④ Click OK.

TRY THIS: Click anywhere in the chart. Click the Chart Wizard button on the Standard toolbar. Step through the Chart Wizard again and make some modifications to the chart, including the chart type, the data you're using, the titles and other labels, and whether the chart is to be an object on the worksheet or on its own chartsheet. Click Finish to modify the existing chart based on your settings in the Chart Wizard.

TIP: The Chart Type button on the Chart toolbar gives you quick access to several chart types. It doesn't offer the same wide range of options that you'll find in the Chart Type dialog box, but it's a quick way to choose among various chart styles for your data.

CAUTION: You can use a different type of chart for each individual data series within one chart, so— unless that's your intention—be sure to select the entire chart area instead of only a data series.

SEE ALSO: For information about using different chart types in one chart, see "Customizing a Chart" on page 140.

Customizing a Chart

Sometimes a series of columns, bars, or lines doesn't properly express your data. To create the most informative chart possible, you might want to combine different chart types within a single chart. You can even add one or more axes so that your data can be presented with different scales. When you add an axis, that axis will be used for the data series that has the different chart type.

Change a Data Series Chart

① On the Chart toolbar, select the data series.

CAUTION: Some chart types are incompatible, so Excel might not allow you to add one type of chart to another. In this case, you'll need to experiment with different combinations of chart types to find out which ones work together.

TIP: The chart types on the Custom Types tab of the Chart Type dialog box provide several combination charts that incorporate two chart types for different data series.

② Choose Chart Type from the Chart menu to display the Chart Type dialog box.

③ Select both the chart type and the subtype that you want to use for the selected series.

④ Select the Apply To Selection check box.

⑤ Click OK.

Add an Axis

1 Choose Chart Options from the Chart menu, and click the Axes tab of the Chart Options dialog box.

4 On the Titles tab, add the title or titles you want for the new axis or axes.

! TIP: To change the axis on which a data series is plotted, select the series on the Chart toolbar, and click the Format Data Series button. On the Axis tab, select the axis you want to use for the series, and click OK.

2 Specify whether you want a second X-axis and, if so, the way you want the values to be categorized.

5 Click OK.

3 Specify whether you want a second Y-axis.

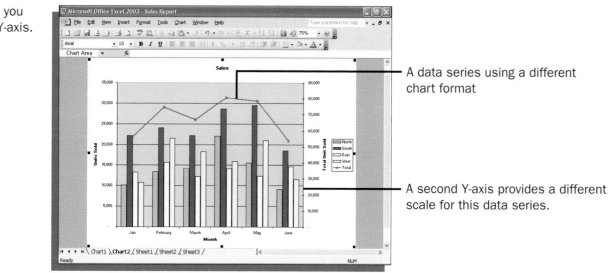

A data series using a different chart format

A second Y-axis provides a different scale for this data series.

Changing the Order of a Series

Excel is very logical, so it plots your data series in the order in which it encounters them. When you're putting your presentation together, however, you might realize that your data will be clearer if you arrange the series in a different order. It's a simple matter to change the order in which the data series is displayed.

SEE ALSO: For information about displaying one series using a different chart type or a different axis scale, see "Customizing a Chart" on pages 140–141.

For information about removing a series from a chart, see "Adding or Removing Data" on the facing page.

Change the Order

① On the Chart toolbar, select any one of the data series.

② Click the Format Data Series button.

③ On the Series Order tab of the Format Data Series dialog box, select the data series you want to move.

④ Click the Move Up or the Move Down button to move the data series in the list. Continue clicking the buttons until you've arranged the data series as desired.

⑤ Repeat steps 3 and 4 for any other data series you want to move.

⑥ Click OK when you've finished.

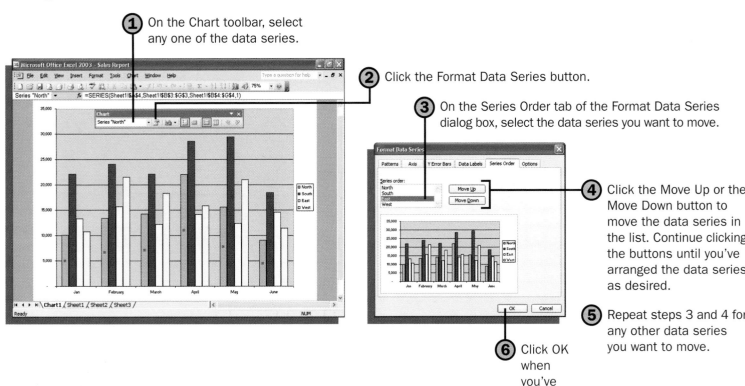

Adding or Removing Data

To achieve the perfect chart, you'll often need to make a few changes to the data you've included. After you've created the chart, you can easily add or delete rows of data or even whole series of data.

Add or Remove Data

TIP: To add data to the chart from a location other than the source of your main data, choose Add Data from the Chart menu. To quickly delete a data series, choose Source Data from the Chart menu, and, on the Series tab of the Source Data dialog box, select the series and click Remove.

(1) Choose Source Data from the Chart menu, and click the Data Range tab of the Source Data dialog box.

(2) Click to minimize the dialog box and access the worksheet.

(3) Drag over the entire range you want to use in your chart, adding or removing data as desired.

(4) Verify that the range reference is correct.

(5) Click to restore the dialog box.

(6) Click OK.

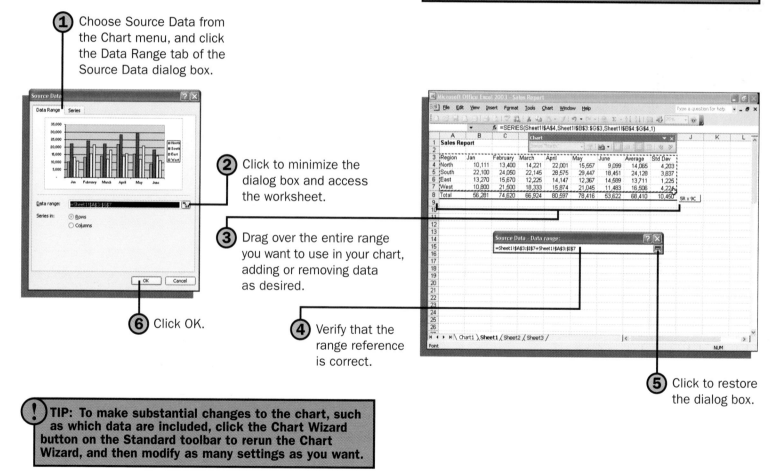

TIP: To make substantial changes to the chart, such as which data are included, click the Chart Wizard button on the Standard toolbar to rerun the Chart Wizard, and then modify as many settings as you want.

Adding a Trendline to a Data Series

A trendline is the plotting of a statistical analysis of a data series. In plainer English, a trendline is a graphic representation of a trend in a data series. You can also use a trendline to examine past performance and to forecast future values.

> **TIP:** For the statistically inclined, a trendline is the fitting of the least squares through the points, using a function based on the type of trend you've selected. The Linear trend is a simple linear regression.

Add a Trendline

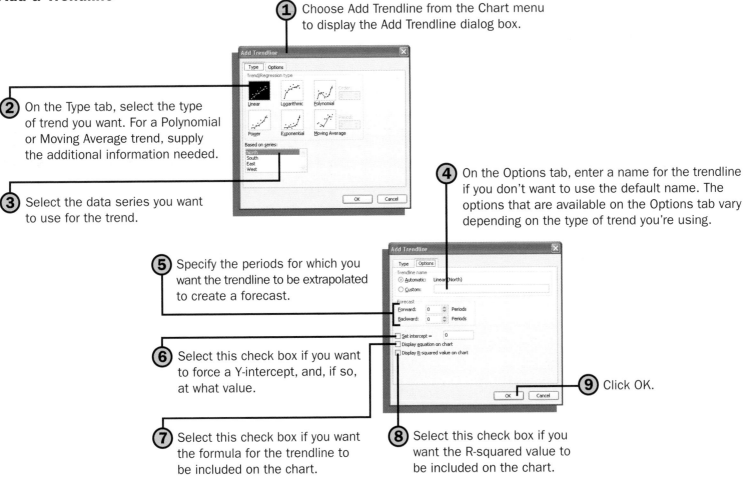

1 Choose Add Trendline from the Chart menu to display the Add Trendline dialog box.

2 On the Type tab, select the type of trend you want. For a Polynomial or Moving Average trend, supply the additional information needed.

3 Select the data series you want to use for the trend.

4 On the Options tab, enter a name for the trendline if you don't want to use the default name. The options that are available on the Options tab vary depending on the type of trend you're using.

5 Specify the periods for which you want the trendline to be extrapolated to create a forecast.

6 Select this check box if you want to force a Y-intercept, and, if so, at what value.

7 Select this check box if you want the formula for the trendline to be included on the chart.

8 Select this check box if you want the R-squared value to be included on the chart.

9 Click OK.

Adding Error Bars

Adding error bars to a chart is a great way to show how much confidence you have in the data. You can base the error bars on a fixed value, on the values in a worksheet, on a percentage of a data point's value, or on standard deviation or standard error. If you like statistics, you'll *love* error bars! If you're leery about someone else's data, including error bars when you chart the data will let you determine how much you can trust the data and the conclusions.

① TIP: You can add Y error bars to most two-dimensional charts, and you can add both X and Y error bars to scatter charts and bubble charts.

Add Error Bars to a Series

① On the Chart toolbar, select the data series to which you want to add error bars, and click the Format Data Series button to display the Format Data Series dialog box.

② On the Y Error Bars tab, select the type of error bar you want to use.

③ Specify the type of value you want to use.

Use Custom to set different positive and negative values, or to set the values to the value of cells in the worksheet.

④ Supply any additional information required for that type of value.

⑤ If the chart type supports X error bars, click the X Error Bars tab, and select the type of error bars and the type of value you want to use. Supply any additional information required for that type of value.

⑥ Click OK.

⑦ Repeat steps 1 through 6 for any other data series to which you want to add error bars.

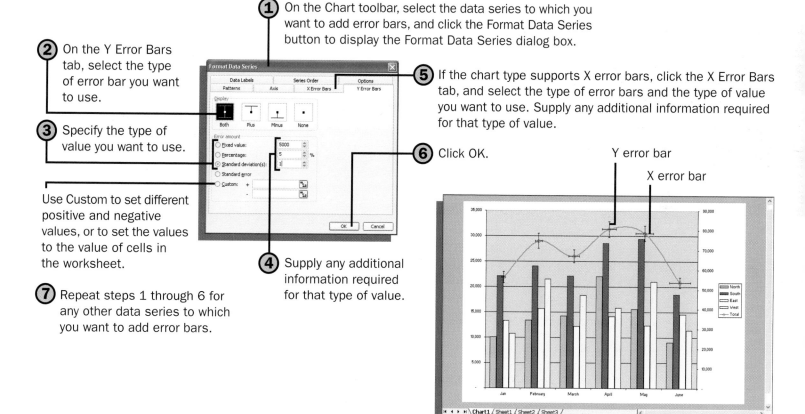

Working with a 3-D Chart

Excel's three-dimensional charts can look really impressive and can add all sorts of eye-popping effects to even the most boring of data presentations. You can also manipulate all three axes of the chart so that the chart represents your data with the greatest possible clarity.

TRY THIS: Choose Corners from the Chart Objects list on the Chart toolbar. Drag a corner of the chart, and note the way the chart moves. Drag a different corner for more changes. Choose 3-D View from the Chart menu, and note the values for all the different types of rotation.

Modify Your Chart

(1) Create a 3-D chart by using the Chart Wizard and choosing a 3-D chart subtype. Then choose 3-D View from the Chart menu to display the 3-D View dialog box.

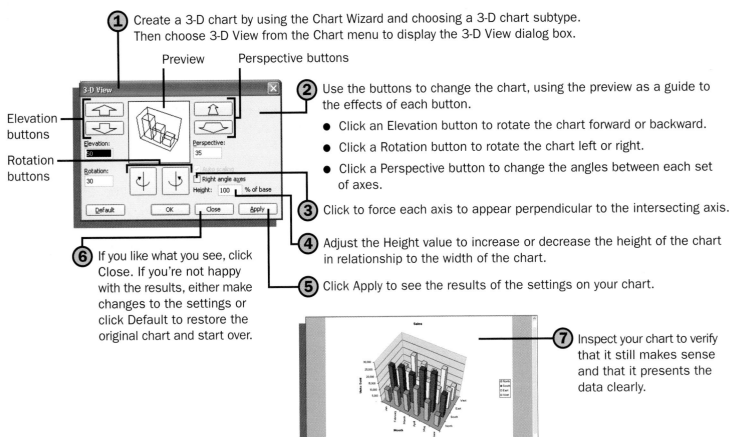

Preview   Perspective buttons

Elevation buttons

Rotation buttons

(2) Use the buttons to change the chart, using the preview as a guide to the effects of each button.

● Click an Elevation button to rotate the chart forward or backward.

● Click a Rotation button to rotate the chart left or right.

● Click a Perspective button to change the angles between each set of axes.

(3) Click to force each axis to appear perpendicular to the intersecting axis.

(4) Adjust the Height value to increase or decrease the height of the chart in relationship to the width of the chart.

(5) Click Apply to see the results of the settings on your chart.

(6) If you like what you see, click Close. If you're not happy with the results, either make changes to the settings or click Default to restore the original chart and start over.

(7) Inspect your chart to verify that it still makes sense and that it presents the data clearly.

Moving a Chart

When you create a chart, Excel offers you a couple of options: You can place the chart as an object on an existing worksheet, or you can place it on its own chartsheet. If you put the chart in one place and then decide that you'd prefer to locate it somewhere else, you can easily move it.

Change the Location

TRY THIS: Want the chart in both places? With the chart on a chartsheet and the chartsheet selected, choose Move Or Copy Sheet from the Edit menu. In the Move Or Copy dialog box, select the Create A Copy check box, and click OK. In the new copy of the chartsheet, choose Location from the Chart menu, select the option to place the chart as an object in the worksheet that is the chart's data source, and click OK.

1. Click in the chart to activate it.

2. Choose Location from the Chart menu to display the Chart Location dialog box.

3. Do either of the following:
   - To move a chart from a worksheet to a new chartsheet, select As New Sheet, and enter a name for the new sheet.
   - To move a chart from a chartsheet to an existing worksheet, select As Object In, and select the worksheet in which you want to insert the chart.

4. Click OK.

TIP: For a special effect, you can move a chart as an object onto another chartsheet.

Saving a Custom Chart Design

You've worked tirelessly for long hours, and you've created the perfect chart! It looks gorgeous, with its mixed chart types and stunning backgrounds, but you're not sure that you want to go through all that work again if you need to create a similar chart. Well, you don't have to—you can simply save the design and apply it to your new data.

> (!) **TIP:** If you designate the custom chart as the default, it will be the default selection when you use the Chart Wizard to create a new chart. If you don't make it the default, you can use it by clicking the Custom Types tab of the Chart Type dialog box and selecting the User-Defined option.

Save the Design

(1) Make sure the chart is exactly the way you want it.

(2) Choose Chart Type from the Chart menu, and click the Custom Types tab of the Chart Type dialog box.

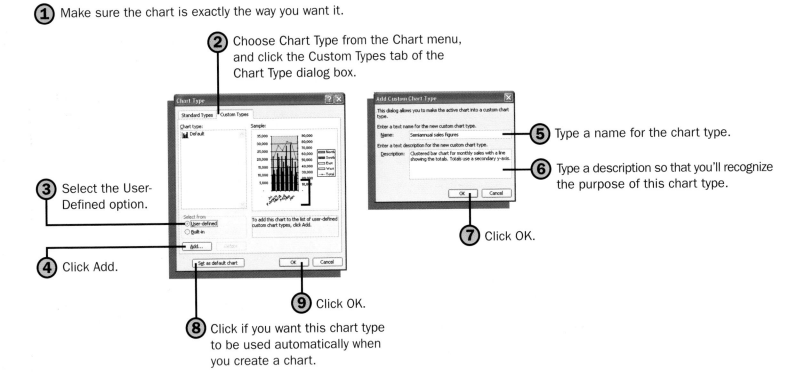

(3) Select the User-Defined option.

(4) Click Add.

(5) Type a name for the chart type.

(6) Type a description so that you'll recognize the purpose of this chart type.

(7) Click OK.

(8) Click if you want this chart type to be used automatically when you create a chart.

(9) Click OK.

9 Communicating Using Outlook

Microsoft Office Outlook 2003 is a combination of programs and features. In addition to its primary function, which is sending and receiving e-mail, Outlook also does double duty as a sort of combined office assistant and social secretary. It will help you to keep a record of your contacts, your work schedules as well as your playtimes, and your other activities or obligations, including those on your " to do" list and those you've already accomplished. Right now, though, we're going to concentrate on Outlook's e-mail functioning, and we'll deal with its scheduling and organizing features in the next section of the book.

The ability to communicate electronically is one of a computer's most used and most valued features. You'll find that you can enhance the power and flexibility of your e-mail by using Microsoft Office Word in conjunction with Outlook. For example, you can format your e-mail messages with your favorite fonts and colors, you can design a signature that can be added automatically to your messages, you can use Word's powerful spelling and grammar checkers to correct any errors, and you can enclose files—or *attachments*—with your messages. (Be aware, however, that Outlook e-mail can work in several different ways, depending on how it's configured and whether you're working through a Microsoft Exchange Server or using other Internet services.)

If you have an account with an Internet fax service provider, you can send faxes directly from your Office programs over the Internet. You'll save money by avoiding those long-distance phone charges, and you won't need a dedicated fax phone line.

What's Where in Outlook Mail?

Outlook, like most Office programs, is easily adaptable to the way you like to work. Here's a look at the standard appearance of Outlook's e-mail function. However, you can create many different looks for Outlook; the program is highly customizable, so you can set it up exactly the way you want. For example, you can position the Reading pane at the bottom of the window instead of on the right side, or you can turn it off completely; you can use AutoPreview to view the first few lines of each e-mail message in your Inbox; you can change which buttons are displayed in the Navigation pane or simply not display the Navigation pane at all; and you can organize your messages by date, by subject, by importance, or in just about any configuration you like.

Standard toolbar

Navigation pane

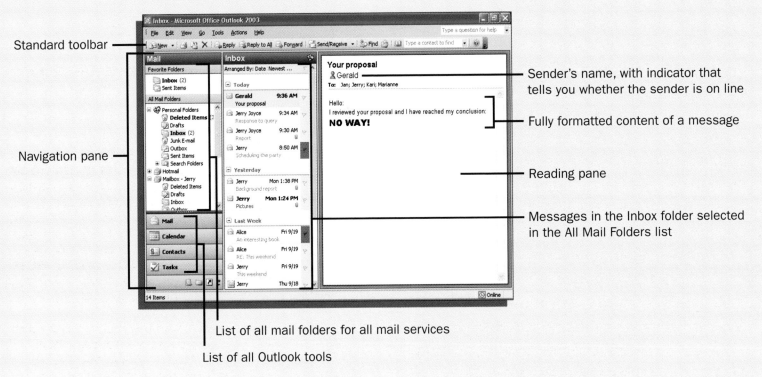

Sender's name, with indicator that tells you whether the sender is on line

Fully formatted content of a message

Reading pane

Messages in the Inbox folder selected in the All Mail Folders list

List of all mail folders for all mail services

List of all Outlook tools

Setting Up an E-Mail Account

When you're installing Outlook for the first time, the E-Mail Accounts Wizard guides you through the series of steps required to set up one or more e-mail accounts. As time goes by, you might want to add new accounts or delete accounts you don't use.

Set Up a New Account

1 Choose E-Mail Accounts from the Tools menu to start the E-Mail Accounts Wizard.

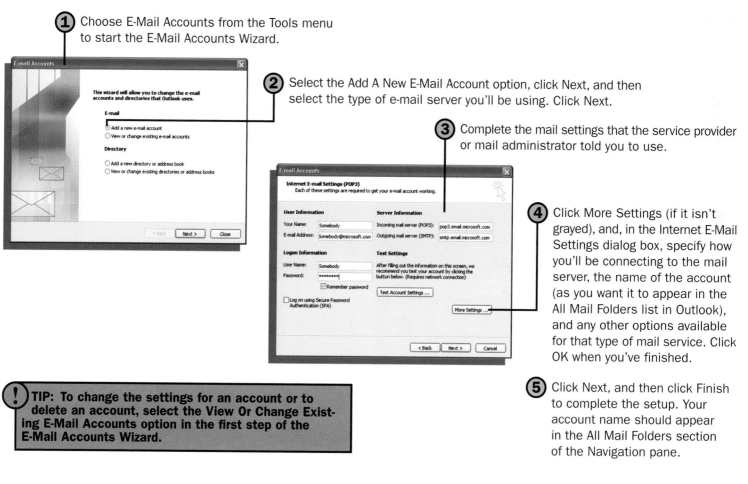

2 Select the Add A New E-Mail Account option, click Next, and then select the type of e-mail server you'll be using. Click Next.

3 Complete the mail settings that the service provider or mail administrator told you to use.

4 Click More Settings (if it isn't grayed), and, in the Internet E-Mail Settings dialog box, specify how you'll be connecting to the mail server, the name of the account (as you want it to appear in the All Mail Folders list in Outlook), and any other options available for that type of mail service. Click OK when you've finished.

5 Click Next, and then click Finish to complete the setup. Your account name should appear in the All Mail Folders section of the Navigation pane.

Sending E-Mail

You don't have to address an envelope or trek to the mailbox on a cold, rainy day. All you do is select a name, create a message, and click the Send button. Outlook and your mail server do the rest. What could be more convenient?

Create a Message

(1) In Outlook, click the Mail button in the Navigation pane if your mail folders aren't displayed, click the Inbox, and then click New.

(2) Start typing the message recipient's name. Press Enter when Outlook completes the name based on the names in your Contacts list or Address Book, or continue typing if the proposed name is incorrect. To add more recipients' names, type a semicolon (;), and then start typing the next name.

(3) Press the Tab key to move to the CC field, and type the names of the people who are to receive a copy of the message.

(4) Press the Tab key to move to the Subject line, type a subject, and press Tab again to move into the message area.

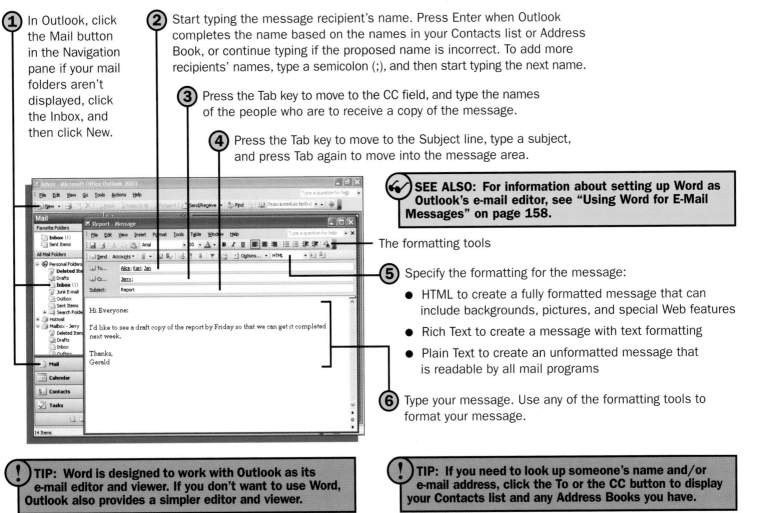

SEE ALSO: For information about setting up Word as Outlook's e-mail editor, see "Using Word for E-Mail Messages" on page 158.

The formatting tools

(5) Specify the formatting for the message:

- HTML to create a fully formatted message that can include backgrounds, pictures, and special Web features
- Rich Text to create a message with text formatting
- Plain Text to create an unformatted message that is readable by all mail programs

(6) Type your message. Use any of the formatting tools to format your message.

! TIP: Word is designed to work with Outlook as its e-mail editor and viewer. If you don't want to use Word, Outlook also provides a simpler editor and viewer.

! TIP: If you need to look up someone's name and/or e-mail address, click the To or the CC button to display your Contacts list and any Address Books you have.

Customize and Send Your Message

(1) If you have multiple e-mail accounts, specify which account you want to use to send the message.

(2) If you want, you can click to indicate whether the message is of high or low importance.

(3) Click to display the Flag For Follow Up dialog box.

(8) Click Send to send the message to your Outbox.

(7) Click if you want to change the security or delivery options, add an e-mail signature, use background stationery, or include a BCC or From line in the address.

(4) Select a type of flag if you want to flag the message.

(5) Specify the date and time by which the selected flag must be acted upon.

(6) Click OK.

(!) TIP: Most company e-mail systems are set up to send and receive messages automatically at a preset interval, as well as whenever you send mail to your Outbox. If your system doesn't use these automatic settings, click the Send/Receive button to send or receive your e-mail.

(!) TIP: The BCC line is used to send a "blind copy," which means that although a copy of the message is sent to the person listed on the BCC line, the other recipients of the message don't see that person's name in their copies of the message.

Receiving and Reading E-Mail

Outlook lets you specify how frequently you want it to check for incoming e-mail, and it notifies you when you receive new mail. You can look at your Inbox and see at a glance which messages have and haven't been read, or you can set the view to list unread messages only.

> **TIP:** You might want to send and receive your mail either automatically or manually, depending on your mail setup, your accounts, and the way you like to work. To customize the way your mail is delivered, choose Options from the Tools menu, and, on the Mail Setup tab, click the Send/Receive button.

Read Your Messages

(1) Switch to the Inbox of the mail service you want to view if it isn't the currently active folder.

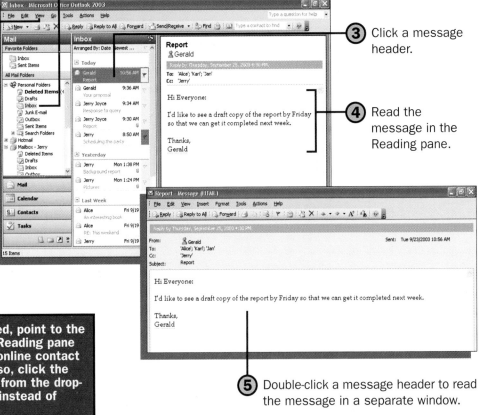

(2) On the View menu, point to Arrange By, and, from the submenu, choose how you want to view your messages:

- Choose the way you want the messages to be ordered.

- Point to Current View, and choose the type of messages you want to be displayed.

- Point to Reading Pane, and specify whether you want the Reading pane to be displayed and, if so, where.

- Click AutoPreview if you want to see the first line or two of the content of each message displayed in the Inbox pane.

(3) Click a message header.

(4) Read the message in the Reading pane.

(5) Double-click a message header to read the message in a separate window.

> **TRY THIS:** In a message you've received, point to the icon next to the sender's name in the Reading pane to determine whether that person is an online contact and whether he or she is on line now. If so, click the icon, and choose Send Instant Message from the drop-down menu to use Windows Messenger instead of sending an e-mail response.

Replying to or Forwarding a Message

When you receive an e-mail message that needs a reply or that you want to forward to someone else, all it takes is a click of a button to create a new message. But be careful when you use the Reply All button—your message could be received by a lot of people for whom it wasn't intended!

> **(!) TIP: When you reply to a message that has an attached file, the attachment isn't included with your reply. When you forward such a message, though, the attachment is included so that the recipient can open or save it.**

Answer or Forward a Message

(2) Click the appropriate button:

- Reply to send your reply to the writer of the message only
- Reply All to send your reply to the writer of the message and to everyone listed in the original message's To and CC lines
- Forward to send a copy of the message to another recipient

(3) Add names to or delete names from the To and CC lines.

(4) Type your reply message or any note associated with the forwarded message.

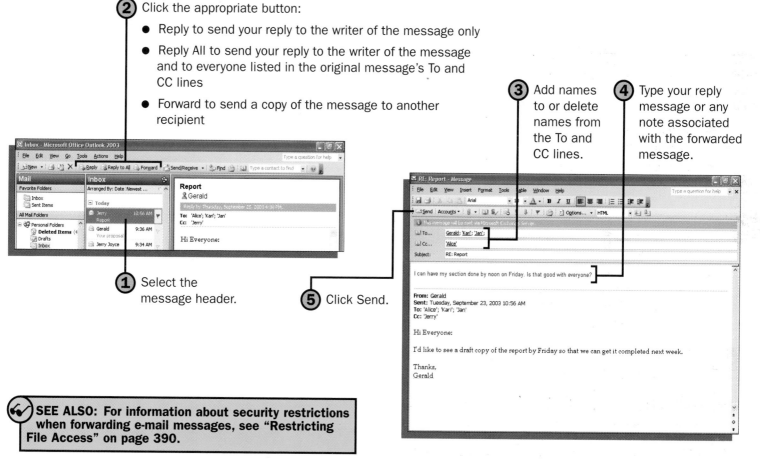

(1) Select the message header.

(5) Click Send.

> **(✓) SEE ALSO: For information about security restrictions when forwarding e-mail messages, see "Restricting File Access" on page 390.**

Sending or Receiving a File

A great way to share a file—a Microsoft Office Excel worksheet or chart, a Word document, or a drawing or photograph, for example—is to include it as part of an e-mail message. The file is kept as a separate part of the message—an attachment—that the recipient can save and open at any time.

TRY THIS: Open a folder window, hold down the Ctrl key, and select two or more files. Right-click one of the files, point to Send To on the shortcut menu, and choose Mail Recipient from the submenu.

Send a File by E-Mail

3 Click the Insert File button.

1 Start a new e-mail message.

7 Click Send.

The options differ depending on the type of file you're sending and the type of e-mail system you're using.

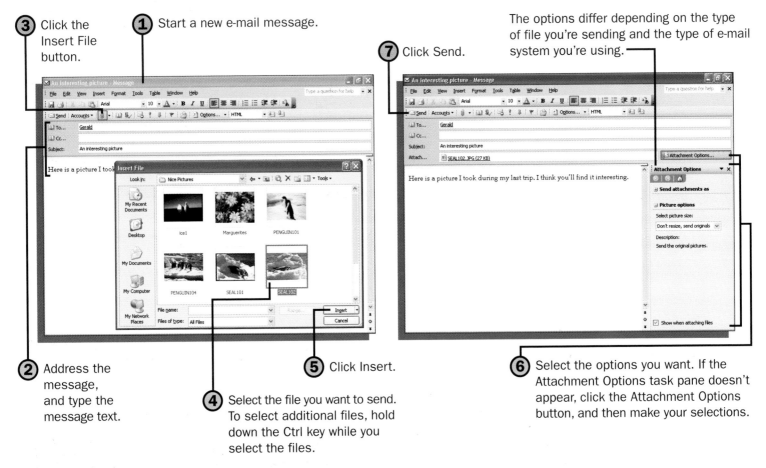

2 Address the message, and type the message text.

5 Click Insert.

4 Select the file you want to send. To select additional files, hold down the Ctrl key while you select the files.

6 Select the options you want. If the Attachment Options task pane doesn't appear, click the Attachment Options button, and then make your selections.

Receive an Attachment

(1) Select a message you've received that contains an attachment.

SEE ALSO: For information about working with a file attachment that was sent out for review, see "Sending Out a File For Review" on pages 350–351, "Reviewing Document in Word" on page 352, and "Reviewing a File in Excel or PowerPoint" on page 353.

For information about verifying the source of a file, see "Verifying a File by Using a Signature" on page 387.

(2) Right-click the Attachment icon, and, from the shortcut menu that appears, choose

- Open to open the file.
- Print to open the file in its default program and then send the file to the default printer.
- Save As to save the file to a disk without opening the file.

(3) Specify where you want to save the file.

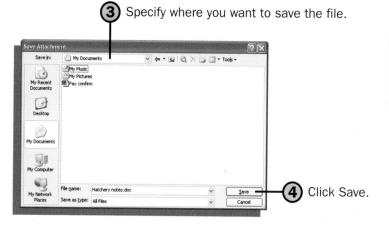

(4) Click Save.

TIP: Some mail systems can't accommodate attachments larger than about 1 MB, and some types of files can be corrupted when they're sent as attachments. In those cases, you might be able to compress the file before you send it, by using either a file-compression program or compressed folders that are integrated in Windows. You can use other file-transfer methods too, such as those available in Windows Messenger, or you can connect to a Web site that supports FTP file transfers.

CAUTION: Viruses are often distributed in attached files. *Never* open an attachment you aren't expecting without first verifying its source, and always use a virus-scanning program on your computer.

Using Word for E-Mail Messages

If you're using Outlook as your e-mail program, you can (and should) use the power of Word to compose and read your e-mail messages. Doing so allows you to use many of Word's invaluable features, such as spelling and grammar checking, AutoCorrect and AutoFormat options, AutoText, and even Word's smart tags.

> **SEE ALSO:** For information about setting up a default format for your e-mail messages in Word, see "Setting the Default Formatting for E-Mail Messages" on pages 160–161.

Configure Outlook

(1) In Outlook, choose Options from the Tools menu to display the Options dialog box. Click the Mail Format tab.

(3) Select these check boxes for editing and reading your messages in Word.

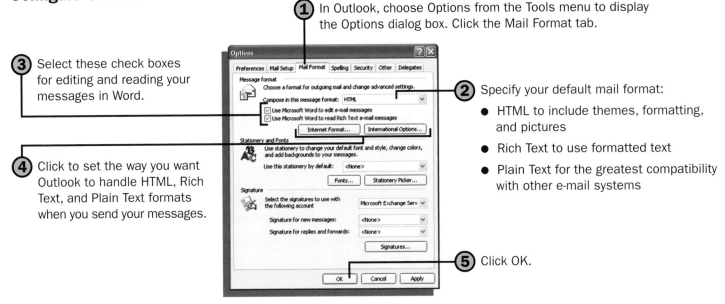

(2) Specify your default mail format:

- HTML to include themes, formatting, and pictures
- Rich Text to use formatted text
- Plain Text for the greatest compatibility with other e-mail systems

(4) Click to set the way you want Outlook to handle HTML, Rich Text, and Plain Text formats when you send your messages.

(5) Click OK.

> **TRY THIS:** Configure Outlook to use Word as its e-mail editor. Start a new message, and, in the text of the message, include your name or the name of someone in your Contacts list or Address Book. If the name becomes underlined, indicating that it's a smart tag, click the Actions button and see the various tasks you can accomplish using the smart tag that Word inserted. Easy to see why it's called a *smart* tag, isn't it?

Sending a File as E-Mail

If you've created a file in an Office program, and you want to send that file to friends or coworkers, you don't have to send it as an attachment to an e-mail message. Instead, you can transform the file itself into a formatted e-mail message. To do this, you simply add an e-mail header to the file, and then you can send a copy of the entire document as the body of the message. You can also add a brief introduction to the file if you want.

> **TIP:** When you send a file as an e-mail message, the mailing information is saved with the file. The next time you open the document and click the E-Mail button, the address information is still there, along with the date and time you sent the message. It's a really efficient way to keep track of when and to whom you sent certain files.

Send the Text of a File

(2) Click the E-Mail button on the Standard toolbar to display the e-mail header. If you're asked what you want to send, select the option to send the content as part of the message body.

(5) Click to send your message, which now includes the full text of the document.

(4) Insert some introductory text if you want. This text and a signature, if you add one, will precede the text of the document.

(1) In your Office program, create and save a file, or open an existing file.

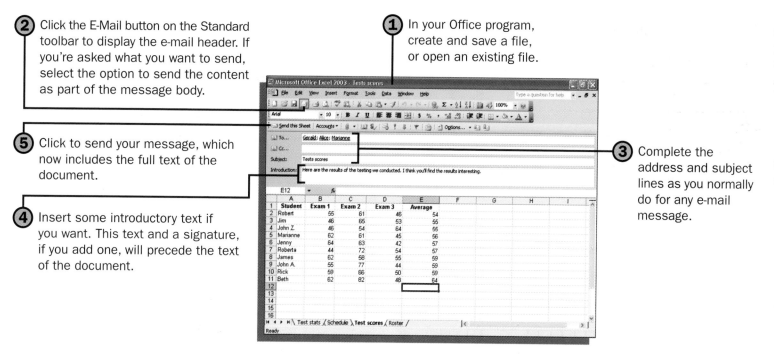

(3) Complete the address and subject lines as you normally do for any e-mail message.

> **SEE ALSO:** For information about sending out a file for review, see "Sending Out a File for Review" on pages 350–351.

> **TRY THIS:** In your Office program, point to Send To on the File menu, and see all the different ways you can send the file to a mail recipient.

Setting the Default Formatting for E-Mail Messages

When you use Word to compose your e-mail messages, you can format the way your messages look. Be aware, though, that no matter how gorgeous a message looks when you send it, it might not look the same when it's received! For that to happen, the recipient must be using an e-mail program such as Outlook or Outlook Express that can display your formatting in all its glory.

Format the Message

(2) On the Personal Stationery tab, click Theme to add specially designed formatting, including a background picture or pattern.

(1) In Word, choose Options from the Tools menu to display the Options dialog box. On the General tab, click the E-Mail Options button to display the E-Mail Options dialog box, and review the settings.

(4) If you want to use a fonts other than those designated for the theme, click to use your own fonts.

(5) Click to specify which fonts to use for your messages.

(3) Select the theme you want, and then preview it. If you're satisfied with it, click OK.

(6) Select this check box to have your name (or any name you type) included in any comments you make in a message.

(7) Select this check box to use an unused color for your text in a reply so that it can be easily identified.

(8) Click to specify a font that you want to use in any Plain Text messages.

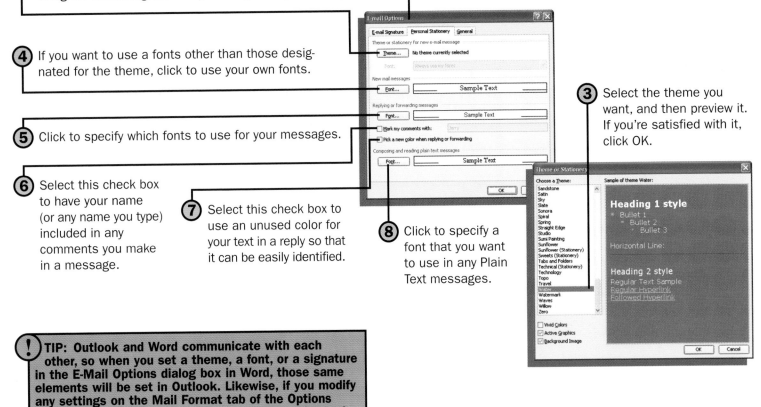

> **!** **TIP: Outlook and Word communicate with each other, so when you set a theme, a font, or a signature in the E-Mail Options dialog box in Word, those same elements will be set in Outlook. Likewise, if you modify any settings on the Mail Format tab of the Options dialog box in Outlook, those settings will be changed in Word.**

Add Your Signature

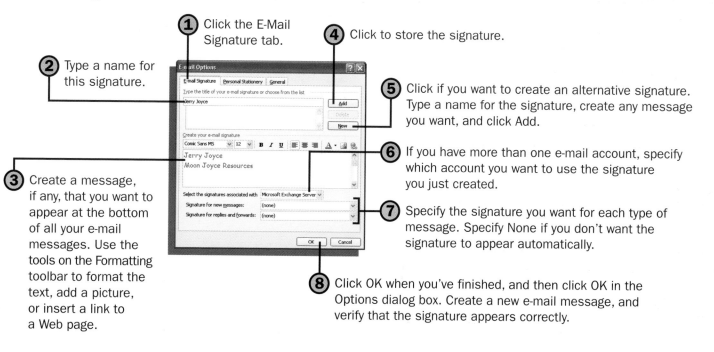

(1) Click the E-Mail Signature tab.

(2) Type a name for this signature.

(3) Create a message, if any, that you want to appear at the bottom of all your e-mail messages. Use the tools on the Formatting toolbar to format the text, add a picture, or insert a link to a Web page.

(4) Click to store the signature.

(5) Click if you want to create an alternative signature. Type a name for the signature, create any message you want, and click Add.

(6) If you have more than one e-mail account, specify which account you want to use the signature you just created.

(7) Specify the signature you want for each type of message. Specify None if you don't want the signature to appear automatically.

(8) Click OK when you've finished, and then click OK in the Options dialog box. Create a new e-mail message, and verify that the signature appears correctly.

TRY THIS: Create two or more e-mail signatures. Start a new e-mail message, and note your signature. Right-click the signature, and choose the alternative signature.

TIP: If you're not using Word as your e-mail editor, you can still set the default formatting and create a signature in Outlook. Just choose Options from the Tools menu, and make your changes on the Mail Format tab.

TIP: Your signature might look different from what you specified, depending on the format you use to send your messages. For example, if you send your messages as Plain Text, your signature won't include any text formatting, pictures, or links.

Sending a File as a Fax

You can create an Office file in Word, Excel, PowerPoint, or Document Imaging and then send it out as a fax over the Internet by using an Internet fax service provider. Depending on the services provided, you can also receive a fax, which is forwarded to you as an e-mail message by the fax service provider. Using the Internet, not only will you avoid those long-distance phone charges that mount up so quickly when you use a fax modem, but also you won't need a dedicated fax phone line.

Send an Internet Fax

> **!** **TIP:** You can send a fax via a fax modem directly from Word by pointing to Send To on the File menu, choosing Recipient Using A Fax Modem from the submenu, and then stepping through the Fax Wizard that appears.

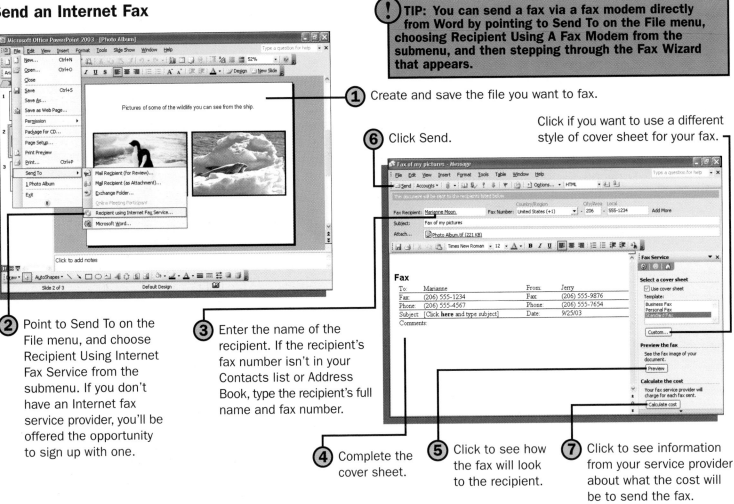

1 Create and save the file you want to fax.

6 Click Send.

Click if you want to use a different style of cover sheet for your fax.

2 Point to Send To on the File menu, and choose Recipient Using Internet Fax Service from the submenu. If you don't have an Internet fax service provider, you'll be offered the opportunity to sign up with one.

3 Enter the name of the recipient. If the recipient's fax number isn't in your Contacts list or Address Book, type the recipient's full name and fax number.

4 Complete the cover sheet.

5 Click to see how the fax will look to the recipient.

7 Click to see information from your service provider about what the cost will be to send the fax.

10 Managing with Outlook

In the previous section we talked about e-mail, the most commonly used feature of Microsoft Office Outlook 2003. In this section, we'll introduce Outlook's lesser-known but extraordinarily useful features.

You can use the Calendar to schedule anything and everything. If you need to plan staff meetings, you and your group can share your Calendars to compare schedules and find a date and time when everyone's available. If you play tennis on Thursdays and take a cooking class on Saturdays, tell Outlook to schedule those recurring appointments for you *and* give you an early reminder.

If you've been using Outlook for your e-mail, you already know how useful the Contacts list and Address Book are. It's a great convenience to be able to list so many details about a person or a business on an Address Card and then retrieve all the information with a click or two. We also like the ability to automatically add a new contact based on the e-mail address in a received message, and being able to create a *distribution list* to send a single message to a group of people.

Are you tired of seeing sticky notes on your computer, your refrigerator door, or stuck to the bottom of your shoe? Banish those stickies from your life, or at least reduce their numbers, with Outlook's Tasks list and Notes feature. Use the Tasks list to jot down all the stuff you need to do, along with due date, start date, and any other details. Use the Notes feature to write…well, notes. As with the Calendar, you can share your Tasks list and your notes with friends and coworkers. Last but not least, use the Journal to record your hours or keep a record of your activities.

What's Where in Outlook?

Outlook does a lot more than just handle your e-mail!
Outlook also provides the following useful tools:

- A scheduling tool that presents multiple views of your own Calendar, as well as the Calendars of your friends and coworkers

- A detailed, well-organized Contacts list and Address Book

Calendar in the
Navigation pane

Switch to weekly or monthly views.

Click to select
a different view.

View an Address Card for each person
or business in your Contacts list.

An appointment
with a reminder

Daily schedule

- A Tasks list that helps you schedule work, play, and everything in between

- A nice little electronic Notes feature that you can use instead of cluttering up your monitor with all those sticky notes.

Click to select a different view.

Your Tasks list

Click to select a different view.

A note, with its first few words visible

Keeping Track of Your Schedule

If you're so busy that you need to keep track of every moment in your day, or if you're just a bit forgetful and need to write everything down, let Outlook do your organizing for you. Enter all your appointments, vacation schedules, business trips, birthdays, anniversaries, and so on, and the Outlook schedule not only will keep everything up to date but will remind you of your obligations ahead of time. You can even tell Outlook to schedule certain appointments for you when they occur at the same time each week or each month.

TRY THIS: In the Day view of the Calendar, point to an area at the top or bottom of a scheduled appointment. When the mouse pointer turns into a two-headed arrow, drag the boundary of the appointment up or down to change the length of the appointment. Switch to the Week view, and point to the appointment. When the mouse pointer turns into a four-headed arrow, drag the appointment to another day. Double-click the appointment, and note how the time and day have changed.

Record an Appointment

(2) Select the time for the appointment, right-click the time, and choose New Appointment from the shortcut menu to display the Appointment dialog box.

(9) Click Save And Close.

(1) Click Calendar in the Navigation pane if the Calendar isn't displayed, and then click the date of the appointment.

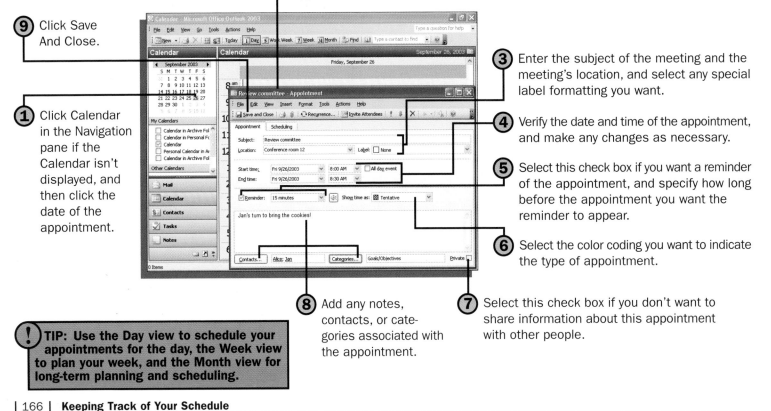

(3) Enter the subject of the meeting and the meeting's location, and select any special label formatting you want.

(4) Verify the date and time of the appointment, and make any changes as necessary.

(5) Select this check box if you want a reminder of the appointment, and specify how long before the appointment you want the reminder to appear.

(6) Select the color coding you want to indicate the type of appointment.

(8) Add any notes, contacts, or categories associated with the appointment.

(7) Select this check box if you don't want to share information about this appointment with other people.

TIP: Use the Day view to schedule your appointments for the day, the Week view to plan your week, and the Month view for long-term planning and scheduling.

Schedule a Recurring Appointment

(1) Select the time for the first occurrence of the appointment, right-click the selection, and choose New Recurring Appointment from the shortcut menu to open the Appointment Recurrence dialog box.

(8) Click Save And Close.

(2) Verify the time and duration of the appointment.

(4) Specify on which day of the week the appointment takes place.

(3) Specify the frequency of the appointment.

(5) Specify the appointment's range of recurrence.

(7) Complete any additional information about the appointment.

(6) Click OK.

! TIP: If you're sharing Calendars or scheduling information with other people, you can see their availability by clicking the Scheduling tab of the Appointment dialog box.

! TIP: If an appointment is based on information in an e-mail message, drag the message onto the Calendar button. The Appointment dialog box that opens will contain the full text of the e-mail.

⊘ SEE ALSO: For information about sharing Calendars, see "Sharing Calendars" on page 168.

Sharing Calendars

We're all so busy living our lives that it can be a real scheduling problem to get a group of people together for an event, whether it's an important business meeting, a baby shower, or simply a coffee break or lunch date. You can reduce the frustration by having each person set up his or her individual Calendar to be shared, and *voilà!* No more "telephone tag." You just glance at each other's Calendars to see who's free and when. To accomplish this, however, your network needs to be using Microsoft Exchange Server.

> ⚠️ **TIP: When you're setting the permission level, you can select more than one person at a time and set the same permission level at one time for all those selected.**

Share Your Calendar

(1) Click the Calendar button in the Navigation pane, and then click Share My Calendar.

(2) In the Calendar Properties dialog box, click Add.

(3) In the Add Users dialog box, double-click the name of each person to whom you'll grant permission to see your shared Calendar.

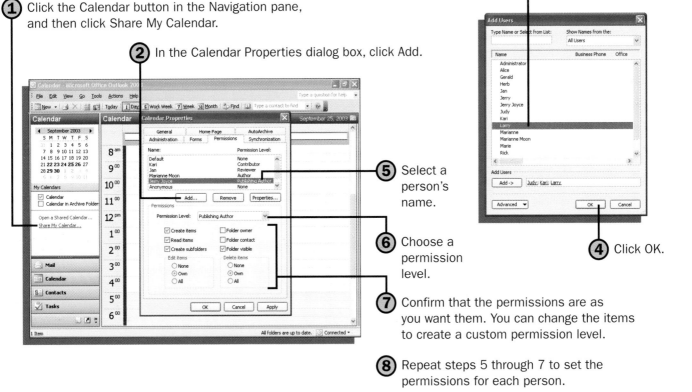

(5) Select a person's name.

(6) Choose a permission level.

(4) Click OK.

(7) Confirm that the permissions are as you want them. You can change the items to create a custom permission level.

(8) Repeat steps 5 through 7 to set the permissions for each person.

View a Shared Calendar

1 Click Open A Shared Calendar.

TIP: If you don't want to share every detail of your life, create a second Calendar for your more personal details. To do so, in the Folders list in the Navigation pane, right-click the Calendar folder, choose New Folder from the shortcut menu, and create and name a new folder. This will be your unshared personal Calendar that you alone will be able to view.

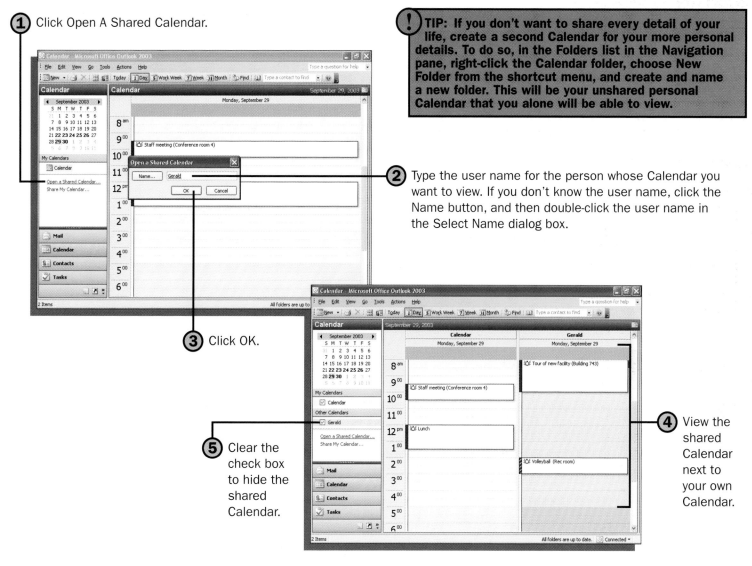

2 Type the user name for the person whose Calendar you want to view. If you don't know the user name, click the Name button, and then double-click the user name in the Select Name dialog box.

3 Click OK.

5 Clear the check box to hide the shared Calendar.

4 View the shared Calendar next to your own Calendar.

Creating an Internet Calendar

Outlook can automatically post your scheduling information to an Internet Calendar by using the Microsoft Office Internet Free/Busy Service. This service lets you share your scheduling information with other people by displaying the times that you're free or busy, and it also enables you to see someone else's posted schedule.

SEE ALSO: For information about creating a group schedule, see "Viewing Your Group's Schedule" on the facing page.

For information about creating a meeting request, see "Scheduling a Meeting" on pages 172–173.

Set Up an Internet Calendar

(1) In Outlook, choose Options from the Tools menu, and click the Calendar Options button on the Preferences tab of the Options dialog box.

(2) Click the Free/Busy Options button in the Calendar Options dialog box.

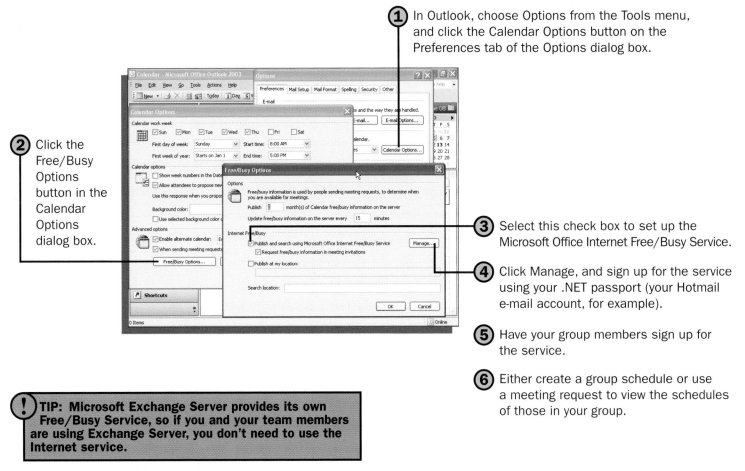

(3) Select this check box to set up the Microsoft Office Internet Free/Busy Service.

(4) Click Manage, and sign up for the service using your .NET passport (your Hotmail e-mail account, for example).

(5) Have your group members sign up for the service.

(6) Either create a group schedule or use a meeting request to view the schedules of those in your group.

TIP: Microsoft Exchange Server provides its own Free/Busy Service, so if you and your team members are using Exchange Server, you don't need to use the Internet service.

Viewing Your Group's Schedule

If you need to know who is or isn't free to attend an impromptu meeting, conduct an interview with a possible new hire, or have a quick lunch, you can take a look at your group's schedules to see what's on everyone's agenda.

TIP: To be able to see everyone's scheduling information, you and the other members of the group need to be using either Microsoft Exchange Server or Microsoft Office Internet Free/Busy Service.

Set Up Your Group

1 Click Calendar in the Navigation pane, and then click View Group Schedules on the Standard toolbar.

2 Click New, enter a name for the group in the Create New Group Schedule dialog box, and click OK.

3 In the dialog box that appears, click Add Others, and then choose Add From Address Book from the drop-down menu.

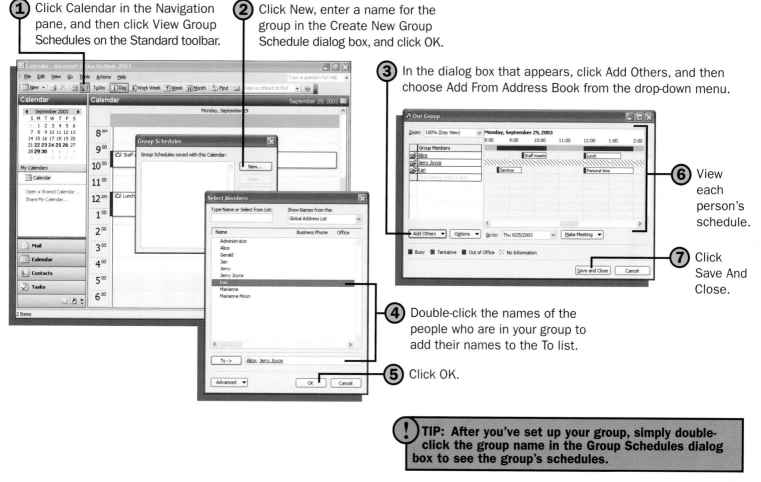

6 View each person's schedule.

7 Click Save And Close.

4 Double-click the names of the people who are in your group to add their names to the To list.

5 Click OK.

TIP: After you've set up your group, simply double-click the group name in the Group Schedules dialog box to see the group's schedules.

Scheduling a Meeting

Having the ability to view other people's schedules makes it relatively easy to get people together for a meeting. All you need to do is compare schedules, find a time when everyone who should attend the meeting will be free to do so, and then send e-mail inviting the members of your group to attend the meeting.

Set Up a Meeting

(1) Click Calendar in the Navigation pane, and select the date and time you'd like to hold the meeting. Right-click the date and/or time when you're planning to have the meeting, and choose New Meeting Request from the shortcut menu to display the Meeting dialog box.

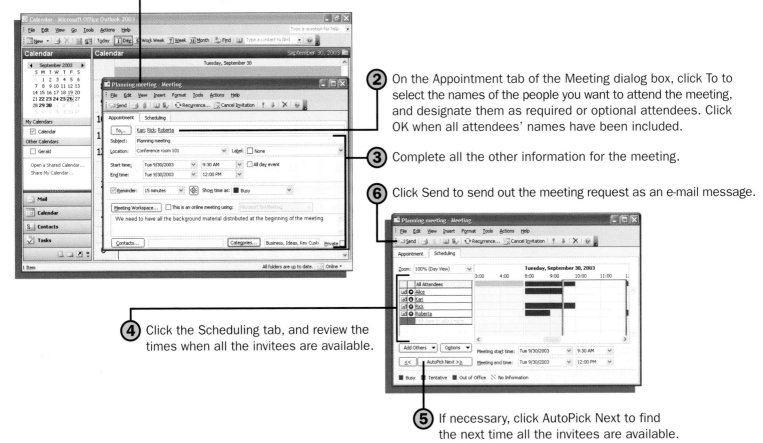

(2) On the Appointment tab of the Meeting dialog box, click To to select the names of the people you want to attend the meeting, and designate them as required or optional attendees. Click OK when all attendees' names have been included.

(3) Complete all the other information for the meeting.

(6) Click Send to send out the meeting request as an e-mail message.

(4) Click the Scheduling tab, and review the times when all the invitees are available.

(5) If necessary, click AutoPick Next to find the next time all the invitees are available.

Finalize the Meeting

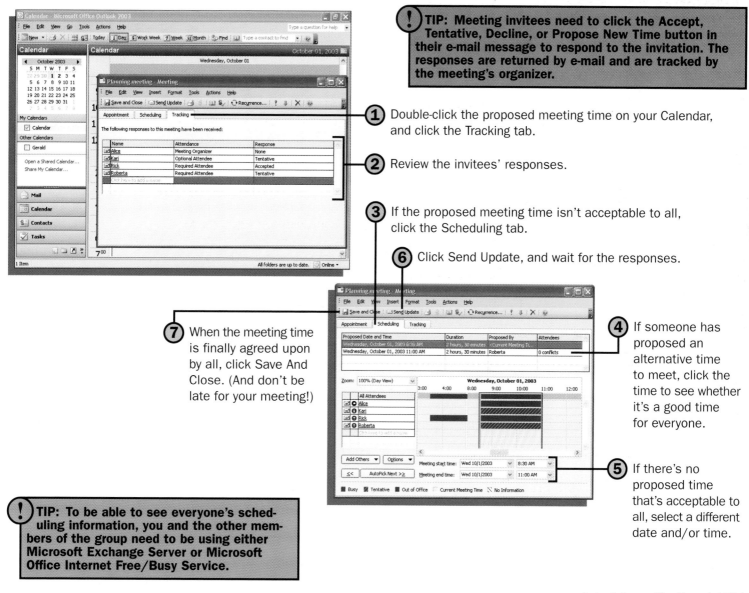

TIP: Meeting invitees need to click the Accept, Tentative, Decline, or Propose New Time button in their e-mail message to respond to the invitation. The responses are returned by e-mail and are tracked by the meeting's organizer.

(1) Double-click the proposed meeting time on your Calendar, and click the Tracking tab.

(2) Review the invitees' responses.

(3) If the proposed meeting time isn't acceptable to all, click the Scheduling tab.

(6) Click Send Update, and wait for the responses.

(7) When the meeting time is finally agreed upon by all, click Save And Close. (And don't be late for your meeting!)

(4) If someone has proposed an alternative time to meet, click the time to see whether it's a good time for everyone.

(5) If there's no proposed time that's acceptable to all, select a different date and/or time.

TIP: To be able to see everyone's scheduling information, you and the other members of the group need to be using either Microsoft Exchange Server or Microsoft Office Internet Free/Busy Service.

Managing Your Contacts

Your Contacts list is one of your best friends—the latest and greatest place to keep all the information you need about all your business and personal contacts. On a single Address Card, you can store everything you need to know about a person or a business: e-mail addresses, phone and fax numbers, mailing addresses, birthdays, anniversaries, and many more details. Also, if you often send one message to the same group of people, you can gather all their addresses into a distribution list, and then all you need to find and use is that one address item. It's a real time-saver.

Create a New Contact

> ❗ **TIP:** To add someone's name to your Contacts list based on the e-mail address in a message you've received, right-click the e-mail address or name in the message, and choose Add To Outlook Contacts from the shortcut menu. You can also use this technique to add the address to your Messenger Contacts list or to open the contact information for that individual.

> ❗ **TIP:** When you send or receive an Address Card, it's called a *vCard,* or virtual card, and it's a file that contains all the contact information for an individual.

① In Outlook, click Contacts in the Navigation pane, and then click New.

⑤ To enter another contact who has the same company information, choose New Contact From the Same Company from the Actions menu, and repeat steps 2 through 4 to complete the fields that haven't already been completed automatically by Outlook.

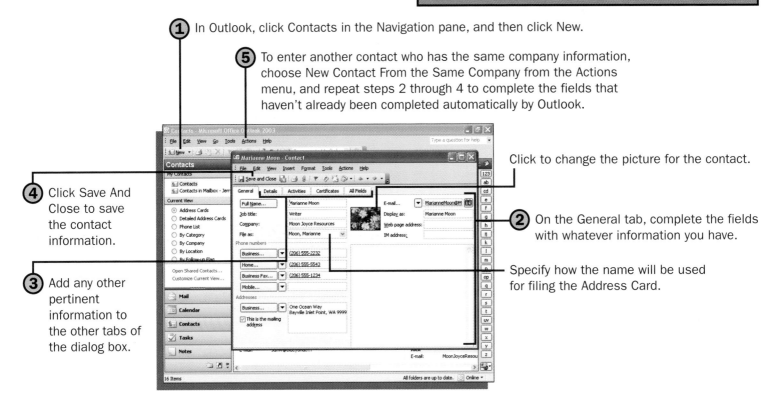

④ Click Save And Close to save the contact information.

③ Add any other pertinent information to the other tabs of the dialog box.

Click to change the picture for the contact.

② On the General tab, complete the fields with whatever information you have.

Specify how the name will be used for filing the Address Card.

Create a Distribution List

(8) Click Save And Close to create and save the distribution list.

(1) Choose New Distribution List from the Actions menu to display the Distribution List dialog box.

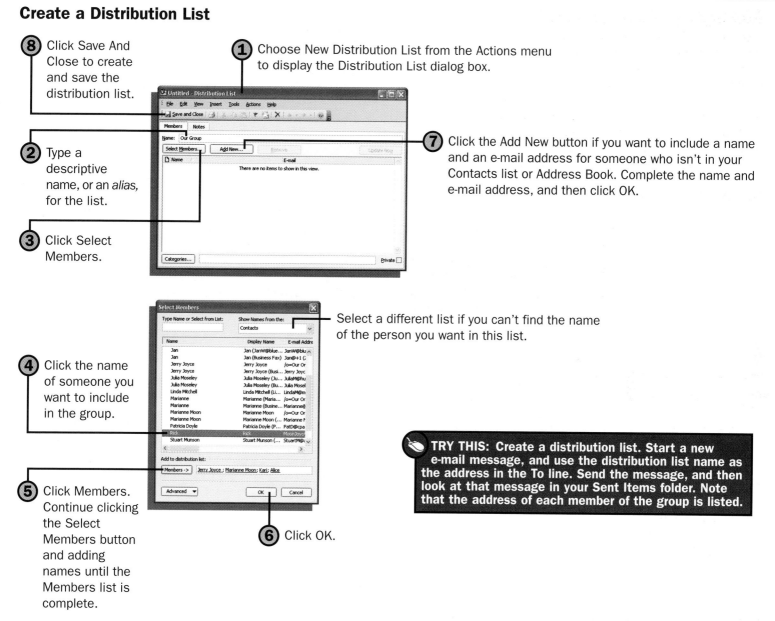

(2) Type a descriptive name, or an *alias,* for the list.

(3) Click Select Members.

(7) Click the Add New button if you want to include a name and an e-mail address for someone who isn't in your Contacts list or Address Book. Complete the name and e-mail address, and then click OK.

Select a different list if you can't find the name of the person you want in this list.

(4) Click the name of someone you want to include in the group.

(5) Click Members. Continue clicking the Select Members button and adding names until the Members list is complete.

(6) Click OK.

> **TRY THIS: Create a distribution list. Start a new e-mail message, and use the distribution list name as the address in the To line. Send the message, and then look at that message in your Sent Items folder. Note that the address of each member of the group is listed.**

Keeping Track of Your Tasks

If your computer monitor is surrounded by what we call "the ring of fire"—those sticky notes you attach at eye level to remind you of the zillions of tasks you have to complete—we're going to recommend a better (not to mention tidier) way to keep track of such details. Let Outlook do it for you!

SEE ALSO: For information about tracking your business tasks using the Microsoft Business Manager addition to Outlook, see "Working with Business Manager" on pages 358–359.

Record a Task

1 In Outlook, click Tasks in the Navigation pane, and then click the New button.

2 Type a subject for the task.

3 Specify the task's due date and start date.

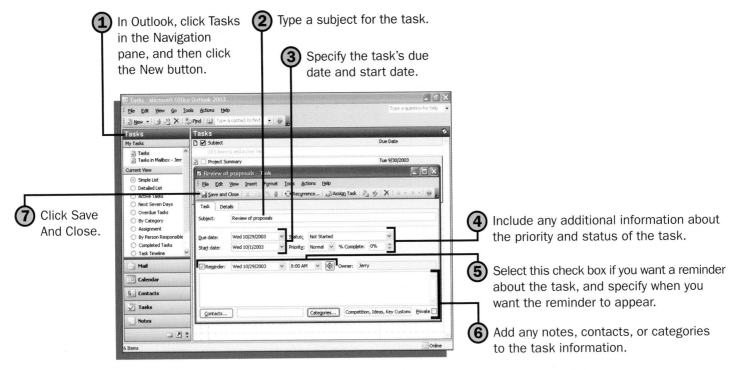

7 Click Save And Close.

4 Include any additional information about the priority and status of the task.

5 Select this check box if you want a reminder about the task, and specify when you want the reminder to appear.

6 Add any notes, contacts, or categories to the task information.

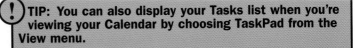

TIP: You can also display your Tasks list when you're viewing your Calendar by choosing TaskPad from the View menu.

Track Your Tasks

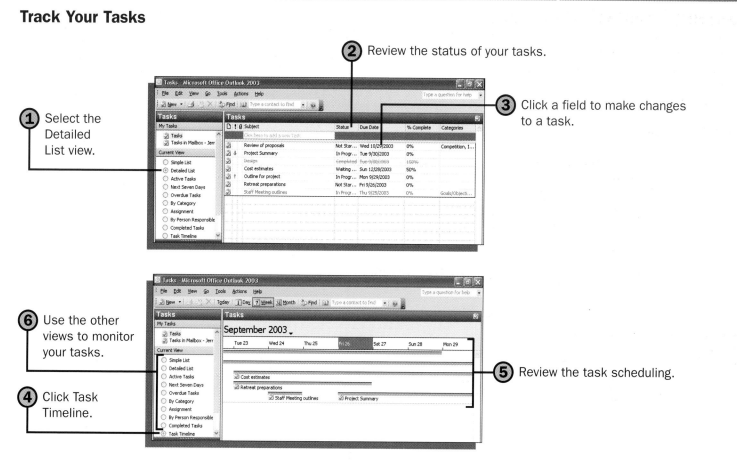

② Review the status of your tasks.

① Select the Detailed List view.

③ Click a field to make changes to a task.

⑥ Use the other views to monitor your tasks.

④ Click Task Timeline.

⑤ Review the task scheduling.

TRY THIS: Under Current View in the Navigation pane, select the Simple List view. Select the check box for each task you've completed. Click in the top line of the Tasks list, and enter the subject and due date for a new task. Click Detailed List, and complete the other fields. Double-click the new task to open the Task dialog box, add more details, and then click Save And Close.

TIP: To sort the tasks by subject, due date, or any of the other fields, in Detailed List view, click the field name at the top of the Tasks list.

Assigning Tasks

The key to success? Delegate! With Outlook, it's easy to delegate all those responsibilities by assigning tasks to your coworkers.

Assign a Task to Someone

1 In Outlook, click Tasks in the Navigation pane, right-click the task, and choose Assign Task from the shortcut menu to display the Task dialog box. (If the task has already been assigned, the Assign Task command won't be listed on the shortcut menu.)

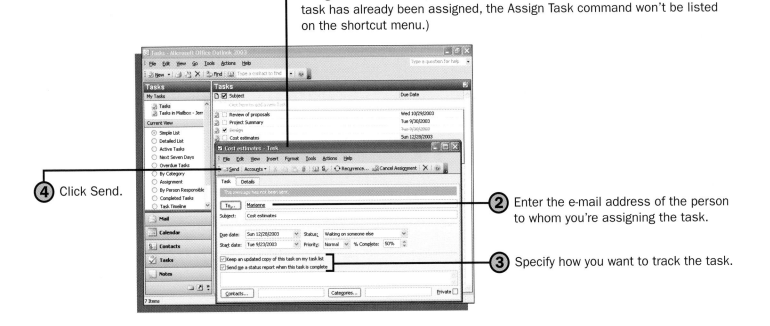

4 Click Send.

2 Enter the e-mail address of the person to whom you're assigning the task.

3 Specify how you want to track the task.

TIP: When you assign a task, the recipient can accept or decline the task in the e-mail he or she receives. If the task is accepted, the recipient can send updates on the progress of the task by clicking the Send Update button in the Task dialog box.

TRY THIS: Click the Calendar button in the Navigation pane. Drag an appointment onto the Tasks button in the Navigation pane. Complete the information in the Task dialog box, click the Assign Task button to assign the task to someone, and then send the message.

Taking Notes

If you're hooked on those ubiquitous little sticky notes to keep track of everything from shopping lists and "to do" lists to sudden inspirational thoughts or little poems, you might want to try Outlook's electronic equivalent.

Create a Note

① In Outlook, click Notes in the Navigation pane, and then click New.

② Type your note.

③ Click the Close button to save and close the note.

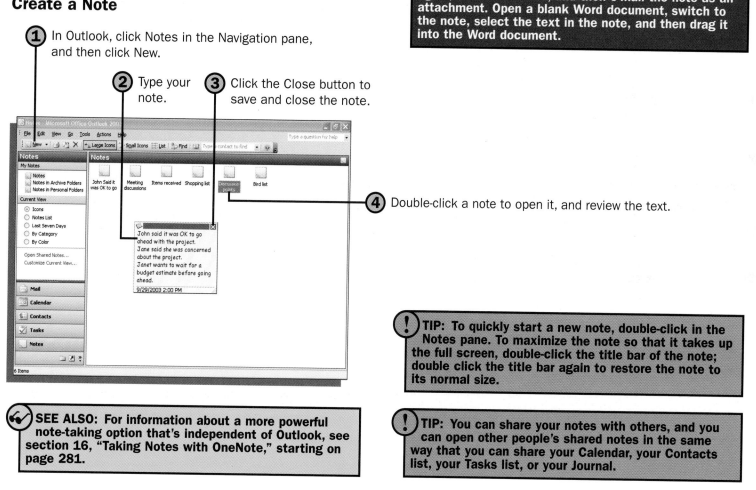

④ Double-click a note to open it, and review the text.

TRY THIS: Create a new note or open an existing one. Minimize Outlook. Click the Note icon in the top-left corner of the note. Choose Save As from the shortcut menu, and save the note. Click the Note icon again, choose Forward, and then e-mail the note as an attachment. Open a blank Word document, switch to the note, select the text in the note, and then drag it into the Word document.

TIP: To quickly start a new note, double-click in the Notes pane. To maximize the note so that it takes up the full screen, double-click the title bar of the note; double click the title bar again to restore the note to its normal size.

SEE ALSO: For information about a more powerful note-taking option that's independent of Outlook, see section 16, "Taking Notes with OneNote," starting on page 281.

TIP: You can share your notes with others, and you can open other people's shared notes in the same way that you can share your Calendar, your Contacts list, your Tasks list, or your Journal.

Reviewing Your Actions

If you need to track your activities for billing purposes, to keep a record of your overtime hours, or just to prove that you actually sat at your desk and did some work, you can tell Outlook to automatically record all your e-mail and Office program activities in Outlook's Journal. You can also use the Journal to manually record other activities.

TIP: The Journal isn't enabled by default, because its use is fairly limited and it can be rather cumbersome. If you don't need a detailed record of your daily activities, you might want to forget about the Journal. To track your activities related to a specific contact, double-click the contact in the Contacts list, and review your history with that person on the Activities tab.

Set Up Your Record

① Click Journal in the Navigation pane. If the Journal isn't listed in the Navigation pane, choose Journal from the Go Menu.

③ Select the Outlook items you want to record.

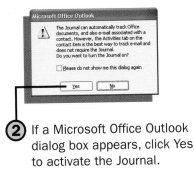

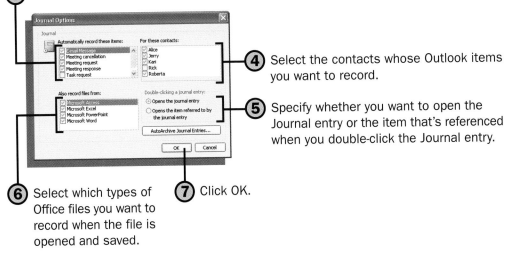

④ Select the contacts whose Outlook items you want to record.

⑤ Specify whether you want to open the Journal entry or the item that's referenced when you double-click the Journal entry.

② If a Microsoft Office Outlook dialog box appears, click Yes to activate the Journal.

⑥ Select which types of Office files you want to record when the file is opened and saved.

⑦ Click OK.

TIP: To change the items being logged, choose Options from the Tools menu, and, on the Preferences tab, click the Journal Options button.

Create a Journal Entry

 With Journal selected in the Navigation pane, click New on the Standard toolbar to display the Journal Entry dialog box.

⑥ Click Save And Close when you've finished.

⑦ To modify an entry, double-click it, and make changes in the Journal Entry dialog box.

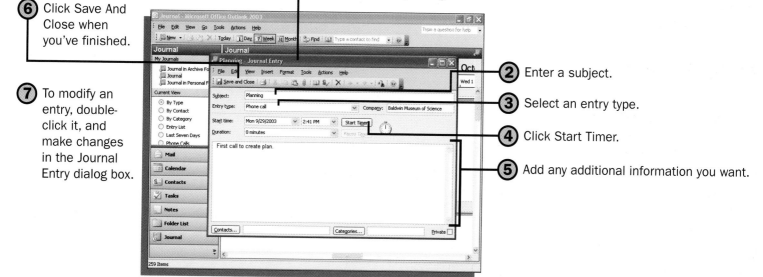

② Enter a subject.

③ Select an entry type.

④ Click Start Timer.

⑤ Add any additional information you want.

> **SEE ALSO:** For information about sharing Calendars, see "Sharing Calendars" on pages 168–169.

> **TIP:** You can share your Journal with others in the same way that you can share your Calendar, your Contacts list, your Tasks list, and your notes.

> **TIP:** To add the Journal to the Navigation pane, click the Configure Buttons button at the bottom-right of the Navigation pane, click Navigation Pane Options, select the Journal check box, and click OK.

Using Public Folders

If you're using Microsoft Exchange Server, you'll find that using public folders in Outlook is one of the most powerful ways to communicate with your group, to create a place to post messages and notes, to conduct discussions, to share contacts, and to display a group calendar, a list of tasks, or a journal of activities. You create your own folder and designate what type of work it will be used for, and then you can let others in your group use the folder to organize the details of a specific project.

> **TRY THIS:** Create a new public folder for e-mail and post items, and give members of your group access to the folder. Right-click the folder in the Folder List, and choose Send Link To This Folder from the shortcut menu. Send an e-mail containing the link to the members of your group. Select the folder again, and click New on the Standard toolbar. Create a welcoming message for the folder, and click Post. The folder is now ready to host all the messages and discussions your group needs to work effectively.

Create a Folder

1 Click Folder List in the Navigation pane, right-click the public folder in which you want to create your new folder, and choose New Folder from the shortcut menu to display the Create New Folder dialog box.

6 Right-click the new folder in the Folder List, and choose Properties from the shortcut menu to display the Reviews Properties dialog box.

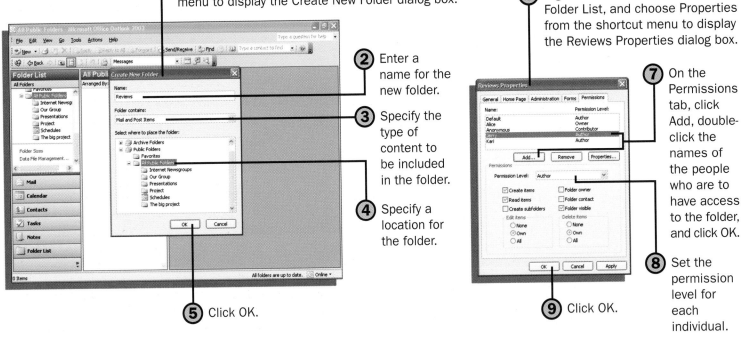

2 Enter a name for the new folder.

3 Specify the type of content to be included in the folder.

4 Specify a location for the folder.

5 Click OK.

7 On the Permissions tab, click Add, double-click the names of the people who are to have access to the folder, and click OK.

8 Set the permission level for each individual.

9 Click OK.

11 Working with a Database

If you've worked with an electronic list of items—customers' names and addresses, parts lists, and sales records, for example—you've worked with a database, maybe by entering items in specific places on one or more predesigned forms. What happens to the information you've entered is that someone—perhaps you, perhaps a coworker—eventually manipulates the data to achieve a variety of specific results.

So, if you're the owner of a small business, how will a database help you? Let's say you own a children's shoe store, and every six months you want to send a note out to the parents who've purchased their children's shoes from you, reminding them that it's time to have the children's feet remeasured. You can create a series of tables in a Microsoft Office Access 2003 database that will help you do just that. One table will contain the name and address of the parent who purchased the shoes; another table will list all your sales invoices, including date of purchase, shoe size and style, child's name, and so on; another will contain your shoe inventory; another your sales revenues; another the names and addresses of your salespeople. You can create as many tables as you need—you might even want a table listing the children's names and birthdays so that you can send birthday cards. The fact that you're working with a *relational database* means that you can extract whatever parts of the information you want for whatever reason you need them. For example, you can track your inventory, find out which shoe styles were your best sellers, which didn't sell, and so on. How do you create the relationship among your tables that makes all this possible? Read on.

What's Where in Access?

Access provides you with a variety of components, all of which are designed to record, investigate, and report your data. To do this, each component of the program displays two faces—one that you use to work with the data, and the other that you use for designing your database. Take a look at the graphic below, which displays all the different types of Access windows, opened and arranged in the main Access window.

With the exception of the Database window, the other windows show a table, a query, a form, and a report, all of which are ready to be used. The Database window works differently from the other windows because it's the control center through which you access all the items in the database, open an existing form or table, or create a new table or query.

Database window

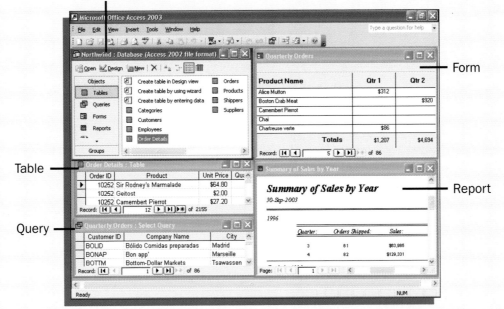

Form

Table

Query

Report

Now take a look at the graphic below. These are the same windows as those displayed in the graphic on the facing page, but—with the exception of the Database window, which looks the same because it has only one view—they all look completely different because you're now seeing them in Design view. You use Form Design view to add labels that help you understand what goes where, and to add data fields

that are your connection to the table. Similarly, you use Table Design view to create and modify the tables that store the data. You use Query Design view and Report Design view in similar ways: In Query Design view you design the way you interrogate your database and extract information from it, and in Report Design view you design your printed report and designate the information it contains.

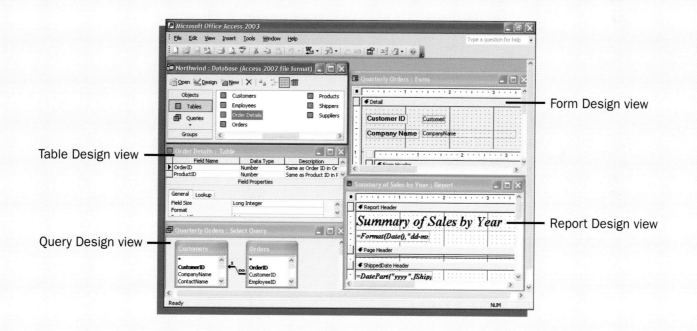

Table Design view

Query Design view

Form Design view

Report Design view

What Is a Relational Database?

Microsoft Access lets you create and use a relational database. What's the purpose of a relational database, and why would you use one? The short answer is that a relational database lets you organize your data logically and efficiently and lets you extract the information it contains in many different ways. Now here's the long answer.

A *table* is a container for data, and your database can contain several tables. One table might contain names, addresses, and other contact information about your clients. Another table might contain a list of your company's products and their unit costs. A third table might be your inventory, a fourth table your sales records for the year, and a final table your sales staff's contact information. As you can see, the information in all the tables is related. The power of an Access database is realized when you use its tools to explore the relationships among the data in the tables. For example, you might want to assess how product sales are doing in a specific market and how the sales are affected by the unit prices of the items. You can easily draw out that information by gathering up and comparing data from different tables.

An Access table with its columns and rows looks similar to an Excel worksheet, but it has substantially different properties. Each column is a data category called a *field*— for example, PartNumber, Description, Dimensions, Weight, and so on. Each row is a *data record,* which contains data for a single item in a data field—for example, the data for PartNumber 17843. Each table needs a field that contains a unique identifier, called the *primary key,* for each data record. This could be a part number or an employee identification number, or you could simply number each record consecutively. The concept of the primary key can be confusing, but you actually use one every day. For example, when you dial a phone number, the number works as a primary key to identify a specific phone line.

The way you extract data from the database depends on the type of information you want. A *form* is an easy-to-use interface that shows one record at a time, whether the fields are from one table or several. A form is also a good way to add, change, or delete the information in a table.

For more complex relational questions, a *query* is handy. A query means that you ask conditional questions of, and/or perform mathematical operations on, the data. A query can be as simple as calculating the total sales for a particular product, or it can be extremely complex. The results of a query are placed in the table format, and you can use them in the same way you use other tables.

To summarize information from the database and have the summary set up in a printable form, you create a *report*. A report is a reliable, permanent record of your data and your analysis of the data. You can do some organizing of the data in a report, but a report that requires extensive analysis of the data is usually based on the results of a query rather than on the results of data extracted directly from the tables.

There are even more parts to a database. A *data access page* is similar to a form, but it's designed to record data to and display data from the database using a Web page instead of working directly in Access. A *macro* is a (usually) little program that automates or expands the operations in Access—connecting to an external database or doing specialized formatting, for example. A *module* contains programming code that executes special actions in Access.

Intimidating, isn't it? But Access is extremely scalable— that is, doing something simple is usually quite simple, and doing something complex is probably quite complex. So stick to the simple stuff, and use the wizards whenever you can. When you're ready to explore the more complex aspects of Access, open the Help menu, point to Sample Databases, and click Northwind Sample Database to see an example of how to set up and work with a substantial database.

Using an Existing Database

Most of your database work is probably going to be done on an existing database in which you'll add, update, or extract information from the data. To use the database, just open it up and start working.

Use a Form

① Open the database you want to use.

② Click Forms in the database window.

③ Double-click the form you want to use.

④ Use the Navigation buttons to display the record you want.

First record

Previous record

Next record

Last record

Command button

⑦ Close the form when you've finished.

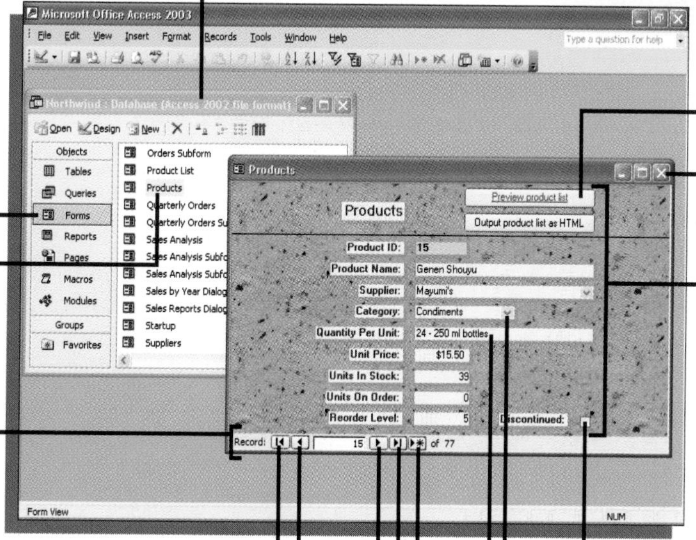

⑤ Do any of the following:

- Change any of the text or numbers in a text box to correct the data.
- Select a different item from a drop-down list to change the data.
- Select a check box or option button to specify a choice.
- Click a command button to execute an action.

Check box

Drop-down list box

Text box

⑥ Click the New Record button to enter data in a new record.

!TIP: The interface for an Access database is extremely customizable. Many large databases use an additional form called a Switchboard form to access other parts of the database, so if you're working on a database that looks substantially different from the one shown here, follow the instructions that accompany that database.

!TIP: Databases can have high security levels, so you might not have permission to make changes to the existing data. If you need to make changes but are denied access to do so, contact the owner or administrator of the database.

Creating a Database from a Template

Access provides a selection of templates that make it quick and easy for you to create the most common types of databases.

When you open a template, the Database Wizard starts up and walks you through the process of creating a customized database.

Select a Database Template

① In Access, choose New from the File menu.

④ Verify from the preview that the database contains the elements you need.

③ On the Databases tab, select the template you want to use.

② In the Templates section of the New File task pane, choose On My Computer to display the Templates dialog box.

⑤ Click OK.

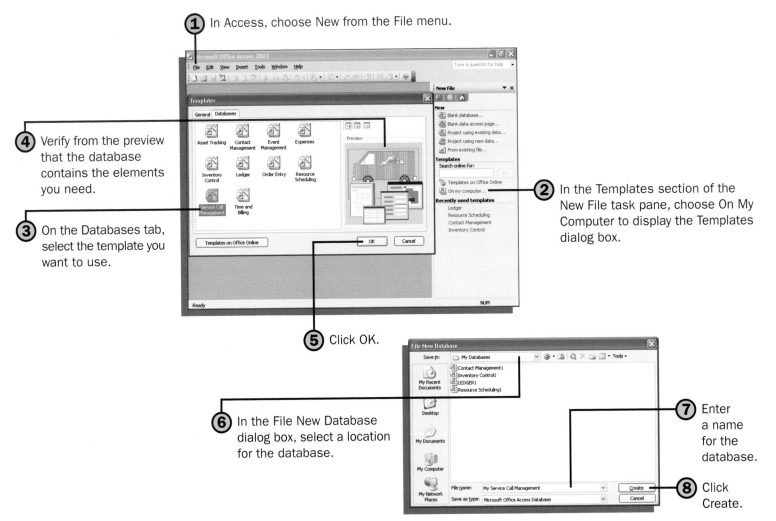

⑥ In the File New Database dialog box, select a location for the database.

⑦ Enter a name for the database.

⑧ Click Create.

Customize the Database

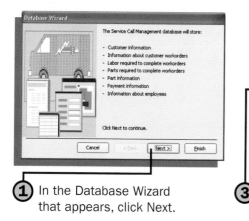

(2) With the first table selected, select or clear the check boxes to indicate which fields you want to include in the table.

(1) In the Database Wizard that appears, click Next.

(3) Select the next table, and specify the fields to be included. Continue selecting tables and specifying the fields for all the tables in the list.

(4) Click Next, and select the style you want for the screen displays. Click Next, and select the style you want for the printed reports. Continue through the wizard, naming the database and specifying the formatting you want. Select the option to start the database, and click Finish.

(5) Wait while the database is being created. Supply additional information if requested to do so, and then use the database as you would any other database.

TIP: Many of the database templates create an additional form called a Switchboard form. This is used to simplify executing tasks and navigating in the database. If you don't want to use the Switchboard form, close it, and use the main database window to open tables and forms.

CAUTION: Depending on the template you choose, you might not be permitted to clear the check boxes for certain fields in the Database Wizard. Don't try to remove any of these fields after you've created the database unless you're absolutely certain that you know what you're doing!

Adding a Table to a Database

Whether you're creating a new database or modifying an existing one, you can add a table of your own design to store data that you haven't already included in the database. When you use the Table Wizard to add the table, you can just specify which fields you want to include, and Access does the rest for you.

Create a Table

(1) In the database window, click Tables.

(2) Double-click Create Table By Using Wizard to start the Table Wizard.

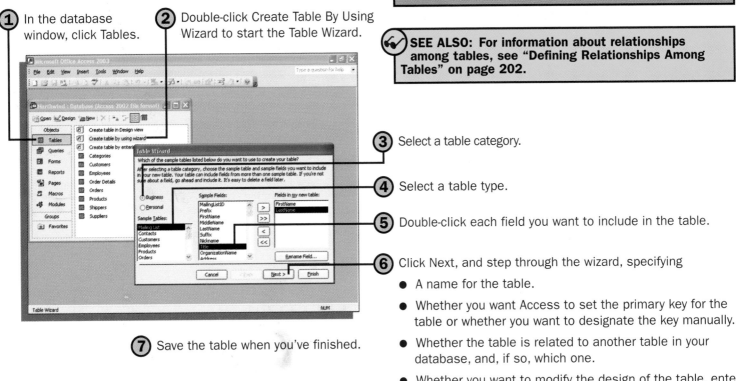

(7) Save the table when you've finished.

> **! TIP:** A primary key is a field in each record that uniquely identifies that record. If you let Access create the primary key, it inserts an ID field that uses the AutoNumber data type to consecutively number the records. Use your own primary key if the data already contain a unique identifier for the record—a part number or an employee identification number, for example.

> **✓ SEE ALSO:** For information about relationships among tables, see "Defining Relationships Among Tables" on page 202.

(3) Select a table category.

(4) Select a table type.

(5) Double-click each field you want to include in the table.

(6) Click Next, and step through the wizard, specifying

- A name for the table.
- Whether you want Access to set the primary key for the table or whether you want to designate the key manually.
- Whether the table is related to another table in your database, and, if so, which one.
- Whether you want to modify the design of the table, enter the data, or have Access create a form on which you can enter the data.

Modifying a Table

If you used the Table Wizard but it didn't produce exactly the type of table you wanted, you can use Design view to modify the table so that it contains the elements you want. While you're there, you can also add other information to customize the table and to help maintain the quality of the data.

> **TIP:** To get information about each field property—for example, the Caption property or the Indexed property—click in the property's field, and press the F1 key.

Make Changes to a Table

1 Open the table if it isn't already open.

> **TIP:** To delete a field, right-click it, and choose Delete Rows from the shortcut menu. To add a new field, click in the blank row below the last entry, and enter a field name. To move a field, select the entire row, and drag it to the location where you want it.

2 Click the View button on the Table Datasheet toolbar to switch to Design view.

3 Click in a field name, and change the field name if you want to rename it.

4 Click in the data type for a field, click the down arrow that appears, and select the type of data to be used if the default type is incorrect.

5 To provide additional information about the field, enter a description for it.

7 Save the table.

8 Click the View button on the Table Design toolbar to return to your form.

6 Complete the additional information about the field properties.

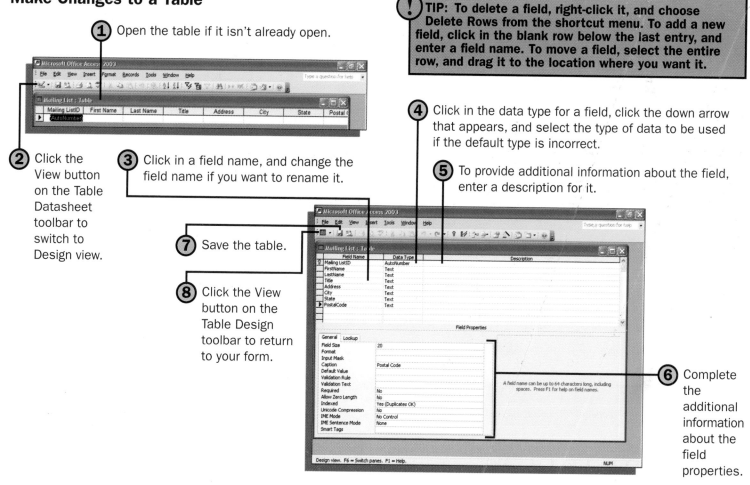

Adding Data to a Table

There are two ways to enter data in a table: either working directly in the table, or using a form. Working directly in the table might be the faster method of data entry, but we think that using a form makes the data easier to work with and understand.

! TIP: To use a Microsoft Office Excel worksheet that already contains data as the source for an Access table, point to Get External Data on the File menu, choose Import from the submenu, and step through the Import Spreadsheet Wizard.

Add Data Directly

(1) Click Tables, and then double-click the table you want to open.

(3) If the selected field reads "AutoNumber," press Tab to move to the next field.

(8) Close the form when you've finished.

(4) Enter the data for the field. If the field displays a down arrow, click it, and select the data you want from the list. Press Tab to move to the next field.

(5) Continue entering the data for each field in the record, pressing Tab to move to the next field.

(2) Click the New Record button.

(6) After you've completed the last field of the record, press Enter.

(7) Repeat steps 3 through 6 if you want to insert data for additional records.

! TIP: You can use either of the data-entry methods described here to edit fields in existing records.

Add Data by Using a Form

1 Click Forms, and then double-click the form you want to use.

Type text or numbers in a text box.

Click the down arrow, and select an item in a list box or combo box.

Select or clear a check box.

3 Complete the information in each field of the form, pressing Tab to move to the next field.

Select an option button.

Click a command button.

2 Click the New Record button.

4 Click the New Record button to enter data for the next record.

SEE ALSO: For information about creating a form, see "Creating a Form" on page 194.

For information about entering data into or retrieving data from a database using a data-access page on a Web page, see "Creating a Data-Access Page" on page 263.

Creating a Form

A form is an efficient way to enter, edit, or review the data in a table. A form simplifies data entry because it displays only one record at a time, so it's easy to see what you're doing. If you want to add a little interest to your data-entry work, you can even add some special formatting.

> **TIP:** To quickly create a form that has minimal formatting and that contains all the fields of a table, click the table on which you want to base the form in the database window, and choose AutoForm from the Insert menu.

Create a Form for a Table

(2) Double-click Create Form By Using Wizard to start the Form Wizard.

(1) In the database window, click Forms.

(3) Select the table on which you want to base the form.

(4) Select one of the fields you want to include.

(5) Click the Add button. Continue selecting tables and fields, clicking the Add button to add all the fields you want to the form.

Click to add all the fields at one time.

(6) Click Next, and continue through the wizard, specifying the layout and style for the form, and entering a name for the form. Click Finish to complete the form.

> **SEE ALSO:** For information about creating relationships among tables, which is required if you want to use fields from different tables, see "Defining Relationships Among Tables" on page 202.

(7) Save the form.

Modify a Form

1 In the open form, click the View button on the Form View toolbar to switch to Design view.

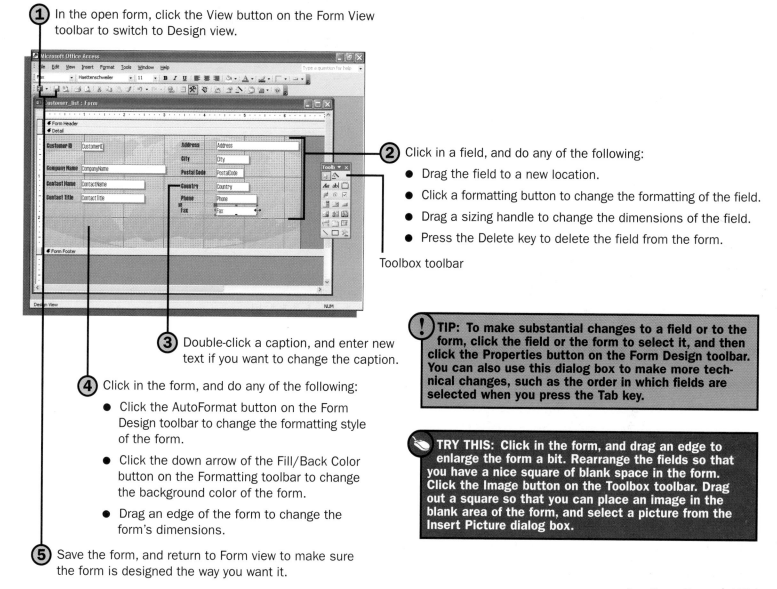

2 Click in a field, and do any of the following:
- Drag the field to a new location.
- Click a formatting button to change the formatting of the field.
- Drag a sizing handle to change the dimensions of the field.
- Press the Delete key to delete the field from the form.

Toolbox toolbar

3 Double-click a caption, and enter new text if you want to change the caption.

4 Click in the form, and do any of the following:
- Click the AutoFormat button on the Form Design toolbar to change the formatting style of the form.
- Click the down arrow of the Fill/Back Color button on the Formatting toolbar to change the background color of the form.
- Drag an edge of the form to change the form's dimensions.

5 Save the form, and return to Form view to make sure the form is designed the way you want it.

! TIP: To make substantial changes to a field or to the form, click the field or the form to select it, and then click the Properties button on the Form Design toolbar. You can also use this dialog box to make more technical changes, such as the order in which fields are selected when you press the Tab key.

TRY THIS: Click in the form, and drag an edge to enlarge the form a bit. Rearrange the fields so that you have a nice square of blank space in the form. Click the Image button on the Toolbox toolbar. Drag out a square so that you can place an image in the blank area of the form, and select a picture from the Insert Picture dialog box.

Creating a Report from the Data

The ability to use forms, tables, queries, and the other powerful features Access provides gives you a great deal of flexibility in your work with databases, but how do you get that information out of the computer and onto a piece of paper that you can share with others? Access gives you an easy solution by creating a report.

⚠️ **TIP: To create a basic report based on a table, click the table in the database window, and choose AutoReport from the Insert menu.**

✅ **SEE ALSO: For information about creating relationships among tables, which is required if you want to use fields from different tables, see "Defining Relationships Among Tables" on page 202.**

Create a Report

1 In the database window, click Reports.

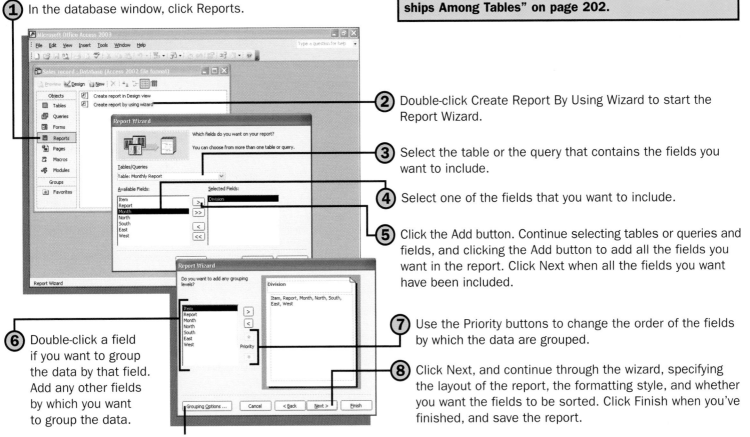

2 Double-click Create Report By Using Wizard to start the Report Wizard.

3 Select the table or the query that contains the fields you want to include.

4 Select one of the fields that you want to include.

5 Click the Add button. Continue selecting tables or queries and fields, and clicking the Add button to add all the fields you want in the report. Click Next when all the fields you want have been included.

6 Double-click a field if you want to group the data by that field. Add any other fields by which you want to group the data.

7 Use the Priority buttons to change the order of the fields by which the data are grouped.

8 Click Next, and continue through the wizard, specifying the layout of the report, the formatting style, and whether you want the fields to be sorted. Click Finish when you've finished, and save the report.

Click if you want to change the way the items are grouped.

Modify a Report

(1) With the report open, click the View button on the Print Preview toolbar to switch to Design view.

(2) Click in a field, and do any of the following:
- Drag the field to a new location.
- Click a formatting button to change the formatting of the field.
- Drag a sizing handle to change the dimensions of the field.
- Press the Delete key to delete the field from the form.

(6) Choose Print Preview from the View menu to see the results of your changes.

(3) To add a field to the report, click the Field List button on the Report Design toolbar if the Field List isn't displayed. Drag the field from the Field List to the part of the report where you want it.

(5) Click Save to save the report.

(4) To add other elements to the report—a picture, for example—click the element on the Toolbox toolbar, and drag out the area in the report where you want to place the element.

TIP: To change the way the data are grouped and/or sorted, click the Sorting And Grouping button on the Report Design toolbar, and make your changes in the Sorting And Grouping dialog box.

Extracting Information from a Database

The most powerful tool in a database is the query. Using a query you can ask such questions as "Which companies have placed more than 10 orders?" or "What's the average length of time between the date an order is placed and the date it's shipped?" The trick is to figure out the data you need and how to ask the appropriate questions. Until you've become well acquainted with query structure, you'll probably need to do some trial-and-error querying: creating a query, modifying it, and possibly having to delete it and try again. When you get your queries working properly, however, you'll be amazed by what you can do.

> **!** **TIP: To use fields from different tables, you need to assign relationships to the tables so that Access can determine which data to use from each table.**

> **✓** **SEE ALSO: For information about defining the relationships among tables, see "Defining Relationships Among Tables" on page 202.**

Create a Query

1 In the database window, click Queries.

2 Double-click Create Query By Using Wizard to start the Simple Query Wizard.

3 Select the table or the query that contains the fields you want to use in the query.

4 Select one of the fields that you want to include in the query.

5 Click the Add button. Continue selecting fields and clicking the Add button to add all the fields you want to include in the query.

6 Click Next when all the fields you want have been included.

7 Specify whether you want Access to show all the records that are returned by the query, or to include only summary data.

Click to specify the way you want Access to summarize the data.

8 Click Next, name the query, and click Finish to open the query.

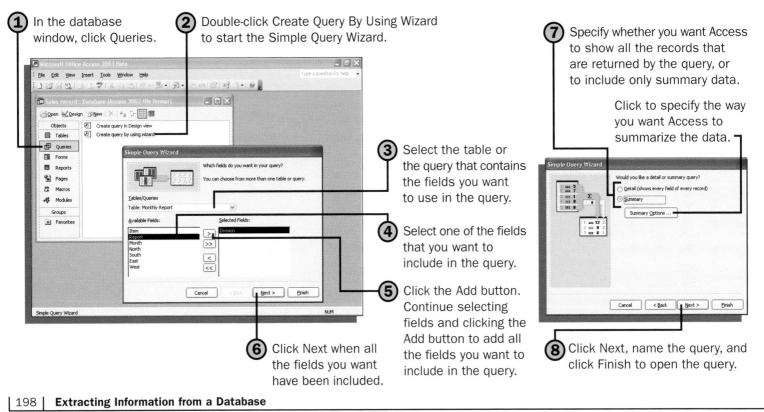

Define the Questions

 1 With the query open, click the View button on the Query Datasheet toolbar to switch to Design View.

The results of the query

2 Click in the Sort property for a field, click the down arrow that appears, and select the type of sort if you want the results of the query to be sorted by this field.

3 Clear the check box if you don't want the results for this field shown in the query results.

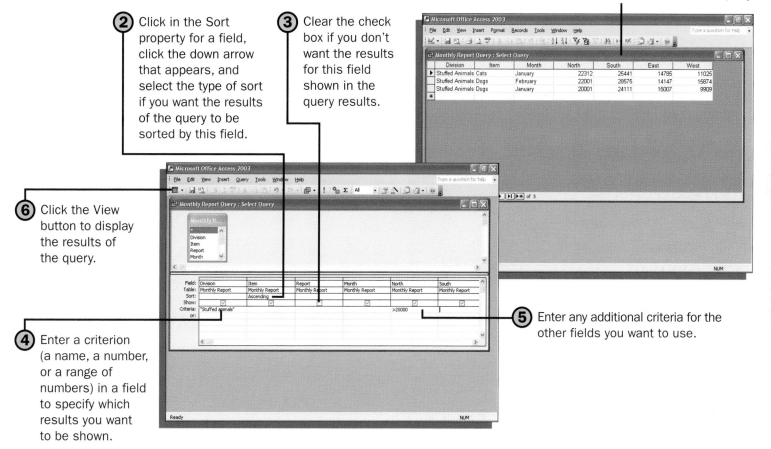

6 Click the View button to display the results of the query.

4 Enter a criterion (a name, a number, or a range of numbers) in a field to specify which results you want to be shown.

5 Enter any additional criteria for the other fields you want to use.

> **TIP:** If you're familiar with the SQL programming language, you can modify the query by clicking the down arrow of the View button, choosing SQL View, and editing the SQL code.

> **TIP:** For help in creating an expression as the criterion, click the Build button on the Query Design toolbar, and use the Expression Builder dialog box to create the expression.

Analyzing Data with a PivotChart

A PivotChart is a way to selectively view the graphing of specific parts of your data. When you create the chart, you choose the fields that are used in the chart. After you've created the chart, you can specify which portions of that data are displayed so that you can examine the relationships among the data.

Create a PivotChart

1 Open the table or the query that you want to use to produce the PivotChart.

2 Choose PivotChart View from the View menu.

Use a major classification to separate the data into logical pages.

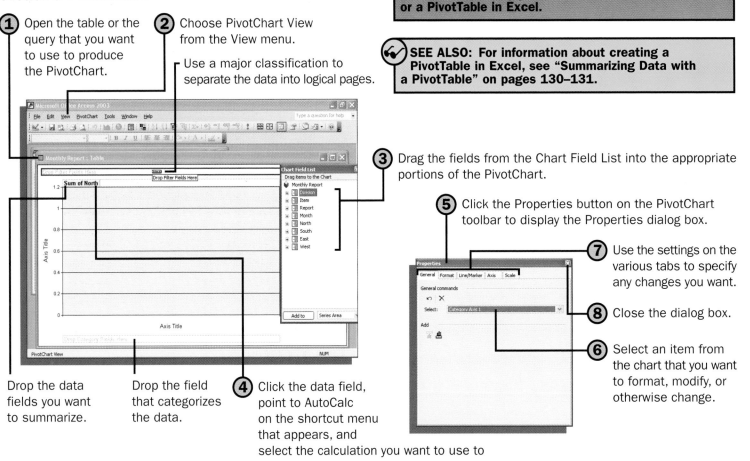

Drop the data fields you want to summarize.

Drop the field that categorizes the data.

4 Click the data field, point to AutoCalc on the shortcut menu that appears, and select the calculation you want to use to summarize the data from the submenu.

> ! **TIP:** To utilize the full power of Access, try basing your PivotChart on a query so that you can customize the data before you create the chart.

> ! **TIP:** You can also create a PivotTable in Access; it's similar to the way you create a PivotChart in Access or a PivotTable in Excel.

> ✓ **SEE ALSO:** For information about creating a PivotTable in Excel, see "Summarizing Data with a PivotTable" on pages 130–131.

3 Drag the fields from the Chart Field List into the appropriate portions of the PivotChart.

5 Click the Properties button on the PivotChart toolbar to display the Properties dialog box.

7 Use the settings on the various tabs to specify any changes you want.

8 Close the dialog box.

6 Select an item from the chart that you want to format, modify, or otherwise change.

Use the PivotChart

① Click the down arrow in the Page field, select the item you want to be displayed, and click OK.

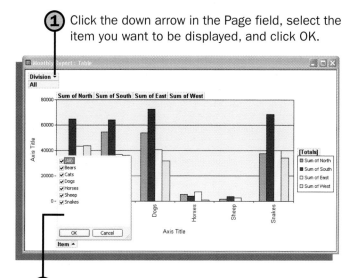

② Click in a Category field, clear the All check box, select the items you want to be displayed, and click OK.

④ Save and close the PivotChart when you've finished.

③ Do any of the following:

● Drag other fields from the Chart Field List onto the chart, and set the calculation for summarizing the data to add other series to the chart.

● Click the Multiple Charts button, and drag a field from the Chart Field List to the Drop MultiChart Fields Here section to create a separate chart for each item in the Multichart field or fields.

● Click the Multiple Plots Unified Scale button to force the scale to be the same for each chart when you're using multiple charts.

● Click the Properties button, select the Plot Area for a chart, and change the chart type on the Type tab. Close the Properties dialog box.

● Click Properties, select any of the plot components, and make any changes you want to that component using the different tabs of the Properties dialog box. Close the Properties dialog box.

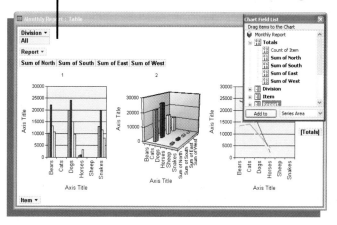

!) TIP: If the Chart Field List isn't displayed, click the Field List button on the PivotChart toolbar.

Defining Relationships Among Tables

If your tables are going to be spending time together, they need a formal introduction so they'll know how to relate to each other. This introduction takes a unique identifier from one table (usually the primary key) and an equivalent—although not usually unique—identifier from another table (technically called a *foreign key*). After you've established the proper relationship, you can create queries, forms, reports, and even Access data pages that are based on fields from different tables.

> **(!) TIP: The ability to define relationships among tables requires some advance planning in the design of your tables; you need to give Access some sort of reference as to how to find the data that link the tables. For example, if your inventory table uses ProductNumber as its primary key, you'll probably want to include the product number in your sales table. That way, you can create a relationship between the two tables using the ProductNumber field in both tables.**

Define the Relationship

(1) Choose Relationships from the Tools menu to display the Show Table dialog box.

(2) Double-click each table for which you want to define a relationship.

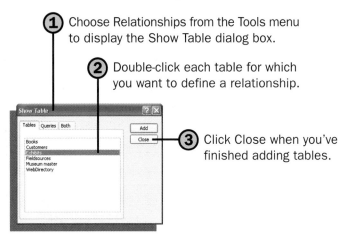

(3) Click Close when you've finished adding tables.

(5) In the Edit Relationships dialog box that appears, confirm the relationship field.

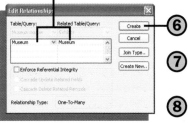

(6) Click Create.

(7) Repeat steps 4 through 6 to create any other relationships among different tables.

(8) Save and close the relationships.

(4) Drag the field from one table onto the related field in another table.

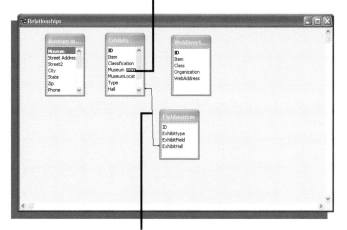

The line shows the relationship between the tables and identifies the fields that are connected.

12 Creating a PowerPoint Presentation

When you create a slide show in Microsoft Office PowerPoint 2003, you have several choices as to how you present your slides. You can take your presentation to a service bureau that can convert the electronic slides into 35mm photographic slides, and then you can project them onto a screen using a conventional slide projector. You can print your slides as a series of transparencies that you display by using an overhead projector. The method you might be most familiar with, however, is running an onscreen presentation from your computer and showing it on a large screen in a classroom or conference room.

You can create your entire presentation from scratch, or, if you're not sure where to begin, you can use PowerPoint's AutoContent Wizard. It creates a generic slide show for you, and all you need to do is add your own slides and text. Then, however you initially created your presentation, you can make any changes you like: adding or deleting slides, changing the text, re-ordering the slides, and so on. PowerPoint also provides stunning special effects that add a professional touch to your presentation. We're certain that you'll try out every one of the text animation and transition effects—we did! Just don't use too many of them in one presentation.

You can set the timing so that each slide advances automatically after a specified period of time, or you can advance the slides manually. You can add music and/or a narration to liven up an onscreen presentation, and, if you're taking your show on the road, you can record the entire production on a CD and then run it on an unfamiliar computer even if that computer isn't running PowerPoint.

What's Where in PowerPoint?

The PowerPoint program is designed to create slide presentations. A presentation can have several components—the main one, of course, being the slides that display your pictures, text, charts, videos, and so on. In addition, PowerPoint can help you create handouts that include printed versions of your slides with accompanying text, and a script—that is, printed notes to assist you with your presentation. You'll spend most of your time, however, working with the slides—modifying them to achieve the consistent look that results in a polished presentation, and rearranging them so that they're shown in the most logical order.

You create the individual slides in Normal view (shown below), adding text and graphics, tweaking the color scheme, and adding any new slides.

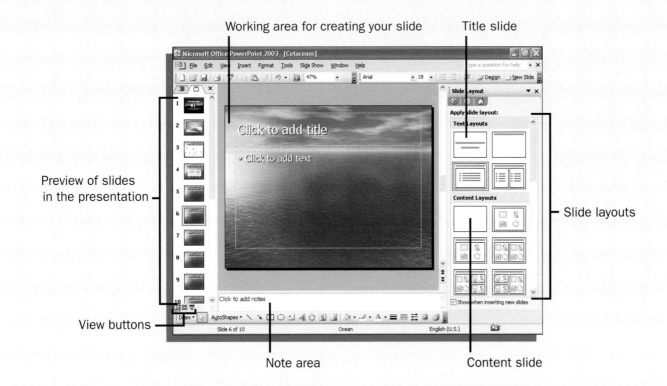

Working area for creating your slide

Title slide

Preview of slides in the presentation

Slide layouts

View buttons

Note area

Content slide

You use Slide Sorter view (shown below) to organize your entire presentation and to make sure all the design elements have a consistent look. You can also use Slide Sorter view as a kind of "storyboard" for reviewing your presentation: Just double-click a slide, and it will open in Normal view, ready for editing. Slide Sorter view is also a good view to use when you're setting up your slide show's properties—for example, the animation scheme for your slides, if you're using one,

and/or the transition effects as one slide advances to the next.

There are a couple of other views—Slide Show view and Notes Page view—that we haven't shown here. Slide Show view is self-explanatory, and Notes Page view is similar to Normal view, except that it's formatted as a printed page, showing a printed version of the slide and including an area where you can type your notes.

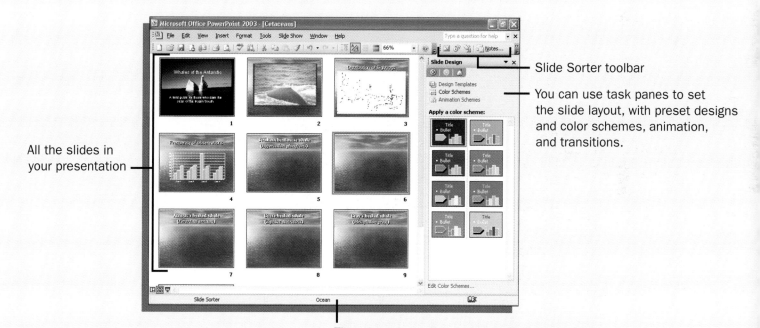

Slide Sorter toolbar

You can use task panes to set the slide layout, with preset designs and color schemes, animation, and transitions.

All the slides in your presentation

The status bar tells you which design template has been applied to the selected slide.

Creating a Presentation

When you start PowerPoint, it displays the default design for a title slide. Starting from there, you can add text and formatting, insert new slides, add color schemes, or use a predesigned template for your presentation.

Start the Presentation

(1) Choose Page Setup from the File menu. Make sure that your slides are sized for the proper type of presentation and that you're using the orientation you want. Click OK.

TIP: When you add a design template to a presentation, PowerPoint applies the design to all the slides in the presentation. If you want to apply the design to a single slide, select the slide, point to the template, click the down arrow button that appears, and choose Apply To Selected Slides from the drop-down menu that appears.

(2) In Normal view, with the default title slide displayed, choose Slide Layout from the Format menu.

(4) Click the Design button to display the Slide Design task pane.

(5) Select the design template you want to use for your presentation.

(3) In the Slide Layout task pane, select the layout you want.

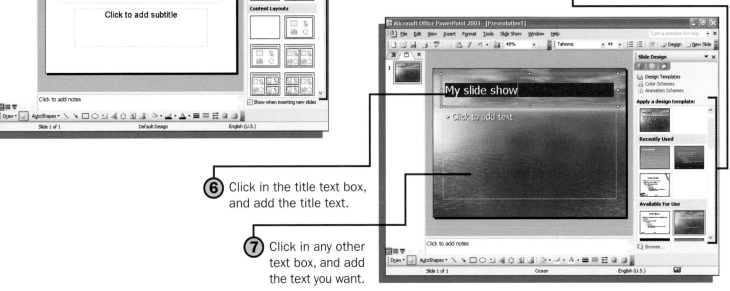

(6) Click in the title text box, and add the title text.

(7) Click in any other text box, and add the text you want.

Add Slides

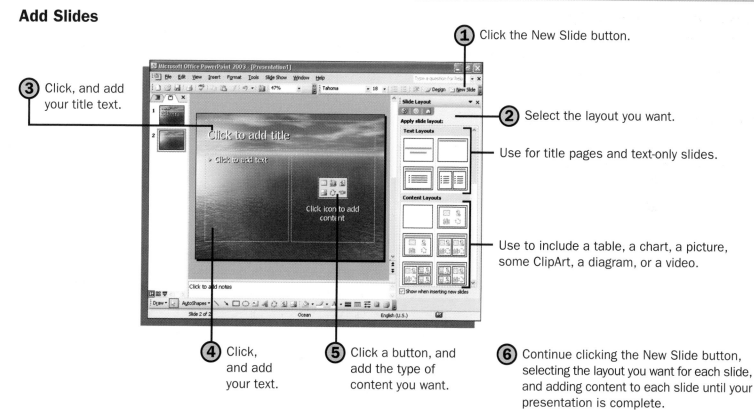

① Click the New Slide button.

③ Click, and add your title text.

② Select the layout you want.

Use for title pages and text-only slides.

Use to include a table, a chart, a picture, some ClipArt, a diagram, or a video.

④ Click, and add your text.

⑤ Click a button, and add the type of content you want.

⑥ Continue clicking the New Slide button, selecting the layout you want for each slide, and adding content to each slide until your presentation is complete.

CAUTION: One of the worst kinds of mistakes you can make when you're creating an onscreen presentation—especially when the presentation will be projected during a large conference or meeting—is to put too much text on a slide or to include charts or pictures that are too detailed to be seen clearly. PowerPoint slides don't cost anything, so use as many additional slides as you need to decrease the amount of text on a single slide or to ensure that your charts or pictures are large enough for your audience to see.

TRY THIS: Right-click a blank spot on a slide, and choose Background from the shortcut menu. In the Color drop-down box, choose Fill Effects. On the Picture tab of the Fill Effects dialog box, select a picture, and click OK. In the Background dialog box, click Apply. If you don't like the result, use the Undo button to revert to the slide's original design.

Using a Predesigned Presentation

You have an important presentation to make at a big conference, but where do you begin? PowerPoint can get you started. When you use the AutoContent Wizard, PowerPoint creates a generic slide show, to which you can then add your own content.

Customize the Presentation

SEE ALSO: For information about changing the content and the order of the slides, see "Editing a Presentation" on page 210.

For information about creating a presentation based on a Word document, see "Using Word to Prepare PowerPoint Text" on page 296.

(1) In PowerPoint, choose New from the File menu to display the New Presentation task pane.

(2) Click From AutoContent Wizard, and click Next when the AutoContent Wizard appears.

(4) Select the type of presentation you want.

(3) Select a category for your presentation.

(5) Click Next, and step through the wizard, specifying the presentation method, the presentation title, and the content to be displayed in the footer of each slide. Click Finish when you've completed the wizard.

(6) Edit the content of each slide, and re-order the slides if necessary.

Creating a Photo Album

Do you have a huge collection of photographs that you keep vowing to organize "someday"? A PowerPoint photo album is a really great way to display all those pictures you've amassed, whether you want to show them on the screen as a slide show, put the slide show on a CD to send to friends and family, or print them out for posterity.

> **! TIP:** To modify the photo album layout after you've created it, choose Photo Album from the Format menu, make your changes, and click Update.

Create an Album

3 Click the appropriate button, as follows, and then use the dialog box that appears to insert your content:

- File/Disk to display the Insert Picture dialog box, where you can locate and select the picture files you want

- Scanner/Camera to scan photos or download them from your camera

- New Text Box to insert a blank text box that you can later use as a title page

7 Specify whether you want the file names to be included as captions under all your pictures, and whether you want to convert your color pictures into black-and-white versions.

4 Use the Order buttons to re-order the pictures, or the Remove button to remove a picture from the album.

1 In PowerPoint, choose New from the File menu to display the New Presentation task pane.

2 Click Photo Album.

5 Use the picture controls to rotate a selected picture or to change the contrast or brightness of the picture.

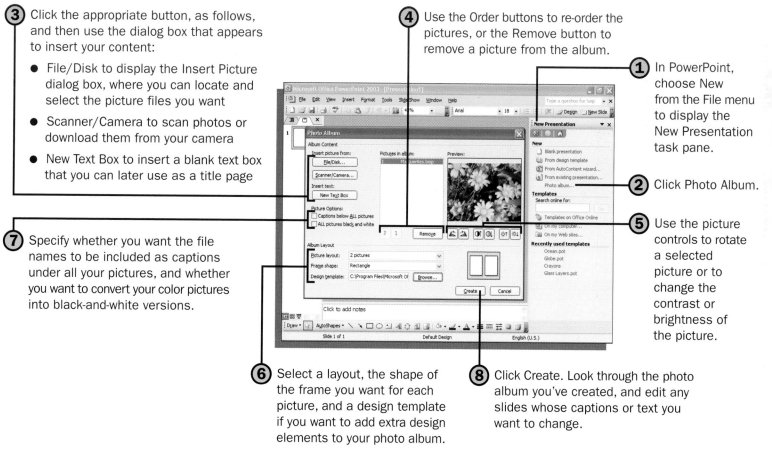

6 Select a layout, the shape of the frame you want for each picture, and a design template if you want to add extra design elements to your photo album.

8 Click Create. Look through the photo album you've created, and edit any slides whose captions or text you want to change.

Editing a Presentation

Whether you created your slide presentation from scratch and need to tweak a few elements, or used a wizard that inserted generic text, you can easily edit and modify your PowerPoint presentation using two extremely helpful organizational tools: the Outline and the Slide Sorter.

Change the Content of Slides

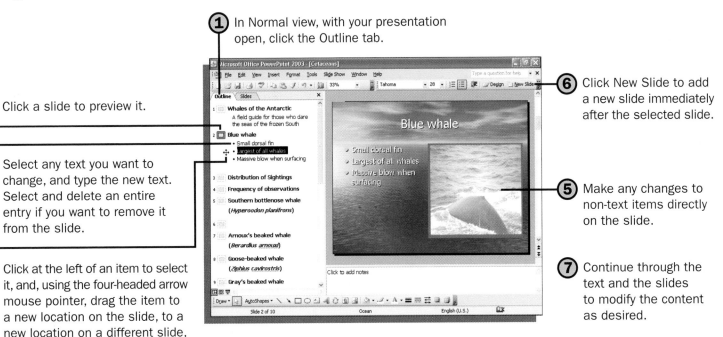

(!) TIP: When the Slides tab is displayed, the Outline tab's label is truncated and shows only an icon. When you switch to the Outline tab, the Outline tab's label gets bigger, and the tab now reads "Outline." If the Slides and Outline tabs aren't visible, choose Normal View (Restore Panes) from the View menu.

(1) In Normal view, with your presentation open, click the Outline tab.

(2) Click a slide to preview it.

(3) Select any text you want to change, and type the new text. Select and delete an entire entry if you want to remove it from the slide.

(4) Click at the left of an item to select it, and, using the four-headed arrow mouse pointer, drag the item to a new location on the slide, to a new location on a different slide, or to the left or right to promote or demote the item in a list.

(6) Click New Slide to add a new slide immediately after the selected slide.

(5) Make any changes to non-text items directly on the slide.

(7) Continue through the text and the slides to modify the content as desired.

(!) TIP: To change the default formatting of all your slides, point to Master on the View menu, and choose Slide Master from the submenu. You can then make formatting and layout changes for all your slides or for the title slides only.

Change the Order of Slides

(3) If there's a slide that you don't want to include in this slide show but that you don't want to delete, select it, and click the Hide Slide button. To return the hidden slide to the slide show, select it, and click the Hide Slide button again.

(4) To permanently delete a slide, select it, and press the Delete key.

(5) To add a slide, right-click the slide that will precede the new slide in the slide show, and choose New Slide from the shortcut menu.

(1) Click the Slide Sorter View button to switch to Slide Sorter view.

(2) Drag a slide that you want to display in a different part of the slide show to the spot where you want it.

TRY THIS: In Slide Sorter view, select all the slides that relate to a single topic by holding down the Ctrl key while you click each slide. Click the Summary Slide button on the Slide Sorter toolbar to create a slide that summarizes the topic of the selected slides. Move the summary slide into the position in the slide show where you want it. Double-click the new slide to review it, and, if necessary, to edit it in Normal view. Return to Slide Sorter view, and create another summary slide for a different group of slides.

TIP: You can change the order of slides in Normal view by selecting a slide on either the Slide tab or the Outline tab, and then dragging the slide to a new location on that tab. Slide Sorter view, however, lets you see more of your slides at one time than you can see in Normal view.

Adding Text Animation Effects

A text animation scheme can make an onscreen slide presentation come alive with some very professional looking effects. You can make your text fade in or out, slither in from the top or bottom of a slide, appear one letter at a time, bounce up and down, and do a number of other remarkable tricks. After you've applied an animation scheme, you can modify the way the animation works: You can choose an overall theme to apply to all the lines at one time, or you *can* give each line a different scheme. As a general rule, however, spare your audience's collective eyesight and *don't* do the latter!

Animate the Text

(1) In Normal view, choose Animation Schemes from the Slide Show menu.

(2) Click the slide whose text you want to animate.

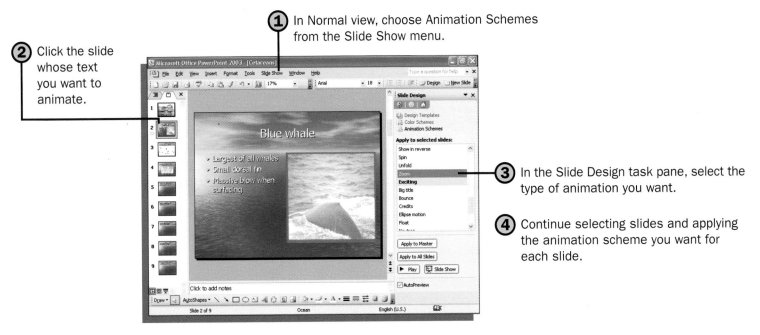

(3) In the Slide Design task pane, select the type of animation you want.

(4) Continue selecting slides and applying the animation scheme you want for each slide.

TIP: Try limiting any fancy animation to title slides and using the same simple animation scheme for the rest of the slides.

CAUTION: Don't ruin a good presentation by using too many animation effects! With text swirling around and flashing and fading, your audience will be too distracted by the effects to grasp your points.

Customize the Animation

(1) Choose Custom Animation from the Slide Show menu to display the Custom Animation task pane.

(2) Select the line of text whose animation you want to change.

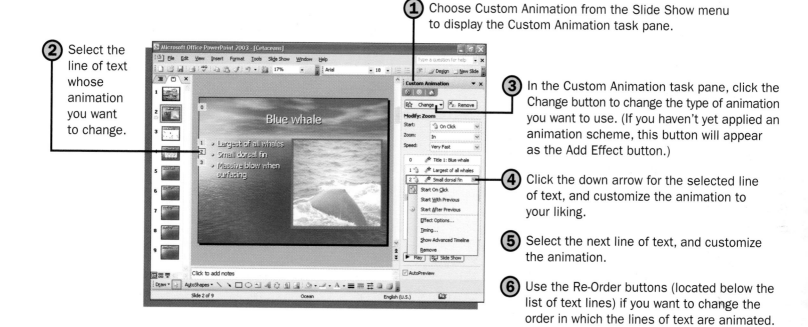

(3) In the Custom Animation task pane, click the Change button to change the type of animation you want to use. (If you haven't yet applied an animation scheme, this button will appear as the Add Effect button.)

(4) Click the down arrow for the selected line of text, and customize the animation to your liking.

(5) Select the next line of text, and customize the animation.

(6) Use the Re-Order buttons (located below the list of text lines) if you want to change the order in which the lines of text are animated.

TRY THIS: On a slide that has several bulleted lines of text, select the first bulleted item, and click the Change button in the Custom Animation task pane. Point to Motion Paths on the drop-down menu, and click Spiral Right. Add a different motion path to each of the other lines of text. Now play the slide, and see what you *can* do, while observing the reality of what you *shouldn't* do for an effective presentation! In other words, more isn't better!

TIP: Apply an animation scheme to all your slides before you do any customizing of the animation. That way, you'll start out with some consistency in the animation throughout the slide show.

Adding Transition Effects

When you develop an onscreen slide show, you might want to include some special effects as you make the transition from one slide to the next. When a new slide appears, your audience sees a transition effect—for example, a dissolve, a checkerboard, a "newsflash" effect—and/or a sound. You can also specify whether you want the next slide to advance automatically after a preset time or whether you want to switch to the next slide manually with a mouse-click. Note, however, that these effects will be lost if the slide show is converted to 35mm slides or printed out on paper or as transparencies.

> **CAUTION:** As with the text effects, don't use a lot of different transitional effects. They can make your presentation seem chaotic, and an audience might find them quite distracting.

> **TIP:** It's usually best to apply the transitions after you've added all the slides to the slide show; however, you can add the transition effects at any time if you prefer.

Set the Transitions

(2) Click the slide to which you want to add the transition.

(1) In Normal view, choose Slide Transition from the Slide Show menu to display the Slide Transition task pane.

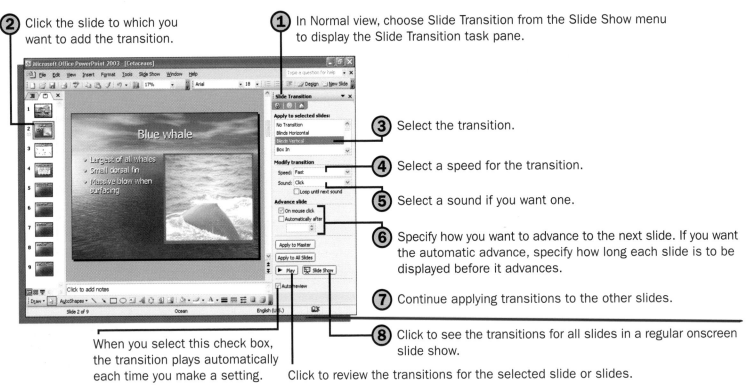

(3) Select the transition.

(4) Select a speed for the transition.

(5) Select a sound if you want one.

(6) Specify how you want to advance to the next slide. If you want the automatic advance, specify how long each slide is to be displayed before it advances.

(7) Continue applying transitions to the other slides.

(8) Click to see the transitions for all slides in a regular onscreen slide show.

When you select this check box, the transition plays automatically each time you make a setting.

Click to review the transitions for the selected slide or slides.

Adding Special Content

A PowerPoint presentation can include a lot more than just text and backgrounds. You can increase your audience's understanding of your topic—and increase their interest in your presentation—by incorporating pictures or charts into all types of slide presentations, and videos or sound clips into onscreen presentations.

> **SEE ALSO:** For more information about working with pictures, diagrams, WordArt, and other types of objects, see section 18, "Working with Graphics and Objects," starting on page 305.

Add the Content

(1) Click the New Slide button, and, in the Slide Layout task pane, create a slide that has either a content-only or a text-and-content layout.

(2) Click in the content area.

(3) Click the type of item you want to add to the slide, or choose the type of item from the Insert menu. Use any dialog box that appears (or use a worksheet to insert a chart) to insert the item you want.

(4) Use the sizing handles to change the dimensions of the item.

(5) Right-click the item, and use the specialized commands that are available to edit or modify the item.

(6) Drag the item to where you want it on the slide.

Adding Notes and Handouts

Notes are designed to help you (or a presenter) with the details of the presentation. Your notes can be quick reminders about what to say, or they can be as organized as a detailed script. You can add the notes as you design each slide or as you review the finished slide show. Handouts are printed copies of your presentation that PowerPoint can generate automatically. After you've completed the notes and set up your slide show, you can print the notes and handouts for easy reference during the presentation.

> ⚠️ **TIP:** To make format or layout changes to all the notes (the *notes master*) or all the handout pages (the *handout master*), point to Master on the View menu, and choose either Notes Master or Handout Master from the submenu. Make your changes to the master, and then close Master View. To make formatting or content changes to individual notes, choose Notes Pages from the View menu.

Create Notes and Handouts

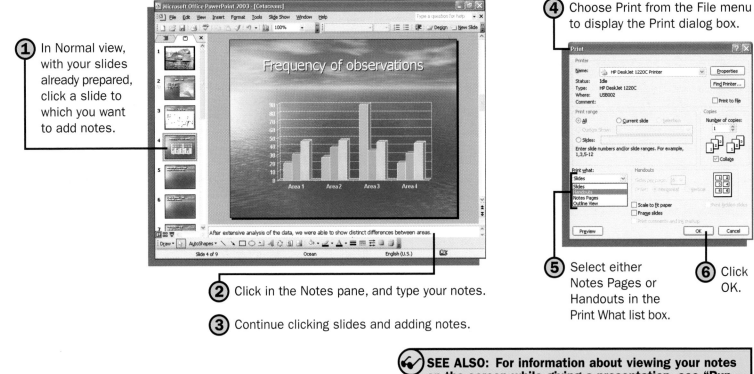

① In Normal view, with your slides already prepared, click a slide to which you want to add notes.

② Click in the Notes pane, and type your notes.

③ Continue clicking slides and adding notes.

④ Choose Print from the File menu to display the Print dialog box.

⑤ Select either Notes Pages or Handouts in the Print What list box.

⑥ Click OK.

> ✓ **SEE ALSO:** For information about viewing your notes on the screen while giving a presentation, see "Running a Slide Show Using Dual Monitors" on page 221.

Including a Slide from Another Presentation

If a slide that's part of one slide presentation would work well in another presentation, you can copy the slide to your new presentation and use it wherever you need it.

! TIP: You can use the same slide more than once in a presentation. To do so, in Slide Sorter view, right-click the slide to be duplicated, and choose Copy from the shortcut menu. Right-click where you want the duplicated slide to appear, and choose Paste from the shortcut menu.

Include a Slide

1 In your current presentation, click the slide that you want to appear in front of the slide or slides to be inserted.

2 Choose Slides From Files from the Insert menu to display the Slide Finder dialog box.

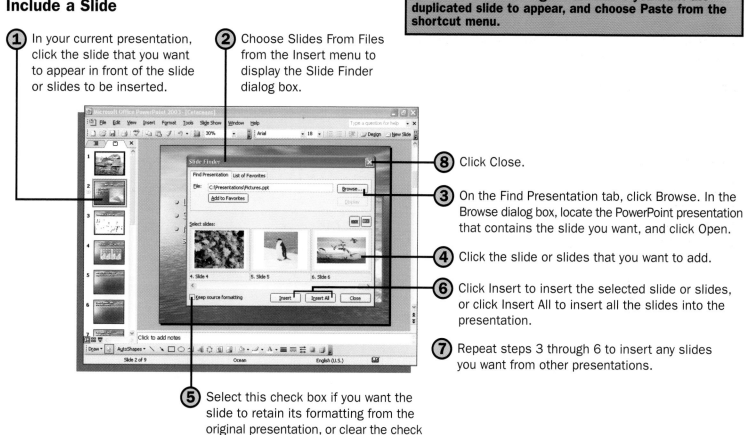

8 Click Close.

3 On the Find Presentation tab, click Browse. In the Browse dialog box, locate the PowerPoint presentation that contains the slide you want, and click Open.

4 Click the slide or slides that you want to add.

6 Click Insert to insert the selected slide or slides, or click Insert All to insert all the slides into the presentation.

7 Repeat steps 3 through 6 to insert any slides you want from other presentations.

5 Select this check box if you want the slide to retain its formatting from the original presentation, or clear the check box if you want the slide to take on the formatting of the new presentation.

Running a Slide Show Automatically

If you're tired of saying the same old thing every time you present your slide show, why not record your talk so that your presence isn't required for the presentation? By setting the timing, you can also automate the advance of each slide, which can be a great help if you're scheduling your presentation at a large meeting or conference: You know exactly how long it takes the entire slide show to run and that it takes the same amount of time every time.

Narrate and Time Your Presentation

! TIP: To delete a narration from a slide, in Normal view, click the sound icon at the bottom right of the slide, and press the Delete key.

! TIP: To set the timing for advancing each slide without recording a narration, in Slide Sorter view, click the Rehearse Timings button on the Slide Sorter toolbar, step through the slide show, and save the timings when you've finished.

(2) Choose Record Narration from the Slide Show menu to display the Record Narration dialog box.

(3) If you haven't previously set up a narration on this computer, click each button, and make your recording settings.

(1) In Slide Sorter view, click the first slide to select it.

(4) Click OK.

(5) Record your narration for the first slide, and click anywhere on the screen when you're ready to move to the next slide. Continue recording your narration until you've completed the slide show.

(6) When PowerPoint asks you whether you want to save the timings for the slide show, click Save.

(7) Run the slide show to make sure it's being presented just the way you want.

Customizing a Slide Show

When you've finished putting all the bits and pieces of your slide presentation together and you're ready for the big show, you need to tell PowerPoint just how you want to run the presentation.

SEE ALSO: For information about using Presenter view, see "Running a Slide Show Using Dual Monitors" on page 221.

Set Up the Show

(1) Choose Set Up Show from the Slide Show menu to display the Set Up Show dialog box.

(2) Specify the way you want the show to be displayed.

(3) Select this check box to have the slide show run continuously until you (or a presenter) press the Esc key.

(4) Select either of these check boxes if you want to omit any narration or animation from the show.

(5) Select the range of slides you want to include in the show.

(6) Specify the way you want each slide to be advanced.

(7) If the computer is equipped with two or more monitors, specify which monitor is to display the show and which monitor is to show Presenter view.

(8) Click OK.

Clear this check box if you don't want to display Presenter view on one monitor while the slide show is displayed on a second monitor.

(9) Run the slide show to make sure that it's presented just as you want it.

TIP: If you want to enhance your slide show by customizing its content even further, you can download Producer, a free add-in to PowerPoint, from the Microsoft Online Web site. Producer is geared toward professional content providers, but it can be used by anyone to improve a presentation. Be aware, however, that the program is quite large and that some of its features can be a bit complex to use.

Running a Slide Show Using a Single Monitor

A large part of a successful slide show is the way you deliver the presentation. If you're using a single monitor, you interact with the same display that everyone sees. Fortunately, there are some tools to help you run the show.

(!) TIP: If you use any of the annotation tools, you can save the annotations so that they will appear in your next slide show.

Give a Presentation

(!) TIP: You can start the slide show by pressing the F5 key, and you can end the show at any time by pressing the Esc key.

(3) To modify the presentation, move the mouse if the mouse pointer and the command buttons aren't visible on the screen, and do any of the following:

- Click the Back button to return to the previous slide.

- Click the Pointer button, choose the type of pointer you want to use, and specify whether you want to use the pointer to annotate the slides with highlighting or with drawings.

- Click the Show button to open a menu to move to a different slide, to change what's shown on the screen, or to end the show.

- Click the Next button to move to the next slide.

(1) With PowerPoint running and your slide show open, choose View Show from the Slide Show menu to start the presentation.

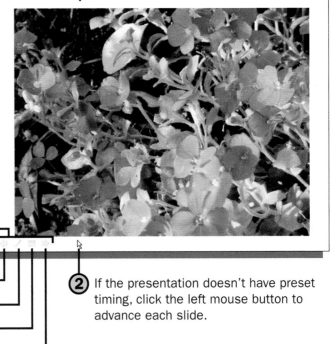

(4) Continue through the show until you reach the end, or use a command to end the show.

Back button ———
Pointer button ———
Show button ———
Next button ———

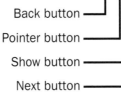

(2) If the presentation doesn't have preset timing, click the left mouse button to advance each slide.

Running a Slide Show Using Dual Monitors

If the computer system you're using for your slide show is set up with dual monitors, you're in luck! You use one monitor in Presenter view, which gives you a variety of tools with which to present the slide show, along with a view of all your notes, and the second monitor to display the slide show for the audience.

Control the Show

(1) With PowerPoint running and your presentation open, press the F5 key to start the slide show. Make sure that your monitor shows Presenter view and that the monitor the audience sees displays the slide show.

SEE ALSO: For information about customizing a dual-monitor setup for the presentation and how to specify which monitor displays the slide show, see "Customizing a Slide Show" on page 219.

(2) Preview the slide that's being shown.

(8) Use the End Show button if you have to terminate the show before you reach the end.

(7) Use the Black Screen button to pause the show and display a blank black screen. Click the mouse button to resume the show.

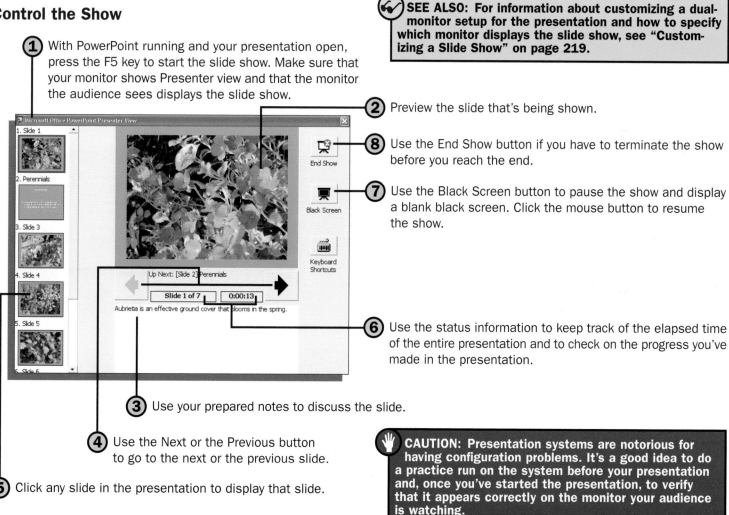

(6) Use the status information to keep track of the elapsed time of the entire presentation and to check on the progress you've made in the presentation.

(3) Use your prepared notes to discuss the slide.

(4) Use the Next or the Previous button to go to the next or the previous slide.

(5) Click any slide in the presentation to display that slide.

CAUTION: Presentation systems are notorious for having configuration problems. It's a good idea to do a practice run on the system before your presentation and, once you've started the presentation, to verify that it appears correctly on the monitor your audience is watching.

Taking a Slide Show on the Road

How's this for a worst-case scenario? You take your slide show on the road—let's say to a conference or an important meeting. You put your presentation on an unfamiliar computer, start running the show, and oh, the horror! Either your show doesn't run at all, or some of its components—the narration, the video, or the background sound—won't work. You can ensure that this doesn't happen to you by copying all the items, including all the linked files for the presentation, onto a CD. PowerPoint also includes a PowerPoint Viewer in case the computer you're using for the slide show doesn't have PowerPoint installed.

> **TIP:** Make sure your presentation is perfect before you copy it; once it's copied, you won't be able to edit it on the CD.

> **CAUTION:** To copy your presentation directly onto a CD, your computer must be running Windows XP or later and must have a CD burner installed.

Package Your Presentation

(1) With PowerPoint running and your presentation open, choose Package For CD from the File menu to display the Package For CD dialog box.

(2) Type a descriptive name for the CD.

(3) Click to add files to the CD. (These files don't have to be part of your presentation.)

(4) Click to display the Options dialog box.

(7) Do either of the following:

- Click Copy To Folder, and specify the folder name and location to store the files in a folder for later transfer to a CD.

- Click Copy To CD to copy directly to the CD, and complete the required information.

(8) Click Close to complete the process.

(5) In the Options dialog box, do any of the following:

- Select the first check box if you want to include the PowerPoint Viewer.

- Specify the way you want the CD to play.

- Specify which types of files are to be included.

- Set a password to open or modify the files.

(6) Click OK.

> **TIP:** To broadcast your slide show over either the Internet or an intranet, you'll need to download the Online Broadcast tools from Microsoft Office Online, which you can access from the Help menu.

13 Creating a Publication in Publisher

Saying that Microsoft Office Publisher 2003 is a layout program for creating publications is about as descriptive as saying that Hollywood makes movies or that artists paint pictures. The range of options Publisher gives you is nothing short of breathtaking, and trying to describe everything you can do in Publisher is impossible in these few pages. Fortunately, the background wizards make the predesigned publications so easy to work with that you really can jump right in and create professional looking publications with little outside assistance, even if you have no design experience whatsoever.

The best way to get to know Publisher is to start it up and look around. You'll see dozens of different ready-made designs for print publications: certificates, brochures, greeting cards, menus, newsletters, advertisements, catalogs, and so on. Likewise, you'll find a huge variety of ready-made designs for Web pages and e-mail publications. There are design sets for holidays (cards, invitations, thank-you notes) and similar sets for other special events. All you have to do is choose a design and insert your own content. If you're creative and you'd prefer to design your own publications from scratch, go right ahead. You can insert your own pictures or drawings, pop in some ClipArt, or choose something from Publisher's extensive Design Gallery. It's fun, it's easy, and it's extremely rewarding.

We haven't described any one type of publication in the procedures that follow. You can apply the general discussions in this section to any type of publication in Publisher, and we're sure you'll be surprised and delighted with the results.

What's Where in Publisher?

When you work in Publisher, you work with *objects*. What, exactly, *is* an object? Let's say you want to insert some text. In Publisher, you'll need to create a container for it—called a *text-box object*—and you'll place your text inside that object. To include a picture, you'll create a *picture-frame object,* and you'll place your picture inside that object. Some objects, however, come with their own containers: When you insert a piece of ClipArt or WordArt, for example, it goes onto the page as a ClipArt or WordArt object, already nestled in its own container. Each page of your publication is a container for all the objects you place on it. After you've created these self-contained objects, you can move each one around and/or resize it to create your arrangement on the page. The result is a polished publication that your readers see as a cohesive whole rather than a collection of separate objects.

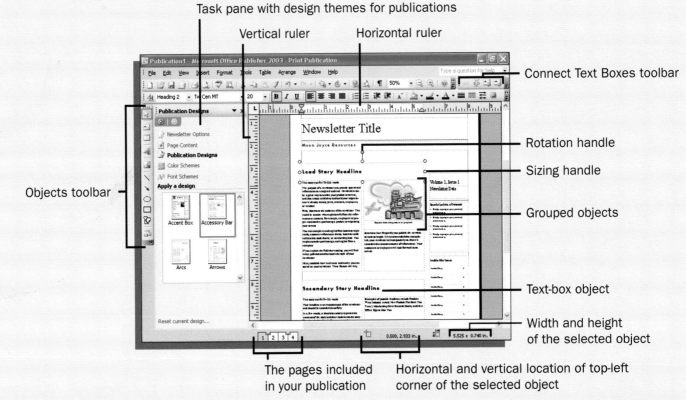

Task pane with design themes for publications

Vertical ruler

Horizontal ruler

Connect Text Boxes toolbar

Objects toolbar

Rotation handle

Sizing handle

Grouped objects

Text-box object

Width and height of the selected object

The pages included in your publication

Horizontal and vertical location of top-left corner of the selected object

Creating a Publication from Scratch

If you feel confident enough to express your creativity unfettered by the restraints of other people's design concepts, you'll enjoy the challenge of creating a publication from scratch. You can add as few or as many objects as you want, and you have the freedom to arrange them any way you like.

Set Up Your Publication

> **SEE ALSO:** For more information about inserting text boxes and pictures, see "Adding Text" on pages 228–229 and "Adding a Picture" on page 234.
>
> For information about creating a Web site using Publisher, see "Creating a Web Site in Publisher" on page 264.

(2) Choose Page Setup from the File menu to display the Page Setup dialog box.

(3) On the Layout tab, select the type of publication you want to create.

(4) If necessary, modify the page dimensions.

(1) In the New section of the New Publication task pane, click Blank Print Publication. If the New Publication task pane isn't displayed, choose New from the File menu, and click Blank Print Publication.

(5) Select your layout's orientation: Portrait (for a page that's taller than wide) or Landscape (for a page that's wider than tall).

(6) On the Printer And Paper tab, select the printer you'll be using to print your publication.

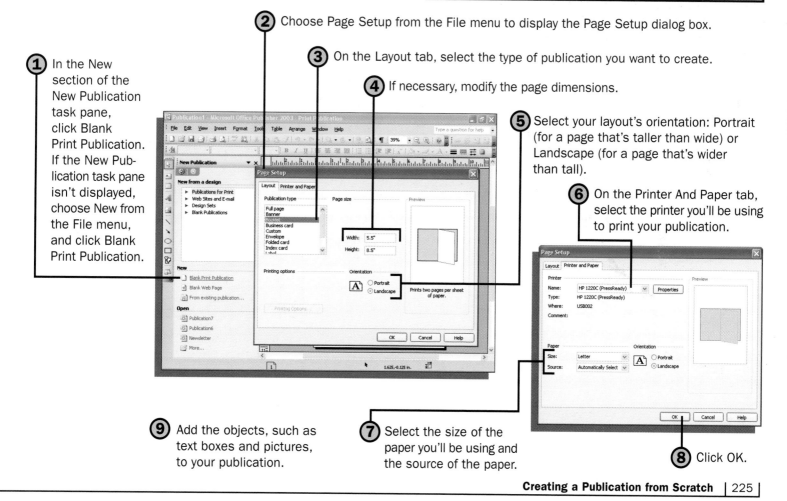

(9) Add the objects, such as text boxes and pictures, to your publication.

(7) Select the size of the paper you'll be using and the source of the paper.

(8) Click OK.

Creating a Publication from a Design

Consistency of design is critical in producing an attractive publication that will be inviting enough to command your readers' attention. No matter how compelling the content of your story, its credibility will suffer if it's poorly presented. If you need some assistance in the area of design, you can use one of Publisher's many predesigned publications, each suited to a specific purpose. To use a design, simply select it, and then replace the placeholder items with your own material.

CAUTION: If you'll be printing your publication, be sure to select the printer you'll be using to print the final version of your publication. Do this in the Page Setup dialog box while you're designing your page. Otherwise, what you see on the screen might not be what you'll see when you print the publication.

Use a Design

① If the New Publication task pane isn't visible, choose New from the File menu to open the task pane.

⑥ Save the publication.

② Specify how you're going to use the publication—that is, as a print publication, as a Web page, as e-mail, and so on.

③ Select a publication type.

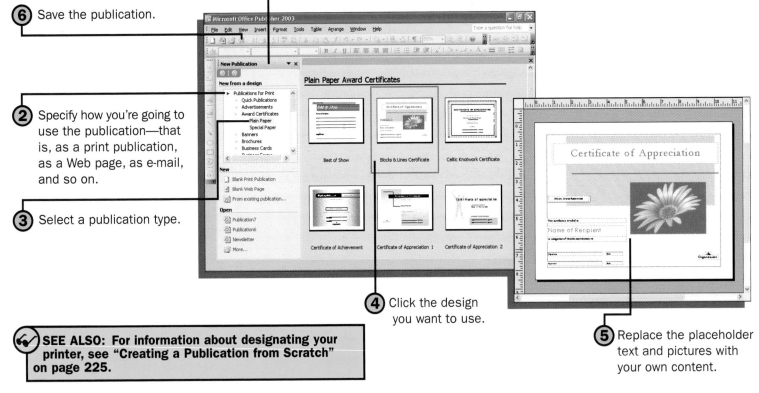

④ Click the design you want to use.

⑤ Replace the placeholder text and pictures with your own content.

SEE ALSO: For information about designating your printer, see "Creating a Publication from Scratch" on page 225.

Repeating Objects on Every Page

If you want certain design objects to repeat on every page of your publication—for example, a picture, a logo, a background pattern, and so on—you can place the object on a *master page*. Then, whenever you create a new page, the material on the master page is included on the new page.

SEE ALSO: For information about creating running headers or footers in Word, a process very similar to creating running headers or footers in Publisher, see "Numbering Pages and Creating Running Heads" on page 77.

Add the Repeating Objects

1 With your publication open in Publisher, choose Master Page from the View menu.

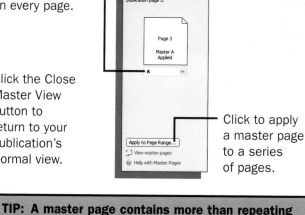

3 Add the object or objects you want to repeat on every page.

4 Click if you want to create an additional master page in order to create a different layout in part of your publication, and add to that page the objects you want to repeat.

2 Click if you want to create a two-page-spread master page instead of a single-page master page.

5 Click the Close Master View button to return to your publication's Normal view.

6 With a page of your publication selected, specify which master page you want to be applied to the page or whether the master page is to be ignored. If the Apply Master Page task pane isn't displayed, choose Apply Master Page from the Format menu. Continue selecting pages and applying the master page you want to use.

Click to apply a master page to a series of pages.

> **TIP:** A master page contains more than repeating objects; it controls the margins, the layout grid, the background color, and any headers and footers that you're using.

Adding Text

All the text in a Publisher publication is contained in text boxes. To add text to your publication, you first insert a text box, and then put your text inside the text box. If there's too much text to fit into the text box, you can make the text box bigger, reduce the size of the text, or have the text continue in another text box—possibly on a different page if there's not enough space on the current page.

Add a Text Box

Zoom Out button — ┌ Zoom In button

(1) With your publication open in Publisher, click the Zoom In or Zoom Out button so that you can see the entire area in which you're going to place the text box.

Rotation handle ┐ ┌ Sizing handle

(2) Click the Text Box button on the Objects toolbar.

(3) In your publication, drag out a text box to the approximate dimensions you want.

(4) Do any of the following to adjust the text box to suit your needs:

- Point to a boundary of the text box, and drag the text box to the location where you want it.

- Drag a sizing handle to fine-tune the dimensions of the text box.

- Drag the Rotation handle to change the orientation of the text box.

SEE ALSO: For information about using Word and Publisher together, see "Using Word to Prepare Publisher Text" on page 299.

Add Text

(1) Click in the text box to activate it.

(2) Type or paste your text.

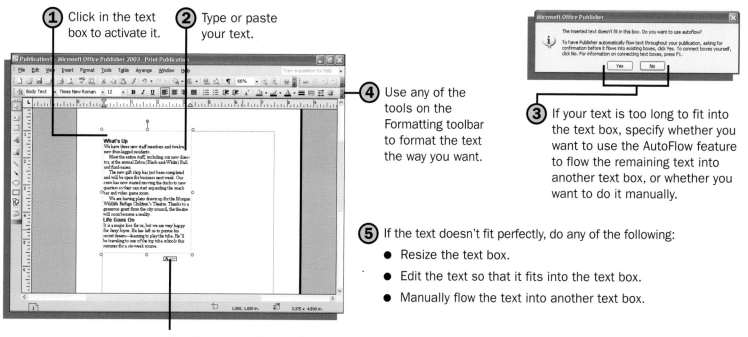

(4) Use any of the tools on the Formatting toolbar to format the text the way you want.

(3) If your text is too long to fit into the text box, specify whether you want to use the AutoFlow feature to flow the remaining text into another text box, or whether you want to do it manually.

(5) If the text doesn't fit perfectly, do any of the following:
- Resize the text box.
- Edit the text so that it fits into the text box.
- Manually flow the text into another text box.

The Text In Overflow indicator shows you that there's too much text to fit into the text box.

SEE ALSO: For information about using AutoFlow to flow text, or to manually flow text into another text box, see "Flowing Text Among Text Boxes" on page 230.

For information about inserting WordArt text, see "Creating Stylized Text with WordArt" on pages 306–307.

For information about formatting text boxes and other types of objects, see "Formatting an Object" on page 319.

TRY THIS: Right-click the text box, and choose Format Text Box from the shortcut menu. On the Text Box tab, set the alignment and margins for the text box. Click the Columns button, select the number of columns you want, and click OK. Click OK in the Format Text Box, and see how your text layout has changed.

Flowing Text Among Text Boxes

The way to position a long story in a publication is to use two or more connected text boxes so that the story flows from one box to the next. In that way, you can continue a story from one side of a page to the other, from one sidebar to the next, or from one page to another. You can use AutoFlow to automatically flow text that's too long for one text box into another text box, or you can manually flow the text by connecting the text boxes that will contain the rest of your story.

> **TIP:** You can connect text boxes before you add any text. Then, when you add your text, it will automatically flow from one text box to the next.

> **TIP:** If you're using AutoFlow and you haven't created enough text boxes for all the text to fit into, Publisher will create another text box, which you'll need to resize and position.

AutoFlow the Text

1 Create your text in Word, and select and copy it (Ctrl+C).

2 With your Publication open in Publisher, create the text boxes you'll need for your story.

3 Click in the first text box, and paste your text (Ctrl+V).

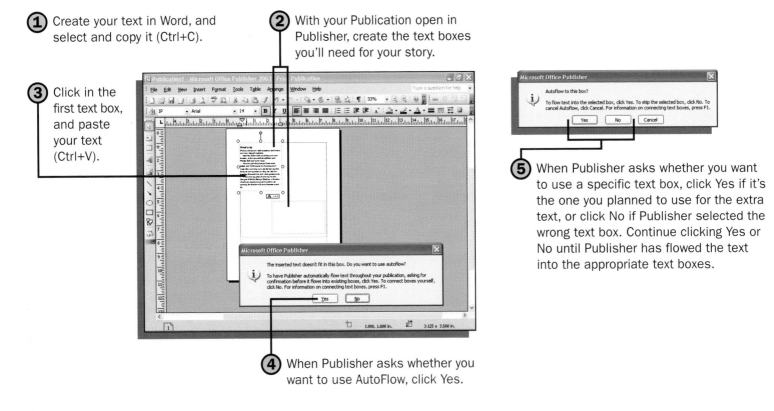

4 When Publisher asks whether you want to use AutoFlow, click Yes.

5 When Publisher asks whether you want to use a specific text box, click Yes if it's the one you planned to use for the extra text, or click No if Publisher selected the wrong text box. Continue clicking Yes or No until Publisher has flowed the text into the appropriate text boxes.

Manually Flow the Text

(1) In your publication, create a second text box if you haven't already created it.

(2) Click in the first text box (the one that contains the text that's too long).

(3) Click the Create Text Box Link button on the Connect Text Boxes toolbar.

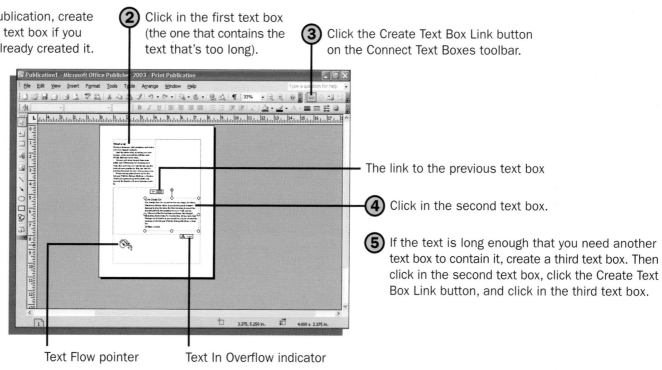

The link to the previous text box

(4) Click in the second text box.

(5) If the text is long enough that you need another text box to contain it, create a third text box. Then click in the second text box, click the Create Text Box Link button, and click in the third text box.

Text Flow pointer   Text In Overflow indicator

TRY THIS: Create a publication that has two pages, with a text box on each page. Click in the first text box, and choose Text Box from the Format menu. On the Text Box tab of the Format Text Box dialog box, select the Include "Continued On Page..." check box, and click OK. Click in the second text box, open the Format Text Box dialog box again, and, on the Text Box tab, select the Include "Continued From Page..." check box, and click OK. In the first text box, paste some text that's too long for the text box, and use AutoFlow to flow the text into the second text box. Observe the result.

! TIP: Use the Previous Text Box and the Next Text Box buttons on the Connect Text Boxes toolbar to review the entire set of connected text boxes. Use the Break Forward Link button to remove the link from one text box to the next.

Tweaking Your Text

The text is usually the largest part of most publications, and if the text doesn't look good, the publication doesn't look good. Of course, you need to start by choosing a clear, easy-to-read font for your story—for example, you wouldn't use a script font or any other fancy font because large blocks of such fonts are difficult to read. Then you can improve the overall look of your text by tweaking some subtle but important details: namely, the *scaling, tracking,* and *kerning* of the characters. Sometimes it's the small details that make a big difference.

Improve the Look of the Text

1 Select the text whose appearance you want to improve.

2 Choose Character Spacing from the Format menu to display the Character Spacing dialog box.

3 Adjust the percentage if you want to scale—that is, shrink (condense) or stretch (expand)—the width of the selected characters and their spacing without changing the height of the characters.

4 Select a type of tracking, or enter a percentage, to adjust the distance between all the characters of the selected text.

5 Select a type of kerning, and the amount of kerning, to fine-tune the space between two selected characters without changing the dimensions of the characters themselves.

6 Select the Kern Text At check box, and set the minimum point size for character pairs that tend to look "gappy" because of their shapes (for example, VA, WA, To, Te) so that they'll always be automatically kerned.

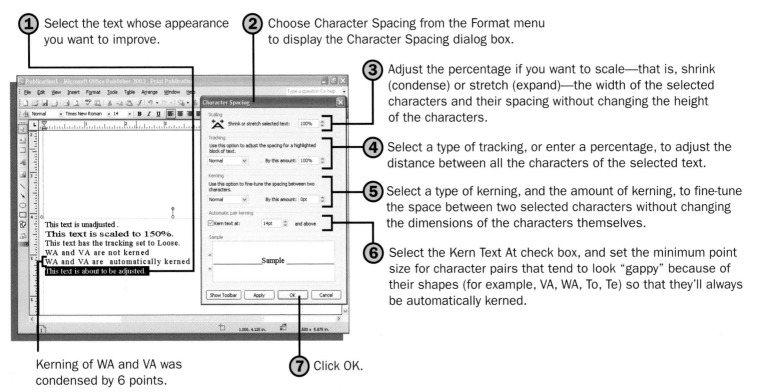

Kerning of WA and VA was condensed by 6 points.

7 Click OK.

Adding a Table

Creating a table is often the best way to organize and present certain types of information with the greatest possible clarity in a publication. Publisher comes with a series of design formats that help you create exactly the type of table you need for your specific purpose.

! TIP: To change the format of the table, choose Table AutoFormat from the Table menu.

Insert a Table

(1) With your publication open in Publisher, click the Insert Table button on the Objects toolbar, and drag out a table in the approximate dimensions you need.

(2) In the Create Table dialog box that appears, select the number of rows and columns you want for the table.

(5) Add your content to the table, using the tools on the Formatting toolbar to modify the formatting of the table.

Rotation handle

(6) Use the sizing handles to change the size of the table or the Rotation handle to change the orientation of the table.

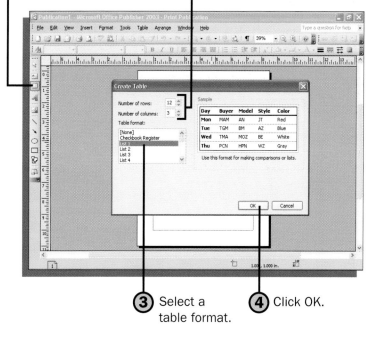

(3) Select a table format.

(4) Click OK.

Sizing handle

TRY THIS: Create a table, drag the sizing handles to create fairly large cells, and then click in one cell. Choose Cell Diagonals from the Table menu, select Divide Down in the Cell Diagonal dialog box, and click OK. Now add text to both sides of the diagonal in the one cell.

Adding a Picture

You can add a great deal of interest, color, and visual appeal to a publication by using pictures, whether they're photographs, drawings, or ClipArt. When you're working in Publisher, first you create a picture frame to contain the picture, and then use Publisher's tools to customize the picture.

Insert a Picture

(1) With your publication open in Publisher, click the Picture Frame button on the Objects toolbar.

(2) Choose the type of picture and its source:

- Choose ClipArt, and use the ClipArt task pane to locate and insert the ClipArt picture you want.
- Choose Picture From File, drag out a picture frame in the publication, and use the Insert Picture dialog box to locate and insert a picture.
- Choose Empty Picture Frame, and drag out a placeholder picture frame in the publication.
- Choose From Scanner Or Camera to display the Scanner Or Camera dialog box to scan or download the picture, and then drag out a picture frame in the publication.

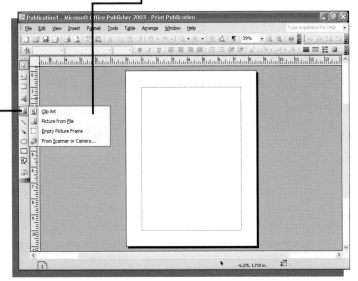

The Picture toolbar appears automatically whenever you insert or select a picture or picture frame.

(3) Use the sizing handles to change the dimensions of the picture and/or the picture frame; use the Rotation handle to change the orientation of the picture; or use the tools on the Picture toolbar to adjust the picture or picture frame.

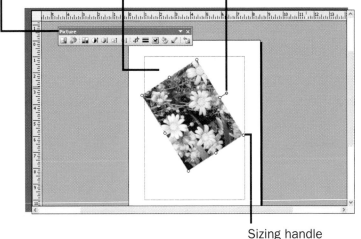

Rotation handle

Sizing handle

> **SEE ALSO: For information about inserting ClipArt, see "Inserting ClipArt" on page 308.**
>
> **For information about modifying a picture, see "Editing a Picture" on pages 316–317.**

Adding a Design Object

If you need some fresh ideas, take a look at Publisher's Design Gallery! It provides a huge variety of design objects that were created to complement Publisher's design themes. You'll find that some of these objects are inserted automatically when you apply a design theme to a publication, but you can add any of the objects yourself, even if you're not using the design for which that particular object was intended.

> **TIP:** Many of the objects in the Design Gallery are actually collections of different design objects that have been grouped together. In some cases, you might want to ungroup the items to modify or delete an item or to add other items. You can easily regroup the items when you've finished.

Insert a Design Object

(1) With your publication open in Publisher, click the Design Gallery Object button on the Objects toolbar to display the Design Gallery dialog box.

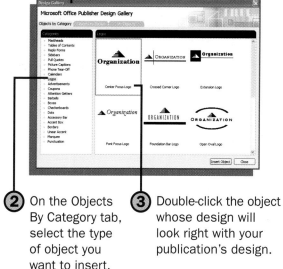

(2) On the Objects By Category tab, select the type of object you want to insert.

(3) Double-click the object whose design will look right with your publication's design.

(4) Move and size the object to fit into your publication.

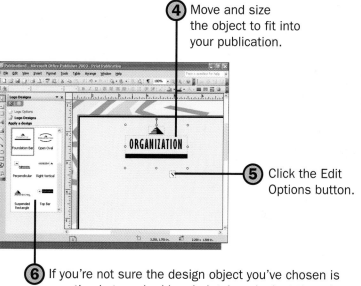

(5) Click the Edit Options button.

(6) If you're not sure the design object you've chosen is exactly what you had in mind, take a look at the other designs for this type of object, and, if you see one you prefer, click the design.

(7) If necessary, edit the content of the object to fit your publication.

> **SEE ALSO:** For information about grouping and ungrouping objects, see "Stacking and Grouping Objects" on page 238.

Arranging Objects on the Page

Misalignment of the items on a page can make your publication look sloppy and amateurish. By using Publisher's arranging tools, you can produce a professional looking publication whose objects are precisely placed for maximum design impact. Use the margin guides to determine the amount of space between your content and the edge of the page; use the grid guides to line up objects either horizontally or vertically; use the baseline guides so that the lines of text align vertically across the page even if they're in different text boxes; and use the ruler guides to align each object to a specific measurement.

Set Up Your Grid

(1) With your publication open in Publisher, choose Layout Guides from the Arrange menu to display the Layout Guides dialog box.

(2) On the Margin Guides tab, set the margins you want for the page.

(7) Point to Snap on the Arrange menu, and choose To Guides from the submenu.

(8) Drag or resize an object in your document, and note how it aligns with the grid guidelines.

(3) On the Grid Guides tab, select the number of column guides and row guides you want.

(4) Set the spacing (the distance from the guide with which an object will align) for both column guides and row guides.

(5) On the Baseline Guides tab, specify the spacing for the baseline of your text, and set the offset distance that you want between the first baseline and the top margin guide.

(6) Click OK.

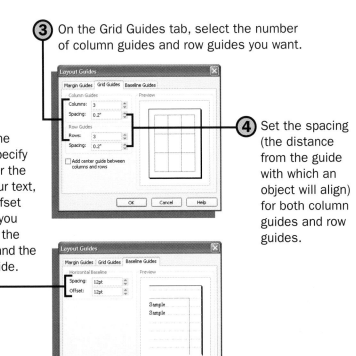

Position an Object at an Exact Location

1 Point to the horizontal ruler, and drag out a horizontal ruler guide to the location you want, as shown on the vertical ruler. Drag out and position as many horizontal ruler guides as you want.

2 Point to the vertical ruler, and drag out a vertical ruler guide to the location you want, as shown on the horizontal ruler. Drag out and position as many vertical ruler guides as you want.

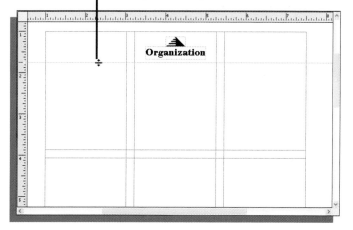

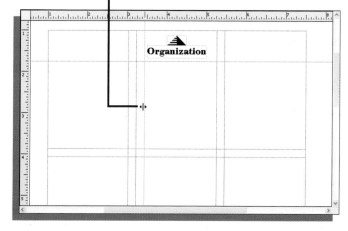

3 Point to Snap on the Arrange menu, and choose To Ruler Marks from the submenu.

4 Move or resize an object so that its boundaries snap to a horizontal or vertical ruler guide, or to the intersection of a horizontal and a vertical guide.

> **SEE ALSO: For information about creating a style in Word, a process very similar to creating a style in Publisher, see "Creating Your Own Styles" on pages 54–55.**

> **TRY THIS: Point to Toolbars on the View menu, and choose Measurement from the submenu. Click to select an object, and note the information about its position, dimensions, and font characteristics. Point to Nudge on the Arrange menu, and drag the top of the submenu so that it becomes a floating toolbar. Move the selected object by clicking the Nudge buttons.**

> **TIP: To move the entire ruler instead of creating ruler guides, point to the ruler, hold down the Shift key, and drag the ruler to a new position.**

Stacking and Grouping Objects

One of Publisher's most powerful features is the ability it gives you to stack, or layer, several different objects, and to adjust the order in which they're stacked. After you've assembled the objects you've chosen into the arrangement you like, you can group them so that they function as a single unit that you can then easily move around or resize.

Arrange the Objects

(1) In a publication that contains all the objects you want to stack and arrange, point to Order on the Arrange menu, and drag the submenu away from the menu to create the Order toolbar.

TIP: To change the arrangement of objects that you've grouped, select the group, and then choose Ungroup from the Arrange menu.

TIP: When you're working with several stacked objects that you want to group, it can be difficult to select an object that's stacked underneath other objects by clicking it. To select all the objects, use the mouse to drag a selection rectangle around all the objects, and then group them.

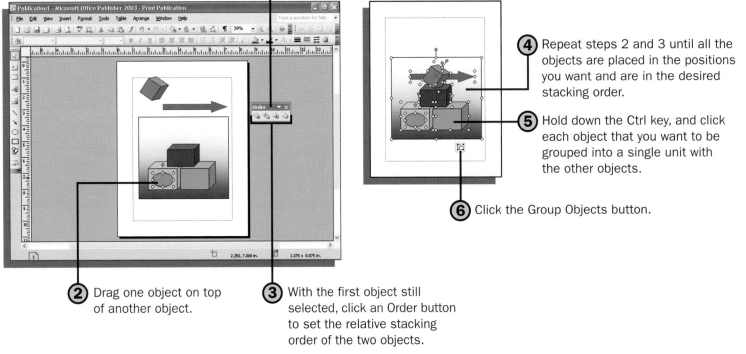

(4) Repeat steps 2 and 3 until all the objects are placed in the positions you want and are in the desired stacking order.

(5) Hold down the Ctrl key, and click each object that you want to be grouped into a single unit with the other objects.

(6) Click the Group Objects button.

(2) Drag one object on top of another object.

(3) With the first object still selected, click an Order button to set the relative stacking order of the two objects.

Flowing Text Around an Object

You can add style and sophistication to your publication by flowing the text of your story around an object—picture or an AutoShape, for example. You do this by setting the text wrapping for the object that the text wraps around.

Set the Text Wrapping

(1) In a publication that contains a text box and the object you want the text to wrap around, right-click the object, and choose Format from the shortcut menu to display the Format dialog box. (The name of the dialog box changes depending on the type of object selected.)

(2) On the Layout tab, select the text-wrapping style you want.

(3) Specify how you want the text to wrap around the object.

(4) If you chose the square wrapping style and would rather not use the automatic setting, clear the Automatic check box, and set the values for how closely the text will wrap around the object.

(5) Click OK.

(6) Drag the object onto a text box that contains text, and adjust the position of the object so that the text wraps around the object in exactly the way you want.

I awoke. The sun shone brightly as I squinted across the water, looking for a sail on the distant horizon. I knew the ship would come, sooner or later. They had promised to return and I trusted them—I know not why. All I had for company was a broken radio, a waffle iron, and my 3-D glasses. The land provided for all my needs but none of my wants.

The sand stood in sweeping mounds as if to mock me. As I fell upon a dune, the sand poured through my fingers like the sand of an hourglass. I knew, however, that my wait would not be measured in hours. The sand grew in front of me, a 25 cm. testament to the time I have lost and will never regain.

> **TRY THIS:** Set the text wrapping to Tight for an object, and drag the object onto a text box that contains text. Point to Text Wrapping on the Arrange menu, and choose Edit Wrap Points from the submenu. Drag a square black wrapping point into a new location to change the way the text wraps around the object. Continue moving wrapping points until you get the wrapping effect you want. Click outside the object when you've finished.

Double-Checking Your Publication

You worked long hours on a publication that you thought would be a joy to behold, but what you got when you printed it was a woefully misaligned mess. Your eyes fill with tears of anger and despair as you wail, "What happened?" Don't give up! At this point, you could scroll through your publication to try to detect the problems, but there's a lesson to be learned here: *Before you print, let Publisher do a comprehensive check through your publication to identify any problems.*

Check the Design

 2 Point to a problem that Design Checker has identified, click the down arrow button, and choose

- Go To This Item to jump to the problem item and adjust the problem manually.

- Fix... to automatically fix the problem, bearing in mind that not every problem can be fixed automatically.

- Never Run This Check Again to discontinue using the specific check that reported the problem.

- Explain to display Publisher Help, read why this is a problem, and learn about any automatic or manual fixes.

3 Repeat step 2 for any other identified problems.

4 Click Close Design Checker when you've finished.

1 In your completed and saved publication, choose Design Checker from the Tools menu to display the Design Checker task pane.

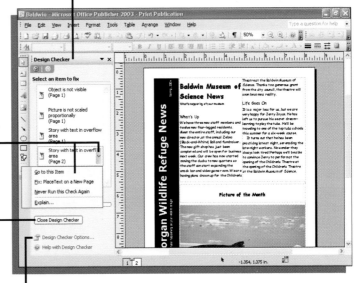

Click to change which items are checked and how they are checked.

SEE ALSO: For information about checking your spelling, see "Correcting Your Spelling" on page 24 and "Proofreading in Another Language" on pages 362–363.

Sending a Publication as E-Mail

If you want to send an unusually elaborate e-mail message, a newsletter, or an announcement, consider creating it in and sending it from Publisher. You have two choices: You can send the publication itself as the message, or you can enclose the publication file as an attachment to an e-mail message. If you send the publication itself as the message, it will be sent in HTML format. This means that the recipient must be running an e-mail program such as Outlook or Outlook Express that can view HTML messages. If you send the publication as an attachment, the recipient must have Publisher on his or her computer to be able to view the file.

E-Mail Your Publication

① Create and save your publication. Point to Send E-Mail on the File menu, and choose E-Mail Preview from the submenu.

② In the Web page preview that appears, verify that the publication contains the information you want, and then close the preview window.

④ Address the message, add a subject line, and click Send.

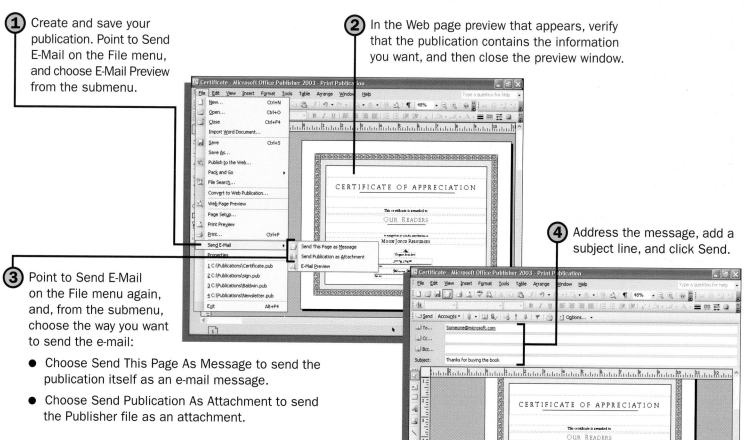

③ Point to Send E-Mail on the File menu again, and, from the submenu, choose the way you want to send the e-mail:

- Choose Send This Page As Message to send the publication itself as an e-mail message.

- Choose Send Publication As Attachment to send the Publisher file as an attachment.

Printing Your Publication

Although you can use Publisher to produce Web pages and e-mail messages, chances are that you're going to print most, if not all, of your publications on paper. You'll find that Publisher gives you exceptionally fine control of the printing process so that you can designate exactly what's printed and how it's printed.

The Final Step: Print It!

TIP: If you've decided to have your publication printed by a commercial printer, first find out about all the settings you need from someone at the print shop. Then point to Commercial Printing Tools on the Tools menu, and use the items on the submenu to make the recommended settings for your publication. Whether or not you use the commercial printing tools, use the Pack And Go command on the File menu whenever you transfer your publication to ensure that all the files you need are included.

1 With your publication proofread, checked by Design Checker, and saved, choose Print from the File menu to display the Print dialog box.

2 Select the printer you're going to use if it isn't already selected. Specify the pages to be printed, the number of copies you want, and whether the copies are to be collated.

3 Click the Advanced Print Settings button.

Click to change the way a page is to be printed on a large sheet of paper (for printers that have this capability).

9 Click OK.

4 On the Separations tab, specify whether you want to print a composite copy of the publication (a final copy showing all the colors together on each page), or the separations (a separate page for each color to check that the color has been applied correctly to every element).

5 Complete the other printing specifications.

6 On the Page Settings tab, specify how you want the pages to be printed, which printer's marks you want, and whether there are any bleeds (color that extends beyond the edge of the page).

7 On the Graphics And Fonts tab, specify how graphics are to be printed and whether you'll allow the printer to substitute its fonts for the fonts in your publication.

Click to read some helpful definitions of the complex terminology used in the printing process.

8 Click OK.

14 Creating Web Pages and Web Sites

Of course you're familiar with Web sites. You've probably visited enough Internet sites to have developed an eye for which sites work and which don't. But how do you create your own Web pages or sites? With the programs in the Microsoft Office System, you have a multitude of Web-development methods at your fingertips. For the greatest control when you're developing a Web site, there's no better tool than Microsoft Office FrontPage 2003. Dedicated solely to Web-site and Web-page authoring, FrontPage can help you produce just about any type of Web site. You can use the templates that come with FrontPage to develop standard Web sites. To develop specialized and highly functional Web pages or sites, you'll need to learn to work with objects and HTML code. FrontPage is also a great way to create a custom SharePoint Web site, where your coworkers can find all the information they need in one convenient spot.

If you don't want to deal with the intricacies of FrontPage, there are simpler ways to create a Web site. Publisher is an easy-to-use tool for creating a personal Web site or a small business site. With Word, you can convert an existing Word document into a Web page. In Excel, you can present your data as a worksheet or a chart, and you can let other people work on the data on the Web page. A PowerPoint Web page is a great way to have a slide show available for anyone to view at any time. With Access, you can create a Web page that's connected to a database so that users can interact with the data over the Internet or an intranet. And if you want to share your personal Calendar or your organization's schedule, you can publish an Outlook Calendar as a Web page.

What's Where in FrontPage?

FrontPage is a powerful Web-authoring tool that utilizes HTML code to develop and customize Web sites, Web pages, and Web services. Did you just say, "Forget it—that's *way* too technical for me!"? Actually, we don't think it is. FrontPage does most of the scary technical stuff behind the scenes: developing the HTML code for you as you add items and modify them on the page, using wizards to develop entire Web sites, and providing all sorts of Web components to add special services and features. And, just like some of the other powerful Office programs, FrontPage is scalable—that is, easy projects are easy to do, and complex projects are quite complex. Stick to the easy projects, and you'll find yourself creating some great Web pages.

Web-page tab

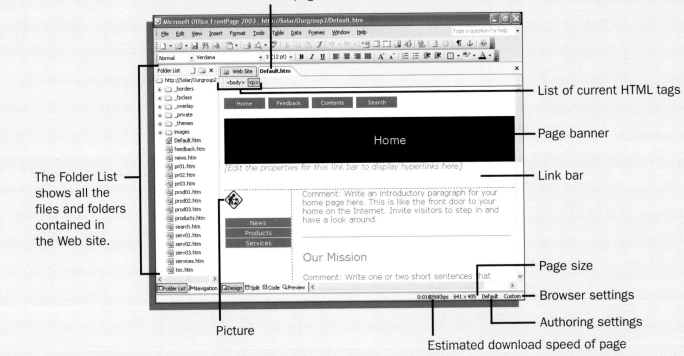

List of current HTML tags

Page banner

Link bar

The Folder List shows all the files and folders contained in the Web site.

Picture

Page size

Browser settings

Authoring settings

Estimated download speed of page

FrontPage provides several views that help you create and organize your Web site. Below is an illustration of the Web-site tree structure that you see in Navigation view, which is the view that shows you how Web pages are related. You can use this view to reorganize the structure of your Web site. The other views are straightforward and mostly self-explanatory: Folders view displays details about all the files and folders in your Web site, Remote Web Site view connects the local copy of your Web site to the remote site from which it's published, Reports view displays a summary report about the health and structure of your site, Hyperlinks view shows the links connected to each individual page of your Web site, and Tasks view lists the tasks that have been assigned to your Web site's contributors and allows you to track the construction and maintenance of the site.

Web Site tab

Top level of tree

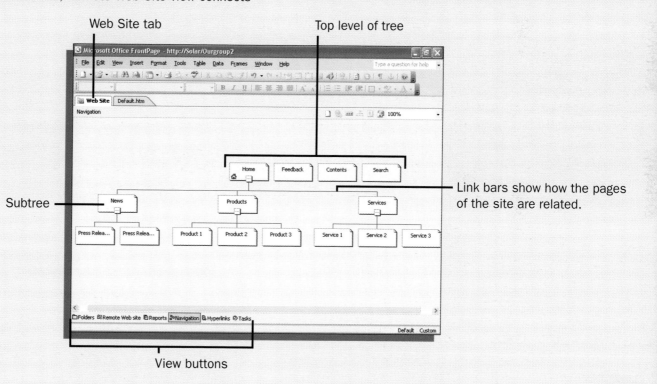

Subtree

Link bars show how the pages of the site are related.

View buttons

Creating a Web Site

When you're creating a Web site, you normally create the entire Web site locally—that is, on your computer. FrontPage simplifies the creation of your Web site's structure by providing a template that you use, and, in some cases, stepping you through a wizard.

After FrontPage has created the structure of the Web site, you then complete the content of the site's pages. When you've completed the site, you place it on the server that will host the Web site.

Start Creating Your Web Site

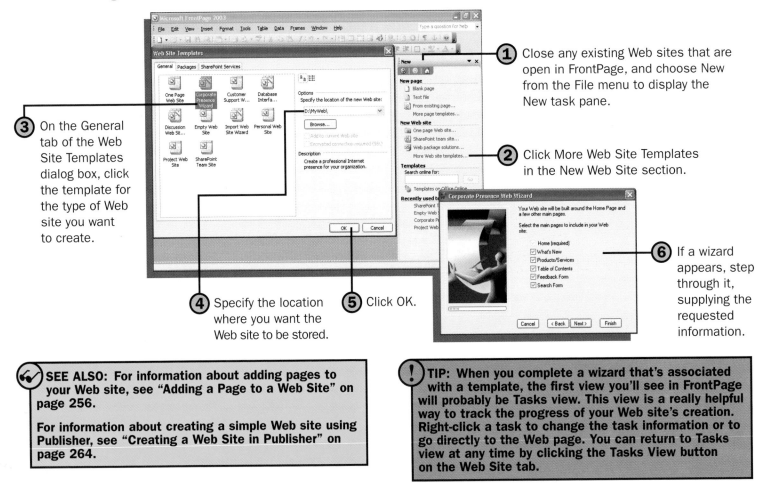

1. Close any existing Web sites that are open in FrontPage, and choose New from the File menu to display the New task pane.

2. Click More Web Site Templates in the New Web Site section.

3. On the General tab of the Web Site Templates dialog box, click the template for the type of Web site you want to create.

4. Specify the location where you want the Web site to be stored.

5. Click OK.

6. If a wizard appears, step through it, supplying the requested information.

SEE ALSO: For information about adding pages to your Web site, see "Adding a Page to a Web Site" on page 256.

For information about creating a simple Web site using Publisher, see "Creating a Web Site in Publisher" on page 264.

TIP: When you complete a wizard that's associated with a template, the first view you'll see in FrontPage will probably be Tasks view. This view is a really helpful way to track the progress of your Web site's creation. Right-click a task to change the task information or to go directly to the Web page. You can return to Tasks view at any time by clicking the Tasks View button on the Web Site tab.

Review the Web Site

(2) Double-click a Web page to open it, and review the content of the page.

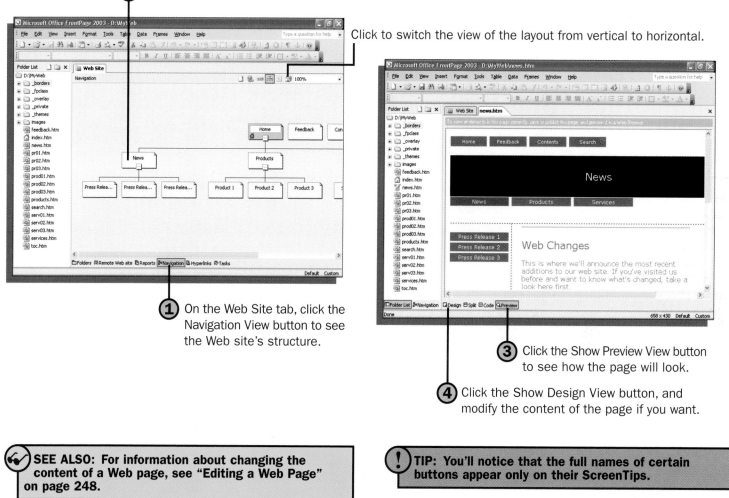

Click to switch the view of the layout from vertical to horizontal.

(1) On the Web Site tab, click the Navigation View button to see the Web site's structure.

(3) Click the Show Preview View button to see how the page will look.

(4) Click the Show Design View button, and modify the content of the page if you want.

SEE ALSO: For information about changing the content of a Web page, see "Editing a Web Page" on page 248.

TIP: You'll notice that the full names of certain buttons appear only on their ScreenTips.

Editing a Web Page

Whether you just created a Web site using one of FrontPage's templates or you have an existing Web site under development, you can easily make changes to any of the site's pages. You can change the content either by changing the value of the properties or by changing the content directly on the Web page.

Change the Properties

TIP: To quickly open a Web page, double-click its title in the Folder List. You can switch to any open Web page by clicking its tab.

TIP: In FrontPage, you're dealing primarily with two different types of content: text and objects. Objects are containers that use code to make them work. A picture, a page banner, and a Web component are all objects. By setting an object's properties, you specify what values it contains, and how it looks and works.

(1) With both your Web site and the Web page to be edited open, point to an object on the page that displays either the Properties pointer or an arrow pointer.

Link bar object

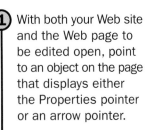

Properties pointer

(2) Double-click that object to display its Properties dialog box.

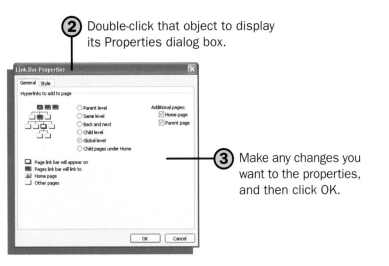

(3) Make any changes you want to the properties, and then click OK.

Change the Content Directly

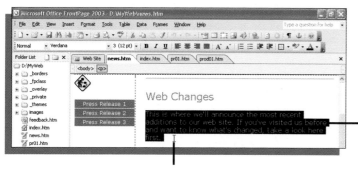

Text Select pointer

TIP: To make sure your Web page or Web site is displayed correctly in different resolutions and/or in different browsers, click the down arrow at the right of the Preview button on the Standard toolbar, and select a browser and/or a resolution. Repeat for different browsers and/or resolutions.

(1) Point to the text on the page, and, with the Text Select pointer (the same I-beam pointer you use in Word), select the text you want to change.

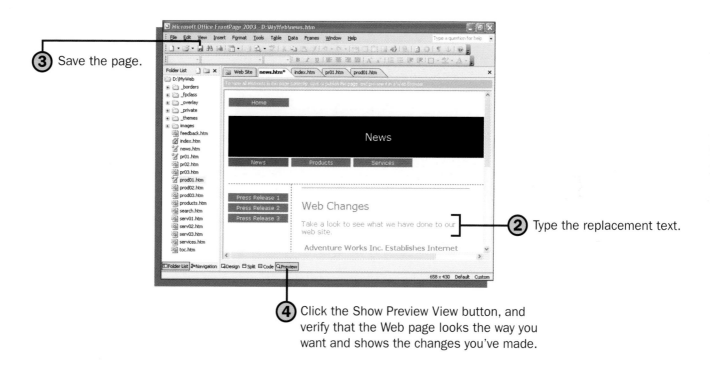

(3) Save the page.

(2) Type the replacement text.

(4) Click the Show Preview View button, and verify that the Web page looks the way you want and shows the changes you've made.

Customizing Your Web Site

A Web site is usually designed to appeal to a select audience in a specific way. You've probably already identified your target audience. Your next step is to get instructions from whoever controls your Web server as to how your site should be constructed for maximum efficiency and impact. You can then construct your Web site using those specific settings, and, at the same time, you can set the values for certain parameters (phone numbers or fax numbers, for example) that are used repeatedly throughout the site.

Modify the Settings

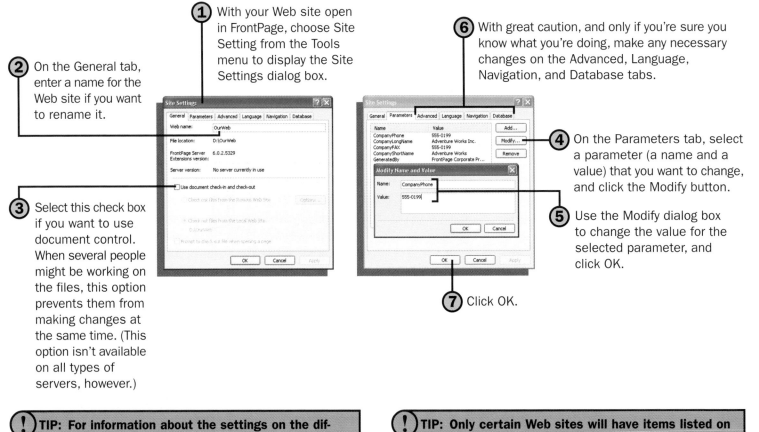

(1) With your Web site open in FrontPage, choose Site Setting from the Tools menu to display the Site Settings dialog box.

(2) On the General tab, enter a name for the Web site if you want to rename it.

(3) Select this check box if you want to use document control. When several people might be working on the files, this option prevents them from making changes at the same time. (This option isn't available on all types of servers, however.)

(6) With great caution, and only if you're sure you know what you're doing, make any necessary changes on the Advanced, Language, Navigation, and Database tabs.

(4) On the Parameters tab, select a parameter (a name and a value) that you want to change, and click the Modify button.

(5) Use the Modify dialog box to change the value for the selected parameter, and click OK.

(7) Click OK.

> **! TIP:** For information about the settings on the different tabs of the Site Settings dialog box, with the dialog box open, press the F1 key for FrontPage Help.

> **! TIP:** Only certain Web sites will have items listed on the Parameters tab. Such items are likely to appear only if you used a wizard to create the site.

Customizing a Web Page

Just as you can customize the settings that affect the entire Web site, you can also customize the settings that affect the individual pages in the site and the resources—such as SharePoint Services and Web components—that are available to the Web pages.

> **! TIP: The ruler and the grid aren't displayed until you open the View menu and choose to display them.**

Make Your Settings

(1) In FrontPage, open the page whose settings you want to change, and choose Page Options from the Tools menu to display the Page Options dialog box.

(2) On the Picture tab, change the default file type for pictures, if necessary.

(3) Click to change the way you want GIF and/or JPG files to be inserted on the page.

(4) On the AutoThumbnail tab, modify the size of the thumbnails that will be generated on the page.

(5) Select this check box if you want the thumbnails to have borders.

(7) Cautiously make any necessary changes on the other tabs to change the way you work when you're dealing directly with the coding for the Web page.

(6) On the Ruler And Grid tab, specify how you want the ruler and the grid to be displayed during the design of the Web page.

(8) Click OK when you've finished.

Creating Hyperlinks

A hyperlink is a word, a phrase, or a picture that, when clicked, takes you to another place on the current Web page or Web site, or transports you to an entirely different Web site.

Create a Hyperlink

1 In FrontPage, open the Web page on which you're going to place the hyperlink. Insert, format, and then select the picture or the text that you want to use for the hyperlink.

2 Click the Insert Hyperlink button on the Standard toolbar to display the Insert Hyperlink dialog box.

3 Select the type of location you want the link to go to:

- Existing File Or Web Page to link to any file you want, regardless of its location

- Place In This Document to link to a bookmark in the current document

- Create New Document to create and link to a new file

- E-Mail Address to start a new e-mail message to the specified e-mail address and to include a predefined subject

4 Select or enter the destination of the link or the e-mail address and the subject of the message.

5 If you're using text for the hyperlink on your page, verify or change the text that will be displayed.

6 Click to create a ScreenTip that will be displayed when the mouse pointer points to the hyperlink.

7 Use the buttons to define the destination, to add code to the action or change existing code, or to change the formatting of the hyperlink.

8 Click OK.

> **TIP:** To go to a specific location on a page, you can create a bookmark at that location. To create a bookmark, select the location on the Web page, choose Bookmark from the Insert menu, enter a name for the bookmark, and click OK.

> **SEE ALSO:** For information about changing an object's properties, see "Editing a Web Page" on pages 248–249.
>
> For information about Web components, see "Adding Web Components" on page 257.

> **TIP:** WebBots are dynamic objects (such as the Web components available in FrontPage) that execute specific actions on a Web page. If you want to add, delete, or change the hyperlinks on a WebBot item, such as a Link bar, you can make changes to the WebBot's properties.

Creating Hotspot Hyperlinks

A hotspot is a special type of hyperlink that's used only in a picture. A hotspot is often located in one small part of a picture, which means that you can put more than one hotspot in a picture.

With multiple hotspots, you can then click specific areas of the picture to jump to as many locations as there are hotspots. Think of the possibilities!

Create a Hotspot

1 With your Web page open in FrontPage, and with the picture you're using formatted and located where you want it, display the Pictures toolbar if it isn't already displayed.

2 Click one of the hotspot buttons to create a hotspot in the shape you want.

4 In the Insert Hyperlink dialog box that appears, specify the location of the hyperlink.

5 Add a descriptive ScreenTip, and click OK.

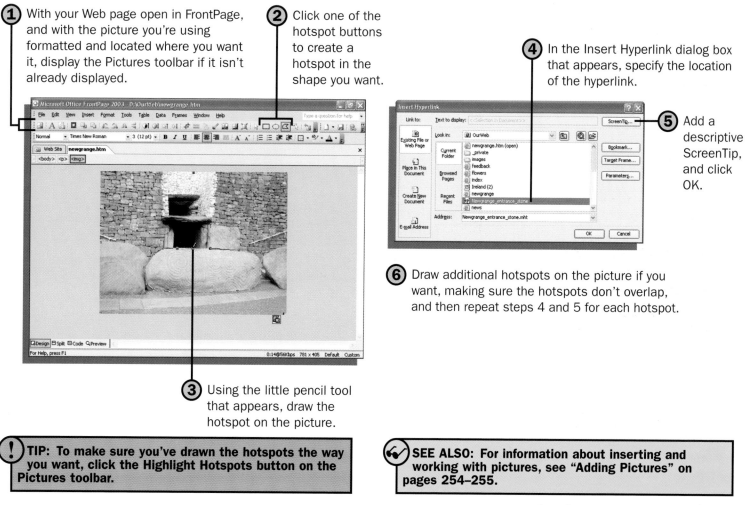

3 Using the little pencil tool that appears, draw the hotspot on the picture.

6 Draw additional hotspots on the picture if you want, making sure the hotspots don't overlap, and then repeat steps 4 and 5 for each hotspot.

> **! TIP:** To make sure you've drawn the hotspots the way you want, click the Highlight Hotspots button on the Pictures toolbar.

> **SEE ALSO:** For information about inserting and working with pictures, see "Adding Pictures" on pages 254–255.

Adding Pictures

Pictures are an integral part of most Web pages. From a single instance of your company's logo to an entire picture gallery of thumbnail images, each of which you click to open a larger version, pictures complement and enhance your written material and add interest and color to your Web pages.

Add a Picture

① With your Web site open in FrontPage, and with the Web page on which you're going to put the picture displayed in Design view, click in the page. Point to Picture on the Insert menu, and choose From File from the submenu to display the Picture dialog box.

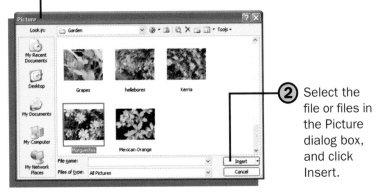

② Select the file or files in the Picture dialog box, and click Insert.

③ Save the Web page, and, when the Save Embedded Files dialog box appears, click OK to save the file or files in your Web site.

④ Position the picture where you want it on the Web page.

SEE ALSO: For information about creating hotspots, see "Creating Hotspot Hyperlinks" on page 253.

For information about using tables for laying out your page, see "Using Tables for Web-Page Layout" on page 258.

⑤ Select the picture, and modify and customize it using the buttons on the Pictures toolbar:

- Use the Text button to add text to the picture (the picture must be in the GIF file format).

- Use the Auto Thumbnail button to create a thumbnail image of the picture; click the thumbnail to show the full picture.

- Use the Position Absolutely button to make the position of the picture exact rather than relative to other items.

- Use the Bring Forward or Send Backward button to set the stacking order of the picture relative to other items.

- Use the Set Transparent Color button to specify a color in the picture that will be transparent on the page (the picture must be in the GIF file format).

- Use the Hotspot buttons to create hyperlink hotspots in the picture.

Text button · Position Absolutely button · Send Backward button · Hotspot buttons

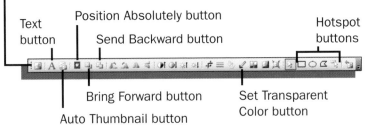

Bring Forward button · Auto Thumbnail button · Set Transparent Color button

⑥ Save the Web page again to make sure that all the changes to the pictures have been saved.

Create a Photo Gallery

① With the Web page that is to contain the photos displayed in Design view, point to Picture on the Insert menu, and choose New Photo Gallery from the submenu to display the Photo Gallery Properties dialog box.

② Click Add, and choose Pictures From Files from the menu that appears. Use the File Open dialog box to select the pictures you want, and then click Open.

③ Select a picture, and use the Move Up or Move Down button to place the picture where you want it. Repeat with the other pictures until the list is in the desired order.

④ Click Edit if you want to change the size or orientation of the selected picture.

⑤ Make any changes you want to the thumbnail size.

⑥ Type a caption for the selected picture.

⑦ Type a description of the picture.

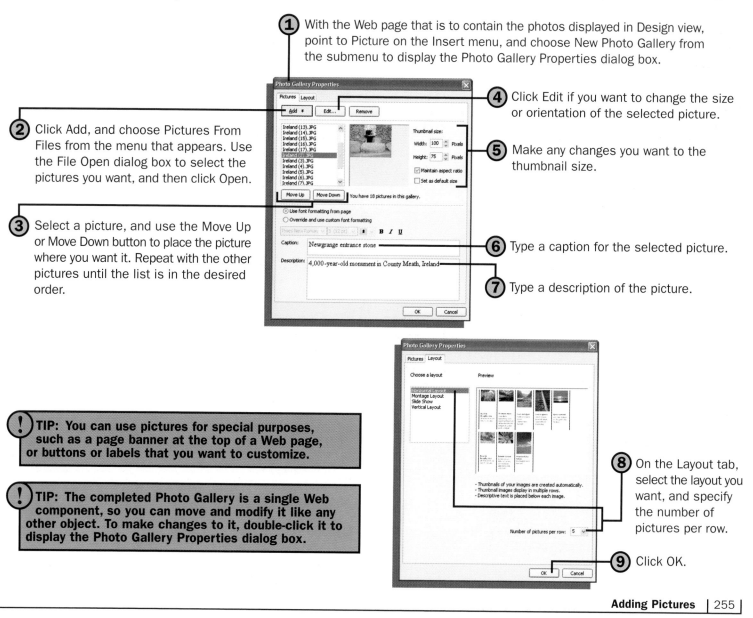

> **!** TIP: You can use pictures for special purposes, such as a page banner at the top of a Web page, or buttons or labels that you want to customize.

> **!** TIP: The completed Photo Gallery is a single Web component, so you can move and modify it like any other object. To make changes to it, double-click it to display the Photo Gallery Properties dialog box.

⑧ On the Layout tab, select the layout you want, and specify the number of pictures per row.

⑨ Click OK.

Adding a Page to a Web Site

Creating a Web site is often a fairly lengthy process, and you'll seldom complete it in one sitting—you're more likely to add pages over a period of time. Even when your site is completed, you'll probably want to update it every so often or modify it in other ways. You can easily add new or existing Web pages to your site without compromising the site's structure.

Add an Existing Page

 TIP: To delete a Web page, right-click it in the Navigation pane, choose Delete from the shortcut menu, and, in the Delete Page dialog box that appears, choose to delete only that page from the current structure or to delete the entire file from the Web site. To add a blank page, click the New Page button in the Navigation pane.

① With your Web site open in FrontPage, choose Import from the File menu to display the Import dialog box.

② Click Add File to add a stand-alone file, click Add Folder to import all the files for a Web page contained in a folder, or click From Site to use the Import Web Site Wizard to download the files. Complete the information to add the file or files, and click OK.

③ Click the Web Site tab to display the content of the Web site if the Web site isn't already displayed.

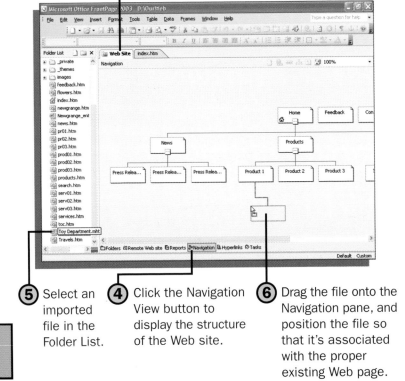

⑤ Select an imported file in the Folder List.

④ Click the Navigation View button to display the structure of the Web site.

⑥ Drag the file onto the Navigation pane, and position the file so that it's associated with the proper existing Web page.

 TIP: You can also use the Navigation pane to move around existing Web pages to change the structure of the Web site.

Adding Web Components

Web components are self-contained objects that usually have a lot of code built into them, which allows them to perform all sorts of automated activities for you. Using Web components is the easiest way to create powerful Web sites.

> **! TIP: In Web-page lingo, many types of Web components are called WebBots.**

Insert a Web Component

2 Click the Web Component button on the Standard toolbar to display the Insert Web Component dialog box.

3 Select the type of Web component you want.

4 Select the component or component style you want.

5 Click Next if the button is available, and complete all the additional information. Click Finish when you've finished.

6 Complete the required information in the Web component's Properties dialog box, or in any other dialog box that appears and requests additional information.

1 With your Web site open in FrontPage, and with the Web page that's going to contain the Web component open in Design view, click in the page where you want to place the Web component.

7 Move or modify the Web component as you would any other object on the page.

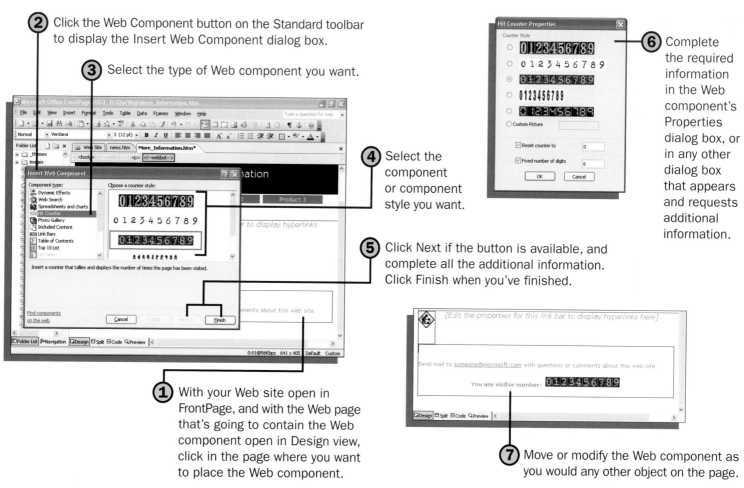

Using Tables for Web-Page Layout

You can employ one of the oldest and best techniques that Web designers use, which is to divide up a Web page by using a table. After you've configured the table, it's a simple process to insert the elements you want into the individual cells of the table and to get everything lined up the way you want it to appear on the page. FrontPage provides a variety of preset layouts, but you can easily customize any of the layouts to create your own design.

> **! TIP:** An alternative layout technique is to use separate frames on your page to hold different content. A table of contents or an index is often placed in a frame at the left side of a standard Web page. Use the Frames menu to insert and use frames.

Insert a Layout Table

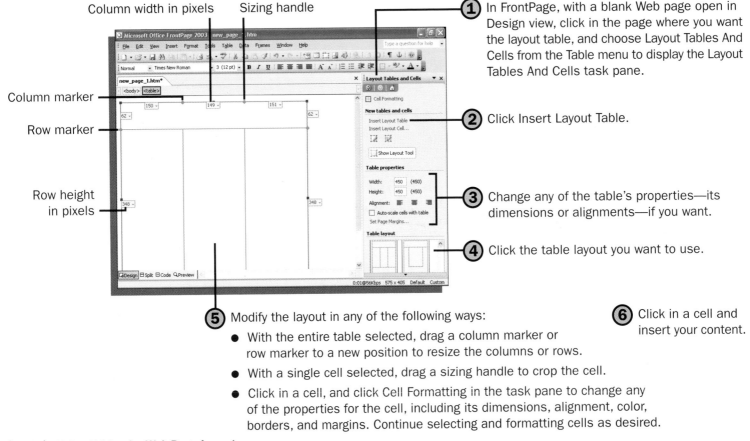

Column width in pixels   Sizing handle

Column marker

Row marker

Row height in pixels

1 In FrontPage, with a blank Web page open in Design view, click in the page where you want the layout table, and choose Layout Tables And Cells from the Table menu to display the Layout Tables And Cells task pane.

2 Click Insert Layout Table.

3 Change any of the table's properties—its dimensions or alignments—if you want.

4 Click the table layout you want to use.

5 Modify the layout in any of the following ways:

- With the entire table selected, drag a column marker or row marker to a new position to resize the columns or rows.
- With a single cell selected, drag a sizing handle to crop the cell.
- Click in a cell, and click Cell Formatting in the task pane to change any of the properties for the cell, including its dimensions, alignment, color, borders, and margins. Continue selecting and formatting cells as desired.

6 Click in a cell and insert your content.

Creating a SharePoint Web Site

Whether your business employs a small staff in one office or has branch offices worldwide, a locally hosted SharePoint Web site is a great way to centralize all the information to which your coworkers need access. You can use FrontPage to create a SharePoint site, which you can then customize to include critical information, schedules, group activities, and whatever other information your group needs.

> **! TIP:** FrontPage is also a great tool for customizing an existing SharePoint Web site.

> **SEE ALSO:** For information about publishing your Web site, see "Publishing Your Web Site" on page 270.
>
> For information about using a SharePoint Web site, see "Sharing a File on a SharePoint Site" on page 337.

Create a Custom SharePoint Web Site

1 In FrontPage, choose New from the File menu to display the New task pane, and click SharePoint Team Site. In the Web Site Templates dialog box that appears, enter the name and location where you want to store the Web site. Double-click the SharePoint Team Site template, and wait for the background wizard to create a generic SharePoint Web site.

2 In the Folder List, double-click the Default.htm file to open the Web site's home page.

3 Double-click a list on the Web page to display the list's List View Properties dialog box.

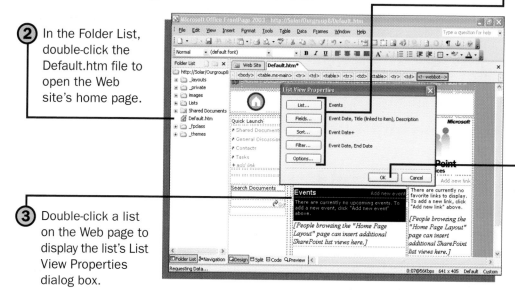

4 Click each button in turn to customize the properties for that list:

- List to select the type of list you want
- Fields to choose which fields of information you want to include in the Web site
- Sort to specify how you want the list to be sorted
- Filter to specify how you want the list to be filtered
- Options to specify the style you want for the list and the toolbar

5 Click OK, and then continue double-clicking lists and setting the properties for each list.

6 Add any other Web objects you want (an interactive button, for example), replace a placeholder picture with your own picture, or add formatting, such as a theme. Add any additional Web pages to your site, and then publish the site.

Creating a Web Page in Word

If you don't want to deal with the intricacies of FrontPage, you can use Word to create a simple Web page. The easiest way to do so is to take an existing Word document and convert it into a Web page. You can create two types of Web page in Word: a standard Web page, all of whose items except the text (pictures, for example) are stored in a separate folder; and a single-file Web page, all of whose items are contained in a single file. The standard page is usually better if you're going to include it in an existing Web site. The single-file Web page is the way to go if you want to e-mail the page to someone or post the page in a shared folder.

> **! TIP:** You can also start with a blank Web page in Word, in which case only the tools and formatting that can be saved in Web-page format will be available. Creating a document in Word and converting it into a Web page, however, ensures that you'll have a backup of the document in Word format.

Convert a Word Document into a Web Page

1 Create and save your document in Word as a Word document, or open an existing Word document.

2 Choose Options from the Tools menu, and, on the General tab of the Options dialog box, click the Web Options button to display the Web Options dialog box.

3 Make the settings that you want for your Web page on the different tabs of the dialog box, and click OK. Click OK to close the Web Options dialog box.

4 Choose Save As Web Page from the File menu to display the Save As dialog box.

5 Open the folder that will contain the Web page and all of its content.

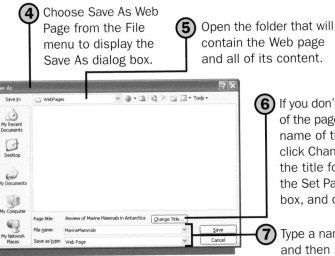

6 If you don't want the title of the page to be the file name of the document, click Change Title, enter the title for the page in the Set Page Title dialog box, and click OK.

7 Type a name for the file, and then save the page as a Single File Web Page or as a Web Page. Click Save.

8 If a dialog box appears, note the items that changed when you saved the page, and click Continue.

9 Preview the page in Word's Web Layout view.

Creating a Web Page in Excel

Getting your data up on the Web is as easy as posting your Excel worksheet or workbook as a Web page. You can specify whether the information is there for reading only, or whether you'll allow others to make any changes to the contents. To make sure that the Web page is working properly, you can publish and view it on your own computer (provided your computer is running Internet Information Services). Then, if you need to modify the worksheet or workbook, you can see the updates on the Web page. After you've finalized the content of the page, you can save the material as a Web page and post it on your main Web server.

> **TIP:** To modify the settings for the way the page works as a Web page, choose Options from the Tools menu, and, on the General tab of the Options dialog box, click the Web Options button.

> **TIP:** You need to publish the Web page to verify that any interactivity is working. If you're not including interactivity, you can preview the page by choosing Web Page Preview from the File menu.

Create an Excel Web Page

(1) Open the Excel workbook you want to use, and choose Save As Web Page from the File menu to display the Save As dialog box. Click the Publish button to display the Publish As Web Page dialog box.

(2) Specify the worksheet or workbook that you want to publish.

(3) Select this check box if you'll allow other people to be able to work with the data on the Web page, and specify the type of interactivity you want. (If you're publishing the entire workbook, interactivity is enabled automatically.)

(4) Click if you want to change the title of the page or the file's location and file name.

(5) Select these check boxes to view the published Web page in your Web browser, and to republish the Web page each time you modify and save the Excel workbook.

(6) Click Publish, and take a look at your Web page.

(7) Continue modifying the file in Excel if necessary, clicking the Save button on the Standard toolbar to save the changes. Keep republishing the page and reviewing it until you're satisfied with it.

Creating a Web Page in PowerPoint

A PowerPoint presentation on a Web site can be an impressive way to share information, allowing a viewer to run your slide show right in his or her Web browser. However, because of its large file size, a PowerPoint Web page can take forever to download unless the viewer has a fast Internet connection. Therefore, if you're going to publish the page on the Internet, you might consider simplifying the presentation so that it's mostly text. If you're posting the presentation on your company's intranet, however, where everyone has a fast connection, you can use pictures and special effects to your heart's content.

Create a PowerPoint Web Page

① Open your PowerPoint presentation in PowerPoint, and choose Web Page Preview from the File menu to display the presentation in your Web browser. Use the tools to preview the presentation.

② Return to PowerPoint, and make any changes you want so that the presentation looks the way you want in the Web browser.

③ With the presentation saved, choose Save As Web Page from the File menu, and click the Publish button to display the Publish As Web Page dialog box.

⑤ Click to specify whether you want navigation controls and animation to be shown, how you want the files to be stored, and whether you want pictures to be resized to fit whatever monitor resolution the viewer is using.

④ Specify what you want to include on the Web page, and which Web browsers are to be supported.

⑥ Click if you want to change the title of the Web page.

⑦ Click Browse to change the file name and/or file location, and to specify whether the presentation is to be saved as a single-file Web page or as a Web file with supporting files stored separately.

Select this check box to view the completed Web page in your Web browser.

⑧ Click Publish to create your Web page.

Creating a Data-Access Page

A data-access page is a Web page containing a form that's connected to an existing Access or SQL database and that gives others access over the Internet or an intranet to whatever parts of the database you want to display. You can set the database to Read-Only if you don't want the data to be changed and/or editable. Like most things in Access, setting all the properties and values can be quite complex. However, if you keep your project simple, the work will be manageable.

> **!TIP:** You can set access to the data at different levels, including permission for users to view or modify the data when connecting; different permission levels you set in the database; and permissions you set at the group level. Make sure you don't create conflicts in permissions; otherwise, users might not be able to access, view, or modify any of the data.

Create an Access Web Page

(1) With Access running, click Blank Data Access Page in the New File task pane. If the New File task pane isn't displayed, choose New from the File menu.

(7) Save the Web page to a location from which you can publish it on the Internet or on your intranet.

(4) Arrange the fields, and add other Web-page elements, including a title, objects, and formatting.

(5) Right-click the area that contains your data fields, and choose Group Level Properties from the shortcut menu.

(6) In the Group Level Properties dialog box that appears, specify whether you'll allow additions, deletions, or edits to be made to the data fields. Make any changes you want to the other properties, and click different elements of the page to set their properties.

(2) In the Select Data Source dialog box, double-click either Connect To New Data Source or New SQL Server Connection, and step through the Data Connection Wizard to connect to the database and set permissions for access to the data. The data-access page appears, listing the tables and queries in the database, and the fields for each table and query.

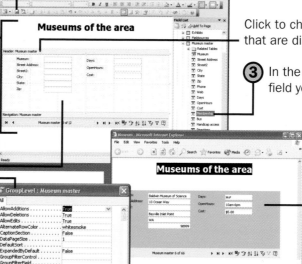

Click to change the sections that are displayed.

(3) In the Field List, double-click each field you want to include in the form.

(8) Click the View button to switch to Page view, and see how the form looks and works. Modify the form if necessary in Design view, and save the page. Run the page in your browser, and test it, test it, test it to make sure it works properly before you allow others access to it.

Creating a Web Site in Publisher

Publisher provides some excellent tools for creating a Web site, even if the site has only one page. Although you can use an existing Publisher publication that was designed for print, you'll find it much easier to start fresh with a publication that's specifically designed for the Web. Then, if you want to, you can simply cut and paste the items that you want to use from your original publication.

Create a Web Site

(1) In Publisher, in the New Publication task pane, click the Web-site type you want in the New From A Design section, and then click the design you want. If the New Publication task pane isn't displayed, choose New from the File menu to display it.

(2) If the Easy Web Site Builder dialog box doesn't appear automatically, click Add Functionality in the Web Site Options task pane to display the dialog box. Select the items you want to add to the Web site, and click OK.

(3) Specify how you want the Navigation bar, which provides links to the other pages of this Web site, to be displayed on all the pages.

(4) Click Page Content to go to the Page Content task pane if you want to change the page layout. Return to the Web Site Options task pane when you've finished.

(7) Click the Save button on the Standard toolbar to save the publication as a Publisher file so that it will be available for any later modifications.

(5) Use the tools on the Web Tools toolbar to customize your Web page.

(6) Replace the placeholder text and graphics with your own content.

(9) Return to your publication, make any changes you want to the Web site, and save it again.

(8) Click the Web Page Preview button on the Web Tools toolbar to preview the Web site in your Web browser.

> **! TIP:** If your Web service provider doesn't support direct connection and publishing from Publisher, choose Save As from the File menu. In the Save As Type list box, select Web Page, and click Save. You can then send the entire folder to your Web server.

> **! TIP:** If none of the available Web-site designs is what you want, click Blank Web Page in the New Publication task pane, and use the Publication Designs, Page Content, and Web Site Options task panes to create an original design for your Web page.

Publish It!

1 Choose Publish To The Web from the File menu. If a dialog box appears and tells you that you need a Web-hosting service, click OK to continue if you already have a Web service, or press the Esc key to cancel the publishing until you've signed up for a Web-hosting service.

2 In the Publish To The Web dialog box, locate your Web site, and click Save without changing the file name. If the Microsoft Office Publisher dialog box appears telling you that a filtered HTML version has been created, read the notice, and click OK.

3 Wait for the files to be uploaded.

4 Go to your Web site, and make sure that everything is working properly.

CAUTION: When you publish your Web site, Publisher gives the file a name. Don't change it unless you've been instructed to do so by the Web-site administrator, or your Web site might not be accessible on the Web server. If you're told that you need to use a specific file name, click the Web Page Options button on the Web Tools toolbar, and enter the name in the File Name box.

Creating a Calendar Web Page

If you want friends and coworkers to have access to your schedule, or if you want to publish a calendar of events for your group or organization, you can create a Web page based on your Outlook Calendar.

Publish Your Calendar

TIP: When you create a Calendar Web page, Outlook creates more than one file. If you're unable to connect directly to the Web site when you're creating the Calendar, create a new folder, save your Calendar Web page in that folder, and then transfer the folder to the Web site.

(1) In Outlook, display the Calendar you want to publish. If more than one Calendar is displayed, click the one you want to publish.

(2) Choose Save As Web Page from the File menu to display the Save As Web Page dialog box.

(3) Set the date range for the Calendar. The Calendar will show at least one month of dates, but only the appointments in the specified date range will be displayed.

(4) Select these check boxes if you want the Calendar to contain a pane with the appointment details, and if you want to have a graphic tiled as a background for the Calendar.

(5) Enter a title for the Calendar.

(6) Enter the Internet or intranet address where you're publishing the Calendar, and its file name.

(7) Select this check box if you want to preview the Calendar Web page.

(8) Click Save.

Working with HTML Code

As you create Web pages, FrontPage generates the Hypertext Markup Language (HTML) code for you. If you're feeling bold and adventurous, you can modify the code directly to expand the capabilities of your Web page. Most of the HTML content consists of a short piece of code, or *tag,* that identifies the type of content, followed by the content itself, and then another tag. Other parts of the code identify an object, such as a picture or a WebBot, and tag its formatting.

TIP: You don't need to split the window to edit one tag at a time. In Design view, click the item, whether it's a text paragraph or an object, and then open the tag at the top of the window. Choose Edit Tag to display the Quick Tag Editor, make your changes, and press Enter. However, if you like working on code by itself, click the Show Code View button at the bottom of the window to show only the code.

Review the Tags

(1) In FrontPage, with the page you want open in Design view, choose Reveal Tags from the View menu to display the tags in your Web page if they aren't already displayed.

(5) Point to the tag, and click the down arrow. Specify what you want to do with the tag.

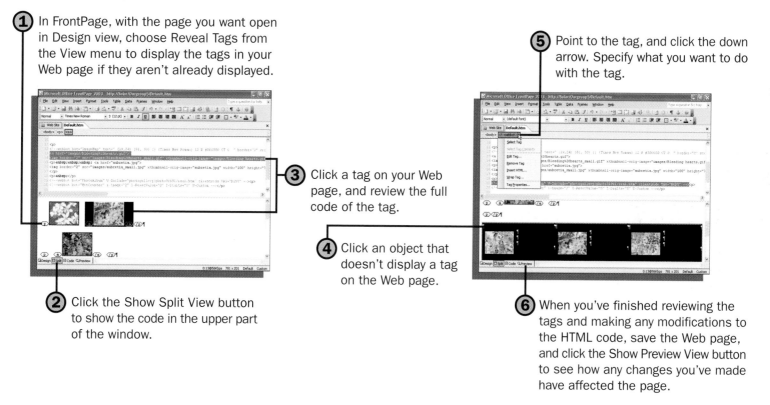

(3) Click a tag on your Web page, and review the full code of the tag.

(4) Click an object that doesn't display a tag on the Web page.

(2) Click the Show Split View button to show the code in the upper part of the window.

(6) When you've finished reviewing the tags and making any modifications to the HTML code, save the Web page, and click the Show Preview View button to see how any changes you've made have affected the page.

Double-Checking Your Web Site

You're almost ready to publish your Web site, and you've probably checked the spelling and grammar and made little tweaks to the fonts, pictures, and so on. But do you really have time to open every page, test every hyperlink, check out every component? And, if there are pages and files that are no longer being used in the Web site but are still stored there, how do you find them so that you can delete them and keep your Web site from ballooning into a monster size? The answer is to let FrontPage do the checking for you so that you can then spend your time fixing problems instead of looking for them.

Check the Site

(2) Review the information in the Site Summary report. If the Site Summary report isn't displayed, click the current report name, and choose Site Summary from the drop-down menu.

(3) Click a topic in the report to review the information about that topic.

(4) Right-click an item in the report, and choose the action you want to take from the shortcut menu.

(5) Click the report name, and choose Site Summary from the drop-down menu to return to your Web site's main summary.

(1) With your Web site open in FrontPage, click the Reports View button on the Web Site tab.

> **! TIP:** A great way to track the progress of your Web site's development is to use Tasks view to keep an interactive record of the progress and responsibilities related to managing each page of the Web site. That way, you can be certain that everyone who developed a page has signed off on it and that you won't be including any incomplete pages.

Review the Structure

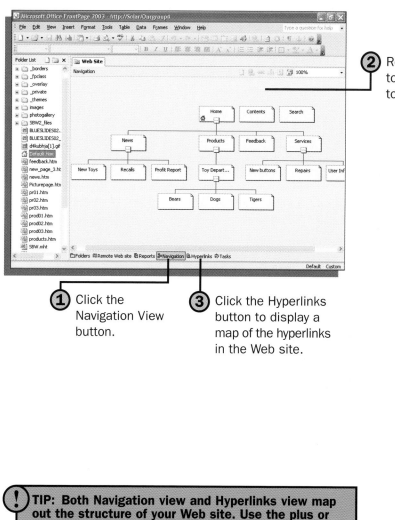

② Review the structure of your Web site, and, if you need to make any modifications to the structure, drag pages to new locations or delete unnecessary pages.

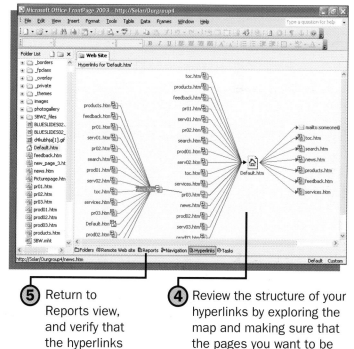

① Click the Navigation View button.

③ Click the Hyperlinks button to display a map of the hyperlinks in the Web site.

⑤ Return to Reports view, and verify that the hyperlinks and all the other elements are properly configured.

④ Review the structure of your hyperlinks by exploring the map and making sure that the pages you want to be linked are linked. Choose Recalculate Hyperlinks from the Tools menu, and, in the Recalculate Hyperlinks dialog box, click Yes to have all the hyperlinks updated. Review the hyperlinks again.

> **TIP: Both Navigation view and Hyperlinks view map out the structure of your Web site. Use the plus or minus sign to expand or collapse the map so that you can see specific sections of the map. At any time, you can review any Web page in Design view by double-clicking the page's icon on the map.**

Publishing Your Web Site

The way you publish your Web site depends on the way the hosting site is set up and the type of access permission you have. With direct access to a Web server, and with the proper permissions, you can connect directly to the Web site and upload updated or new files to the site. You can also use FTP (File Transfer Protocol) to send the files to an FTP site, or you can publish the files to a shared folder on a computer, and then host the Web site on your company's intranet.

Publish Your Files

1 With your finished Web site open in FrontPage, choose Publish Site from the File menu to display the Remote Web Site Properties dialog box.

2 Select the method you need to use to publish your Web site.

3 Enter the address of either the Web site, the FTP site, or the file folder.

4 Select this check box if you're connecting to a Web site that supports SSL encryption and if you want to encrypt the files during transfer for added security.

5 On the Optimize HTML tab, specify whether you want to optimize the HTML code and, if so, how.

6 On the Publishing tab, specify what is to be published and whether you want the changes to the site to be logged so that you can maintain a permanent record of your changes.

7 Click OK.

8 With the Local To Remote option selected, click Publish Web Site, and wait for the files to be transferred.

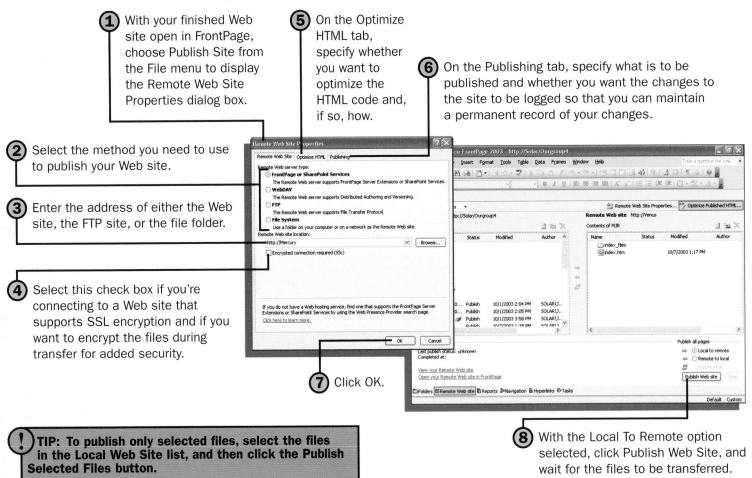

> **TIP:** To publish only selected files, select the files in the Local Web Site list, and then click the Publish Selected Files button.

15

Using Forms with InfoPath

Microsoft Office InfoPath 2003 has one purpose only: to gather and store information using online forms. With InfoPath, you can easily complete an existing form on line or create a form for your own specific purposes. Instead of providing tools to summarize the data you've gathered, InfoPath stores the data in a format that's usable by a variety of programs in the Microsoft Office System, as well as by some other programs. The information in an InfoPath form is stored in the XML format (more about that later in this section).

When you enter and save data on a form, InfoPath gives each piece of data an identifying tag. A form asking for your name might tag the data you entered—your name, for example—with a tag such as *employeename*. When that data file is used in an Office program that's been set up to use corresponding tags, InfoPath automatically inserts the data in the correct location. Fortunately, you don't need to know anything about XML to use InfoPath. You can fill out a form, print a blank or completed form, e-mail a form to someone, or gather information on a series of forms, and then let someone else worry about utilizing the data. In a corporate setting, if your organization has set up InfoPath, you'll probably find a library of forms on your network, each for a specific purpose such as a vacation request, and all you need to do is select and complete the form. If you're working in a smaller setting, or an appropriate form isn't available, you can use one of the forms that come with InfoPath, create your own form by customizing an existing form, create a form based on an existing data file or XML *schema*, or create a form from scratch.

What's Where in InfoPath?

The InfoPath program has two functions, each with its own structure. One part of InfoPath is designed for the filling out of forms by those who will be using the forms; the other part is designed for the creating of forms by those who have a great need to make other people fill out forms. Although the form structure looks like many other online forms, there are some special features that allow you to customize the way forms are filled out. Note the various ways you can complete the information on a form. You can use a Rich-Text box to enter formatted text; a Date Picker, in which a calendar helps you pick a date; and familiar components, such as a text box, a drop-down list, a check box, options buttons, and command buttons. A form can also include special types of tables,

and sections that help keep the form as compact as possible. A *repeating table,* for example, shows only a single row of a table, but you can easily expand the table to add as many rows of information as you need. A *repeating section* works in a similar manner, in that the section—which can contain several components, such as text boxes, check boxes, and whatever else is needed—shows only one set of these controls, but you can create additional sections to contain all the information you need. An *optional section* is hidden, except for a note telling you to click it if you need it. That way, the optional section isn't displayed unless you need to put information in that section.

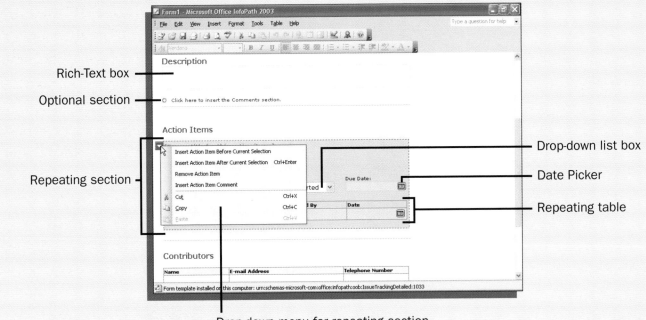

Rich-Text box

Optional section

Repeating section

Drop-down list box

Date Picker

Repeating table

Drop-down menu for repeating section

InfoPath provides a variety of tools that you can use when you're designing a form. Most of the form is based on layout tables that contain and align the controls you use in the form, and on sections that determine the behavior of the controls. You can use a variety of controls in the form—text boxes, list boxes, and so on—but, if you're ambitious, you can also insert command buttons to execute actions;

hyperlinks to take you to other locations in the same form, to jump to another form, or to transport you to just about anywhere you want to go, be it a Web page, a document, or a Help file; or pictures to add style or color to the form. When you add a control to a form, InfoPath assigns the control to a specific data tag in the behind-the-scenes XML structure. In tech-talk this is called *data binding*.

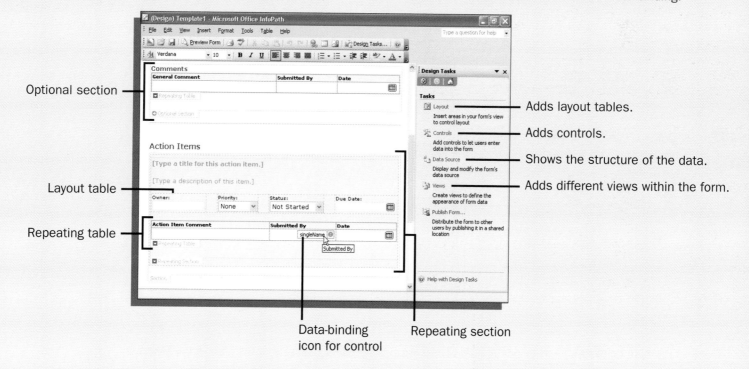

Optional section

Layout table

Repeating table

Adds layout tables.

Adds controls.

Shows the structure of the data.

Adds different views within the form.

Data-binding icon for control

Repeating section

Filling Out a Form

Filling out a form in InfoPath can be a fairly simple process, but, depending on the form's design, you might have to do a few things to get all the information entered. When you've finished filling out the form, you can check it for errors and then save it and, if necessary, send it off to whoever is responsible for reviewing and/or approving the completed form.

Enter the Information

(4) If there are other views for the form that should be completed at this point, choose another view from the View menu, and complete that view.

(2) Complete the first field of the form, pressing the Tab key to move to the next field.

(3) Continue moving through the form, and do any of the following:

- If a down arrow appears, click it, and choose any option you want.

- If the field is a section that's optionally displayed, click it only if you want to record information in that section.

- If the completed field is surrounded by a red border, and either a ScreenTip or a dialog box appears, it means that the field has failed the validation test, and you need to correct the indicated error.

TIP: A form can have more than one view. When you're filling out a form, you complete the first (default) view that appears when you open the form, and then you use any other views for additional details or follow-up information. Provided the form is properly designed, a command button or a hyperlink on the form will take you to the other views of the form, or the form will include instructions for switching to different views. However, you can also switch to another view by choosing it from View menu.

(1) In InfoPath, open the form from the Fill Out A Form task pane. If the task pane isn't displayed, choose Fill Out A Form from the File menu.

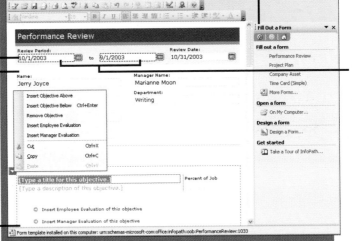

The red borders indicate that both these fields have failed the validation tests that were built into the form and that they probably contain errors.

Review and Save the Form

 ① If you ignored the indicated errors while you were filling out the form, choose Go To Next Error from the Tools menu to find any values that don't conform to the validation tests, and right-click the field for an explanation of the error.

Fields whose errors have been ignored

 ④ If you want to fill out another form using the same template, click the Fill Out A Form button to open another copy of the form, all ready to be completed.

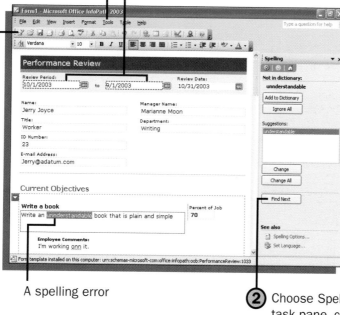

A spelling error

③ Do any or all of the following:
- Click the Print button on the Standard toolbar to print a copy of the form.
- Choose Save from the File menu to save the data to a shared folder or SharePoint Web site.
- Click the Send To Mail Recipient button on the Standard toolbar to send the completed form and the XML data to an e-mail recipient.
- Choose Submit from the File menu to send the data if the form is attached to a database or a Web service.
- Choose Save As from the File menu, and save a copy of the data to a local folder for your records.

② Choose Spelling from the Tools menu, and, in the Spelling task pane, choose Find Next. Correct any spelling errors, and continue searching for errors until the spelling check is completed.

TIP: When you e-mail a form, the completed form is sent in HTML formatting, showing all the completed fields. The XML data is sent as an attachment, and it can be used to modify the contents of the form or can be processed for other purposes.

SEE ALSO: For information about XML, see "What Is XML?" on page 280.

Creating a Form

There are three basic ways to create a form: You can use an existing XML or database file, you can use an existing form and modify it, or you can create a form from scratch. Once you've set up the form, it's stored as a form template, which you then use to generate the actual form.

Start a Form

(3) Click the Save button on the Standard toolbar.

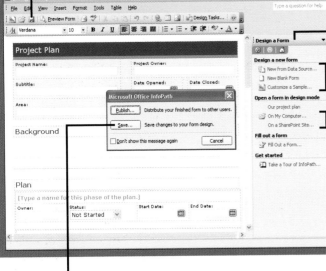

(4) Click Save in the Microsoft Office InfoPath dialog box, and use the Save As dialog box to save your work in progress.

TIP: To create a section for information that doesn't appear unless the person who'll be filling out the form chooses to complete it, you can insert an optional section and add controls to it. To create a table that initially displays only one line but which can be expanded by the user, insert a repeating table. To create a section that the user can add from a menu, insert a repeating section.

SEE ALSO: For information about XML, see "What Is XML?" on page 280.

(1) In InfoPath, choose Design A Form from the File menu to display the Design A Form task pane.

(2) Select the type of form you want to create:

- New From Data Source to create a form from an XML schema or a data file. (You can also create a form from a SQL or Access data file by completing the Data Source Setup Wizard.)
- New Blank Form to create a form from scratch.
- Customize A Sample to open and modify one of the sample forms that came with InfoPath.
- On My Computer to open and modify an existing form on your computer or in a shared network folder.
- On A SharePoint Site to open and modify a form from the Forms Library on a SharePoint site.

TIP: To prevent the person who'll be filling out the form from modifying the form template, choose Form Options from the Tools menu while you're designing the form, select the Enable Protection check box, and click OK.

Modify the Form

(8) Choose Publish from the File menu, and step through the Publishing Wizard to publish the form template to a shared folder, to a SharePoint Forms Library, or to a Web server for others to use.

(7) Click Preview Form to make sure the form looks the way you want.

(!) **TIP:** If you want to draw attention to an abnormal value in a range but don't want to mark it as an error, use conditional formatting instead of a validation rule.

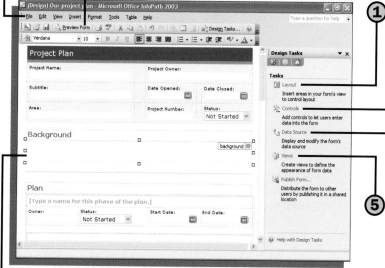

(1) In the Design Tasks task pane, click Layout to add a layout table to your form. Use the Merge And Split Cells section in the Layout task pane to customize the layout table.

(2) Click Controls to display the Controls task pane, and add controls to the form—a text box, a picture, or a repeating table, for example.

(4) Click Data Source to display the Data Source task pane so that you can review and, if necessary, modify the structure of the data source or directly modify the properties of an existing control.

(5) Click Views to display the Views task pane if you want to create additional views of the form, to change the properties of each view, or to create a printed version of the view.

(6) If necessary, move and/or resize any elements on your form.

(3) Double-click one of the controls you added, and complete the Properties dialog box for that control to set its field name, type, default value, format, validation values, placeholder text, size, ScreenTip, tab order, and access key. Click OK when you've finished, and repeat for each control you've added.

(!) **TIP:** To modify a completed form, open the saved form (not the form template), make your changes, and then save the form again.

Using InfoPath Data

In most instances, completing and saving or printing a form are all you'll want to do with the InfoPath data. However, the power of using XML code lets you do a lot more with the data if you want. For example, you can merge the data from different forms in order to review the data from multiple forms in a single table.

Merge Data from Different Forms

1 Fill out, save, and close a series of forms that have merge data enabled and that have repeating sections, repeating tables, or Rich-Text boxes.

2 Open a blank form based on the same template as the series of forms by choosing Fill Out A Form from the File menu, and then choose the template in the Fill Out A Form task pane.

CAUTION: A form can't be merged unless merging was enabled when the form was designed. To enable merging in a form, with the form in Design view, choose Form Options from the Tools menu, select Enable Form Merging on the General tab, and click OK.

SEE ALSO: For information about XML, see "What Is XML?" on page 280.

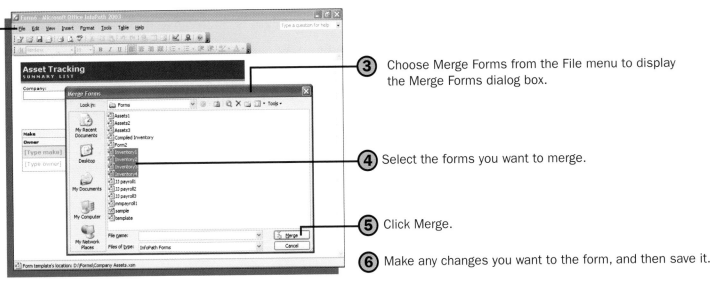

3 Choose Merge Forms from the File menu to display the Merge Forms dialog box.

4 Select the forms you want to merge.

5 Click Merge.

6 Make any changes you want to the form, and then save it.

Review the Data in Excel

(1) Open the form that contains the data you want to export.

! **TIP:** You can also export the data to a single-file Web page if you want to publish the information on the Internet or on your intranet.

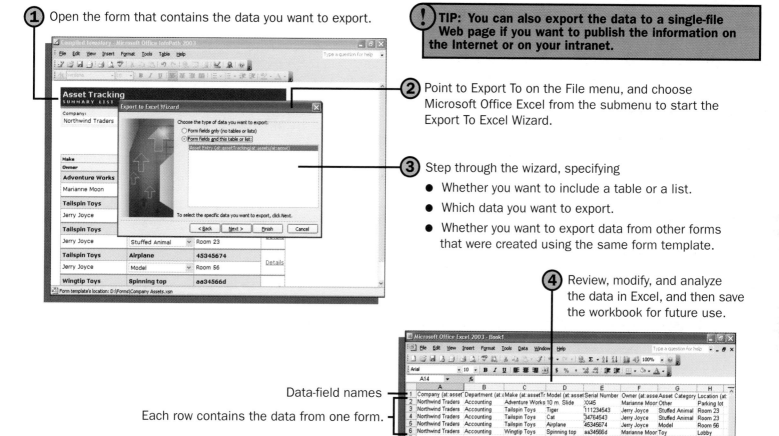

(2) Point to Export To on the File menu, and choose Microsoft Office Excel from the submenu to start the Export To Excel Wizard.

(3) Step through the wizard, specifying

- Whether you want to include a table or a list.
- Which data you want to export.
- Whether you want to export data from other forms that were created using the same form template.

(4) Review, modify, and analyze the data in Excel, and then save the workbook for future use.

Data-field names

Each row contains the data from one form.

What Is XML?

XML (Extensible Markup Language—yes, the "X" comes from "eXtensible") is a format and code whose purpose is to help structure files and data so that the information they contain can be processed, sorted, extracted, queried, and in other ways manipulated. If that's all you can stand to read about it, now's a good time to turn to another page!

XML is an expansion of and an improvement upon HTML (HyperText Markup Language), which is used to create standard Web pages. In HTML code, predefined tags identify the various elements of the Web page—one tag for the beginning of a paragraph and another tag for the end of the paragraph; a tag to identify an image or a graphic; and so on. XML uses tags too, but, unlike HTML's tags, they aren't pre-defined. Instead, a program that uses XML tags the data. So, when you're working with a program in XML—whether what you're working on is a Microsoft Office Word document, an Excel workbook, or a FrontPage Web site—the resulting file will have all sorts of XML tags attached to it, although you won't necessarily be aware of them.

Fear Not the Schema

There's another part of the XML world that's fairly apparent in Office files: the XML schema. This somewhat intimidating term defines the functionality of XML in a file. The schema describes each type of entry—a number, some text, a date or time, for example—and a programmer can specify items such as the default value, validation tests, and even little pieces of programming that you can run or that might run in the background without your even knowing about them.

Arrgh! Why do you need to know this? Actually, in most cases, you don't. It's the programmer's responsibility to create and modify the XML schemas. However, there are some instances in which you might run into an XML schema. If you're creating a new document in Word that will be using

XML resources, for example, you might need to load the proper XML schema into Word. And if you're custom-designing an InfoPath form, you might want to modify the schema a bit to have the form perfectly customized for your needs.

XML and InfoPath

InfoPath is really just a utility that serves as your connection to XML. When you create an InfoPath form, you're creating an XML schema. All the fields in the form are contained in that schema. When you fill out a form, you're automatically recording the data in an XML text file. When you take an XML file and load it into InfoPath, you're creating a new form that incorporates all the data from the XML file.

Putting XML to Work

So, if you've gotten this far in your reading, you're probably wondering how you can make XML work for you. Let's say you've used Word to routinely send personalized letters to your customers or to any large group of people. You've taken a lot of time to format the letters, and perhaps you've included some ancillary information about your company. Without using XML, if you wanted to go back and analyze the data—whom you've contacted and how often, what details you included, and so on—you'd need to enter the information twice: once in Word and again in a data-analysis program such as Excel or Access. But, with XML and a custom XML schema, you can save all the significant data in the Word document as an XML file. Now you can place the XML data in Excel or Access without having to reenter the numbers. This might not be a real time-saver if we're talking about only one or two letters, but think about an office that generates scores of letters every day. In computerese, this is some serious data mining!

16 Taking Notes with OneNote

Microsoft Office OneNote 2003 is simple but difficult, intuitive but confusing, elegant but ungainly. To what does it owe its split personality? It's not the program that's at fault—it's our thinking about the way a program should work. We've learned that everything is linear on a computer: One word follows another, one line follows another, one paragraph follows another. We've also learned that everything is digital on a computer—a letter is simply a character in a specific font at a specific size. However, when we're not in the realm of computers and are jotting down our ideas on paper, those rules don't apply. Sure, we often take notes on consecutive lines, word following word, paragraph following paragraph. But we're also apt to jot down a quick note where there's some space, maybe circle that note for emphasis, add a few more bits of information in the margin, draw a little stick person, and so on.

OneNote is more like that piece of paper than it is like a computer program. Think about it like that, and you'll find it easy to understand and use. If you approach it the way you approach any other program, you might have trouble seeing how it could be useful or save you time. Free yourself from the linear thinking of a computer program and envision OneNote as that familiar notebook on whose pages you can jot down whatever you want, wherever you want. After you've become comfortable with this new way of taking notes, you can explore the digital side of OneNote—check your spelling, copy information to other programs, e-mail your notes, and, if you have a Tablet PC, change your handwriting into computer characters in a specific font and font size.

What's Where in OneNote?

OneNote has two views—the full Notebook view and the smaller Side Notes view. The two views, however, are connected. For example, when you create a side note in the little Side Notes window, the note becomes a new page in the Side Notes section of your OneNote Notebook. When you add a side note to your Notebook, you can review the note in the little Side Notes window. When you maximize the Side Notes window, you'll see your whole OneNote Notebook; restore the size of the maximized window, and you're back to the little Side Notes window.

Click to see a list of all the sections in the Notebook.

The OneNote Notebook

Tabs for the different sections of the Notebook

The title of the current page

Use text to search for a specific note.

Tabs for the different pages in the active section

The page header contains the page title and the date and time the note was created.

The little Side Notes window stays on top of all other program windows unless you change the default setting.

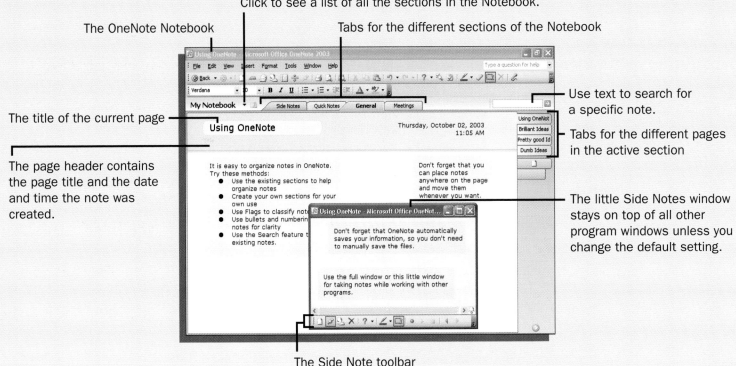

The Side Note toolbar

Typing a Note

OneNote was originally designed primarily as a tool for pen-based computers such as the Tablet PC, but it has proved its functionality for those of us still using keyboards.

> **TIP:** Your notes are automatically saved, so you don't need to save them manually. This can take a bit of getting used to!

Create a Note

(1) With OneNote running, click the tab of the section you want to use.

(3) Type a title for this page if the page header is displayed.

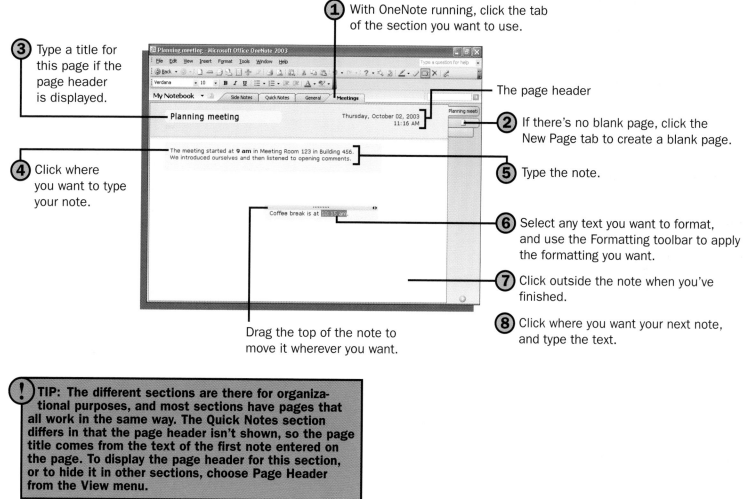

The page header

(2) If there's no blank page, click the New Page tab to create a blank page.

(4) Click where you want to type your note.

(5) Type the note.

(6) Select any text you want to format, and use the Formatting toolbar to apply the formatting you want.

(7) Click outside the note when you've finished.

(8) Click where you want your next note, and type the text.

Drag the top of the note to move it wherever you want.

> **TIP:** The different sections are there for organizational purposes, and most sections have pages that all work in the same way. The Quick Notes section differs in that the page header isn't shown, so the page title comes from the text of the first note entered on the page. To display the page header for this section, or to hide it in other sections, choose Page Header from the View menu.

Using a Side Note

The Side Notes window is a great place for quickly jotting down or recording your notes. The window is always at hand for easy access to all your side notes.

Use the Side Notes Window

TRY THIS: Create a side note in the Side Notes window. Close the window. Open your OneNote Notebook, and open the Side Notes section. Click the page tab of the side note you just created, which you can see has used the beginning text of your note for the page title. Type a new descriptive title in the title section of the page.

(1) In the Notification area of the Windows taskbar, click the Open New Side Note icon to display the Side Notes window.

11:22 AM

(2) Type your note.

(4) Close the window or move it out of the way when you've finished.

With the Keep Window On Top button cli...

With the Keep Window On Top button clicked, this window will stay on top of other program windows, so you can easily take notes just by clicking in this window.

Deletes the entire page.

Moves the current page to a different section.

Keeps the Side Notes window on top of all other program windows.

Activates text selection.

Records an audio note.

Plays an audio note.

Stops playing an audio note.

(3) Use the buttons on the Side Note toolbar to manage your notes.

Displays next page of side notes.

Creates a new Side Notes page.

Designates a pen type for drawing or handwriting.

Displays previous page of side notes.

Applies different types of flags to the note.

TIP: If the Open New Side Note icon isn't visible on the Windows taskbar, in OneNote, choose Options from the Tools menu, and, in the Options dialog box, click Other in the Category section. Select the check box to place the OneNote icon on the taskbar, and click OK.

Drawing a Note

OneNote recognizes two types of penmanship—handwriting and drawing. If you're using a Tablet PC, you can convert your handwriting into text that you can format, search, spell-check, and use in other programs. Without a Tablet PC, you can still use handwriting and do some drawing, but the handwriting won't be converted into text. Although you can write and draw on a standard computer using your mouse, the results will be a lot better if you use some type of pen device—a pen and a digitizing pad, for example.

Draw a Note

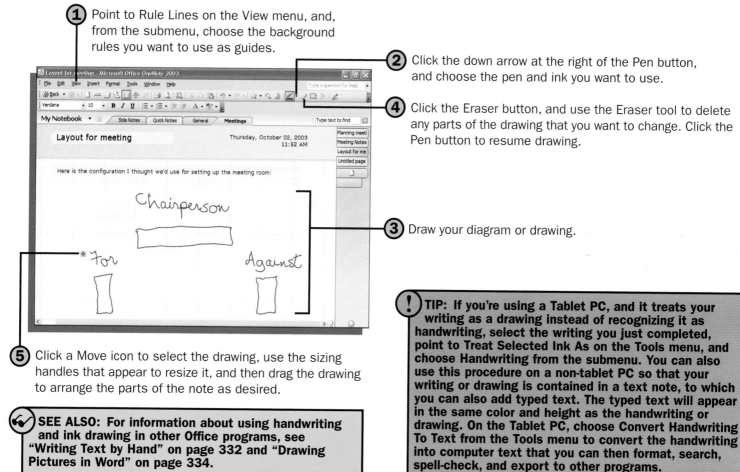

(1) Point to Rule Lines on the View menu, and, from the submenu, choose the background rules you want to use as guides.

(2) Click the down arrow at the right of the Pen button, and choose the pen and ink you want to use.

(4) Click the Eraser button, and use the Eraser tool to delete any parts of the drawing that you want to change. Click the Pen button to resume drawing.

(3) Draw your diagram or drawing.

(5) Click a Move icon to select the drawing, use the sizing handles that appear to resize it, and then drag the drawing to arrange the parts of the note as desired.

SEE ALSO: For information about using handwriting and ink drawing in other Office programs, see "Writing Text by Hand" on page 332 and "Drawing Pictures in Word" on page 334.

TIP: If you're using a Tablet PC, and it treats your writing as a drawing instead of recognizing it as handwriting, select the writing you just completed, point to Treat Selected Ink As on the Tools menu, and choose Handwriting from the submenu. You can also use this procedure on a non-tablet PC so that your writing or drawing is contained in a text note, to which you can also add typed text. The typed text will appear in the same color and height as the handwriting or drawing. On the Tablet PC, choose Convert Handwriting To Text from the Tools menu to convert the handwriting into computer text that you can then format, search, spell-check, and export to other programs.

Recording a Note

A great hands-free way to record a note is to create an audio note. Each page of your Notebook has its own audio file, so any notes that you create on a page are recorded in that page's audio file. You can then play back your audio notes.

Record a Note

 Type or write any information you want in the note.

Start/Stop Recording button

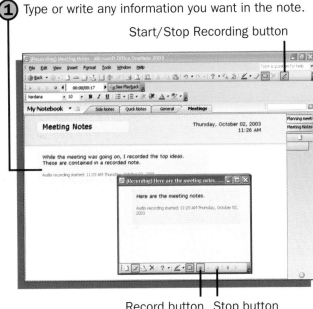

Record button   Stop button

(2) Depending on which view of OneNote you're using, do either of the following:

- In the OneNote Notebook, click the Start/Stop Recording button on the Standard toolbar.
- In the Side Notes window, click the Record button on the Side Note toolbar.

(3) Record your note.

(4) Click either the Start/Stop Recording button on the Standard toolbar or the Stop button on the Side Note toolbar.

Play Back Your Note

(1) Move the mouse pointer over the note that you want to play.

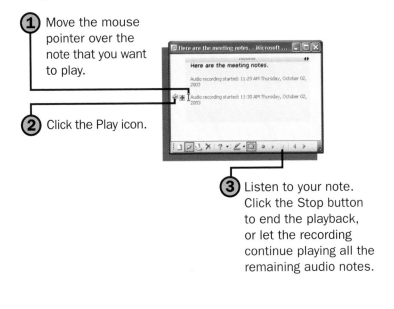

(2) Click the Play icon.

(3) Listen to your note. Click the Stop button to end the playback, or let the recording continue playing all the remaining audio notes.

TIP: Remember that you need a microphone to record a note, and speakers or a headset to play back the note.

Formatting a Note

If you don't really care about the way your notes look, you can simply leave them as they are, just as you'd leave them in a paper notebook. However, if you want to, you can improve both the organization and the readability of your notes by changing fonts and font sizes, adding bullets and numbering, and using an outlining hierarchy.

> **TIP: When you point to an item in a list, a four-headed arrow pointer appears. Use this pointer to drag the item to a different level in the hierarchy, to a different position in the list, to a different list in your note, or to a different note.**

Format Your Note

1 In your OneNote Notebook, select the text whose font or emphasis settings you want to change, and use the tools on the Formatting toolbar to apply the formatting.

3 If you want a bulleted or numbered list, click the down arrow at the right of the Bullets or the Numbering button, and choose the type of bullet or the numbering style you want to use. You can apply the bullets or numbering before you type the list, or after you've completed it, by selecting the text before you click the appropriate button.

5 Click in a note, and use the Expand or the Collapse button on the Outlining toolbar to reveal or hide different levels of a hierarchical list. If the Outlining toolbar isn't displayed, point to Toolbars on the View menu, and choose Outlining from the submenu.

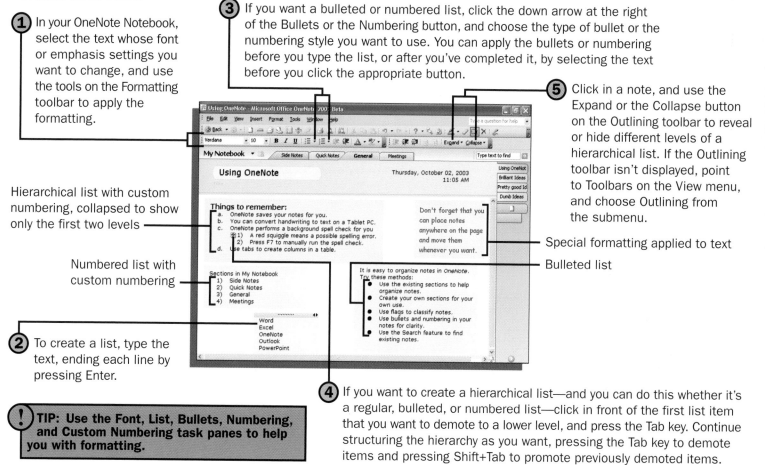

Hierarchical list with custom numbering, collapsed to show only the first two levels

Numbered list with custom numbering

Special formatting applied to text

Bulleted list

2 To create a list, type the text, ending each line by pressing Enter.

> **TIP: Use the Font, List, Bullets, Numbering, and Custom Numbering task panes to help you with formatting.**

4 If you want to create a hierarchical list—and you can do this whether it's a regular, bulleted, or numbered list—click in front of the first list item that you want to demote to a lower level, and press the Tab key. Continue structuring the hierarchy as you want, pressing the Tab key to demote items and pressing Shift+Tab to promote previously demoted items.

Classifying Your Notes

A jumbled hodgepodge of notes makes it difficult for you to keep track of meeting notes, questions, ideas, and other bits and pieces of information. A useful way to track your notes is to classify them with flags and then review them by their flag classifications.

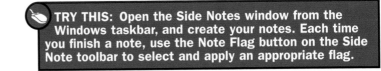

TRY THIS: Open the Side Notes window from the Windows taskbar, and create your notes. Each time you finish a note, use the Note Flag button on the Side Note toolbar to select and apply an appropriate flag.

Flag Your Notes

(1) Point to Toolbars on the View menu, and choose Note Flags to display the Note Flag toolbar if it isn't already displayed.

(3) Click the Note Flag button you want to use.

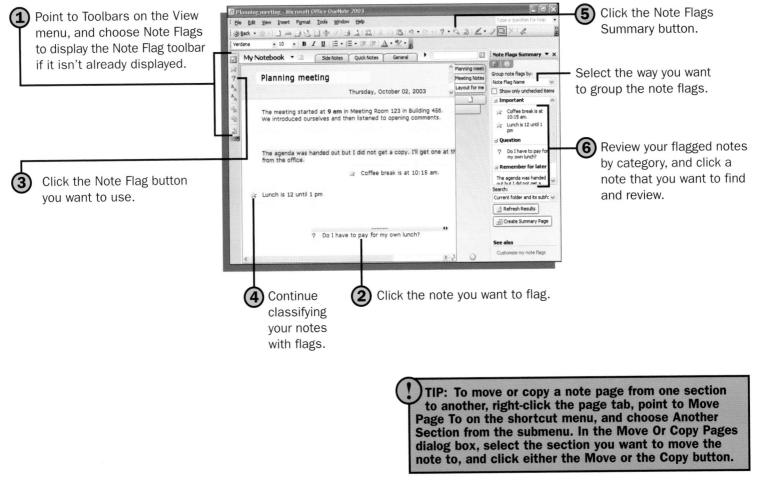

(5) Click the Note Flags Summary button.

Select the way you want to group the note flags.

(6) Review your flagged notes by category, and click a note that you want to find and review.

(4) Continue classifying your notes with flags.

(2) Click the note you want to flag.

> **! TIP:** To move or copy a note page from one section to another, right-click the page tab, point to Move Page To on the shortcut menu, and choose Another Section from the submenu. In the Move Or Copy Pages dialog box, select the section you want to move the note to, and click either the Move or the Copy button.

Transferring Information

One of OneNote's very nice abilities is gathering formatted text or pictures from other programs that you might want to use in your notes or in a different program. You can then transfer whatever material you have in OneNote, whether it's from another program or from your own notes, to other programs.

CAUTION: Most material transfers correctly from OneNote to another program, but some items—a table copied from an Excel worksheet, for example—won't transfer from OneNote to Excel or Word without a substantial loss of formatting. Also, an object in a program, such as an Excel chart, will transfer only as a picture instead of as an object.

Drag Your Material to Another Location

(1) Open a Side Notes window, and then open the program whose material you want to transfer.

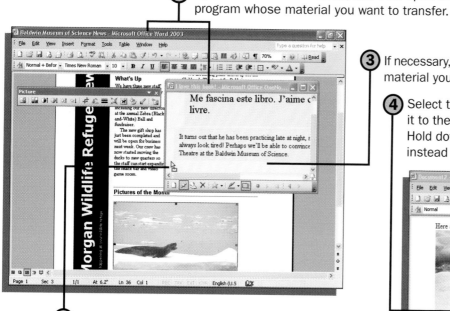

(2) Select the information you want from the program, and drag it into the Side Notes window. To copy the material instead of moving it, hold down the Ctrl key while you drag.

(3) If necessary, edit, reformat, or otherwise customize the transferred material you copied.

(4) Select the material in the Side Notes window, and drag it to the location where you want it in the other program. Hold down the Ctrl key while you drag if you want to copy instead of move the material.

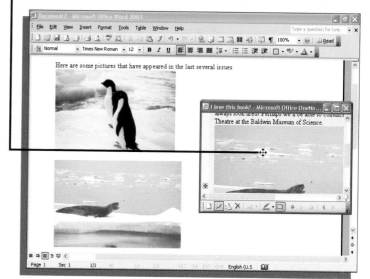

Distributing Notes

Now that you have all your notes organized, how are you going to distribute them to other people, if that's what you want or need to do with them? You could always print them or publish them as a single-file Web page, but one of the easiest ways to distribute them is to send them as Outlook e-mail. That way, the notes are converted into HTML format as the body of the e-mail so that even recipients who don't have OneNote can read them. The OneNote page is then sent as an attachment to the e-mail message so that recipients who do have OneNote can modify the notes in OneNote.

> **! TIP:** You can save an entire section of your OneNote Notebook to a SharePoint Web site or to a shared folder. That way, anyone who has OneNote on his or her computer, and has access to the shared location, will be able to access all the notes in that section. After you've saved the section to the new location, you'll see a new tab at the top of your OneNote Notebook that's a shortcut to the shared notes.

E-Mail Your Notes

(2) Click the E-Mail button on the Standard toolbar.

(3) Complete the addressing information.

(4) Click Send A Copy.

The OneNote file

(1) In OneNote, click the page you want to e-mail.

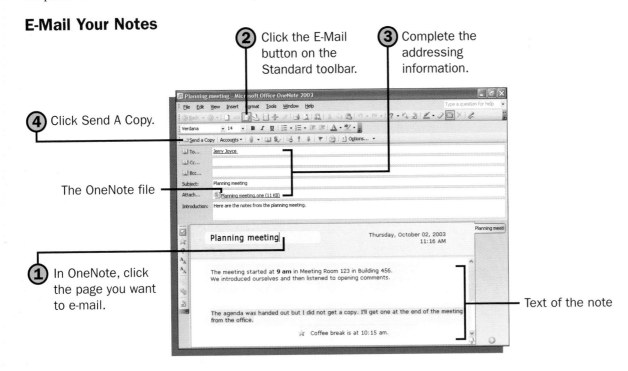

Text of the note

> **! TIP:** To send multiple pages of notes, hold down the Ctrl key as you click the page tabs within a section before you click the E-Mail button.

17 Exchanging Information Among Programs

Each of the programs in the Microsoft Office System was designed to do a specific job, and to do it superbly. However, there are times when the *interoperability* of the programs—that is, the way they work together to enhance each other's performance—can give you even better results than using a single program. And, because of the similarities in structure and functionality among all the Office programs, you'll find that working with more than one program at a time is just as simple as working in a single program. The interaction among programs is almost seamless, and the results are well worth a few extra clicks!

In this section, we'll describe why you might want to exchange information among programs, and then we'll walk you through a few procedures so that you can see how well the programs work together. Let's say that every month you write a company newsletter in Word. It looks fine, but you'd like to give it a more polished look. You could do that in Word, but you don't know much about designing a layout and you don't have time to experiment. Just choose one of Publisher's layout designs for newsletters, and insert your newsletter's text and pictures. The result is a professional looking publication that you'll be proud of. Another example: You're developing a PowerPoint slide show and writing the text for the slides and handouts. In Word, create the look you want for the text, using the formatting, grammar checking, and other tools that aren't available in PowerPoint, and then send the formatted text to PowerPoint. These are only two short examples of many more good ideas you'll find in the pages that follow.

Inserting Excel Data into a Document, Publication, or Presentation

Microsoft Office Excel 2003 is a great tool for collecting and analyzing data, but the information contained in an Excel spreadsheet is often easiest to understand when it's presented along with some explanations or supplemental information. To that end, you can integrate the Excel information into a Microsoft Office Word document, Publisher publication, or PowerPoint presentation. You can include the Excel data in one of several ways. If the Excel information is static—that is, your data collection is complete and the numbers won't change—you can insert the data into a Word document as a table or as text. If your data collection and analysis are still in progress and the information might change, you can link the data to the original Excel file so that any changes to the Excel data will appear in your document, publication, or presentation. If, however, the data or the analysis might change but you won't be able to access the original Excel file, or if you don't want the original Excel file to be changed or played around with by anyone else who has access to it, you can copy the entire Excel worksheet into your document, publication, or presentation, and still use the spreadsheet features to adjust the data.

Copy the Data

(1) In the Excel worksheet, select and copy the cells you want.

(2) In Word, Publisher, or PowerPoint, click in the paragraph, page, or slide where you want to insert the data, and choose Paste Special from the Edit menu to display the Paste Special dialog box.

(3) Specify whether or not you want the inserted table to be linked to the original Excel file. The Paste option inserts data without any connection to the original Excel file. The Paste Link option inserts the data and creates a link to the original Excel file. To link to the original Excel file, make sure that you name and save the file before you copy and link to it. (You can use only certain formats to insert a linked file.)

(4) Select the format you want for the inserted item. Each program offers different choices for the format of the inserted data. Use the information in the Results area to determine the effect of each format.

(5) Click OK.

Inserts a table with Excel formatting.

Inserts data as text with no formatting.

Inserts a table that has Excel formatting but can be reformatted in the receiving program.

Inserts data as an image of the selected portion of the Excel worksheet.

Inserts an object that contains all the Excel information.

Edit the Data

(1) Do any of the following:

- If you pasted the data as an Excel object, double-click the object to open it in your program, and edit the data in the worksheet that appears. Click outside the object to close it.

- If you paste-linked the data as an Excel object, double-click the object to open the original Excel file in Excel, and make your changes in that worksheet. Save and close the workbook when you've finished.

- If you paste-linked the data into Word using a different format—Formatted Text, for example—open the original Excel file, make changes to the worksheet, and save the workbook.

- If you pasted the data in any other format, make the changes to the data in your program. The changes won't be made automatically in the original Excel worksheet. Changes to the Excel worksheet won't be reflected in the data in your document, publication, or presentation.

(2) Position and format the inserted table or object as desired.

(3) Save your document, publication, or presentation.

Results

After completion of the study, we found that the scores ranged from 72 to 42, as shown in the table below.

Student	Exam 1	Exam 2	Exam 3	Average
Robert	55	61	46	54
Jim	46	65	53	55
John Z.	46	54	64	55
Marianne	62	61	45	56
Jenny	64	63	42	57
Roberta	44	72	54	57
James	62	58	55	59
John A.	55	77	44	59
Rick	59	66	50	59
Beth	62	82	48	64

Double-click to Edit Microsoft Office Excel Worksheet

! TIP: When you insert an Excel object, you can work with the worksheet in an Excel window by right-clicking the object in your document, publication, or presentation, pointing to Worksheet Object on the shortcut menu (Microsoft Office Excel Worksheet Object in Publisher), and choosing Open from the submenu. When you've finished, choose Close & Return from the File menu.

TRY THIS: Paste the Excel object. Click to select it, and drag a sizing handle. Note that the size of the text increases. Double-click the object to activate it, and drag a sizing handle. Note that the number of rows and columns that are displayed has changed. Click outside the object to deactivate it.

Inserting an Excel Chart into a Document, Publication, or Presentation

If the final results of your data are contained in an Excel worksheet, but you want to display the data as a chart, you can copy the chart into your Word document, Publisher publication, or PowerPoint presentation. You can insert the chart in one of three ways: as a picture; as a linked Excel object so that changes to the chart in the Excel file will be updated in the chart in your document, publication, or presentation; or as an unlinked (or embedded) Excel object so that the chart resides in your Word, Publisher, or PowerPoint file. The last option lets you edit the chart as necessary, and you no longer need the original Excel file.

Insert a Chart

1 In Excel, create and format your chart. Select and copy it.

2 In Word, Publisher, or PowerPoint, click where you want the chart to appear, and choose Paste Special from the Edit menu to display the Paste Special dialog box.

3 In the Paste Special dialog box, choose one of the following to specify how you want to insert the chart:

- Picture if you're not going to edit the chart and its data.
- Microsoft Office Excel Chart Object, with the Paste option selected, to incorporate all the Excel data so that you can edit the data without access to the original Excel file.
- Microsoft Office Excel Chart Object, with the Paste Link option selected, if you'll need to edit the data and you have access to the original Excel file. If you're linking to the Excel chart, make sure that you've named and saved the Excel file before you insert it.

4 Click OK.

5 Position and format the object as you want.

6 Save your document, publication, or presentation.

> **TIP:** Excel provides many powerful formatting tools. Be sure to format the chart so that it looks the way you want before you insert it. You might need to change the size of the inserted chart to clearly see all the formatting you've applied.

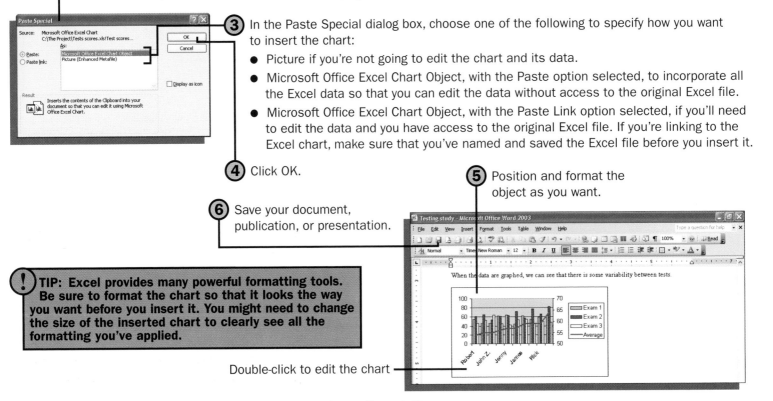

Double-click to edit the chart

Analyzing a Word Table in Excel

You can use Word to generate good-looking tables that present your data cleanly and clearly. However, Word isn't the best tool for summarizing and analyzing that data. If, after you've created a table in Word, you realize that you need to do a bit more analysis of the data, take it to the data-analysis expert: Excel.

TIP: You can also analyze a table from Publisher or PowerPoint in Excel, but in most cases you'll want to have the tables in their final form before you place them in your publication or presentation.

Analyze a Table

(1) In Word, select the table, and click the Cut button on the Standard toolbar (or press Ctrl+X).

Here is a summary of our sales for the first half of the year.

	North	South	East	West
January	10,111	22,100	13,270	10,800
February	13,400	24,050	15,670	21,500
March	14,221	22,145	12,225	18,333
April	22,001	28,575	14,147	15,874
May	15,557	29,447	12,367	21,045
June	9,099	18,451	14,589	9,483

(2) Switch to a blank Excel worksheet, and click the Paste button on the Standard toolbar (or press Ctrl+V) to insert the data from Word.

Microsoft Office Excel 2003 - Sales reviewed

	North	South	East	West	Average	Stnd Dev.
January	10,111	22,100	13,270	10,800	14,070	5,522
February	13,400	24,050	15,670	21,500	18,655	4,957
March	14,221	22,145	12,225	18,333	16,731	4,415
April	22,001	28,575	14,147	15,874	20,149	6,550
May	15,557	29,447	12,367	21,045	19,604	7,477
June	9,099	18,451	14,589	9,483	12,906	4,464
Total	84,389	144,768	82,268	97,035	102,115	29,173

(3) Make whatever changes you want to the table, and save the file.

(5) Click in the Word document to place the insertion point where you want to insert the table, and click the Paste button.

Here is a summary of our sales for the first half of the year.

	North	South	East	West	Average	Stnd Dev.
January	10,111	22,100	13,270	10,800	14,070	5,522
February	13,400	24,050	15,670	21,500	18,655	4,957
March	14,221	22,145	12,225	18,333	16,731	4,415
April	22,001	28,575	14,147	15,874	20,149	6,550
May	15,557	29,447	12,367	21,045	19,604	7,477
June	9,099	18,451	14,589	9,483	12,906	4,464
Total	84,389	144,768	82,268	97,035	102,115	29,173

(4) Select the cells that contain the data you want to return to your Word document, and click the Copy button on the Standard toolbar.

(7) Make any changes you want to the formatting of the table, and save the document.

(6) Click the Paste Options button, and choose one of the following to specify how you want to paste the table:

- Match Destination Table Style to insert the table without staying connected to the Excel worksheet

- Match Destination Table Style And Link To Excel to maintain the connection to Excel so that you can continue to make changes in Excel that will appear in the Word table

Using Word to Prepare PowerPoint Text

When you're developing a PowerPoint presentation, you'll find that preparing the text (but not other content such as tables and pictures) in Word and then sending it to PowerPoint is the easiest and most flexible way to go. You can take advantage of Word's multitude of features to create exactly the look you want for the text of your presentation. As you create your document in Word, you can use the heading styles to tell PowerPoint how you want the information interpreted.

Create the Presentation

1 In Word, choose Options from the Tools menu, and, on the View tab of the Options dialog box, set a value such as 1" in the Style Area Width box. Click OK.

3 With the document saved, point to Send To on the File menu, and choose Microsoft Office PowerPoint from the submenu.

SEE ALSO: For information about designating the outline level for a style, see "Organizing with Styles" on page 74.

TIP: To insert a table from a Word (or an Excel) file, save the file as a Web page (HTML format), and, in PowerPoint, choose Slides From Outline from the Insert menu. In the Insert Outline dialog box, choose All Web Pages from the Files Of Type list, and double-click the Web page.

2 In Normal view, assign styles with the following outline levels:
- Outline Level 1 (such as Heading 1) for a slide title
- Outline Level 2 (such as Heading 2) for the text on the slide
- Outline Level 3 (such as Heading 3) for second-level text under Outline Level 2 text
- Outline Levels 4 through 9 for third- through eighth-level text

Style area

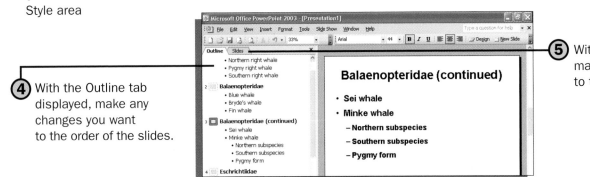

4 With the Outline tab displayed, make any changes you want to the order of the slides.

5 With the Slides tab displayed, make any changes you want to the format of your slides.

Inserting a PowerPoint Slide Show into a Document, Worksheet, or Publication

An ingenious way to create a file that contains a great deal more information than it appears to is to insert one or more PowerPoint presentations into a Word document, an Excel worksheet, or a Publisher publication. With the presentation's only visible sign of existence being an icon, it's hardly noticeable on the page, but double-click the icon, and, presto, there's a slide show!

> ⚠ **TIP:** You can create a Word document containing a single PowerPoint presentation, including notes, and can set it up to be printed instead of being viewed as a slide show. To do so, in PowerPoint, point to Send To on the File menu, and choose Microsoft Office Word from the submenu. In the Send To Microsoft Word dialog box, specify what you want to include in the document.

Insert the Presentation

(1) In your saved document, worksheet, or publication, click where you want to insert the PowerPoint presentation.

(2) Choose Object from the Insert menu to display the Object dialog box.

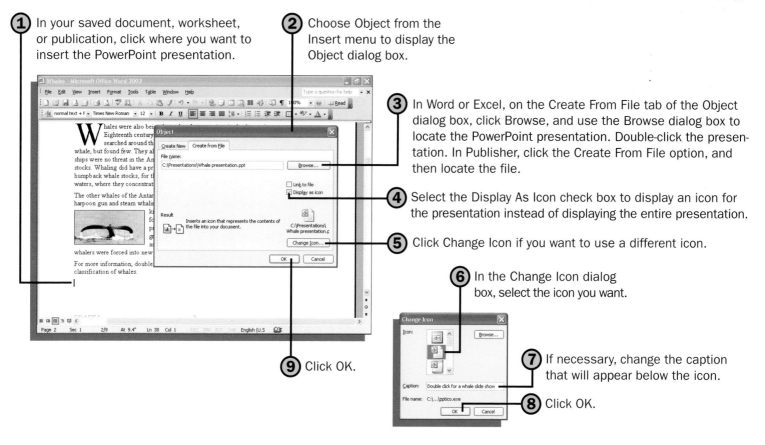

(3) In Word or Excel, on the Create From File tab of the Object dialog box, click Browse, and use the Browse dialog box to locate the PowerPoint presentation. Double-click the presentation. In Publisher, click the Create From File option, and then locate the file.

(4) Select the Display As Icon check box to display an icon for the presentation instead of displaying the entire presentation.

(5) Click Change Icon if you want to use a different icon.

(6) In the Change Icon dialog box, select the icon you want.

(7) If necessary, change the caption that will appear below the icon.

(8) Click OK.

(9) Click OK.

Using Publisher to Present a Word Document

You can do all sorts of tweaking in a Word document to give it a very professional look. However, you'll find that you can do a lot more—and do it more easily—by using Publisher to enhance and fine-tune your document's appearance and design.

Publish Your Document

(1) In Word, write the entire document text, using the formatting and styles you want. Save and close the document.

(2) In Publisher, in the New From A Design section of the New Publication task pane, click Publications For Print to expand the list, and then select Import Word Documents in the list.

(3) Click the design you want, and, in the Import Word Documents dialog box that appears, double-click the Word document you want to use.

> **! TIP:** You'll probably find it easier to add pictures and other types of objects after you've imported the Word document into Publisher rather than including such objects in the original Word document.

> **✋ CAUTION:** Although Word and Publisher work well together, there are substantial differences between them, so an imported Word document might not look quite as you expected, especially if it contains pictures. Always double- and triple-check your publication, and, if necessary, reposition objects such as pictures.

(4) In the Word Import Options task pane, select the printing layout and the page orientation you want, and specify the number of columns on each page and whether you want to include a separate title page. Use the Publisher tools and techniques to complete the publication.

(5) Double-check the layout, and save and print it.

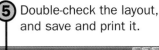

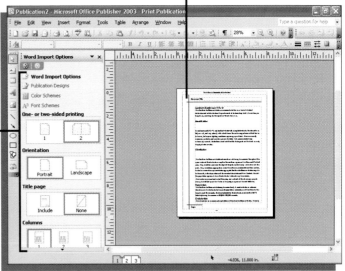

Using Word to Prepare Publisher Text

Trying to compose a lengthy story from scratch in Publisher would be akin to writing a long speech on index cards: impossible to fit everything on one card, and a frustrating waste of time and energy shuffling the cards around. It's a bad idea. Here's a good one: Compose the entire story in Word, using all of Word's tools, and then put the finished, formatted story into Publisher. Then, if you need to, you can do any small edits in Publisher, or you can return to Word for more substantial edits.

Create Your Story

1 In Publisher, design and save the type of publication you want, and lay out your page, with an empty text box (or a text box with placeholder text) ready to contain your story.

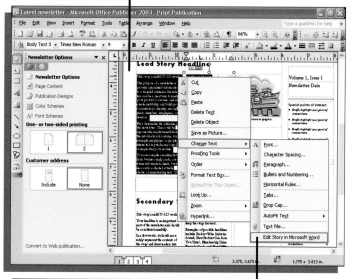

2 Right-click the text box, point to Change Text on the shortcut menu, and choose Edit Story In Microsoft Word from the submenu.

TIP: To insert part of an existing Word file as a story, select the text in Word, copy it, and then paste it into the Publisher text box. To insert an entire Word file, right-click the text box, point to Change Text on the shortcut menu, and choose Text File from the submenu. Double-click the document file in the Insert Text File dialog box.

TIP: You can edit existing text in a text box at any time by choosing Edit Story In Microsoft Word from the Change Text submenu.

4 When you've finished writing, choose Close & Return To from the File menu.

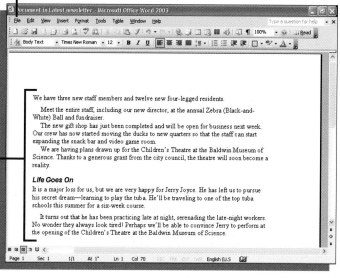

3 In Microsoft Word, delete any existing placeholder text, and write your story, using all the features of Word.

5 In your Publisher publication, modify the dimensions of the text box, and add any formatting you want.

Using Word to Present Access Data

Microsoft Office Access 2003 is the perfect tool for analyzing relational data and for generating good-looking reports on the data. However, when it's time to present the data in a customizable form, along with other relevant information, Access leaves something to be desired. To improve your presentation, you can send the data to Word, where you can manipulate the presentation so that it looks the way you want.

Publish Your Data

① In Access, open the table, query, form, or report that you want to present in Word. If necessary, adjust the item so that it contains the information you want. Save and close the item.

② Select the item in the Database window.

③ Click the down arrow at the right of the OfficeLinks button on the Database toolbar, and choose Publish It With Microsoft Office Word from the drop-down menu.

> **!TIP:** Access creates an RTF (Rich-Text Format) file, and saves it using the name of the item being published from Access (for example, the name of the table). By saving the file with a different name and using the Word Document format, you'll prevent overwriting the file if you publish the same item more than once.

> **!TIP:** Any changes you make to the Word document won't affect the data or the format in the Access database, so you can feel free to delete any rows or columns you don't want.

④ In Word, modify the document as you want, and then choose Save As from the File menu. In the Save As dialog box, save the document in the location you want with the name you want. Set the Save As Type to Word Document.

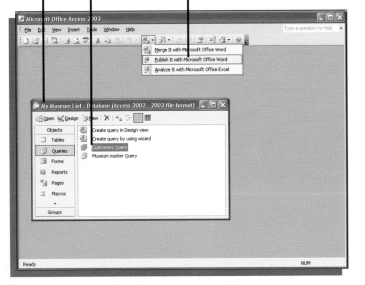

Analyzing Access Data in Excel

The power of Access is its ability to extract information from, and look at relationships in, sets of data. The power of Excel is its ability to perform statistical and other types of analyses on sets of data. You can combine the power of both programs by gathering a data set in Access and then analyzing it in Excel.

Analyze Your Data

① In Access, create and save a query that extracts only the data you want to examine. Display the query in Datasheet view to confirm that the resulting data set is what you want, and then close the query.

② In the Database window, select the query you just created.

③ Click the down arrow at the right of the OfficeLinks button on the Database toolbar, and choose Analyze It With Microsoft Office Excel from the drop-down menu.

⑤ Choose Save As from the File menu, and, in the Save As dialog box, save the workbook in the location you want, using the file name you want.

④ In Excel, use any of the powerful functions to conduct your statistical or other analysis of the data.

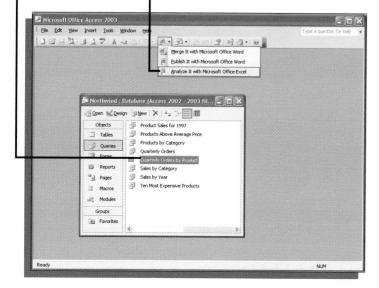

Using Access Data in a Mail Merge

Both Word and Publisher have mail-merge capabilities, and they work in similar ways. When you couple the mail merge with an Access database, you'll be able to create a highly selective mail merge far more easily than if you tried to do a selective mail merge directly in Word or Publisher.

Create a Mail Merge

1 In Access, create and save a query that displays only the records you want to use. Close Access when you've finished.

3 Start the mail merge: In Word, point to Letters And Mailings on the Tools menu, and choose Mail Merge. In Publisher, point to Mail And Catalog Merge on the Tools menu, and choose Mail And Catalog Merge Wizard.

4 Step through the wizard as far as the step in which you select your data source. If you're using Publisher, be sure to select Mail Merge instead of Catalog Merge.

5 Click Browse, and, in the Select Data Source dialog box, double-click the Access database that contains the query you created.

6 In the Select Table dialog box that appears, double-click the query. In the Mail Merge Recipients dialog box that appears, make any necessary changes as to which records are included. Click OK.

SEE ALSO: For additional information about mail merging, see "Mail Merge: The Power and the Pain" on pages 60–61 and "Creating a Form Letter" on pages 62–63.

2 In Word or Publisher, create the document or publication that you want to use as the basis for your mail merge.

7 Insert the fields from the database table or query into your document or publication, and format the fields as you want them to appear in the final document or publication.

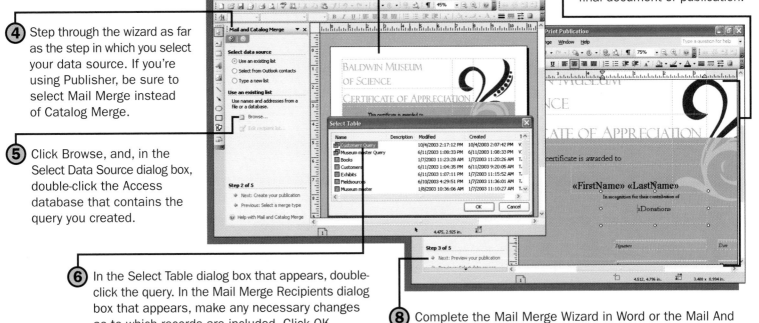

8 Complete the Mail Merge Wizard in Word or the Mail And Catalog Merge Wizard in Publisher, and execute your merge.

Using Access Data to Create a Catalog in Publisher

You can use an Access database as the source for a catalog template in Publisher, and then use that template to create a catalog by merging the data from Access into your template. Once you've created the catalog merge template in Publisher, you can reuse it to create updated catalogs by making changes to the criteria in the Access query.

> **! TIP:** If a text box is already selected in the Catalog Merge Area of your template when you add a field, that field will be added to the text box. If no text box is selected, a new text box is automatically created to hold the field.

Create a Catalog

(1) In Access, create a query that selects the records you want to use in the catalog. Save and close the query.

(2) In Publisher, with a new blank publication open, start the Mail And Catalog Merge Wizard from the Tools menu. Work through the first two steps of the wizard, specifying that you're doing a catalog merge, the name and location of the Access database, the name of the query, and whether you want to exclude any records from the query results.

(3) Point to a field you want to include, click the down arrow, and, on the drop-down menu, select the option to insert the content as text or as a picture. Continue adding the fields that you want to include in the template. Click Next to preview the merge area with real data in the fields.

(4) Arrange and size the fields as you want them in the Catalog Merge Area. Modify the size of the merge area to accommodate your information and to change the number of merge areas that will be printed on one page. Save the completed publication.

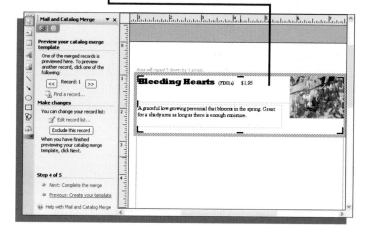

(5) Complete the merge to a new Publisher publication, save it, and review and modify the publication until it looks the way you want.

Adding Excel Data to an Access Database

If you have a large or complex Excel worksheet that you want to use in Access, you don't have to reenter the data in order to use them in Access. You can simply import the data into Access and use them as you'd use any other Access table. When you import the data, you create a copy of the Excel worksheet data. The imported data are independent of the original Excel workbook file, so changes to the data in Access won't change the information in the Excel file.

> **! TIP:** To work interactively with the Excel worksheet, point to Get External Data on the File menu, and choose Link Tables from the submenu. When the Excel worksheet is linked, any changes you make to the table in Access will be saved in the original Excel file. Conversely, any changes you make to the file in Excel will be shown in the Access table.

Get the Excel Data

(1) In Access, with the database you want to use open, point to Get External Data on the File menu, and choose Import from the submenu. In the Import dialog box that appears, select Microsoft Excel in the Files Of Type list box, and then double-click the Excel workbook file that you want to use.

(2) Step through the wizard that appears, specifying
- Which worksheet or named range is to be imported, and whether the first row contains column names.
- The destination of the table.
- The field name and data type for each column in the worksheet, whether the selected column is to be indexed, and whether it should be included when the data are imported.
- The field for the primary key, if any, and the name of the new Access table.

(3) Double-click the new table that you imported.

(4) Examine the table to make sure it's correct, make any modifications you want, and then save the table.

18 Working with Graphics and Objects

Putting pictures and other objects into your documents, presentations, and publications is one of the most exciting and satisfying ways to use today's technology. In the not-too-distant past, combining text and graphics was an expensive and time-consuming process that you simply couldn't do yourself. Type shops were the only businesses that could afford the specialized equipment necessary to successfully unite graphics with text. The ability of today's personal computers to achieve the same professional results has been a blow to those businesses but has transformed an esoteric specialty into an everyday task that enables you to dream up and create unlimited artistic effects.

In this section, we'll explore the various ways you can use the programs in the Microsoft Office System to do a whole lot more than just plop graphics and objects into your Office files. As its name implies, with the alchemy of WordArt you can transmute text into art—and have fun doing it! You can search through vast collections of clip art and choose just the right image to illustrate your text. You can use Auto-Shapes to create drawings: arranging, stacking, coloring, and resizing them, and even putting text inside speech balloons and other shapes. You can use ready-made organization charts and diagram types; insert pictures and photographs, and edit, crop, and recolor them; wrap text around pictures in various ways; and drastically reduce the file size of a picture. And you'll like the way Microsoft Clip Organizer catalogs and organizes all your picture and media files, making them easy to retrieve when you need them.

Creating Stylized Text with WordArt

You can achieve some spectacular effects by creating text as art. Microsoft Office Word, Excel, PowerPoint, Publisher, and FrontPage all can use an accessory program called WordArt that lets you twist your text into weird and wonderful shapes and three-dimensional configurations, and then inserts the result into your document as an object. Try it. But heed our warning—it's highly addictive!

Create Some WordArt

(1) Click the Insert WordArt button on the Drawing toolbar to display the WordArt Gallery dialog box. (In Publisher, click the Insert WordArt button on the Objects toolbar instead of on the Drawing toolbar.)

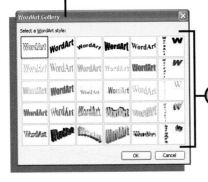

(2) Double-click the WordArt style you want.

TRY THIS: Type the text for your WordArt in the Edit WordArt Text dialog box, and click OK. Double-click the WordArt to open the Edit WordArt Text dialog box again, and make any changes you want to the text, the font, the font size, or the emphasis. Click OK. Click the WordArt Gallery button on the WordArt toolbar to display the WordArt Gallery dialog box again. Click a different WordArt style, and click OK. You'll see how easy it is to change the entire setup of the WordArt you just created.

(3) In the Edit WordArt Text dialog box, specify a font, a font size, and any character emphasis you want. The same formatting will apply to all the text in this piece of WordArt.

(4) Type your text. (Note that WordArt text doesn't wrap automatically; you have to press Enter to start a new line.)

(5) Click OK.

TIP: To transform some existing text into WordArt, select the text before you click the Insert WordArt button on the Drawing toolbar.

Fine-Tune the Result

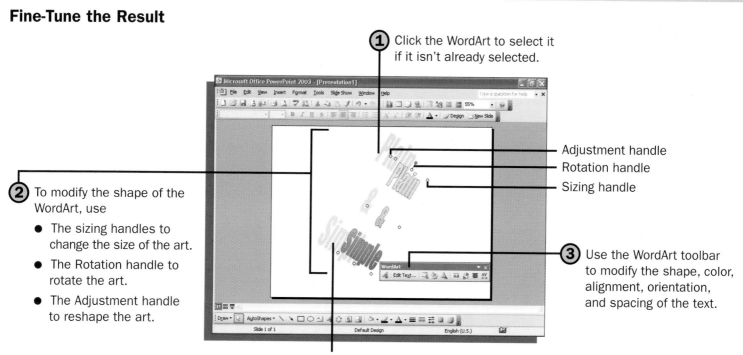

(1) Click the WordArt to select it if it isn't already selected.

Adjustment handle
Rotation handle
Sizing handle

(2) To modify the shape of the WordArt, use

- The sizing handles to change the size of the art.
- The Rotation handle to rotate the art.
- The Adjustment handle to reshape the art.

(3) Use the WordArt toolbar to modify the shape, color, alignment, orientation, and spacing of the text.

Shadow applied to the text

TRY THIS: Create some WordArt, and then use the WordArt toolbar to change the shape, color, and rotation of the text. Use the 3-D button on the Drawing toolbar to apply a three-dimensional effect. Click 3-D Settings on the 3-D button, and use the 3-D toolbar to change the tilt, lighting, and 3-D angle. Amazing, isn't it? And so much fun!

TIP: To change the colors of dual-colored or multi-colored WordArt, click the Format WordArt button on the WordArt toolbar, and use the Fill Effects item in the Color list on the Colors And Lines tab of the Format WordArt dialog box.

TIP: In Word and FrontPage, you can set the text wrapping for the WordArt by clicking the Format WordArt button on the WordArt toolbar and making your settings on the Layout Tab of the Format WordArt dialog box.

Inserting Clip Art

When you're looking for just the right piece of clip art for your project in Word, Excel, PowerPoint, Publisher, FrontPage, or InfoPath, you can hunt through different categories or conduct a search using keywords.

SEE ALSO: For information about adding items to your clip-art collections, see "Managing Pictures, Videos, and Sound Files" on page 320.

Find and Insert Clip Art

(1) Click in your file where you want to place the clip art, point to Picture on the Insert menu, and choose Clip Art from the submenu to display the Clip Art task pane.

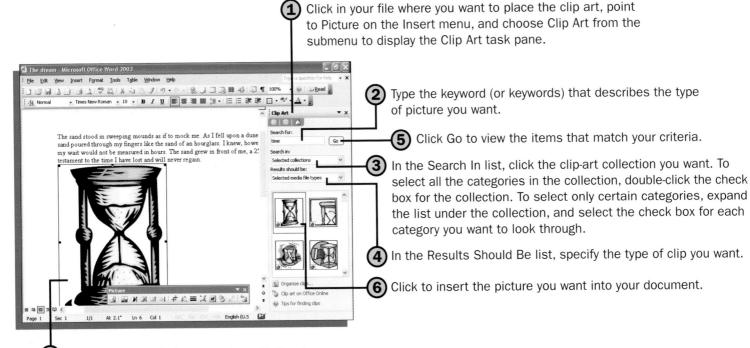

(2) Type the keyword (or keywords) that describes the type of picture you want.

(5) Click Go to view the items that match your criteria.

(3) In the Search In list, click the clip-art collection you want. To select all the categories in the collection, double-click the check box for the collection. To select only certain categories, expand the list under the collection, and select the check box for each category you want to look through.

(4) In the Results Should Be list, specify the type of clip you want.

(6) Click to insert the picture you want into your document.

(7) Click the inserted picture, and modify its size or position as you would any other picture.

Drawing on a Canvas

In Word and FrontPage, you can create a drawing canvas that contains a group of your AutoShapes drawings, as well as pictures, text boxes, and other items, which can all stay together as a single unit. You can move the drawing canvas and its contents and place it wherever you want, and you can even apply formatting to the background drawing canvas. The drawing canvas is optional in Word—you can create AutoShapes in any part of your document with or without the drawing canvas. (You might prefer to use the drawing canvas in Word, though; it helps you manage your drawings as a single unit on the canvas.) However, you must use the drawing canvas in FrontPage if you want to use AutoShapes.

Create a Drawing

SEE ALSO: For information about drawing with Auto-Shapes, see "Drawing AutoShapes" on page 310.

1 Point to Picture on the Insert menu, and choose New Drawing from the submenu to create a new drawing canvas.

6 Use the options on the different tabs to adjust the fill color and transparency, the line color of the borders, the dimensions of the drawing canvas, and the text wrapping. If necessary, on the Web tab, enter text to describe the drawing; this text will be displayed in Web browsers that are unable to display the drawing. Click OK when you've finished.

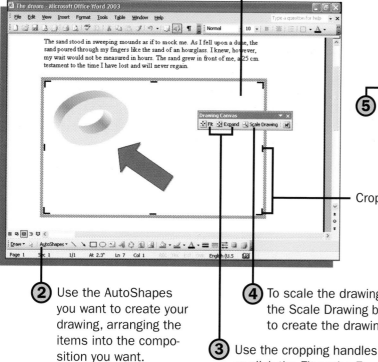

5 Right-click the drawing canvas, and choose Format Drawing Canvas from the shortcut menu to display the Format Drawing Canvas dialog box.

Cropping handles

2 Use the AutoShapes you want to create your drawing, arranging the items into the composition you want.

4 To scale the drawing canvas and everything on it, click the Scale Drawing button, and drag the scaling handles to create the drawing in the size you want.

3 Use the cropping handles to adjust the size of the drawing canvas, or click the Fit or the Expand button to resize the drawing canvas.

Drawing AutoShapes

AutoShapes are drawing objects that you can manipulate in many ways to create unusual and eye-catching effects. You can also use AutoShapes as containers for text, so you can create callouts, pull quotes, advertising blurbs, and so on, to produce all sorts of interestingly shaped special effects. You can use AutoShapes in Word, Excel, PowerPoint, Publisher, and FrontPage.

Draw an AutoShape

TIP: Word normally creates a new drawing canvas when you create a new AutoShape, unless you've clicked inside an existing drawing canvas. You can drag the AutoShape outside the drawing canvas if you want, or you can stop Word from creating the drawing canvas by choosing Options from the Tools menu, and, on the General tab, clearing the check box for automatically creating a drawing canvas.

① Click where you want to insert the AutoShape. (In FrontPage, you must click in an existing drawing canvas.)

SEE ALSO: For information about creating and using a drawing canvas, see "Drawing on a Canvas" on page 309.

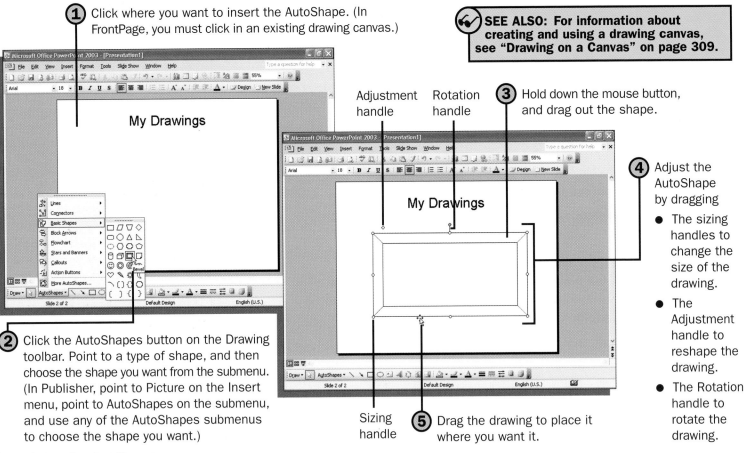

Adjustment handle   Rotation handle

③ Hold down the mouse button, and drag out the shape.

④ Adjust the AutoShape by dragging
- The sizing handles to change the size of the drawing.
- The Adjustment handle to reshape the drawing.
- The Rotation handle to rotate the drawing.

② Click the AutoShapes button on the Drawing toolbar. Point to a type of shape, and then choose the shape you want from the submenu. (In Publisher, point to Picture on the Insert menu, point to AutoShapes on the submenu, and use any of the AutoShapes submenus to choose the shape you want.)

Sizing handle

⑤ Drag the drawing to place it where you want it.

Format the AutoShape

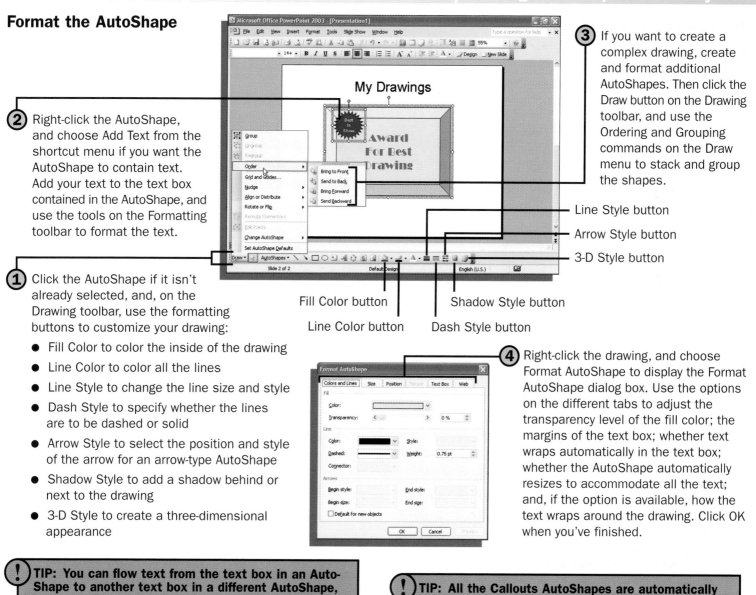

(2) Right-click the AutoShape, and choose Add Text from the shortcut menu if you want the AutoShape to contain text. Add your text to the text box contained in the AutoShape, and use the tools on the Formatting toolbar to format the text.

(3) If you want to create a complex drawing, create and format additional AutoShapes. Then click the Draw button on the Drawing toolbar, and use the Ordering and Grouping commands on the Draw menu to stack and group the shapes.

Line Style button

Arrow Style button

3-D Style button

(1) Click the AutoShape if it isn't already selected, and, on the Drawing toolbar, use the formatting buttons to customize your drawing:

Fill Color button

Shadow Style button

Line Color button

Dash Style button

- Fill Color to color the inside of the drawing
- Line Color to color all the lines
- Line Style to change the line size and style
- Dash Style to specify whether the lines are to be dashed or solid
- Arrow Style to select the position and style of the arrow for an arrow-type AutoShape
- Shadow Style to add a shadow behind or next to the drawing
- 3-D Style to create a three-dimensional appearance

(4) Right-click the drawing, and choose Format AutoShape to display the Format AutoShape dialog box. Use the options on the different tabs to adjust the transparency level of the fill color; the margins of the text box; whether text wraps automatically in the text box; whether the AutoShape automatically resizes to accommodate all the text; and, if the option is available, how the text wraps around the drawing. Click OK when you've finished.

! TIP: You can flow text from the text box in an Auto-Shape to another text box in a different AutoShape, just as you flow text among text boxes in Publisher.

! TIP: All the Callouts AutoShapes are automatically set to contain text.

Inserting a Diagram

Word, Excel, and PowerPoint provide the following six types of diagrams to illustrate relationships and processes: the Organization Chart, the Cycle Diagram, the Radial Diagram, the Pyramid Diagram, the Venn Diagram, and the Target Diagram. All you need to do is choose the appropriate diagram, and then use the tools to customize it for your use.

Create a Diagram

① Choose Diagram from the Insert menu to display the Diagram Gallery dialog box.

Sizing handles for the entire diagram

② Double-click a diagram type to start creating your diagram.

Sizing handle for an individual shape

Adds another diagram element.

Re-orders the elements.

Changes the size and scaling of the diagram.

Changes the style of the diagram.

Changes the type of diagram.

Sets text wrapping when you're working in Word.

④ Use the toolbar to modify the diagram. To modify an individual shape, choose AutoLayout from the Layout menu to turn off the option, and then use the sizing handles around the item to resize or move it.

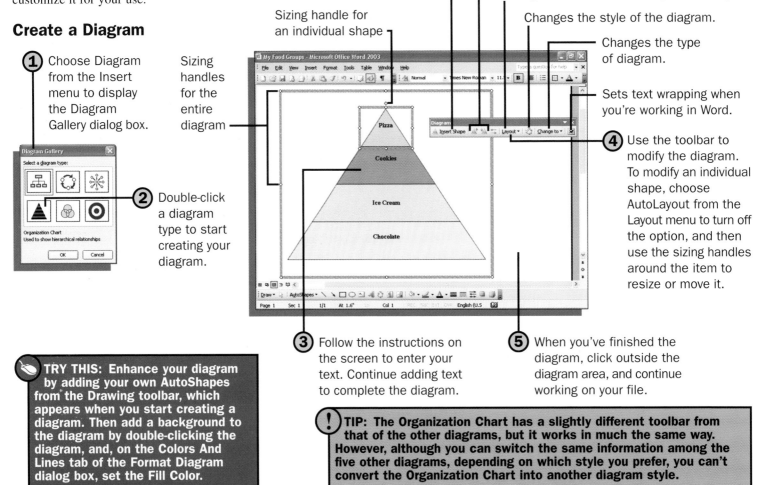

③ Follow the instructions on the screen to enter your text. Continue adding text to complete the diagram.

⑤ When you've finished the diagram, click outside the diagram area, and continue working on your file.

TRY THIS: Enhance your diagram by adding your own AutoShapes from the Drawing toolbar, which appears when you start creating a diagram. Then add a background to the diagram by double-clicking the diagram, and, on the Colors And Lines tab of the Format Diagram dialog box, set the Fill Color.

TIP: The Organization Chart has a slightly different toolbar from that of the other diagrams, but it works in much the same way. However, although you can switch the same information among the five other diagrams, depending on which style you prefer, you can't convert the Organization Chart into another diagram style.

Creating an Equation

It can be difficult to display mathematical equations on a computer, but they can be very useful in Word, Excel, Publisher, PowerPoint, or Access when you're trying to present mathematical or statistical information. For simple equations, you can generally use standard characters and formatting, but for more complex equations, you'll want to use Microsoft Equation Editor 3.0. Be aware, though, that you're simply *constructing* the equation; neither Equation Editor nor your program can do any actual calculations based on the equation.

SEE ALSO: For information about installing Equation Editor if it doesn't appear in the Object Type list, see "Adding or Removing Office Components" on page 374.

TIP: When you're creating an equation in PowerPoint, you work in a separate Equation Editor window that contains the same menus and tools provided in the other Office programs. When you've completed the equation, choose Exit And Return from the File menu.

Create an Equation

1 Choose Object from the Insert menu, and, on the Create New tab of the Object dialog box, select Microsoft Equation 3.0 in the list.

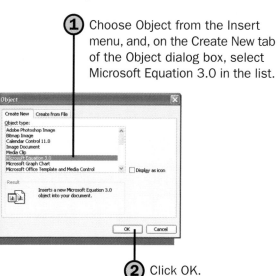

2 Click OK.

3 Use the template menus to insert the symbols with the correct configuration, and use the keyboard to enter characters, keeping these points in mind:

● Work from left to right.

● Use Tab and Shift+Tab to move to different elements and levels.

4 Click outside the equation area when you've finished.

TIP: An equation object, using Equation Editor, is only one type of object that you can insert into your file. Review the Object Type list in the Object dialog box to see other types of objects you can use.

Inserting a Picture

You can add different types of picture files to a single file—photographs and drawings, for example—provided the pictures are in one of the many different file formats the Office programs can use. Some Office programs handle pictures a little differently from others, but the general process is very similar.

Add a Picture

① Click in your file where you want to insert the picture.

② Do either of the following, depending on the program you're using, to display the Insert Picture dialog box:

- In Word, Excel, Publisher, PowerPoint, or InfoPath, point to Picture on the Insert menu, and choose From File from the submenu.

- In Access, Outlook, or OneNote, choose Picture from the Insert menu.

SEE ALSO: For information about using a blank picture frame for layout in Publisher, see "Adding a Picture" on page 234.

For information about using FrontPage to insert a picture into a Web page, see "Adding Pictures" on page 254.

For information about inserting pictures that you cataloged using the Clip Organizer, see "Inserting Clip Art" on page 308.

TIP: To work directly with the picture files and to send one or more pictures to an open or a new Outlook message, a Word document, a PowerPoint presentation, or an Excel worksheet, use the Microsoft Office Picture Manager from the Microsoft Office Tools, which you can access from the Microsoft Office submenu on the Windows Start menu.

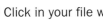

Views button

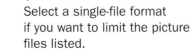

Select a single-file format if you want to limit the picture files listed.

③ Navigate to the folder that contains the picture you want, and select the picture file from the list in the Insert Picture dialog box. If you don't see an image of the picture, use the Views button in the dialog box to switch to Preview or Thumbnails view. (In Outlook, click the Browse button in the Picture dialog box to locate the picture.)

④ Specify how you want to insert the picture:

- In Excel and OneNote, click the Insert button.

- In Outlook, click Open, complete the information in the Picture dialog box, and click OK.

- In Access, click OK.

- In Word, Publisher, PowerPoint, or InfoPath, click the down arrow next to the Insert button, and choose to insert the picture, link to the picture, or (in Word only) to insert and link to the picture.

Wrapping Text Around a Picture

When you position a picture in a Word document, a Publisher publication, an InfoPath form, or a FrontPage Web page, you usually place the picture in line with the regular text so that the picture aligns just like a single text character—albeit a very large one. By changing the text wrapping, you can change the way the picture is positioned in the document or on the Web page.

> **TRY THIS:** In Word, choose Options from the Tools menu, and, in the Insert/Paste Pictures As list on the Edit tab, specify the type of text wrapping you'll want to use for most of the pictures you'll be inserting. Click OK. Now you won't need to change the text-wrapping option each time you insert a picture.

Set the Text Wrapping

(1) Click the picture to select it.

(3) Drag the picture to determine its position in the paragraph and the way you want the text to wrap around it.

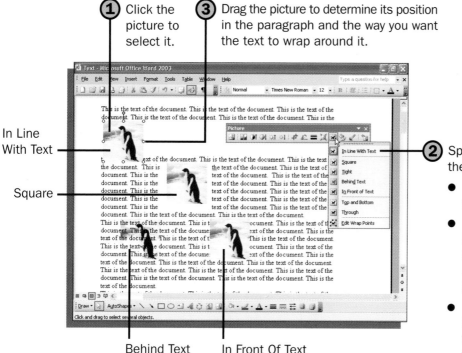

In Line With Text

Square

Behind Text

In Front Of Text

(2) Specify the way you want the text to wrap around the picture:

- In Word or Publisher, click the Text Wrapping button, and specify the text-wrapping option you want.

- In FrontPage, right-click the picture, and choose Picture Properties from the shortcut menu. Select the text-wrapping style you want on the Appearance tab of the Picture Properties dialog box, and click OK.

- In InfoPath, right-click the picture, and choose Format Picture from the shortcut menu. Select the text-wrapping style you want on the Text Wrapping tab of the Format Picture dialog box, and click OK.

Editing a Picture

After you've placed a picture in your Word document, Excel worksheet, PowerPoint presentation, or Publisher publication, or on your FrontPage Web page, you can make substantial modifications to the picture to make it look exactly the way you want. The key to your editing capabilities is the Picture toolbar.

> **! TIP:** Use the Set Transparent Color tool to specify which color in your picture is to be transparent. This tool works well in some types of drawings that have a single background color, and in some black-and-white photographs, but it rarely works well in a color photograph that has many different background colors.

Modify the Color

① Click the picture to select it. If the Picture toolbar doesn't appear, right-click the picture, and choose Show Picture Toolbar (Show Pictures Toolbar in FrontPage) from the shortcut menu to display the Picture toolbar.

② Click the Color button, and choose one of the following to specify how you want the image to appear:

- Automatic to use the original color
- Grayscale to use shades of gray instead of color
- Black & White to use only those two colors
- Washout to create a faint image

③ Click to adjust the contrast and the brightness in the picture.

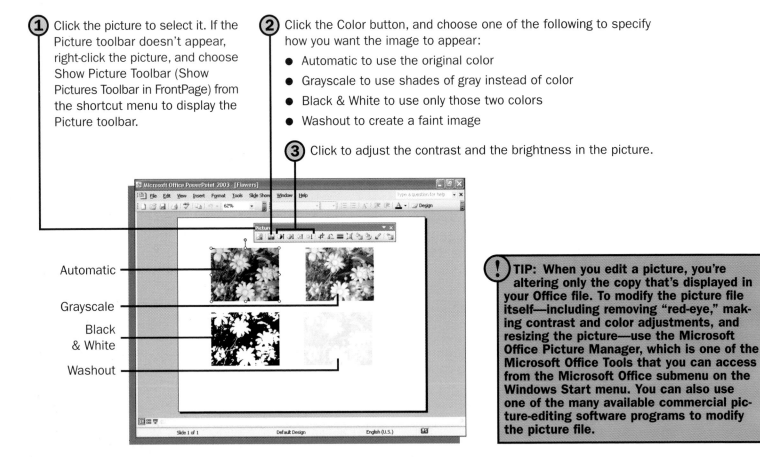

Automatic

Grayscale

Black & White

Washout

> **! TIP:** When you edit a picture, you're altering only the copy that's displayed in your Office file. To modify the picture file itself—including removing "red-eye," making contrast and color adjustments, and resizing the picture—use the Microsoft Office Picture Manager, which is one of the Microsoft Office Tools that you can access from the Microsoft Office submenu on the Windows Start menu. You can also use one of the many available commercial picture-editing software programs to modify the picture file.

Resize the Picture

(1) Click the picture to select it.

Sizing handle

(2) Drag a sizing handle at one of the corners or sides of the picture. Use a corner handle to resize the picture proportionally, or use a side handle to distort the image.

(!) TIP: When you crop a picture, the cropped part isn't deleted unless you tell your Office program to delete it. To restore the cropped part of the picture, use the cropping tool to drag the picture border outward to reveal the entire picture.

SEE ALSO: For information about permanently deleting the cropped portion of a picture, see "Reducing the File Size of a Picture" on page 318.

Crop the Picture

(1) Click the picture to select it and to display the Picture toolbar if it isn't already displayed.

(2) Click the Crop button to use the cropping tool.

(3) Place the cropping pointer over a sizing handle at one of the corners or sides of the picture, and drag the pointer inward to crop the picture. Click outside the picture to turn off the cropping tool.

TRY THIS: With the picture selected, click the Format Picture button on the Picture toolbar. On the Size tab, set a specific height, width, or scaling. On the Picture tab, set the cropping, color, and brightness. Close the dialog box when you've finished. Note the precision of the changes you can make to the picture using the Format Picture dialog box.

Reducing the File Size of a Picture

Pictures are wonderful additions to your document, worksheet, or presentation, but they can make the file size so large that it becomes unwieldy. Fortunately, in Word, Excel, and PowerPoint, you can drastically reduce the file size of a picture by compressing it, by reducing its resolution, and by deleting from the file any part of the picture that was cropped out on the screen.

Reduce the File Size

① Select the picture or pictures to be compressed. If you want to compress all the pictures in your file, you need to select only one picture.

② Click the Compress Pictures button on the Picture toolbar.

TIP: To reduce the file size of a picture in FrontPage, right-click the picture, choose Change Picture File Type from the shortcut menu, and, in the Picture File Type dialog box, choose the file type and the quality setting for the picture. Click OK when you've finished.

TIP: To select multiple pictures, hold down the Ctrl key as you click each picture.

⑦ If you're asked whether you want to compress your pictures and apply changes to the resolution (picture optimization) despite the possibility that this could cause some reduction in the quality of the pictures, click Apply.

③ Specify which picture or pictures you want to compress.

④ Specify whether you want to change the picture resolution for a specific use.

⑤ Clear the appropriate check box if you want to delete only the cropped area without compressing the picture, or want to compress the picture without deleting the cropped area.

⑥ Click OK.

Formatting an Object

In Word, Excel, PowerPoint, and Publisher, you can format the objects you insert into your file—text boxes, pictures, and tables, for example—to give those objects the look you want. Although some types of formatting criteria are common to all objects—height and width, for example—other kinds of formatting are specific to the type of object you're working with. The way you crop a picture or the kind of border art you can use for a text box are just a couple of examples. When you format an object, be sure to explore all the tabs of the Format dialog box to take advantage of the many available formatting tools.

Add Formatting

① Right-click the object, and choose the Format command from the shortcut menu to display the Format dialog box.

③ On the Size tab, specify the height, width, rotation, and scaling for the object.

② On the Colors And Lines tab, specify the Fill (background) color and transparency; the type, color, and size of the lines; and any other features you want to customize.

④ On the Layout tab, choose the layout you want. The options differ depending on the type of object and whether it's situated on a drawing canvas.

⑤ On the Picture tab, specify the cropping and color adjustments you want.

⑥ On the Text Box tab, specify the internal margins and whether you want the text to use word wrap to fit inside the text box.

⑦ On the Web tab, insert text that describes the object if the file will be seen as a Web page and the viewer's Web browser is unable to display the object.

The dialog boxes in some programs, including Excel, contain different tabs to provide formatting specific to those programs.

⑧ Click OK.

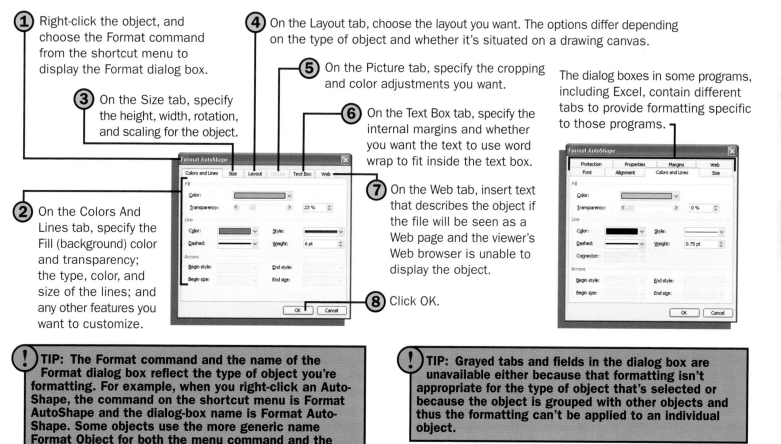

! TIP: The Format command and the name of the Format dialog box reflect the type of object you're formatting. For example, when you right-click an Auto-Shape, the command on the shortcut menu is Format AutoShape and the dialog-box name is Format Auto-Shape. Some objects use the more generic name Format Object for both the menu command and the dialog-box name.

! TIP: Grayed tabs and fields in the dialog box are unavailable either because that formatting isn't appropriate for the type of object that's selected or because the object is grouped with other objects and thus the formatting can't be applied to an individual object.

Managing Pictures, Videos, and Sound Files

Today's computers can store so many pictures and other media files that it can be difficult to find and keep track of them. Fortunately, the Microsoft Clip Organizer catalogs and provides easy access to your media files. The Clip Organizer uses the folders on your computer that contain the media as the basis for cataloging them, treating each folder as a separate collection. You can add custom collections and rearrange the catalog as you want. Then you can access your media files directly from the Clip Art task pane in your program.

Organize Your Clips

(1) In Word, Excel, PowerPoint, Publisher, FrontPage, or InfoPath, click Organize Clips in the Clip Art task pane to display the Microsoft Clip Organizer. If the Clip Art task pane isn't displayed, point to Picture on the Insert menu, and choose Clip Art from the submenu.

(2) To add your picture files and other media files to the Clip Organizer, point to Add Clips To Organizer on the File menu, and choose the way you want to add the clips:

- Automatically to have the Clip Organizer search the hard disk for all picture and media files

- On My Own to manually select the picture and media files that you want to add

- From Scanner Or Camera to add scanned pictures or to download pictures from your camera

(8) Close the Clip Organizer.

(7) Right-click a media file, and use the items on the shortcut menu to move or copy the file to a different collection, or to delete the file from the collection.

(9) Use the Clip Art task pane to locate a media file by searching for its keyword or keywords, just as you'd search for a piece of clip art.

(3) In a collection, right-click a media file, and choose Edit Keywords to display the Keywords dialog box.

(4) Modify the caption and keywords for the media file.

(5) Click Apply.

(6) Click Next to preview the next media file in the collection, and make any changes you want to the caption and keywords. Continue going through all the media files in the collection, and click OK when you've finished.

19

Alternative Ways to Add Content

We had a lot of fun when we wrote this section of the book, and we're sure that you'll be as intrigued as we are by the Microsoft Office System's innovative, imaginative, and timesaving features that take you and your computer to a new level of usefulness and efficiency.

One of our favorites is the AutoCorrect feature, which corrects your own repetitive typing errors and common misspellings as you type. You won't even notice it most of the time, but it's working away in the background, changing *adn* into *and,* capitalizing the first letter of a sentence when you don't, inserting frequently used symbols for you, and much more. Another great feature is Office's ability to translate a few words or an entire document into or from another language—*è meravigliosa! C'est magnifique!*

Yet another bit of wizardry is a feature that allows you to scan a printed document (or use a fax that you've received on your computer) and convert the text into a Word file—a lifesaver if you need to edit a document but don't have access to its original electronic file. And how do you insert symbols such as © or £, or accented characters such as Ä or â, that don't exist on your keyboard? You'll find these and a multitude of others in the Symbol dialog box. And then there's the much-awaited speech-recognition feature—you dictate the text, and your Office program types it for you. You tell your program how you want the text formatted, and it obeys you. What could be better? And we haven't even mentioned the Handwriting feature that lets you insert your own handwriting into a file, or the Drawing Pad for doodling, so read on…

Correcting Text Automatically

Microsoft Office Word, Excel, PowerPoint, Publisher, Access, and OneNote provide an exceptionally useful feature called AutoCorrect that you can set up to automatically correct the common misspellings of certain words as you type them. You can also customize the AutoCorrect feature to include your own common repetitive typing errors (*teh* instead of *the*, for example), and you can make AutoCorrect work even harder for you by defining special AutoCorrect entries.

Add Your Own Misspellings

1 In Word, Excel, PowerPoint, or Access, press the F7 key to display the Spelling (Spelling And Grammar in Word) dialog box.

2 Correct any misspellings until you come to one that you want to add to your AutoCorrect list, and then click the correct spelling in the Suggestions list.

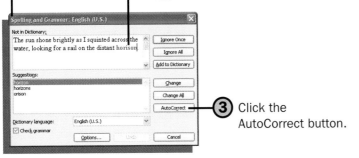

3 Click the AutoCorrect button.

4 Complete the spelling check, adding any other common misspellings or your own repetitive mistakes to your AutoCorrect list.

Add Other Entries

1 Choose AutoCorrect Options from the Tools menu to display the AutoCorrect dialog box.

2 With the Replace Text As You Type check box selected on the AutoCorrect tab, enter the abbreviated or incorrect form of the word or phrase in the Replace column.

3 In the With column, type the correct replacement text.

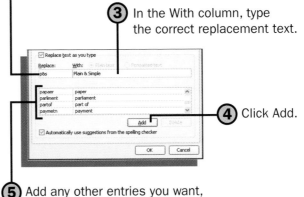

4 Click Add.

5 Add any other entries you want, and click OK when you've finished.

> **TRY THIS: In Word, choose Symbol from the Insert menu. Select the Yen symbol (¥), and then click AutoCorrect. In the Replace box in the AutoCorrect dialog box, type (yn) (include the parentheses), and click OK. Now type (yn) and a space to see the magic of AutoCorrect.**

Control the Corrections

(1) Choose AutoCorrect Options from the Tools menu to display the AutoCorrect dialog box, and—if there's more than one tab in the dialog box—click the AutoCorrect tab.

(2) Select this check box to have AutoCorrect changes marked with an Actions button in your file so that you can reverse the changes if necessary.

(3) Select or clear check boxes to specify the items you want AutoCorrect to correct.

(4) Select this check box to have AutoCorrect replace any item in the list with its correction.

(5) Select this check box to have a misspelling automatically replaced with a correction from the spelling dictionary, provided the correction is unambiguous. (This check box is available in Word and Publisher only.)

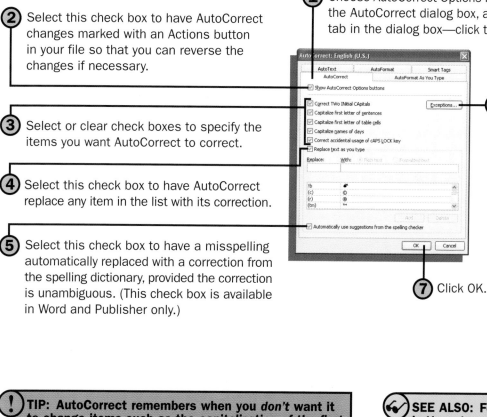

(6) Click Exceptions to specify when a word that would normally start with a capital letter is *not* to be capitalized (for example, after the apparent end of a sentence or after a specified word or abbreviation) or when two capitalized letters in a row are not to be corrected.

(7) Click OK.

TIP: AutoCorrect remembers when you *don't* want it to change items such as the capitalization of the first letter in a sentence, or two initial capital letters at the beginning of a word. However, if you *do* want these changes made on a case-by-case basis, you have two choices: You can use the Backspace key to remove the correction and simply retype the text the way you want it, or you can click the AutoCorrect Options Actions button for the correction, and then use the menu to prevent AutoCorrect from making these corrections.

SEE ALSO: For information about using Actions buttons to reverse automatic changes, see "Formatting as You Compose" on pages 38–39.

Translating Foreign-Language Text

In Word, Excel, PowerPoint, Publisher, and OneNote, and in an Outlook e-mail message, you can translate a word or a common phrase into or from another language by using one of the language dictionaries installed on your computer. If you need to translate into or from a language that isn't included in your installed bilingual dictionaries, your program can use additional resources that are available on line. With these resources, you can translate an extensive amount of text, or even a whole document.

Translate a Word or Phrase

(2) Click the Research button on the Standard toolbar. (In an Outlook message, choose Research from the Tools menu.)

(7) Click the Paste button on the Standard toolbar to replace the text from which you translated with the translated text. To add the translation to the original text instead of using it to replace the original text, click where you want to insert the translation before you click the Paste button.

(1) Select the word or phrase you want to translate.

(3) In the Research task pane, select Translation from the Reference Books drop-down list.

(4) Select the language from which the text is to be translated.

(5) Select the language into which the text is to be translated.

(6) Double-click the translated text to select it; then right-click it, and choose Copy from the shortcut menu.

(8) To translate another word or phrase, type it (or copy and paste it) into the Search For text box, and then click the Start Searching button.

> ✋ **CAUTION:** Don't assume that the computer translation of a phrase or a large amount of text will be absolutely accurate, especially if you've used any idiomatic or colloquial language. If possible, ask a native speaker of the language to proofread the translation to make sure that it doesn't contain any potentially embarrassing, hilarious, or politically incorrect wording.

> ✎ **TRY THIS:** In Word, open your document, and click the Research button. Select Translation in the Reference Books drop-down list, specify the language you want, and click the Translate Whole Document arrow. (If you're connected to the Internet, the text will appear in a Web page.)

Scanning Text

If you want to edit a printed document or just e-mail an interesting article to a friend, but you don't have access to the electronic file, you'll be happy to know that you don't need to laboriously retype the entire document. You can simply scan it, and then let Microsoft Office Document Scanning convert the printed text into a Word file.

Scan a Text Document

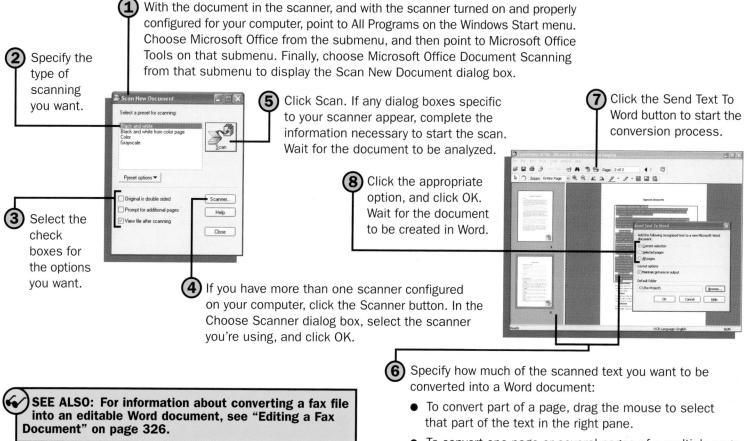

1. With the document in the scanner, and with the scanner turned on and properly configured for your computer, point to All Programs on the Windows Start menu. Choose Microsoft Office from the submenu, and then point to Microsoft Office Tools on that submenu. Finally, choose Microsoft Office Document Scanning from that submenu to display the Scan New Document dialog box.

2. Specify the type of scanning you want.

3. Select the check boxes for the options you want.

4. If you have more than one scanner configured on your computer, click the Scanner button. In the Choose Scanner dialog box, select the scanner you're using, and click OK.

5. Click Scan. If any dialog boxes specific to your scanner appear, complete the information necessary to start the scan. Wait for the document to be analyzed.

6. Specify how much of the scanned text you want to be converted into a Word document:
   - To convert part of a page, drag the mouse to select that part of the text in the right pane.
   - To convert one page or several pages of a multiple-page document, select the page or pages in the left pane. Hold down the Ctrl key, and click to select multiple pages.

7. Click the Send Text To Word button to start the conversion process.

8. Click the appropriate option, and click OK. Wait for the document to be created in Word.

> **SEE ALSO:** For information about converting a fax file into an editable Word document, see "Editing a Fax Document" on page 326.

Editing a Fax Document

When you receive a fax on your computer, you'll notice that the fax is saved as a picture in the TIF file format rather than as a Word document. If you want to edit the contents of the fax, you can use one of the Office tools to convert the fax into text using Optical Character Recognition (OCR), and then you can edit the text in a Word document.

> **TIP:** After OCR has converted the fax into text, you can select a portion of the text by clicking the Select button on the View toolbar, dragging the mouse pointer over the text, and choosing to send only the selected text to Word. However, you might find it easier to send the whole page to Word and then delete the extraneous material.

Convert the Fax

3 Click the Recognize Text Using OCR button on the Standard toolbar.

5 Click the Send Text To Word button.

1 Point to All Programs on the Windows Start menu, point to Microsoft Office on the submenu, point to Microsoft Office Tools on that submenu, and then choose Microsoft Office Document Scanning from the next submenu. In the Microsoft Office Document Imaging window that appears, click the Open button, and open your fax document.

2 If you want to convert a single page or several pages of a multiple-page fax, select the page or pages in the left pane of the window. Hold down the Ctrl key and click to select multiple pages.

6 In the Send Text To Word dialog box that appears, specify whether you want to send the selected text, the selected page(s), or all pages of the fax to the Word document.

7 Select this check box if you want any pictures that are in the fax to be included in the Word document.

8 Specify where you want the new Word document to be stored.

9 Click OK, and then edit the text in the Word document that appears.

4 In the Recognize Text Using OCR dialog box that appears, specify whether you want to convert the selected page(s) or all the pages of the fax, and then click OK.

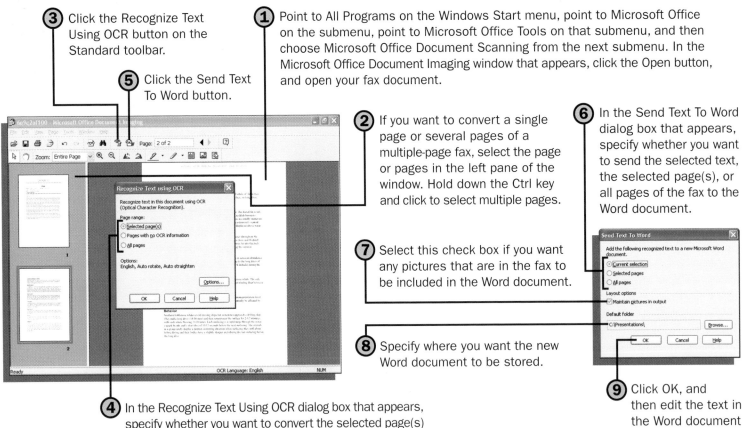

Inserting Special Characters

With at least 101 keys at your fingertips, you'd think that every character you could possibly need would be available on your keyboard. But what about the accented characters in other languages? Different currency symbols? Mathematical symbols? You'd need a keyboard with thousands of keys! Fortunately, Word, Excel, PowerPoint, Publisher, FrontPage, and OneNote all give you access to a huge assortment of symbols and special characters that are contained in all the fonts installed on your computer, and provide several ways to insert them into your files.

Insert a Character

(1) With the insertion point located where you want to insert the character, choose Symbol from the Insert menu, and, if the Symbol dialog box displays more than one tab, click the Symbols tab.

(2) Click Normal Text to insert a character from the font you're currently using, or click a specific font name. Click one of the Symbol fonts for nonstandard characters.

TIP: Some of the characters in the Symbol dialog box might not be supported by all fonts and printers. If you see an empty box instead of a symbol in your document, try using a different font. If you see the symbol on your screen but it doesn't print, try using only the TrueType fonts that came with Office.

TRY THIS: If you have the Handwriting feature installed on your computer, and the Language bar is displayed, click the Handwriting button, and choose On-Screen Symbol Keyboard. Click the keys of that keyboard to insert your symbols.

TIP: Word, Excel, and Publisher each have a Special Characters tab in the Symbol dialog box. This tab provides quick access to typographic characters that can be useful in these programs. The Symbol dialog box in Word also has one button that lets you assign a shortcut key combination to the selected symbol, and another button that lets you quickly add the symbol to your AutoCorrect list.

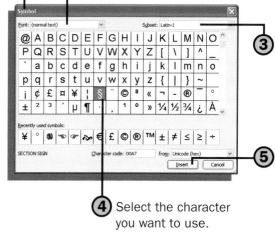

(3) Click the character's category if it's displayed.

(5) Click Insert. To add more characters, click in your file to activate it, click where you want to insert each special character, and then select and insert the character.

(4) Select the character you want to use.

Dictating Your Text

Wouldn't it be great if you could abandon your keyboard and just dictate to your Office program the text you want to enter into your file? Although Office's speech-recognition capabilities might not enable you to send your keyboard and mouse into dusty retirement just yet, you can substantially reduce the amount of typing you need to do by dictating text to your Office program. You can use speech recognition in Word, Excel, PowerPoint, Publisher, Access, FrontPage, and Outlook. However, before you can do any dictation, you'll need to complete a series of training sessions so that

the speech tools can classify and understand the way you speak (your speech profile). These sessions can be a bit time consuming, but they're worth it because they greatly improve the precision of the speech recognition. While you're dictating text, you also use certain commands to help you insert symbols and punctuation, and to help you navigate on the page. We show some of the most common commands here, but, to see a more comprehensive list, search Help for *voice commands*.

Dictate Your Text

(1) Choose Speech from the Tools menu to display the Language bar if it isn't already displayed. (In Excel, point to Speech on the Tools menu, and choose Speech Recognition from the submenu.) If the Speech feature hasn't already been installed, follow the directions on the screen to install it, set up your microphone, and do the training exercises.

CAUTION: You need the proper equipment for successful dictation. If your system doesn't have at least a 400 MHz processor and 128 MB of memory, you won't be able to install Speech capabilities. You also need a good microphone for your dictation to be effective.

Language bar

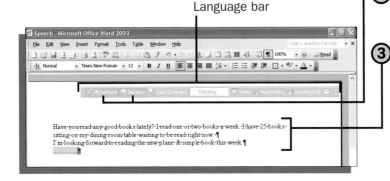

(4) When you've finished dictating, click Microphone, or say **microphone**, to turn off the speech-recognition feature.

(2) Start speaking. If your words aren't being inserted, click the Dictation button on the Language bar. If the Dictation button isn't displayed, click the Microphone button.

(3) Speak as you did in the training exercises, pausing only after completing a phrase or sentence. Word will insert the text after a brief pause.

- To insert a punctuation mark, say the name of the mark—for example, say **period**, **comma**, **question mark**, and so on.
- To insert a number, say the number. Word spells out numbers 0 through 20, and inserts numbers higher than 20 as numerals.
- To insert special characters, say the name of the character—for example, say **quote**, **open parenthesis**, **close parenthesis**, **hyphen**, **ampersand**, and so on.
- To start a new paragraph, say **enter**.
- To move to the next cell in a table or worksheet, or to move to the next field in an Access form, say **tab**.

Correct an Error Manually

Options button

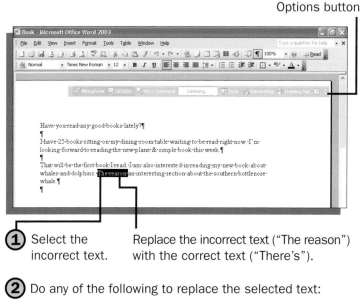

1 Select the incorrect text.

Replace the incorrect text ("The reason") with the correct text ("There's").

2 Do any of the following to replace the selected text:
- Dictate the text again.
- Say **spelling mode**, and spell the word by saying each letter of the word. When you pause, Spelling mode ends automatically.
- Type the text.

> ✋ **CAUTION: Don't let anyone else use your profile to dictate text; doing so will corrupt your speech profile. To switch users, click Tools on the Language bar, point to Users, and choose the appropriate user. To create a new profile for a different user, click Tools on the Language bar, and choose Options from the drop-down menu.**

Choose a Correction

1 In Word or Publisher, if the Correction button isn't displayed on the Language bar, click the little Options button on the Language bar, and choose Correction from the drop-down menu to display the Correction button.

2 Choose the way you want to display a list of corrections:
- If the error was the last word you said, say **correction**.
- If a different word is incorrect, click the word, and then click the Correction button on the Language bar.

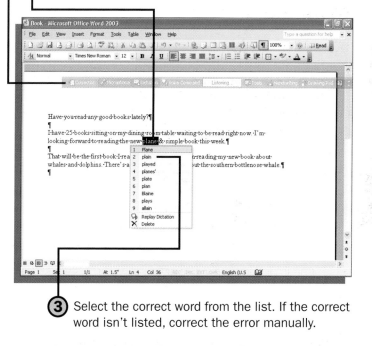

3 Select the correct word from the list. If the correct word isn't listed, correct the error manually.

> ❗ **TIP: To conduct additional training sessions to improve the accuracy of the speech-recognition feature, click Tools on the Language bar, and choose Training from the menu.**

Dictating Custom Text

When you dictate certain text, you might encounter a word that the speech-recognition feature just can't get right no matter how many times you repeat it. When this happens, you can add the word and its pronunciation to a list of custom words so that your Office programs will recognize it in your future dictation sessions.

Add an Unusual Word

1. Click the Tools button on the Language bar, and choose Add/Delete Word(s) from the drop-down menu to open the Add/Delete Word(s) dialog box.

2. Type the word.

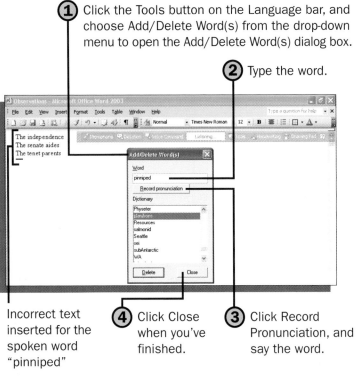

Incorrect text inserted for the spoken word "pinniped"

4. Click Close when you've finished.

3. Click Record Pronunciation, and say the word.

Correct the Pronunciation

1. Select the word in the list, and listen to its pronunciation.

2. If the pronunciation is incorrect, click Record Pronunciation, and pronounce the word correctly.

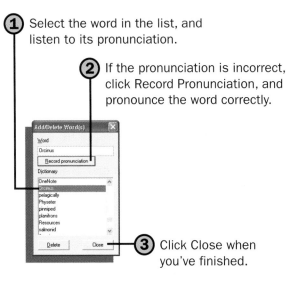

3. Click Close when you've finished.

> **TRY THIS: In Word, open an existing document. Point to Tools on the Language bar, and choose Learn From Document from the drop-down menu. Use the Learn From Document dialog box to specify which words to add to the speech-recognition dictionary. Then use the Add/Delete Word(s) dialog box to specify the pronunciation for the words you added.**

> **(!) TIP: If you have a problem with a word that you're pretty sure you'll be using only once, you might find it fastest to simply type that word instead of trying to correct it in Dictation mode. You can also use Spelling mode to spell out an infrequently used word.**

> **SEE ALSO: For information about using Spelling mode, see "Dictating Your Text" on pages 328–329.**

Telling Your Program What to Do

You can be a ruthless dictator and boss your Office programs around unmercifully, provided you have speech recognition installed. When you're in Voice Command mode, you can choose items from menus, dialog boxes, and task panes, and you can move text around in your file and format it, all with voice commands.

Dictate Your Commands

 Say the commands in your normal voice, as you did in the training exercises. Most commands are the names of items on the screen.

- To select text, say the appropriate commands—for example, **select next word**, **select paragraph**, and so on.
- To move around in the file, say the appropriate commands—for example, **page up**, **page down**, **end**, **back one word**, **go left**, **next cell**, **move up**, and so on.
- To open a menu, say the menu's name. To choose a command from the menu, say the name of the command. To expand a menu, say **expand**.
- To choose a toolbar button, say the name of the button as it's shown on the button's ScreenTip.
- To choose an item in a list, say the full text of the item.
- To format text, select the text you want to format, and then say the names of the formatting buttons.

 When you've finished dictating, click Microphone, or say **microphone**, to turn off the speech-recognition feature.

---

(1) Click the Voice Command button on the Language bar (or say **voice command** if you're in Dictation mode). If the Voice Command button isn't displayed, click the Microphone button first.

! TIP: To change the transparency of the Language bar, its orientation, and whether it displays text labels on each button, right-click the bar, and, from the shortcut menu, choose the changes you want to make.

TRY THIS: In Excel, switch to Voice Command mode. Say file **and then** new. **When the New Workbook task pane opens, say** blank workbook. **Now enter some data, and use the mouse and the keyboard to format and edit some of the cells. Each time you do some editing, note the corresponding voice command in the Speech Message balloon on the Language bar. Now use those voice commands to format the rest of your workbook.**

SEE ALSO: For information about displaying the Language bar and installing the speech-recognition feature if it isn't already installed, see "Dictating Your Text" on pages 328–329.

Writing Text by Hand

If you're tired of typing, or if you simply want to add a little handwriting to your files to give them that personal touch, your Office programs are ready to do your bidding. You can write by hand using a drawing tablet, a tablet PC, or even your mouse. Handwriting recognition will convert your handwriting into regular text or— in Word, if you prefer—will insert your handwriting as is so that your friends and coworkers can behold your exquisite penmanship. Handwriting recognition is available in Word, Excel, PowerPoint, Publisher, FrontPage, OneNote, and InfoPath, and in Outlook e-mail messages.

Write Some Text

(1) Click Handwriting, and, from the drop-down menu that appears, choose the way you want to write your text:

- Writing Pad to use a little window with a baseline to help you write straight
- Write Anywhere to write anywhere in the program window

(3) Use your writing tool to write your text.

(2) Click the Text button, if it isn't already selected, to have your writing transformed into text as you write.

(4) Click the Recognize Now button if your writing isn't immediately converted into text when you've finished.

(5) If the text is recognized too quickly or too slowly, click the Options down arrow, choose Options from the menu that appears, and, in the Handwriting Options dialog box, adjust the Recognition Delay setting.

Write on the Writing Pad...

...or write anywhere in the document.

TIP: In Word, if a word is misinterpreted, right-click it, and choose the correct text from the shortcut menu that appears.

SEE ALSO: For information about adding or removing Office components see "Adding or Removing Office Components" on page 374.

Insert Your Handwriting into a Word Document

(1) Click the Handwriting button on the Language bar, and choose either Writing Pad or Write Anywhere from the drop-down menu.

SEE ALSO: For information about using handwriting in OneNote, see "Drawing a Note" on page 285.

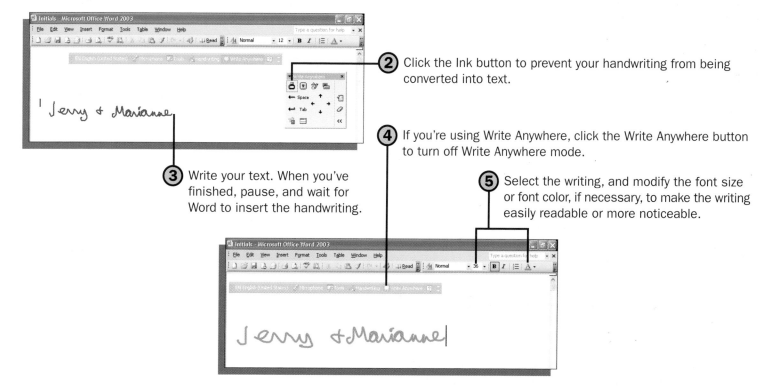

(2) Click the Ink button to prevent your handwriting from being converted into text.

(4) If you're using Write Anywhere, click the Write Anywhere button to turn off Write Anywhere mode.

(3) Write your text. When you've finished, pause, and wait for Word to insert the handwriting.

(5) Select the writing, and modify the font size or font color, if necessary, to make the writing easily readable or more noticeable.

TIP: The Handwriting component isn't always installed in the initial Office installation. To install Handwriting, run the Microsoft Office Setup program to add or remove components, and, under Office Shared Features, expand the Alternative User Input item to find both the Speech and the Handwriting components. Set the Handwriting item to Run From My Computer.

TIP: Handwriting is inserted in line with the text. To format your handwriting with text wrapping, either insert the handwriting into a text box, or use a frame to position it.

Drawing Pictures in Word

If you like the idea of adding quick illustrations, simple drawings, or just a few little doodles to your document, you can do so in Word—and in Outlook if you're using Word as your e-mail editor—by using the Drawing Pad.

TIP: You can use your mouse to create simple drawings, but, if you have a good drawing tablet, you can create illustrations that go well beyond the scope of doodles and stick people.

Do Some Drawing

TIP: If the Picture toolbar isn't displayed when you select your drawing, right-click the drawing, and choose Show Picture Toolbar from the shortcut menu.

(1) Click Handwriting on the Language bar, and choose Drawing Pad from the drop-down menu.

(2) Draw your picture on the Drawing Pad.

(3) When you've finished, click the Insert Drawing button to insert the picture into your document.

(5) Use the tools on the Picture toolbar to modify the drawing and to specify the text wrapping you want, if any.

TIP: You must have the Handwriting feature installed on your computer to be able to use the Drawing Pad.

(4) Click the picture to select it.

20 Working with Others

The ability to collaborate on line with coworkers and business partners is a necessity in today's wired business environment, and the programs in the Microsoft Office System are designed with this goal in mind. With Microsoft Windows SharePoint Services—a Web service that's designed to work especially well with Office files—you and your colleagues can use a Web site on your company's intranet or one provided by an Internet service provider. From this site, you and your group can access and share the files and the information everyone needs to keep your business running smoothly. A SharePoint site is highly customizable, so you can suit it to your needs, making it the vital hub for all workgroup- or company-related business and communications. Office programs also contain quick links to other means of collaboration provided by the Windows operating system, including the ability to start up and participate in online meetings using NetMeeting, or to conduct online conversations using Windows Messenger. We discuss SharePoint in this section because the service is so tightly integrated with Office, but if you want information about NetMeeting and Windows Messenger, you'll find it in our book *Microsoft Windows XP Plain & Simple*.

Even without a SharePoint site, however, Office still makes it possible for you to share files so that you and your coworkers can work on them separately or simultaneously. You can also send Excel, Word, and PowerPoint files out for comments or in-depth reviews by colleagues or independent reviewers, and then you can use the Office tools to accept or reject whatever praise or criticism is heaped upon you!

What's Where in SharePoint?

Microsoft Windows SharePoint Services allows you to create and manage a Web site that's designed for collaborating with your coworkers. SharePoint servers depend on services provided by Microsoft Windows Server 2003, so you'll need to be working on a network that has that server installed, or with an Internet service provider that offers SharePoint Services.

Using SharePoint Services, you can create a site on your company's intranet for use as a central storage and communications location for a single project, for a workgroup, or even for an entire company. In the site, you can include an assortment of document libraries and discussion boards; lists of announcements, contacts, tasks, and any other type of list you want to create; and links to other sites, forms, and surveys. One of the most useful aspects of a SharePoint site is that it's fully customizable, so you can include only the items you want.

Creates a new Web page.

Click to change user access, laying out of pages, and other administrative tasks.

Displays the document libraries and lists.

Displays the discussion boards.

Quick Launch toolbar

Announcements list

Events list

Customized page content

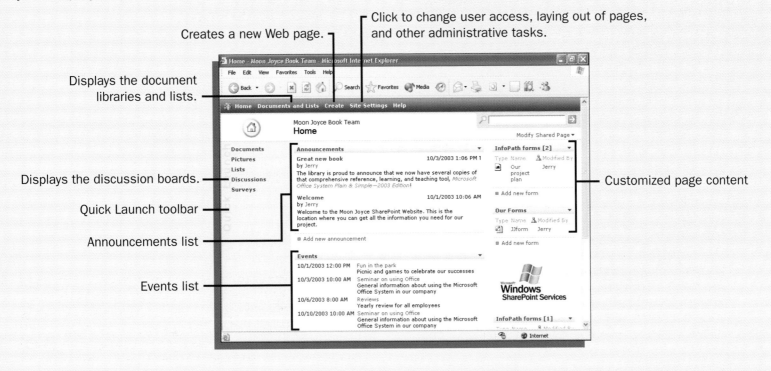

Sharing a File on a SharePoint Site

Microsoft SharePoint Services is a Web service that helps you work and share files with others. If SharePoint is available, either on your company intranet or through an Internet service provider—and provided you're a member of the SharePoint Web site—you can save your files to the Web site so that your coworkers can access them.

Save a File to a Shared Documents Library

(1) Choose Save As from the File menu to display the Save As dialog box.

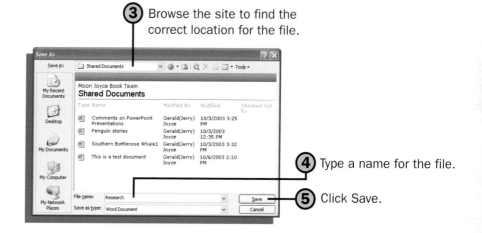

(2) Click My Network Places (or Web Folders, depending on your operating system) in the list, and navigate to your SharePoint Services Web site. If you don't see a shortcut to the SharePoint site, use the Add Network Place or the Add Web Folder item on the drop-down Tools menu of the Save As dialog box to create a shortcut to the Web address (the URL) that was provided to you by the Web site's host.

TRY THIS: Use your Internet browser to go to your SharePoint site. Click the Documents And Lists link in the top Navigation bar, and click the document library in which you want to store a file. Click the Upload Document link, and, on the Upload Document page, use the Browse button to locate the file you want to save. Click Save And Close to transfer and save the file to that document library.

(3) Browse the site to find the correct location for the file.

(4) Type a name for the file.

(5) Click Save.

TIP: SharePoint is fully customizable, so what you see in your SharePoint Web site might differ from what we show here. If that's the case, explore the site to find corresponding areas, or contact the site administrator and ask, "What's where?"

Accessing a Shared File

You can use the Open dialog box to open a shared file from a SharePoint site, just as you can use the Save As dialog box to save a file to a SharePoint site. However, you can also open a shared file directly from the SharePoint Web site. Doing so allows you to browse the document libraries and files to make sure you're opening the file you want.

> **! TIP:** Check to see whether the Quick Launch tool-bar at the left of the Home page has a link to the document library you want; if so, you can open that library with a single click.

Find and Open a File

1 Use your Web browser to go to the SharePoint Services Web site, and click Documents And Lists on the Navigation bar at the top of the Home page.

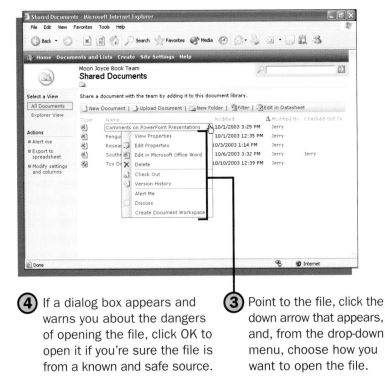

2 Click the name of the document library that contains the file you want.

3 Point to the file, click the down arrow that appears, and, from the drop-down menu, choose how you want to open the file.

4 If a dialog box appears and warns you about the dangers of opening the file, click OK to open it if you're sure the file is from a known and safe source.

Sharing Information with Your Group

SharePoint is much more than a convenient file-storage area. It provides a central location for sharing announcements and contacts, providing news about events, conducting discussions, and including just about anything else you might want to share with or communicate to your group. You can add your own information, read what other people have posted, and even upload or download events and contacts to or from your own Outlook program.

> (!) **TIP: Each of the lists contains different views that help you find and use the information you want. You can also use filtering to display selected items, or view and edit the list in Datasheet view.**

Review and Add Items

(1) On the Home page of the SharePoint site, click Documents And Lists on the top Navigation bar to display the Documents And Lists Web page.

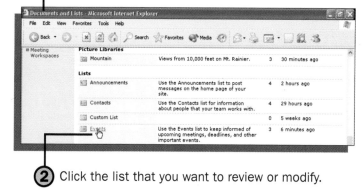

(2) Click the list that you want to review or modify.

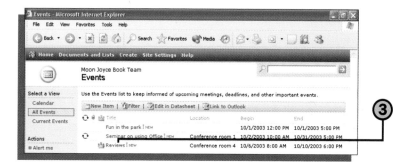

(4) Continue reviewing and modifying the items in the lists:

- In the Contacts list, click Link To Outlook to link the SharePoint Contacts list to Outlook so that those contacts will be included in your Outlook Contacts list.

- In the Contacts list, click Import Contacts to import your Outlook personal Contacts list into the SharePoint Contacts list.

- Click a contact in the Contacts list, and click Export Contact to export the information as a vCard into your Outlook personal Contacts list or to send the vCard to someone else.

- In the Events list, click Link To Outlook so that the events appear in an additional Calendar in your Outlook program.

- Click an item in the Events list, and then click Export Event to create an iCalendar file you can distribute to others so that they can view the Calendar event and add it to their own Outlook Calendars.

(3) Click any item in the list to review, edit, add, or delete an item, or to specify that you want to receive an e-mail if/when the item changes. Use the Go Back To List link in the top Navigation bar to return to your list.

Working in a Shared Workspace

A shared workspace is a Web subsite contained in a SharePoint Web site. You and your coworkers use this shared workspace to work on a specific file or group of files. The shared workspace has its own set of lists and features, announcements, tasks, links, and so on. When you open a file in Microsoft Office Word, Excel, PowerPoint, or OneNote, and that file has been saved in a shared workspace, the Shared Workspace task pane appears and provides you with access to the workspace.

> **!TIP:** If you have permission to create a new workspace, you can do so in a few different ways: by sending the file as an attachment to an Outlook e-mail message, and, in the Attachment Options task pane that appears, specifying that the attachment is shared; by using the Shared Workspace task pane in Word, Excel, or PowerPoint, and specifying the new work-space; or by clicking the down arrow for the file in a SharePoint document library and selecting Create Document Workspace from the drop-down menu.

Use the Shared Workspace

(1) Open a file that's shared in a SharePoint Web site by using the link to the file in an e-mail message inviting you to join the workgroup, by using the Open command on the File menu, or by opening the file directly from the SharePoint site.

(2) In the Shared Workspace task pane that appears, click the Status button to see information about the open file—whether it has been checked out by a coworker, for example.

(3) Click the Members button to see the names of the members of the workspace, and to find out which of them are currently on line.

(4) Click the Tasks button to see all the tasks that have been assigned in the workspace, including any that have recently been assigned to you.

Click to open the SharePoint site in your Web browser.

(5) Click the Document Information button to see who created and modified the file, when it was modified, and all the other properties of the file.

(6) Edit the file, and save the changes to update the file in the shared workspace. Close the file when you've finished.

Click to refresh the information in the task pane.

Work with a Workspace File

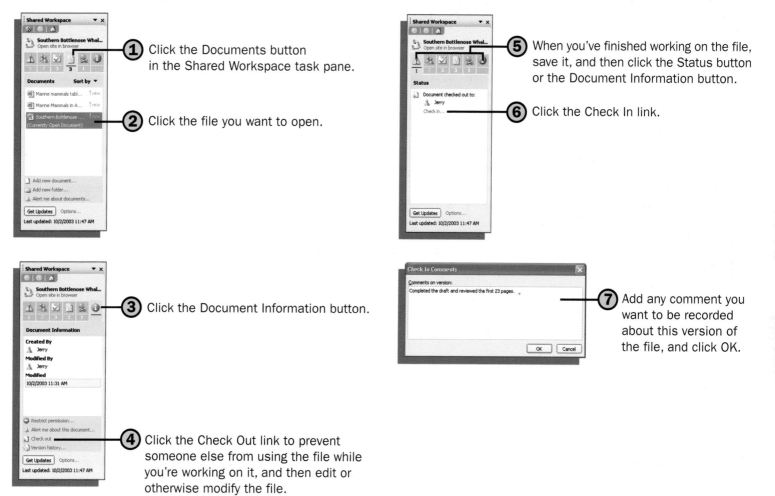

(1) Click the Documents button in the Shared Workspace task pane.

(2) Click the file you want to open.

(3) Click the Document Information button.

(4) Click the Check Out link to prevent someone else from using the file while you're working on it, and then edit or otherwise modify the file.

(5) When you've finished working on the file, save it, and then click the Status button or the Document Information button.

(6) Click the Check In link.

(7) Add any comment you want to be recorded about this version of the file, and click OK.

> (!) TIP: If you close the Shared Workspace task pane before you've finished editing your file, choose Shared Workspace from the Tools menu to display the task pane again.

Managing Your SharePoint Site

One of the great things about a SharePoint site is how easily you can customize it. What you're allowed to do, however, depends on the permissions you've been granted by the site administrator, so you might have to experiment to see what you can and can't do. You can control many individual items on different pages, but the most powerful control you can have, of course, is the ability to administer the entire site.

☑ SEE ALSO: For information about using FrontPage to create and customize a Web site, see "Customizing Your Web Site" on page 250, "Customizing a Web Page" on page 251, and "Creating a SharePoint Web Site" on page 259.

Administer the Site

① With the SharePoint Web site open in your Web browser, click the Site Settings link in the top Navigation bar to display the Site Settings page.

② In the Administration section, click a link to add or change permissions for members of the site, to add or delete subsites and workspaces, to specify who can create and modify subsites and workspaces, or to manage all aspects of the site.

③ In the Customization section, click a link to modify the general appearance of the site, to modify each library and list, or to modify the Home page content and design.

④ In the Manage My Information section, click a link to change the way your name is displayed; to specify your e-mail address and password, and which alerts you want to receive; and to view the entire list of users for the site.

Working Simultaneously on a File

When a file is available to a group of coworkers on a network or on a SharePoint Services Web site, there's always a possibility that more than one person will want to work on the same file at the same time. To avoid the confusion and problems that can result from simultaneous editing by several people, Word and Excel provide a document-management service to help you maintain an orderly transition of the file from one person to another.

Work on an Open File

1 Open the file from the shared folder or Web site.

2 In the File In Use dialog box, select one of the following option buttons in Word or command buttons in Excel:

- The Open A Read-Only Copy option in Word or the Read Only button in Excel to review the file without saving any changes

- The Create A Local Copy... option (available in Word only) to copy the contents of the file to your computer as a Read-Only file, and later to merge the new document with the original document

- The Receive Notification... option in Word or the Notify button in Excel to open the file as a Read-Only file, and to receive a message so that you can edit the file when the current user has closed it

> **TIP:** If you make changes to a Read-Only document in Word, you should save the document using a different file name or in a different location from that of the original document. Using the Compare And Merge Documents command on the Tools menu, you can later combine the changed document with the original one.

> **SEE ALSO:** For information about working on a shared Excel workbook, see "Working Simultaneously on a Shared Excel Workbook" on page 345.
>
> For information about working in Word, Excel, and PowerPoint with merged documents and tracked changes, see "Sending Out a File for Review" on pages 350–351.

3 If you chose to open the Word document as a local copy, save the document after the current user has closed it, and then click Merge.

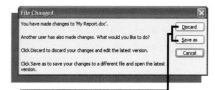

4 If you chose to be notified when the file was available, click Read-Write in the File Now Available dialog box when it appears so that you can open and edit the document.

5 If the File Changed dialog box appears, click Discard to discard any changes you made to the Read-Only file and to open the original file for editing; or click Save As to save the file with your changes, using a different file name.

Comparing Documents and Presentations

If you've ever stared at two or more copies of a Word document or a PowerPoint presentation and wondered which one contained the correct updated information, or if other people have edited a Word document and returned it to you without having used the Track Changes feature, don't despair! Your program is ready to come to your rescue. Provided you have both the original file and the revised file, your program can mark all the changes for your review so that you can compare the revised file with the original one.

SEE ALSO: For information about reviewing a file that contains tracked changes, see "Reviewing a Review in Word" on page 354 and "Reviewing a Review in PowerPoint" on page 356.

TIP: You can compare and merge workbooks in Excel, provided that both are shared workbooks, are copies of the same original workbook, and are stored in the same folder.

Compare Two Documents

1. Open the revised document in your program.

2. Do either of the following:
   - In Word, choose Compare And Merge Documents from the Tools menu to open the Compare And Merge Documents dialog box.
   - In PowerPoint, choose Compare And Merge Presentations to open the Choose Files To Merge With Current Presentation dialog box.

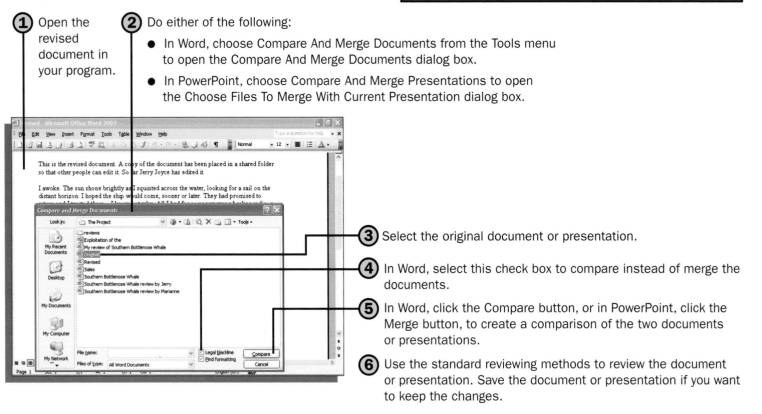

3. Select the original document or presentation.

4. In Word, select this check box to compare instead of merge the documents.

5. In Word, click the Compare button, or in PowerPoint, click the Merge button, to create a comparison of the two documents or presentations.

6. Use the standard reviewing methods to review the document or presentation. Save the document or presentation if you want to keep the changes.

Working Simultaneously on a Shared Excel Workbook

If you need to work on an Excel workbook at the same time others
are working on it, you can set up the workbook to be shared so that
everyone's changes are saved in the workbook.

Share Your Excel Workbook

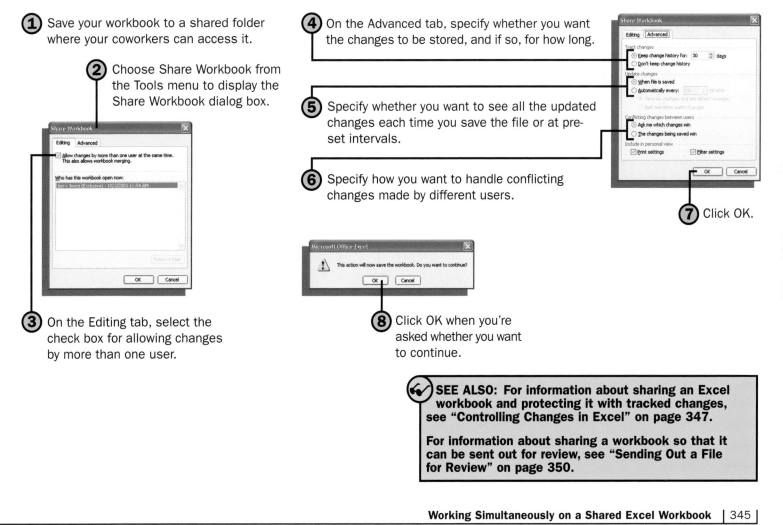

(1) Save your workbook to a shared folder
where your coworkers can access it.

(2) Choose Share Workbook from
the Tools menu to display the
Share Workbook dialog box.

(3) On the Editing tab, select the
check box for allowing changes
by more than one user.

(4) On the Advanced tab, specify whether you want
the changes to be stored, and if so, for how long.

(5) Specify whether you want to see all the updated
changes each time you save the file or at preset intervals.

(6) Specify how you want to handle conflicting
changes made by different users.

(7) Click OK.

(8) Click OK when you're
asked whether you want
to continue.

> **SEE ALSO:** For information about sharing an Excel
> workbook and protecting it with tracked changes,
> see "Controlling Changes in Excel" on page 347.
>
> For information about sharing a workbook so that it
> can be sent out for review, see "Sending Out a File
> for Review" on page 350.

Controlling Changes in Word

When you make a Word document available to others for their review, whether the document is located in a shared folder or sent out in an e-mail message, you can control what those reviewers are allowed to do to the document when they review it.

✓ SEE ALSO: For information about using advanced protection to prevent unauthorized copying or forwarding of your files, see "Restricting File Access" on pages 390–391.

Set the Access in Word

(8) Click OK, and save the document.

(1) Open the document that's going to be reviewed, and choose Protect Document from the Tools menu to display the Protect Document task pane.

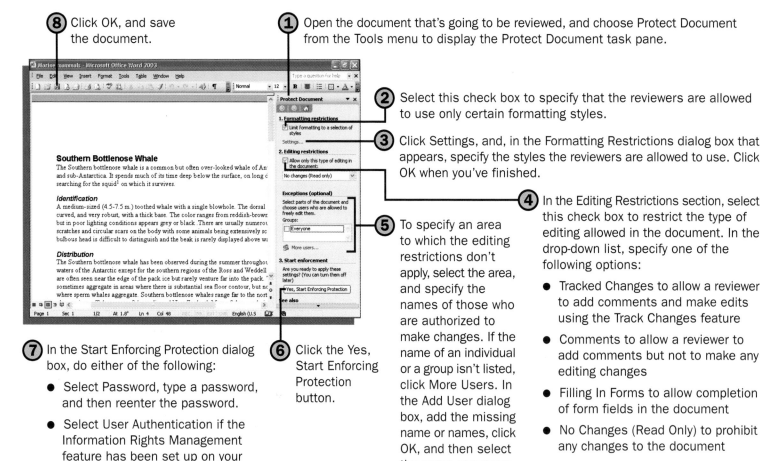

(2) Select this check box to specify that the reviewers are allowed to use only certain formatting styles.

(3) Click Settings, and, in the Formatting Restrictions dialog box that appears, specify the styles the reviewers are allowed to use. Click OK when you've finished.

(4) In the Editing Restrictions section, select this check box to restrict the type of editing allowed in the document. In the drop-down list, specify one of the following options:

- Tracked Changes to allow a reviewer to add comments and make edits using the Track Changes feature

- Comments to allow a reviewer to add comments but not to make any editing changes

- Filling In Forms to allow completion of form fields in the document

- No Changes (Read Only) to prohibit any changes to the document

(5) To specify an area to which the editing restrictions don't apply, select the area, and specify the names of those who are authorized to make changes. If the name of an individual or a group isn't listed, click More Users. In the Add User dialog box, add the missing name or names, click OK, and then select the name or names in the Groups list.

(6) Click the Yes, Start Enforcing Protection button.

(7) In the Start Enforcing Protection dialog box, do either of the following:

- Select Password, type a password, and then reenter the password.

- Select User Authentication if the Information Rights Management feature has been set up on your computer and you want to use it.

Controlling Changes in Excel

When you allow others to access your Excel workbooks, you'll undoubtedly want to control the types of changes your coworkers are allowed to make. Excel provides you with powerful tools to protect portions of a worksheet, a whole worksheet, or an entire workbook. If you decide to share a workbook, you can keep an eagle eye on all your coworkers' proposed changes by using the Track Changes feature.

> **TIP:** To lock or unlock specific cells and to hide or unhide the formulas contained in the cells, select the cells, choose Cells from the Format menu, and, on the Protection tab of the Format Cells dialog box, specify whether you want the cells to be locked and/or the formulas to be hidden. Then choose the Protect Sheet command from the Protection submenu to protect the worksheet.

Protect the Data

(1) In the saved workbook to which you're allowing access, point to Protection on the Tools menu, and, from the sub-menu, choose the type of protection you want to apply:

- Protect Sheet to display the Protect Sheet dialog box, in which you can create a password that's required to unprotect the sheet, and where you can specify what levels of editing users are permitted to do without using the password

- Allow Users To Edit Ranges to display the Allow Users To Edit Ranges dialog box, in which you can specify the regions of the worksheet where individuals who have the proper password or have been given specific permission can make their edits

- Protect Workbook to display the Protect Workbook dialog box, in which you can prevent anyone from deleting, hiding, inserting, moving, renaming, or unhiding a worksheet, and/or can choose to keep the workbook window in its current size and position each time it's opened

- Protect And Share Workbook to display the Protect Shared Workbook dialog box, in which you can choose to share the workbook with others, using the Track Changes feature to accept or reject the proposed changes they've made in the shared worksheet

(2) Repeat step 1 to apply additional levels of protection (for example, to protect both the worksheet and the workbook) so that you have the protection levels you want.

(3) If you want to remove any of the protections you've set, point to Protection on the Tools menu, and, from the submenu, use the Unprotect commands to remove the levels of protection you no longer want.

Discussing a File On Line

With SharePoint Services available on your intranet or through an Internet service provider, you and your team can hold online discussions about a file in Word, Excel, or PowerPoint—even if the file isn't stored in the SharePoint site—and can store participants' discussions on a message board. In Word, you can also choose to have the discussions placed within the document.

Discuss a File

1 With the file you want to discuss open and saved, point to Online Collaboration on the Tools menu, and choose Web Discussions from the submenu to display the Web Discussions toolbar.

✋ **CAUTION: All participants in the discussion must have access to the same discussion server to be able to view each other's comments.**

❗ **TIP: If the file under discussion isn't located in a SharePoint Web site, you might need to specify a discussion server the first time you try to insert a discussion into the file. To specify a discussion server, click the Discussions button on the Web Discussions toolbar, and choose Discussion Options from the drop-down menu.**

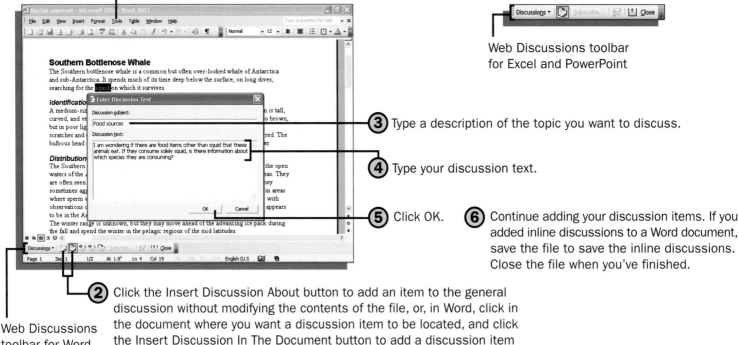

Web Discussions toolbar
for Excel and PowerPoint

3 Type a description of the topic you want to discuss.

4 Type your discussion text.

5 Click OK.

6 Continue adding your discussion items. If you added inline discussions to a Word document, save the file to save the inline discussions. Close the file when you've finished.

Web Discussions toolbar for Word

2 Click the Insert Discussion About button to add an item to the general discussion without modifying the contents of the file, or, in Word, click in the document where you want a discussion item to be located, and click the Insert Discussion In The Document button to add a discussion item (called an *inline discussion*) directly to the document.

Review the Discussions

1 Open the file that's being discussed. If the Web Discussions toolbar isn't displayed, point to Online Collaboration on the Tools menu, and choose Web Discussions from the submenu.

CAUTION: Don't rename the document or save it to another location after you've made your discussion entries. If you do, you'll lose the discussions.

TIP: Click the Subscribe button on the Web Discussions toolbar to receive an e-mail notification whenever someone else makes changes to the file.

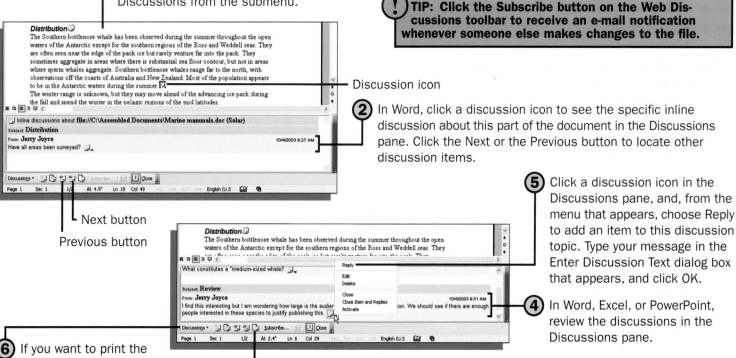

Discussion icon

Next button

Previous button

2 In Word, click a discussion icon to see the specific inline discussion about this part of the document in the Discussions pane. Click the Next or the Previous button to locate other discussion items.

5 Click a discussion icon in the Discussions pane, and, from the menu that appears, choose Reply to add an item to this discussion topic. Type your message in the Enter Discussion Text dialog box that appears, and click OK.

4 In Word, Excel, or PowerPoint, review the discussions in the Discussions pane.

6 If you want to print the discussions, click Discussions, and choose Print Discussions from the drop-down menu.

3 In Word, click the Show General Discussions button to see the general discussions in the Discussions pane.

7 If you've entered any inline discussions into the Word document, save and close the file.

Sending Out a File for Review

When you want your colleagues to review a Word document, an Excel workbook, or a PowerPoint presentation, you have a couple of choices: You can e-mail the file to all the reviewers at once and have their changes and comments added to the file en masse, or, in Word and Excel, you can route the file to individual reviewers in a specific sequence.

Send the File to All the Reviewers

(1) If you're sending an Excel workbook, point to Protection on the Tools menu, and choose Protect And Share Workbook from the submenu (or choose Protect Shared Workbook if you've already shared the workbook). Select the Sharing With Track Changes check box, and supply a password in the Protect Shared Workbook dialog box.

(2) Click OK, and save the file when you're asked to do so.

(3) In Word, Excel, or PowerPoint, with the file completed and saved, point to Send To on the File menu, and choose Mail Recipient (For Review) from the submenu to create a mail message with the file attached.

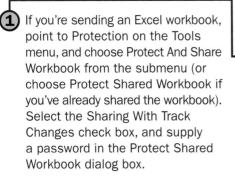

(5) Click Send.

(4) Address the mail message to the reviewers.

Assemble the Reviews

(1) Open a returned file.

(2) When you're asked whether you want to merge the changes with the original document, click Yes.

(3) Repeat steps 1 and 2 to incorporate the returned reviews from other reviewers. After you've included all the reviews, click the End Review button on the Reviewing toolbar.

> **SEE ALSO:** For information about providing additional protection for your Word document or your Excel workbook when it's being reviewed, see "Controlling Changes in Word" on page 346 and "Controlling Changes in Excel" on page 347.

> **TIP:** If the file to be reviewed is stored in a SharePoint Web site, a link to the file is automatically included in your e-mail message, with a request for the review to be made using Web discussions.

> **TIP:** If you want to send out an Excel workbook to be reviewed using the Track Changes feature, the workbook must be both shared and protected for tracked changes.

Route a File for Sequential Reviews

1 With your Word document or Excel workbook file completed and saved, point to Send To on the File menu, and choose Routing Recipient from the submenu to open the Routing Slip dialog box.

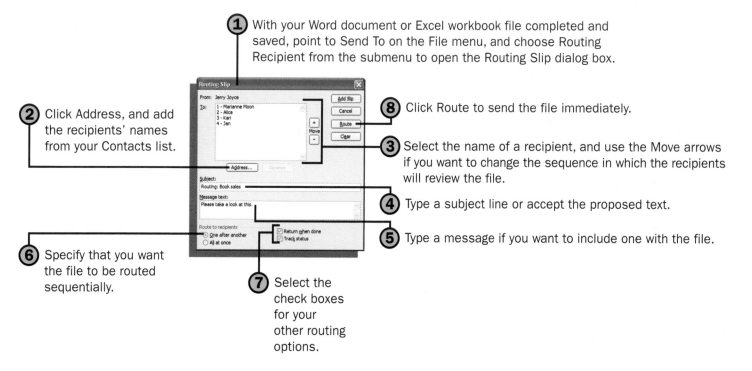

2 Click Address, and add the recipients' names from your Contacts list.

8 Click Route to send the file immediately.

3 Select the name of a recipient, and use the Move arrows if you want to change the sequence in which the recipients will review the file.

4 Type a subject line or accept the proposed text.

5 Type a message if you want to include one with the file.

6 Specify that you want the file to be routed sequentially.

7 Select the check boxes for your other routing options.

SEE ALSO: For information about editing files that have been returned to you after reviewing, see "Reviewing a Review in Word" on page 354, "Reviewing a Review in Excel" on page 355, and "Reviewing a Review in PowerPoint" on page 356.

TIP: If the file was routed sequentially, and if you made no changes to the original document while it was being routed, there's no need to merge the returned document with the original document. All the comments and changes are contained in the returned document.

Reviewing a Document in Word

When you've received a Word document to review, the person who sent it to you might request anything from an in-depth edit to a few comments. You can view the document in different reviewing displays: the original document or the final version with all your changes marked, for example. When you return the document, the Track Changes feature allows the owner of the document to accept or reject your changes and to consider your comments.

Review a Document

(1) Open the document to be reviewed. If the Reviewing toolbar isn't displayed, right-click any toolbar, and choose Reviewing from the shortcut menu.

> (!) TIP: In Normal view, all your changes are marked in the document, and the descriptions and comments are displayed in the Reviewing pane at the bottom of the window.

Insert Comment button   Highlight button

Deleted content noted

(3) Switch to other displays of the document to see how it will look with your changes included, how it looked before your changes, and to see your changes marked on the original.

Identification of the Southern Bottlenose whale

The Southern bottlenose whale (*Hyperodon planifrons*) is a medium-sized (4.5-7.5 m.) toothed whale with a single blowhole.
The whale cannot be identified solely by its blow.
Note these points:
- The blow is low and wispy.
- It is often visible in the Antarctic and subAntarctic but normally not in warmer waters.
- The blow is similar in size, shape, and duration to the blows of minke and killer whales.

Deleted: ¶

Deleted: :

Comment [jj1]: Can this be expanded and describe how it can be identified?

Formatted: Highlight

(2) Modify the content as you want:

- Edit the content as usual. Note that text you insert is underlined, and text you delete appears in a balloon in the margin.

- To insert a comment, select the text you want to comment on, and click the Insert Comment button. Type your comment in the balloon that appears.

- Click the down arrow on the Highlight button, select a highlight color, and drag the mouse pointer over any content you want to highlight.

Highlighted text   Inserted content   A comment

(4) When you've finished, complete the reviewing process as follows:

- Save the file if you want to keep a copy of your own comments.

- If there's a Reply With Changes button on the Reviewing toolbar, click the button to e-mail the file back to the sender. If the button is grayed or nonexistent, close the file. If you're prompted to send the file to the next person on the routing slip, click Yes to e-mail the file; otherwise, return the file as an attachment to the sender.

Reviewing a File in Excel or PowerPoint

When you've been asked to review an Excel worksheet (or workbook) or a PowerPoint presentation, and the file has been protected to use the Track Changes feature, all your changes are automatically recorded. When you return the file to the person who sent it to you, all your changes are marked, and the owner of the file can decide to accept or reject your changes.

> **TIP:** If you want to review an Excel workbook using tracked changes, but the workbook hasn't been protected for sharing with tracked changes by its owner, point to Track Changes on the Tools menu, and choose Highlight Changes. Select your highlighting options in the Highlight Changes dialog box, and then edit the workbook.

Review a File

(1) Open the file to be reviewed. If the Reviewing toolbar isn't displayed, right-click any toolbar, and choose Reviewing from the shortcut menu.

(5) When you've finished, click Reply With Changes to create a new e-mail message containing the changed file. Send the file back to the person who sent it to you.

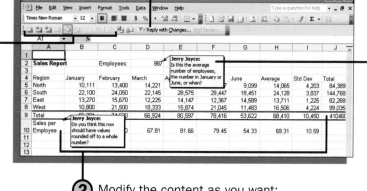

(4) Use the tools on the Reviewing toolbar to locate, edit, or delete any of your comments.

(3) Type a comment, and click outside the comment when you've completed it.

In PowerPoint, you don't see the annotations for your changes, and any comments you make are marked with icons.

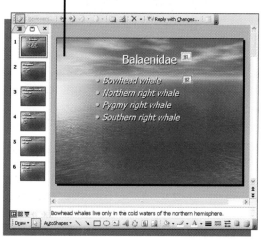

(2) Modify the content as you want:

- Edit the content as you'd normally edit the content in your own file.

- Select the text or the cell you want to comment on, and click the Insert Comment button to insert a new comment.

Reviewing a Review in Word

When a file you've sent out for review has been returned, you can easily review the comments and changes the reviewers have added. As you review, you can incorporate the brilliant and relevant comments, delete the useless or inappropriate ones, and accept or reject the reviewers' changes.

Review the Document

1 Open the document to be reviewed. If the Reviewing toolbar isn't displayed, right-click any toolbar, and choose Reviewing from the shortcut menu.

2 Switch to Final Showing Markup view if that view isn't already displayed.

3 If the document is set for tracked changes, click the Track Changes button to turn off the tracking so that the changes you accept or reject now will be incorporated into the document.

4 Click Show, and select the check box on the drop-down menu for each item you want displayed. Click Show again, point to Reviewers, and choose which reviewers' changes and/or comments you want to see.

5 Click the appropriate reviewing button: Previous to review a change or comment that was skipped, Next to review the next change, Accept Change to incorporate the change into your document, or Reject Change/Delete Comment to restore the original version or to delete a comment

6 If you routed the document for review using the Send To Mail Recipient (For Review) command, and you don't want to incorporate any more returned reviews and changes into this document, click End Review. Save and close the document.

Insertions made by different reviewers are shown in different colors.

> **TIP:** When you're reviewing a document, you can use four reviewing displays: Original, in which all the changes are hidden; Original Showing Markup, which is the same as Original except that the proposed changes are visible; Final, in which the text appears as though all the changes have been accepted; and Final Showing Markup, which is the same as Final except that all the proposed changes are visible.

Reviewing a Review in Excel

When a shared Excel workbook that you've sent out for review—and that you've protected to include tracked changes—is returned to you, you can review the changes after you've merged the reviewed copy into the original workbook.

Review the Changes to the Data

(1) Open the workbook to be reviewed, point to Track Changes on the Tools menu, and choose Accept Or Reject Changes from the submenu to display the Select Changes To Accept Or Reject dialog box.

SEE ALSO: For information about sending out a file for review and combining multiple reviews into a single file, see "Sending Out a File for Review" on pages 350–351.

TRY THIS: Open a workbook that contains tracked changes. Point to a cell that displays a triangular marker in the top-left corner. Note the description of the change in the ScreenTip that appears.

(2) Select the check boxes for the conditions you want to use in the review, and set the conditions for each item you want to use. Click OK when you've finished.

Selection shows the changed cell being reviewed.

(3) In the Accept Or Reject Changes dialog box, note the change that was made by the reviewer.

(6) When you've accepted or rejected all the changes, click End Review on the Reviewing toolbar to incorporate the changes. If you want, you can also select the option to remove the history of tracked changes and to stop sharing the workbook.

(4) Click the Accept button to accept the change, or the Reject button to reject the change.

(5) Continue reviewing the changes until you've completed the workbook.

Reviewing a Review in PowerPoint

PowerPoint provides a handy tool—the Revisions task pane—for reviewing suggested changes to a presentation. The Revisions task pane lets you see the changes that your reviewers have made to both the content and the presentation of a slide. You can then accept or reject the changes.

> ! **TIP: The Gallery tab of the Revisions task pane displays a thumbnail image of the slide, showing the changes made by the reviewers.**

Review the Changes to the Presentation

1 Open the presentation to be reviewed. If the Reviewing toolbar isn't displayed, right-click any toolbar, and choose Reviewing from the shortcut menu. If the Revisions task pane isn't displayed, click the Revisions Pane button on the Reviewing toolbar.

6 When you've accepted or rejected all the changes you want, click End Review to remove all the rejected changes.

Revisions Pane button

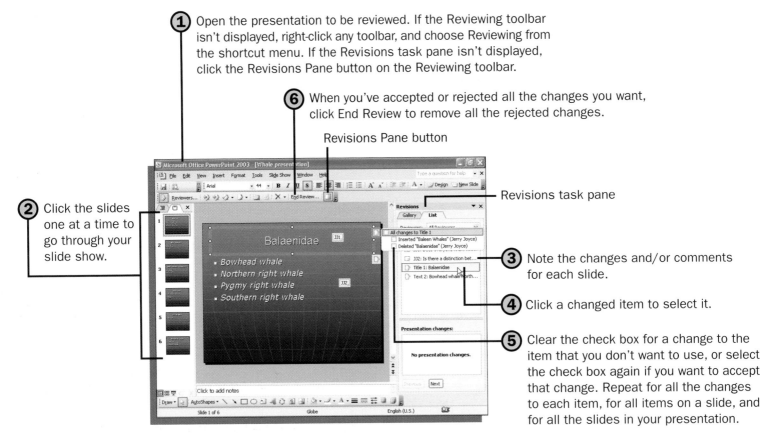

Revisions task pane

2 Click the slides one at a time to go through your slide show.

3 Note the changes and/or comments for each slide.

4 Click a changed item to select it.

5 Clear the check box for a change to the item that you don't want to use, or select the check box again if you want to accept that change. Repeat for all the changes to each item, for all items on a slide, and for all the slides in your presentation.

Combining Reviews in Word or PowerPoint

If you sent out a document or presentation for review without using the Send To Mail Recipient (For Review) command, you'll probably end up with several separate reviewed and/or edited copies of your document or presentation. However, if the reviewers used Word's Track Changes feature, or if you sent out separate copies of the PowerPoint presentation, you can combine all the reviewers' changes and comments by merging the separate documents or presentations into one document or presentation to easily create a final version.

Merge the Documents

1 Open the original document or presentation, and choose Compare And Merge Documents (in Word) or Compare And Merge Presentations (in PowerPoint) from the Tools menu to open the Compare And Merge Documents dialog box (in Word) or the Choose Files To Merge With Current Presentation dialog box (in PowerPoint).

TIP: When you use the Send To Mail Recipient (For Review) command, the returned document or presentation can be merged automatically with its original. However, if you receive a late review that you want to incorporate after you've clicked the End Review button on the Reviewing toolbar, use the procedure on this page to incorporate those additional changes.

TIP: If you use the procedure on this page to combine separate Word files, and your reviewers didn't use the Track Changes feature, the text from all the documents will be included, so you might have repetitive edits for the same parts of the original document.

SEE ALSO: For information about comparing documents and presentations in which the Track Changes feature wasn't used, see "Comparing Documents and Presentations" on page 344.

2 Select one of the revised documents or presentations.

3 In Word, clear this check box to merge the documents.

4 Complete the merge:

- In Word, click the down arrow at the right of the Merge button, and choose Merge Into Current Document from the drop-down menu to merge the changes you want from the revised document into the original document.

- In PowerPoint, click the Merge button, and then click Continue when you're advised that the presentation wasn't sent by using the Send To command.

5 Repeat steps 2 through 4 to merge any other reviews into the original document or presentation. Use the standard reviewing methods to review the changes to the document or presentation.

Working with Business Manager

Business Manager, an Office program that works with Outlook, is a powerful tool that you can use to organize your business accounts, leads, and contacts; your work-related opportunities and tasks; and all your business communications. Business Manager associates your e-mail messages and phone calls with each of your business accounts so that you can easily see and track how your efforts are doing. The power of Business Manager is a behind-the-scenes database that connects and tracks all this information for you. Of course, before you can put Business Manager to work, you first need to populate the various lists and sections with your data, and then you can associate all your activities.

Gather Your Data

1 In Outlook, with Business Manager running, and if your accounts and contacts information is located in a database or another type of data file, point to Import And Export on the File menu, and choose Business Contact Manager from the submenu.

4 Choose either Accounts or Business Contacts from the Business Tools menu (depending on the items you just imported), and review the new list.

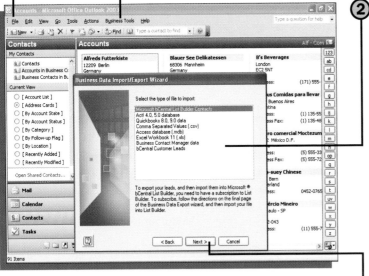

2 Step through the Business Data Import/Export Wizard that appears, and specify

- That you want to import a file.

- The database, workbook, or file from which you want to import information.

- The file name and location.

- Whether to import duplicates (information about an account, a contact, or a lead that's already included in your Outlook files) and whether to create separate entries for accounts, leads, or contacts that have the same name.

- Which section or sections (for example, a database table or an Excel worksheet) you want to use.

- How you want the data from your file to be classified (mapped) to the data fields in Business Manager.

3 Complete the wizard to import the information into the Business Manager database.

5 To manually add data to your business database, point to New on the File menu, and choose the type of information you want to add. Complete the form that appears, and then click the Save And Close button to record the data.

Use Your Information

1 Click the type of information you want to view from the Business Tools menu:

- Accounts to see all your business accounts
- Business Contacts to see all the contacts in your Business Contacts list
- Opportunities to see all the business opportunities you've embarked on

2 Select the item you want to use.

3 Click to specify the way you want to sort the list.

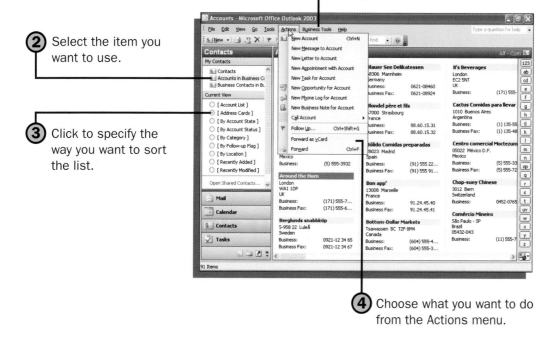

4 Choose what you want to do from the Actions menu.

> **TIP:** When you e-mail a client, Business Manager automatically associates the e-mail with the business account, using the Company field in the Business Contacts list. Make sure that the information in the Company field is complete and that it matches your accounts information.

Reviewing Your Business Information

Business Manager can do a lot more than just organize your business information. Because it utilizes a database, you can have it examine your data, extract the information you need, and produce a detailed report for you.

Create a Report

Shows or hides the grouping structure.

Refreshes the data in the report.

① Point to Reports on the Business Tools menu, point to the type of information you want on the submenu, and then, from the submenu, choose the type of report you want to create and display.

Sorts the information.

Lets you customize what is included.

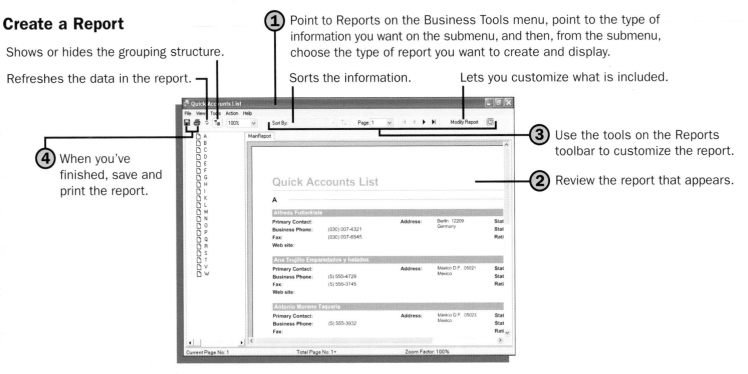

④ When you've finished, save and print the report.

③ Use the tools on the Reports toolbar to customize the report.

② Review the report that appears.

> **TIP:** You can use either your Accounts list or your Contacts list as your data source in order to provide specialized information for a Word or Publisher mail merge.

> **TIP:** To generate the best and most powerful reports, make sure that you include as much information as possible in your Accounts, Business Contacts, and Opportunities lists. With substantial data, you'll find that these groupings are a powerful means of revealing information about your business activities.

21 Fine-Tuning Your Work

We all know that glaring errors in a file—spelling mistakes, poor grammar, and so on—can seriously compromise the credibility of our work. How many of us have never smacked ourselves in the head and howled, "How did I miss *that*?" after seeing an especially egregious mistake in an important file? Fortunately, the programs in the Microsoft Office System provide a variety of tools that help you make your work inviting to look at, easy to read, and error free. When you use the proofing tools, you can be fairly confident that your file won't contain misspelled words or, in Word, any grammatical errors. You can even tailor the levels of spelling and grammar checking so that they're appropriate for certain types of documents—for example, you can have the grammar checker in Word point out gender-specific words, colloquialisms, jargon, and so on. When your tired brain can't come up with that elusive perfect word, you can trust your program's synonym finder or thesaurus to find it for you. And, if you use foreign words or phrases in your writing, your program's multilingual abilities can ensure that you don't make any embarrassing *faux pas*.

Of course, the appearance of your layout is every bit as important as your file's content, and your Office program provides all the tools you need to check and refine the look of your file. You can ensure, for example, that your reader never finds a heading at the bottom of the page and the relevant text on the next page! If you've used a variety of different styles, you can unify your file's appearance by applying consistent formatting to each design element. And before you finalize your work, you can double-check all the details in your program's Preview view.

Proofreading in Another Language

Your Office programs can speak many languages, provided you tell them to use those languages. When you use Office's language tools, Microsoft Office Word, PowerPoint, Publisher, and OneNote can identify selected text as being in a specific language. With the proper dictionaries and proofing tools installed, these programs can use the spelling checker, hyphenation, thesaurus, and Auto-Correct features in a multilingual document, using the correct proofing tools for each language.

> **TIP:** Office comes with a limited number of foreign-language proofing tools (the English release comes with French and Spanish proofing tools, as well as the English tools), but you can purchase and install proofing tools for other languages. If your file contains any text in a language for which you don't have proofing tools installed, that text will be ignored in any spelling and grammar checking you do.

Turn On Office's Language Tools

(1) Close any open Office programs.

(2) On the Start menu, point to All Programs, point your way through Microsoft Office and Microsoft Office Tools, and finally choose Microsoft Office 2003 Language Settings from the submenu to open the Language Settings dialog box.

(3) On the Enabled Languages tab, specify the languages you want your programs to use and for which you have the appropriate dictionaries installed.

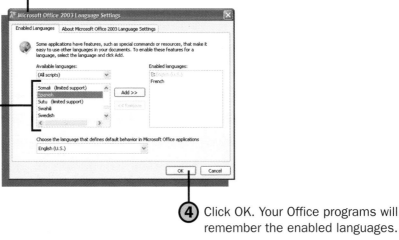

(4) Click OK. Your Office programs will remember the enabled languages.

Work in Different Languages

TIP: Word provides even more powerful language tools than do the other Office programs. When you select the Detect Language Automatically check box in the Language dialog box, Word detects which language is used in a paragraph, provided you've enabled that language.

(1) Select the text you want identified as being in a specific language.

(2) Display the Language dialog box, as follows:

- In Word and Publisher, point to Language on the Tools menu, and choose Set Language from the submenu.

- In PowerPoint, choose Language from the Tools menu.

- In OneNote, choose Set Language from the Tools menu.

(3) Select the language:

- In the Language dialog box in Word, Publisher, and PowerPoint, double-click the language you want to use.

- In OneNote, click the language in the Set Language task pane.

The OneNote Set Language task pane

(4) Repeat steps 1 through 3 for other parts of your file.

TIP: To conduct a spelling check in a different language in Excel or Access, choose Options from the Tools menu, select the language in the Dictionary Language list on the Spelling tab of the Options dialog box, and click OK. In Microsoft Office InfoPath, you can set the language for an entire form by choosing Set Language from the Tools menu and double-clicking the language you want in the list.

Controlling What's Checked

Checking your spelling is definitely a safeguard against discovering embarrassing errors in your final file. However, there are times when a file might repeatedly fail the spelling check because it contains large blocks of text in which technical, legal, or otherwise uncommon words appear frequently. Rather than your being distracted by extensive red squiggles all over the file—and without skipping the spelling check for the entire file—you can tell Word, PowerPoint, Publisher, or InfoPath to ignore the spelling check for those areas of the file.

Specify What Isn't to Be Checked

(1) Select the text that you don't want to be checked.

(3) To prevent the selected text from being proofed:

- In Word, select the Do Not Check Spelling Or Grammar check box.

- In Publisher and PowerPoint, select (No Proofing) in the Mark Selected Text As list.

- In InfoPath, select <None> in the Mark Current Form As list.

> **TIP:** In InfoPath, you can set the language—and therefore the proofing restrictions—for the entire form only. However, if necessary, you can disable the spelling checker for some forms and enable it for others.

> **TIP:** If you frequently use the same unusual words, it's a good idea to add them to your custom dictionary instead of marking them to be skipped. You can add items to your dictionary while you're conducting a spelling check by choosing Add To Dictionary from the shortcut menu, or by clicking the Add To Dictionary button in the Spelling dialog box.

(2) Display the Language dialog box:

- In Word and Publisher, point to Language on the Tools menu, and choose Set Language from the submenu.

- In PowerPoint, choose Language from the Tools menu.

- In InfoPath, choose Set Language from the Tools menu.

The Language dialog box in Word

The Language dialog box in PowerPoint and Publisher

The Language dialog box in InfoPath

(4) Click OK.

(5) Repeat steps 1 through 4 for text in other parts of your file.

Improving the Layout with Hyphenation

Sometimes the right edges of left-aligned paragraphs look ragged and uneven. Justified paragraphs can contain big white spaces between words, especially in columnar text. You can easily repair these common problems with automatic hyphenation. Word and Publisher will do the work for you by inserting *optional hyphens* wherever they're needed. An optional hyphen shows up only when a whole word won't fit on a line, so if a hyphenated word moves from the end of a line because of changes in your text, the optional hyphen will disappear.

> **(!) TIP:** If you don't want to use automatic hyphenation, click the Manual button in the Hyphenation dialog box, and use the Manual Hyphenation dialog box to step through the file and specify which words within the hyphenation zone should be hyphenated, and where to "break" the word and place the hyphen.

> **(!) TIP:** To insert an optional hyphen, press Ctrl+hyphen (-). To insert a nonbreaking hyphen, press Ctrl+Shift+hyphen (-).

Set Automatic Hyphenation

(1) Click in the document (or, in Publisher, in the text box to be hyphenated), point to Language on the Tools menu, and choose Hyphenation from the submenu to display the Hyphenation dialog box.

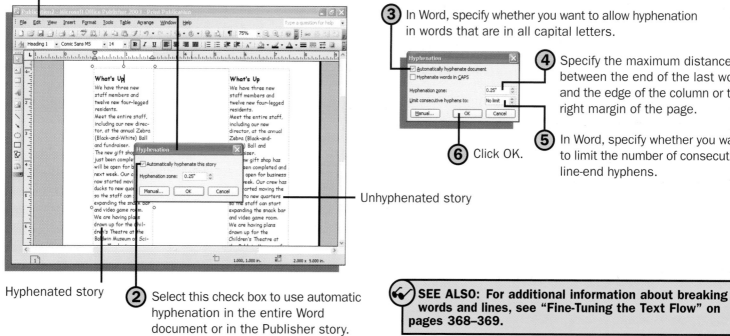

(3) In Word, specify whether you want to allow hyphenation in words that are in all capital letters.

(4) Specify the maximum distance between the end of the last word and the edge of the column or the right margin of the page.

(5) In Word, specify whether you want to limit the number of consecutive line-end hyphens.

(6) Click OK.

Unhyphenated story

Hyphenated story

(2) Select this check box to use automatic hyphenation in the entire Word document or in the Publisher story.

> **(✓) SEE ALSO:** For additional information about breaking words and lines, see "Fine-Tuning the Text Flow" on pages 368–369.

Reviewing Your Grammar in Word

Word, like most Office programs, can check your spelling for you. To create a quality document, however, you need to make sure that your grammar is as correct and consistent as your spelling. Word's powerful and customizable grammar checker will point out any errors and inconsistencies for you, and will even tell you about the grammar problem it's trying to correct.

TIP: If the Spelling And Grammar dialog box doesn't appear when you click the Spelling And Grammar button, choose Options from the Tools menu, and click the Spelling & Grammar tab of the Options dialog box to make your changes to the settings.

Check Your Grammar

(1) With your document open, click the Spelling And Grammar button on the Standard toolbar to display the Spelling And Grammar dialog box.

(3) Review your document until you encounter a grammatical error. Note the highlighted text indicating the error.

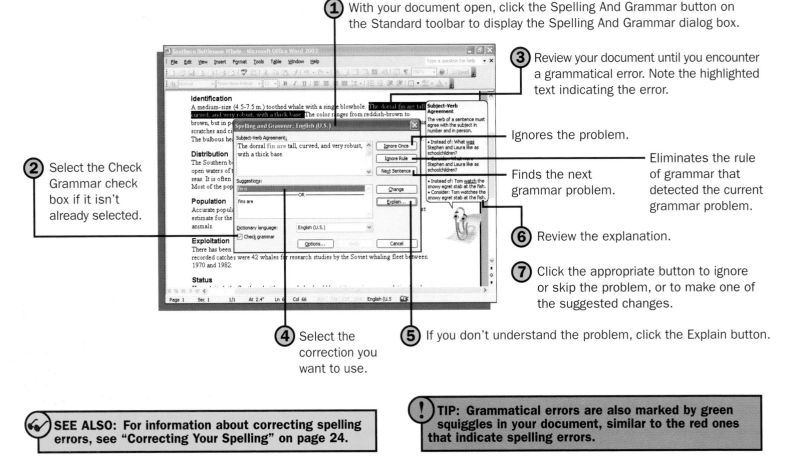

Ignores the problem.

Eliminates the rule of grammar that detected the current grammar problem.

Finds the next grammar problem.

(2) Select the Check Grammar check box if it isn't already selected.

(6) Review the explanation.

(7) Click the appropriate button to ignore or skip the problem, or to make one of the suggested changes.

(4) Select the correction you want to use.

(5) If you don't understand the problem, click the Explain button.

SEE ALSO: For information about correcting spelling errors, see "Correcting Your Spelling" on page 24.

TIP: Grammatical errors are also marked by green squiggles in your document, similar to the red ones that indicate spelling errors.

Set the Grammar Rules

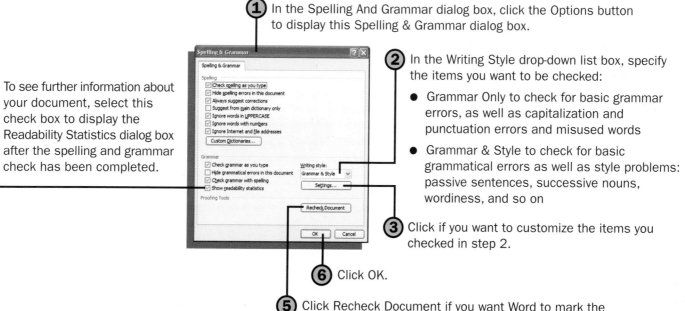

1 In the Spelling And Grammar dialog box, click the Options button to display this Spelling & Grammar dialog box.

2 In the Writing Style drop-down list box, specify the items you want to be checked:

- Grammar Only to check for basic grammar errors, as well as capitalization and punctuation errors and misused words

- Grammar & Style to check for basic grammatical errors as well as style problems: passive sentences, successive nouns, wordiness, and so on

4 To see further information about your document, select this check box to display the Readability Statistics dialog box after the spelling and grammar check has been completed.

3 Click if you want to customize the items you checked in step 2.

6 Click OK.

5 Click Recheck Document if you want Word to mark the corrections you told it to ignore in your previous review.

If you choose to display it, the Readability Statistics dialog box provides statistics about your document.

TRY THIS: If you have any paragraphs in a Word document whose spelling and grammar you don't want Word to check, click the Styles And Formatting button on the Standard toolbar, and click New Style in the Styles And Formatting task pane. Type a name for the new style you're going to create, click the Format button, and choose Language from the drop-down menu that appears. In the Language dialog box, select the Do Not Check Spelling Or Grammar check box, and click OK. Click OK to create the new style, and then apply it to the paragraphs you don't want to be checked.

Fine-Tuning the Text Flow

In Word and Publisher, you can adjust the flow of your text—especially when a paragraph "breaks" across pages or text boxes—to improve the look of your document or publication. Word and Publisher do much of this automatically, but you can make a few adjustments yourself.

Control Widows and Orphans

(1) In Word, switch to Print Layout view if you're not already in that view; in Publisher, adjust the Zoom setting on the Standard toolbar so that you can see the entire text box, and select the paragraph or paragraphs in which you want to make changes.

(3) On the Line And Page Breaks tab, select or clear this check box to control the way paragraphs break across a page in Word or across linked text boxes in Publisher.

(4) Select this check box if you never want a paragraph to break across a page in Word or between text boxes in Publisher.

The Paragraph dialog box in Word

(2) Choose Paragraph from the Format menu to display the Paragraph dialog box.

(5) Select this check box if the paragraph is a heading that must always be on the same page as the beginning of the following paragraph in Word or in the same text box in Publisher.

(6) Select this check box if you always want the paragraph to start on the next page in Word or in the next linked text box in Publisher.

(7) Click OK.

The Paragraph dialog box in Publisher

> **!** **TIP:** There are many definitions of the sad terms "widow" and "orphan" in the publishing world. In Office's world, widows and orphans are single lines that get separated from the paragraph to which they belong and become marooned alone at the top (orphan) or bottom (widow) of a page. Widows and orphans are considered aesthetically undesirable in both worlds.

> **!** **TIP:** To manually insert a column break in Word or a column section break in Publisher, press Ctrl+Shift+Enter. To insert a page break in Word or a text-box section break in Publisher, press Ctrl+Enter.

> **!** **TIP:** Breaking manually means that when you don't like the place where Word or Publisher automatically ended—or broke—a line (or a word, column, or page), or flowed the text into the next text box, you can change the break yourself.

Break Lines

Before fine-tuning

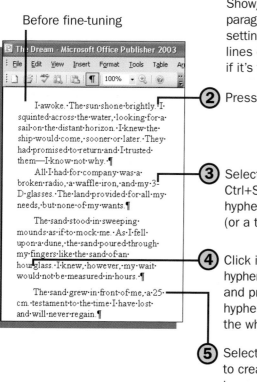

The result after
a little tweaking

(1) In Word, switch to Print Layout view if you're not already in that view. In Word or Publisher, click the Show/Hide ¶ button on the Standard toolbar if the paragraph marks aren't displayed, adjust the Zoom setting so that you can see the entire length of the lines of text, and turn off automatic hyphenation if it's turned on.

(2) Press Shift+Enter to create a manual line break.

(3) Select an existing hyphen, and press Ctrl+Shift+hyphen (-) to create a nonbreaking hyphen that will keep a hyphenated word (or a telephone number) all on one line.

(4) Click in a long word where it can be correctly hyphenated (consult a dictionary if you're not sure), and press Ctrl+hyphen (-) to create an optional hyphen. (An optional hyphen appears only when the whole word won't fit on the line.)

(5) Select a space, and press Ctrl+Shift+Spacebar to create a nonbreaking space that will keep two words or elements that shouldn't be separated on the same line.

(6) Inspect the finished result, and determine whether you need to make any adjustments or undo any of the adjustments you just completed.

CAUTION: Always apply manual column breaks, section breaks, and page breaks as the very last adjustment you make to a file before you print it. Editing a file after you've applied any of these breaks can result in an unacceptably short page or text box, an extra blank page, or even the loss of some text.

TIP: When you manually adjust line breaks in a left-aligned paragraph, try to get the resulting paragraph edges into the shape of a backward letter "C"—that is, try to make the first and last lines of the paragraph a bit shorter than the other lines.

Getting the Results You Want

You worked long and hard on your file, and you can't wait to distribute it. Whether your goal is to print a publication, share a database, or post a Web site, you're eager to see the final result, and when you do...oh, the anguish! How did your masterpiece turn into this ugly mess? We'll try to provide some answers here.

Use the Tools

There are several ways to avoid problems before it's too late. The Office programs provide special tools to help you check your file so that you can produce the results you want. All you need to do is use these tools, together with all the other proofing tools and techniques we've discussed in this section, on your nearly completed file.

- In Word, choose Reveal Formatting from the Format menu, and use the Reveal Formatting task pane to examine your formatting to verify that paragraphs that are supposed to have the same formatting really are consistently formatted.

- In Word, choose Options from the Tools menu, and, on the Edit tab of the Options dialog box, select both the Keep Track Of Formatting and the Mark Formatting Inconsistencies check boxes. Click OK, and then right-click any text in your document that's marked with a squiggly blue underline (indicating a formatting problem) to see suggestions for fixing the problem.

- In Excel, choose Options from the Tools menu, and, on the Error Checking tab of the Options dialog box, select the items you want checked; click OK. In your worksheet, click in a cell that contains an error, click the Error Actions button that appears, and use the drop-down menu to determine the type of error and how to fix it.

- In Access, point to Analyze on the Tools menu, and, from the submenu, choose Table to run the Table Analyzer Wizard, choose Performance to run the Performance Analyzer, or choose Documenter to run the Documenter. Review the results of each type of analysis.

- In PowerPoint, choose Options from the Tools menu, and, on the Spelling And Style tab of the Options dialog box, select the Check Style check box. Click the Style Options button, and choose the capitalization, punctuation, and visual clarity setting you want checked; click OK. The Office Assistant will display any problems that affect the style of your presentation.

- In Publisher, choose Design Checker from the Tools menu, and use the Design Checker task pane to locate a problem, to learn why it's a problem, and to see a proposed fix.

- In FrontPage, choose Accessibility from the Tools menu to display the Accessibility dialog box. Specify which pages you want to be checked and what to check for, and click the Check button. Click an item in the report to see a description of the problem, or double-click an item to select the area of the Web page in which the problem occurs. Close the Accessibility dialog box when you've finished.

As you might expect, Office contains tools other than those listed here. All the programs in the above list provide Preview views so that you can see how a Word document will look when you print it, for example, or how a FrontPage Web page will look in various different browsers. You can also use the preview to make changes to page breaks in Excel, and to run a slide-show preview in order to make any tweaks to a PowerPoint presentation.

Know Your Printer

Some of the worst problems occur when you're printing your file, largely because different printers have different capabilities. Some print in color; some print on both sides of the paper; some use the PostScript printer language; some use their own fonts; and, because some printers can't print close to the edges of the paper, you'll need to set wide margins in your file. Make sure the printer is properly set up on your computer and that you've specified the correct printer in the Print dialog box. If the file is being sent out to a printer that isn't connected to your computer or that isn't accessible on your network, set up the printer to print to a file, and then use the Print dialog box to print to that printer (in Publisher, use the Pack And Go tools on the File menu). If you switch printers in the Print dialog box, reexamine your file in Print Preview before you print it.

Know Your Fonts

The file you see on your screen is displayed using *screen fonts;* the printed version is created with *printer fonts.* The trick is to get the screen fonts and the printer fonts to match each other. All TrueType and OpenType fonts have corresponding screen and printer fonts, but some other fonts don't, so you can't be certain that what you see on the screen is what will be printed. You can avoid nasty surprises by using only TrueType fonts, which you can identify by the double "T" next to their names in the Font list. (Note that OpenType fonts are listed as TrueType fonts in all Office programs except Access, where they're identified by a capital "O.") If your Word, Publisher, or PowerPoint file isn't going to be printed or displayed from your computer, you can include the TrueType and OpenType fonts in the file by selecting the Embed TrueType Fonts check box on the Save tab of the Options dialog box in Word and PowerPoint. (In Publisher, point to Commercial Printing Tools on the Tools menu, choose Fonts from the submenu, and then select the Embed TrueType Fonts When Saving

Publication check box in the Fonts dialog box.) If you'll be using a commercial printing service, talk to a representative and make sure you know what's required of you—some commercial printers don't use TrueType fonts and will ask you to use Type 1 PostScript fonts.

Know What's in Your File

Items you've forgotten about can affect the final appearance of your file. If you've tracked changes or added comments, click the Next button on the Reviewing toolbar to see whether such items are still unresolved. If several people worked on the file and several different versions of it exist, make sure you're using the correct version! Also, make sure the content of your file is consistent with the way you're going to present it—check for items such as backgrounds or animated text that won't print correctly, or colored text that won't provide adequate contrast when printed or displayed.

Print What You Want

Sometimes a file is printed in a strange format or contains information you didn't intend to be printed. Before you print, check your settings. For example, in Word, on the Print tab of the Options dialog box, verify that the Draft Output check box is cleared. If you always want information in fields and links to be updated, make sure you've selected both the Update Fields and the Update Links check boxes. Open the Print dialog box and verify that you've designated the correct printer. Make sure that you're printing what you want—if there's a Print What box or section in the Print dialog box, specify exactly what you want printed so that you don't print the entire file when all you want is one page. If there's an Advanced Print Settings button, click it, and verify that your settings are correct. Then sit down and read the file carefully. All the spelling, grammar, and formatting checkers in the world can't outdo the human brain. Remember, the computer is smart, but you're smarter!

Finding Alternative Wording

If you find that you're using the same word repeatedly in one sentence or paragraph (or even too many times in one file), or if a word doesn't express your meaning precisely enough or provide the impact you want, Word, Excel, Publisher, PowerPoint, and OneNote can come to your rescue by providing you with a wide choice of similar words.

> **TRY THIS:** In a Word document or a PowerPoint presentation, right-click the word for which you want to find a synonym. Point to Synonyms on the shortcut menu, and click the synonym you want to use from the submenu. Easy, isn't it!

Choose an Alternative Word

(1) Right-click the word you want to replace, and choose Look Up from the shortcut menu to display the Research task pane.

(2) In the Research task pane, make sure the correct thesaurus is selected. Choose a different thesaurus if necessary.

(3) Click the Start Searching button to execute the search if the results aren't already displayed.

(4) Point to the word you want to use or the one that's closest to the meaning you're looking for.

(5) Click the down arrow, and choose the action you want from the drop-down menu:

- Insert to replace the selected word in your text
- Copy to copy the word from the thesaurus onto the Windows Clipboard so that you can insert it elsewhere in your file
- Look Up to find other synonyms of the word

> **TIP:** In FrontPage, select the word for which you want to find a synonym, and choose Thesaurus from the Tools menu. Use the Thesaurus dialog box to select your synonym.

22 Customizing Office

You can customize the programs in the Microsoft Office System in a multitude of different ways. To see what we mean, choose Options from the Tools menu, and look through all the choices on the different tabs of the Options dialog box. Do you want white text on a blue background instead of the same old black-on-white text in a Word document? Do you want your program to automatically save AutoRecovery information every few minutes? With just a few clicks, you can make it so. This section explores only the most common types of customization that you make using the Options dialog box. We'll also talk about customizing elsewhere in your programs—adding components you need or deleting those you never use, and specifying exactly how you want various elements in your programs to be displayed, stored, and accessed.

You can make significant changes to your programs' menus and toolbars too: changing the way they look, moving them into different positions, putting toolbar buttons on menus and putting menu commands on toolbars—in other words, making these items work the way *you* want them to. You can even create your own *macros*. (Don't be scared—it's easy!) Of course, you can work productively in your Office programs without changing anything, but if there are some aspects of a particular program you'd like to change, it's good to know that you probably can. One caution: If your computer is part of a network on which company system policies are used, check with the network administrator before you attempt to make any changes. System policies usually set what you can and can't customize, so you'll avoid considerable frustration by being forewarned.

Adding or Removing Office Components

Office contains such an abundance of components that you probably haven't needed or wanted to install all of them on your computer. You can install additional components on an as-needed basis, and you can remove components that you never use so as to save some hard-disk space.

> **!) TIP: When a component is set to be installed on first use, it's automatically installed when you need it. When you manually add or remove components, you'll find that Word, Excel, PowerPoint, Outlook, Publisher, Access, InfoPath, Office Shared Features, and Office Tools are part of the Microsoft Office program installation, while all other Office programs have their own installation in the Add Or Remove Programs dialog box.**

Add or Remove Components

1 With all your Office programs closed, open the Control Panel from the Windows Start menu, and double-click Add Or Remove Programs. Click the Change Or Remove Programs button, click the Office program you want to modify in the list, and click the Change button.

2 Click the Add Or Remove Features option, and click Next.

3 If a program you want isn't installed, select its check box. To remove an installed program, clear its check box.

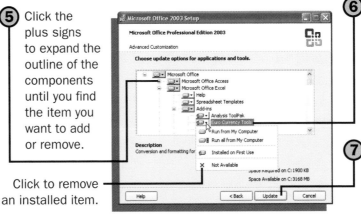

4 Select this check box to specify which components you want to install—shared tools and optional parts of programs, for example—and then click Next.

5 Click the plus signs to expand the outline of the components until you find the item you want to add or remove.

6 Click the down arrow to display the installation choices, and specify a choice. Repeat for any other components you want to change.

Click to remove an installed item.

7 Click Update, and wait for the installation to be completed.

> **!) TIP: You'll probably need to be logged on as a member of the Administrators group to install additional components.**

Changing the Location of Saved Files

If you don't like the locations in which your Office program proposes to store your files or the way in which it gives you access to the files you need to work with in that program, you can change those locations and create the organization that works best for you.

In several programs, you can also specify the default format in which you want the file to be saved, although you can always change this format when you're saving the file.

Change the File Location

① Choose Options from the Tools menu to display the Options dialog box, click the file's location, and then change it, as follows:

- In Microsoft Office Word, click the File Locations tab, double-click the type of file to be saved, and use the Modify Location dialog box to designate the file's new location.

- In Microsoft Office Excel, click the General tab, and enter a new location for the file in the Default File Location text box.

- In Microsoft Office Access, click the General tab, and enter a new location for the file in the Default Database Folder text box.

- In Microsoft Office Publisher, click the General tab, double-click the type of file to be saved, and use the Modify Location dialog box to designate the file's new location.

- In Microsoft Office PowerPoint, click the Save tab, and enter a new location for the file in the Default File Location text box.

- In Microsoft Office OneNote, click the Open And Save category, double-click the type of file to be saved, and use the Select Folder dialog box to designate the file's new location.

Double-click the file's location in a list... **②** Click OK.

...or type the full path to the location.

> **! TIP:** To change the default format for saving a file in Word or PowerPoint, select the format you want to use on the Save tab of the Options dialog box. You can, of course, save a file in a format different from that of the default format by choosing the format you want in the Save As Type list in the Save As dialog box.

Managing Toolbars and Menus

Your Office programs provide quite a few options that let you manage the way your toolbars and menus are displayed. You can make some really significant changes to these components, so it's a good idea to experiment with them to see which settings are right for your working style.

Set the Options

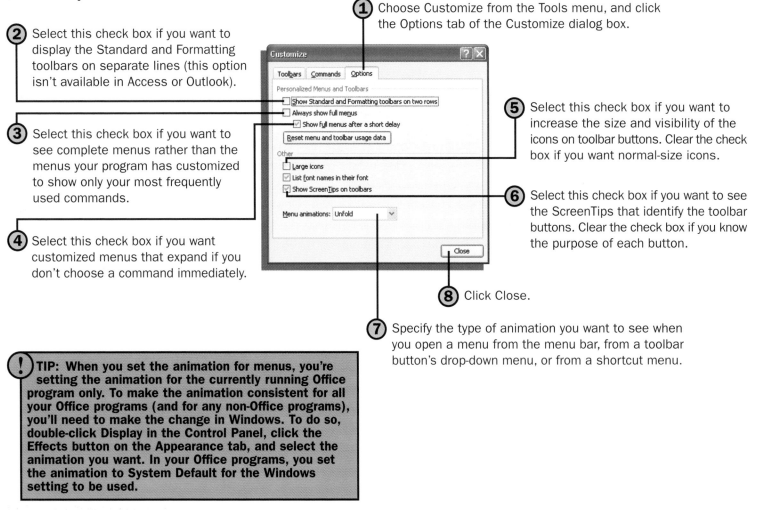

① Choose Customize from the Tools menu, and click the Options tab of the Customize dialog box.

② Select this check box if you want to display the Standard and Formatting toolbars on separate lines (this option isn't available in Access or Outlook).

③ Select this check box if you want to see complete menus rather than the menus your program has customized to show only your most frequently used commands.

④ Select this check box if you want customized menus that expand if you don't choose a command immediately.

⑤ Select this check box if you want to increase the size and visibility of the icons on toolbar buttons. Clear the check box if you want normal-size icons.

⑥ Select this check box if you want to see the ScreenTips that identify the toolbar buttons. Clear the check box if you know the purpose of each button.

⑧ Click Close.

⑦ Specify the type of animation you want to see when you open a menu from the menu bar, from a toolbar button's drop-down menu, or from a shortcut menu.

> ⚠ TIP: When you set the animation for menus, you're setting the animation for the currently running Office program only. To make the animation consistent for all your Office programs (and for any non-Office programs), you'll need to make the change in Windows. To do so, double-click Display in the Control Panel, click the Effects button on the Appearance tab, and select the animation you want. In your Office programs, you set the animation to System Default for the Windows setting to be used.

Rearranging Toolbars

Most Office programs have so many toolbars that you'll probably find it necessary to do some toolbar rearrangement. For example, you might want to display three or more toolbars on the same line, or you might want them on different lines stacked one below the other. You might also want to move a toolbar to the side of the window or have it floating free in the window.

> **TIP:** A toolbar is either *docked* or *floating*. A docked toolbar resides at one of the four sides of your program window. A floating toolbar floats over your file's content in a little window of its own.

Move a Toolbar

(1) Point to a blank part of a toolbar or to the little vertical raised bar on the toolbar.

(6) Double-click the raised bar of a toolbar that shares a line with another toolbar to expand the toolbar as much as possible. Drag the raised bar to fine-tune how much of the toolbar is visible.

(2) Drag a toolbar above or below another docked toolbar to stack the toolbars on separate lines.

(3) Drag a toolbar onto the same line as another toolbar to have both toolbars share the line.

(4) Drag a toolbar to any side of the program window to dock the toolbar at that side.

(5) Drag a toolbar into the area of the file you're working on to change the toolbar into a floating toolbar.

(7) If you can't see all the toolbar buttons, click the double chevrons to see the hidden buttons for all the toolbars on that line.

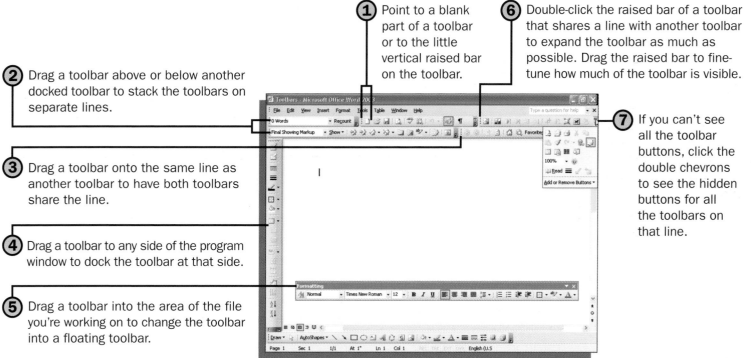

Rearranging Toolbar Buttons and Menus

You don't have to live with the way the toolbar buttons and menus are set up if another arrangement would work more efficiently for you. If you want to move a toolbar button onto a different toolbar or move a menu command onto a different menu, you can easily do so. You can even move toolbar buttons onto menus, and move menu commands onto toolbars.

Move Toolbar Buttons

(1) Choose Customize from the Tools menu, and click the Toolbars tab of the Customize dialog box.

(2) Select the check boxes for the toolbars you want to display and modify.

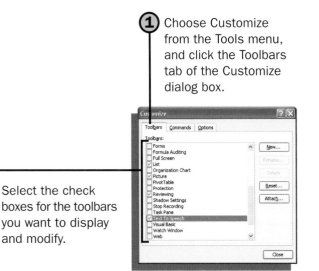

(4) Drag the button from one location to another. You can move buttons within one toolbar or among different toolbars. To copy instead of move a button, hold down the Ctrl key while dragging.

(3) Click a button that you want to move.

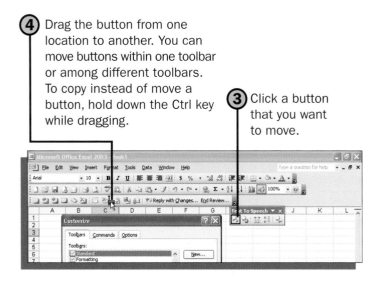

Move Menu Commands

① With the Customize dialog box still open and the Commands tab displayed, click a menu to open it.

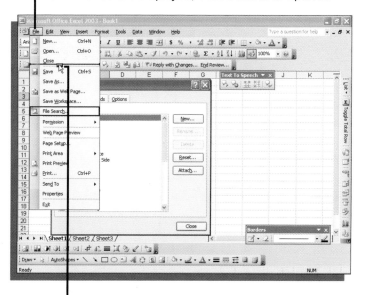

② Drag the menu item to the location you want. You can also move a command onto a different menu or onto a toolbar. To copy a menu item instead of moving it, hold down the Ctrl key as you drag the item.

> **SEE ALSO: For information about adding any items that aren't displayed on the toolbars or menus you're currently using, see "Customizing Toolbars and Menus" on page 380.**

Move Shortcut Menu Commands

① In Word, PowerPoint, or Access, open the Customize dialog box if it isn't already open, click the Toolbars tab, and select the Shortcut Menus check box.

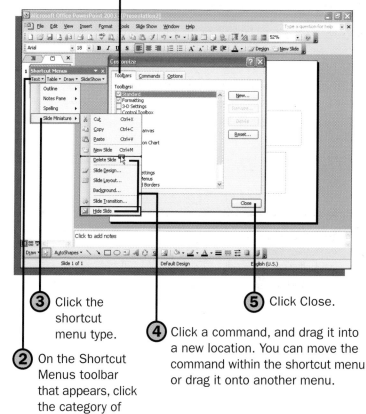

③ Click the shortcut menu type.

② On the Shortcut Menus toolbar that appears, click the category of shortcut menu.

⑤ Click Close.

④ Click a command, and drag it into a new location. You can move the command within the shortcut menu or drag it onto another menu.

Customizing Toolbars and Menus

Why keep your Office programs cluttered up with all sorts of items you never use? And, by the same token, why keep your frequently used items stashed away where they're awkward and time-consuming to get to? You can create a sensible and efficient working environment by customizing your toolbars and menus, adding or removing buttons and commands to create just the balance you want.

Add or Remove Toolbar Buttons

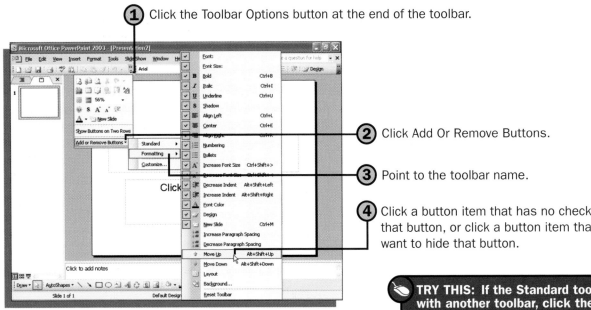

1 Click the Toolbar Options button at the end of the toolbar.

2 Click Add Or Remove Buttons.

3 Point to the toolbar name.

4 Click a button item that has no check box if you want to display that button, or click a button item that has a check box if you want to hide that button.

SEE ALSO: For information about moving existing toolbar buttons into different locations on the same toolbar or onto a different toolbar, see "Rearranging Toolbar Buttons and Menus" on page 378.

TRY THIS: If the Standard toolbar is sharing a line with another toolbar, click the Toolbar Options button, and choose Show Buttons On Two Rows from the drop-down menu to see all the buttons on the Standard toolbar. Click the Toolbar Options button, and add as many other toolbar buttons as you want to the Standard toolbar. Choose Customize from the Tools menu to display the Customize dialog box, and then move buttons around on the toolbar and/or add more commands to the toolbar. Close the Customize dialog box. Click the Toolbar Options button again, and click Reset Toolbar in the list to restore the Formatting toolbar to its original configuration.

Add Different Items to Toolbars or Menus

(1) With any toolbars that you want to modify displayed in the program window, choose Customize from the Tools menu, and click the Commands tab of the Customize dialog box.

(2) Click the category for the command you want to add to the toolbar, or click All Commands to see all the available commands.

(3) Locate the command you want to use.

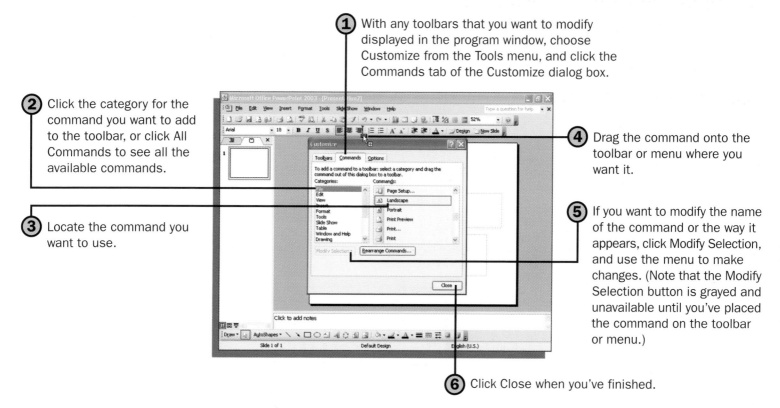

(4) Drag the command onto the toolbar or menu where you want it.

(5) If you want to modify the name of the command or the way it appears, click Modify Selection, and use the menu to make changes. (Note that the Modify Selection button is grayed and unavailable until you've placed the command on the toolbar or menu.)

(6) Click Close when you've finished.

TIP: You're not limited to "standard" commands. You can include macros on a menu or toolbar in the programs that support macros, and, in Word, you can include fonts, AutoText, and styles. In Word, you can also specify in which open template or document you want to save the changes you're going to make (specify Normal to make the changes available to all your documents).

TIP: To delete an item from a toolbar or a menu, drag the item off the toolbar or menu (but make sure you don't drag the item onto a different toolbar or menu).

SEE ALSO: For information about creating macros, see "Creating Your Own Commands" on page 382.

Creating Your Own Commands

If you often find yourself executing the same series of actions over and over again, you can simplify your work and save yourself a lot of time by creating a *macro*. In Word, Excel, and PowerPoint, you can create a macro simply by recording your steps. In Access, Publisher, Outlook, and FrontPage, you'll need to write the macro using the Visual Basic Editor, which is a procedure beyond the scope of this book.

> **TIP:** A macro name must begin with a letter and can be up to 80 characters long, but it can't contain any spaces or symbols. You can assign the macro to a toolbar button in Word or to a shortcut key combination in Word or Excel when you first create it, but you might want to wait to assign the macro until after you've completed it and it has proven its worth.

Set Up a Macro

(1) Click in the file where you want to execute the first of the repetitive actions.

(2) Point to Macro on the Tools menu, and choose Record New Macro from the submenu to display the Record Macro dialog box.

(3) Type a name for the macro, and specify where you want it to be stored. Type a description of what the macro does, and then click OK.

(4) In your file, execute the series of actions you want to record as a macro, using your keyboard to select text and move the insertion point. (Note that, with the exception of clicking a command, most mouse actions aren't recorded.)

(5) If you want to execute any actions in your program without recording them as part of the macro, click Pause Recording. Click Resume Recorder to resume recording your actions.

(6) When you've recorded all the actions that compose the macro, click Stop Recording.

(7) To test your new macro, point to Macro on the Tools menu, and choose Macros from the submenu. In the Macros dialog box, select the macro you just recorded, and click the Run button.

The Recorder mouse pointer reminds you that you're recording all actions.

Any commands you execute and all the settings in dialog boxes are recorded.

> **SEE ALSO:** For information about assigning a macro to a menu or toolbar, see "Customizing Toolbars and Menus" on pages 380–381.

Controlling Your Services

Your Office programs can provide you with a variety of background services, depending on the resources you have or want to use. For example, if you're always connected to the Internet, you can receive updated content directly from Microsoft Office Online. If you're using a shared workspace on a SharePoint Web site, you can specify how often you want to receive updates of your shared files. If you want, you can help Microsoft improve Office by participating in the Customer Experience Improvement Program. Note that when you make changes to the services in one program, those changes are made throughout all your Office programs.

Set the Service Options

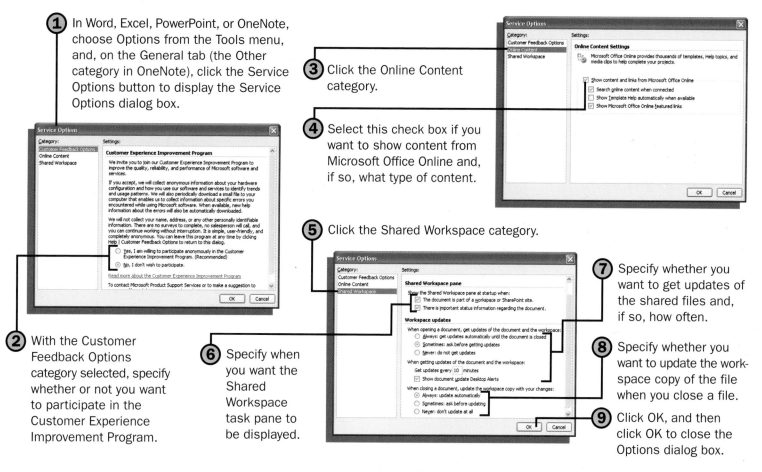

① In Word, Excel, PowerPoint, or OneNote, choose Options from the Tools menu, and, on the General tab (the Other category in OneNote), click the Service Options button to display the Service Options dialog box.

③ Click the Online Content category.

④ Select this check box if you want to show content from Microsoft Office Online and, if so, what type of content.

⑤ Click the Shared Workspace category.

② With the Customer Feedback Options category selected, specify whether or not you want to participate in the Customer Experience Improvement Program.

⑥ Specify when you want the Shared Workspace task pane to be displayed.

⑦ Specify whether you want to get updates of the shared files and, if so, how often.

⑧ Specify whether you want to update the workspace copy of the file when you close a file.

⑨ Click OK, and then click OK to close the Options dialog box.

Controlling the Office Assistant

Some people love their Office Assistant—that little animated character who hangs around on your Desktop waiting to give you advice and answer your questions. Others can't *stand* it, and still others don't even know it exists. Depending on how you feel about the Office Assistant, you can change the way it works, choose your favorite among different Assistants, or banish it forever if it drives you crazy.

> **TIP:** To remove the Assistant temporarily, right-click it, and choose Hide from the shortcut menu. If you do this several times, the Office Assistant will ask you if you want it to turn itself off permanently. Bye-bye!

Design Your Assistant

(1) If the Office Assistant isn't displayed, in Word, Excel, PowerPoint, Publisher, Access, FrontPage, or Outlook, choose Show The Office Assistant from the Help menu to display the Assistant.

(2) Right-click the Assistant, and choose Options from the shortcut menu to display the Office Assistant dialog box.

(4) Click the Gallery tab.

(3) Turn check boxes on or off to specify the way you want the Assistant to work.

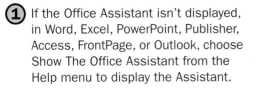

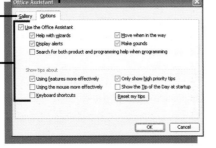

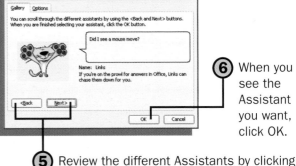

(6) When you see the Assistant you want, click OK.

(5) Review the different Assistants by clicking the Next and Back buttons.

> **TIP:** In a standard installation, only Clippit, the paperclip Office Assistant, is installed. The other Office Assistants are configured for installation on first use. If you decide to install an Office Assistant other than Clippit, you might find that you don't have adequate security permission to install it. If so, contact your network administrator.

> **SEE ALSO:** For information about installing the Office Assistant if it isn't already installed, see "Adding or Removing Office Components" on page 374.

23

Keeping Your Files Secure

No one would question the fact that e-mail and the Internet have put global communications at the fingertips of everyone who owns or works on a computer. You can send an e-mail message to the other side of the world and receive an instantaneous response. You can shop on line, ordering live lobsters from Maine and clothing from Hong Kong. Electronic communications have opened up the world to us. Unfortunately, they've also opened *us* up to the world, invading our privacy and destroying our sense of security. Identity theft is a huge problem. Our Inboxes are clogged with unwanted junk mail. How can we continue to make use of the benefits of e-mail and the Internet without exposing ourselves and our files to harm? This section of the book offers some practical solutions.

One of the simplest precautions you can take is to protect your files with a password, using various levels of protection that dictate the type of access you'll allow and to whom you'll grant it. As an added precaution, you can also specify that personal information be removed from your files. Another way to keep your files secure is to *encrypt* them so that only people who have the correct *digital ID* can read them. To protect your files from viruses and malicious macros, you can set the programs in the Microsoft Office System to screen out these nuisances by specifying a level of security that varies depending on how much or how little you trust certain sources. For the most powerful control, however, there's Information Rights Management, which gives you or a network administrator the ability to use Rights Management certificates to identify users and to restrict or permit access to all your files.

Protecting Your Files

Your files often contain business details or private personal information that you don't want just anyone to be able to read and/or modify. You can protect any such file by assigning it a password. When you require a password to open a file, you're encrypting the file to prevent unauthorized access by those who don't know the password—including anyone who might be trying to hack into the file. When you require a password to modify a file, other people can open and view the file, but they can't save it to the same location with the same file name. You can also make a few additional settings to remove tracked changes and any personal and proprietary information from the file.

CAUTION: Even though it's your own file, you won't be able to open it if you forget the password. Keep a copy of the password in a secure location!

TIP: Microsoft Office Access provides additional levels of protection beyond setting a password to limit individual access; among these is the ability to restrict access to entire groups. To enforce these added security settings, point to Security on the Tools menu, and, from the submenu, choose the type of security settings you want.

Protect a File

1 In Microsoft Office Word, Excel, or PowerPoint, choose Options from the Tools menu, and click the Security tab of the Options dialog box.

4 In Word or Excel, select this check box to advise anyone who opens the file to open it as a read-only document.

2 In Word, Excel, or PowerPoint, enter a password to restrict who can open this file.

3 In Word, Excel or PowerPoint, enter a different password to restrict who can make changes to the file and who can save it to the same location with the same name.

5 In Word, Excel, PowerPoint, or Publisher, select this check box if you want personal information that's normally stored in the file's Properties dialog box to be omitted. (In Access, click the General tab, and choose the same check box on that tab.)

6 In Word, select this check box if you want to make sure that you don't post a file with any tracked changes or comments still visible.

7 Click OK. If you entered any passwords, you'll be prompted to reenter them to confirm them. Do so, and then click OK.

Verifying a File by Using a Signature

Are you sure that file was really sent to you by the person whose name appears on it, and, if it was, how do you know whether anyone else has modified it? You can ensure that your colleagues won't have to ask these same paranoid questions about any files you send them because, when you digitally sign your own files, their origin can be verified by the recipients.

Digitally Sign a File

① With your Word, Excel, or PowerPoint file completed and saved, choose Options from the Tools menu, and, on the Security tab of the Options dialog box, click the Digital Signatures button to display the Digital Signature dialog box. (In InfoPath, with your form completed, click the Digital Signatures button on the Standard toolbar.)

TIP: You must have a *digital certificate* to digitally sign a file. If you don't already have one, click the Help button in the Digital Signature dialog box for information about obtaining a digital certificate.

TIP: A file that has been digitally signed displays the word "Signed" in the program's title bar. To view the signature, open the Digital Signature dialog box, select the signature, and click View Certificate. (In Word, you can also double-click the Digital Signature icon on the status bar.)

② Click Add.

③ Click the signature you want to use.

④ Click OK. Click OK twice more to close the dialog boxes, and then close the file without saving it again.

SEE ALSO: For information about using a digital certificate to sign and encrypt your e-mail messages, see "Encrypting Your E-Mail" on page 394.

Protecting Your System from Malicious Macros

With computer viruses and counterfeit files commonplace, you can take a few steps to protect yourself. One of the greatest vulnerabilities in Word, Excel, Access, PowerPoint, Publisher, and Outlook is for a file to contain a malicious macro. Fortunately, these Office programs can screen out macros that come from unidentified sources.

Set the Macro Security

(1) Point to Macros on the Tools menu, and choose Security from the submenu to display the Security dialog box.

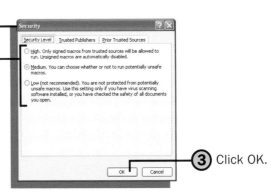

(2) On the Security Level tab, click one of the following options:

- High to disable all macros except those that have been digitally signed by a trusted source

- Medium if your files might contain any macros that were created by you or your coworkers and that have not been digitally signed

- Low only if you're certain that all your macros are safe, if you have an updated virus program installed, or if you have problems with your files and macros when you use either the High or Medium security setting

(3) Click OK.

> **(!) TIP: If you download a file that contains macros from a trusted source and the macros have been digitally signed, a Security Warning dialog box appears. If you're sure you can trust the source of the file, select the Always Trust Macros From This Publisher check box before you click the Enable Macros button. If for some reason you decide that you don't want to trust that source in the future, open the Security dialog box, and, on the Trusted Publishers tab, remove the source from the list.**

(4) If you specified Medium security, and you open a file that contains unsigned macros, in the Security Warning dialog box that appears, click Disable Macros if you're uncertain about the source or the security of a file or template. Click Enable Macros if you're sure of the source of the file and feel confident that all the macros are safe.

What Is Information Rights Management?

Information Rights Management—IRM to its friends—is a service that gives you powerful control over what happens to your Word documents, Excel workbooks, PowerPoint presentation files, and/or Outlook e-mail messages. Without specific and verified permission, a person can't open, read, or forward a file; with permission, that person might be limited to just reading the file, or might be granted the right to edit, save, and print the file. IRM is designed to work with Office 2003 and later programs, but, if you have an earlier version of Office, you can use Microsoft Internet Explorer, with the Rights Management Add-on for Internet Explorer installed, to review a protected file.

The power of IRM is its ability to identify and to assign different levels of access to individual users through the use of secure Rights Management (RM) certificates. IRM is composed of two parts—an IRM server, which issues the RM certificates, and an IRM client on each computer, which uses the RM certificate to identify the user and permit access to the file. Where the IRM server resides depends on your setup: Your company's network might have its own IRM server, or you might need to use a server from an Internet certificate provider. Fortunately, the IRM client can usually detect whether there's an IRM server available, and, if there isn't, can help you obtain your certificate.

Another aspect of IRM is that it can be customized by a network administrator. For example, the basic permissions available are those that restrict access to a file and prohibit its distribution. However, an administrator can add up to 20 customized permissions that are designed to work for the company. For example, the administrator can design a permission that allows only members of the technical team to change a file and/or only supervisors to read a file. These types of custom permissions are added to the Permissions submenu of the File menu in Word, Excel, PowerPoint, and Outlook.

When you open a file that has restricted permissions, you'll find that all the menu commands and toolbar buttons for the actions you don't have permission to do—copy or print, for example—are grayed and unavailable, as shown in the graphic below.

Using IRM, you can be confident that your files are as secure as they can be even in a worst-case scenario: a file placed in the wrong folder on the network, a disk containing sensitive information lost, a confidential file e-mailed and then forwarded around the globe. The list of possibilities is endless and frightening. But you don't need to worry about the consequences if any of these misfortunes occur: Only those people listed as having specific permissions, and producing the RM certificates to verify that they are indeed who they say they are, can access your files.

Restricting File Access

When you use Information Rights Management (IRM) with Word, Excel, or PowerPoint files, or with your Outlook e-mail messages, you can authorize certain individuals to view or edit your files and can specify exactly what they're allowed to do. Using full protection, you can prevent someone from changing a file, from copying or printing any of the file's content, and from forwarding an e-mail message. You need to have the IRM client installed on your computer and you need access to an IRM server to download the Rights Management (RM) certificate that verifies your identity.

> **TIP:** If you don't have an IRM client installed on your computer, the first time you click the Permission button or choose a type of permission from the Permission submenu of the File menu, you'll be prompted to install the client. If you don't have an RM certificate, you'll be prompted to obtain one. If you have more than one RM certificate, the Select User dialog box will appear when you click the Permission button. Select the RM certificate you want to use to identify yourself as the owner of the file, and click OK.

Restrict Access to a File

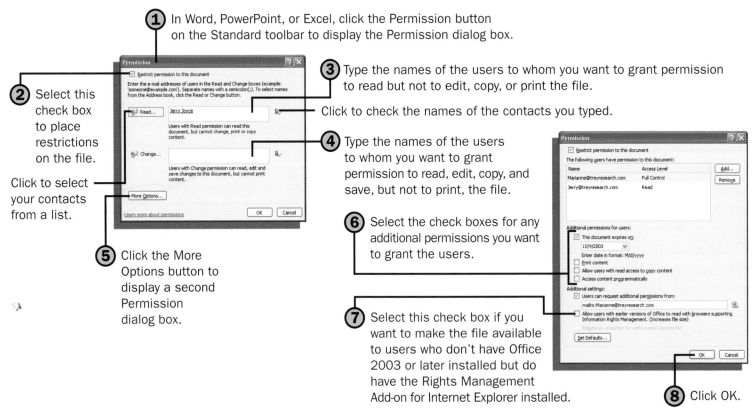

(1) In Word, PowerPoint, or Excel, click the Permission button on the Standard toolbar to display the Permission dialog box.

(2) Select this check box to place restrictions on the file.

Click to select your contacts from a list.

(3) Type the names of the users to whom you want to grant permission to read but not to edit, copy, or print the file.

Click to check the names of the contacts you typed.

(4) Type the names of the users to whom you want to grant permission to read, edit, copy, and save, but not to print, the file.

(5) Click the More Options button to display a second Permission dialog box.

(6) Select the check boxes for any additional permissions you want to grant the users.

(7) Select this check box if you want to make the file available to users who don't have Office 2003 or later installed but do have the Rights Management Add-on for Internet Explorer installed.

(8) Click OK.

Use a Restricted File

1 Open the file that's restricted, and, if necessary, connect to your IRM server to verify your certificate.

TIP: If the Shared Workspace task pane isn't visible, choose Task Pane from the View menu (or press Ctrl+F1) to open the task pane.

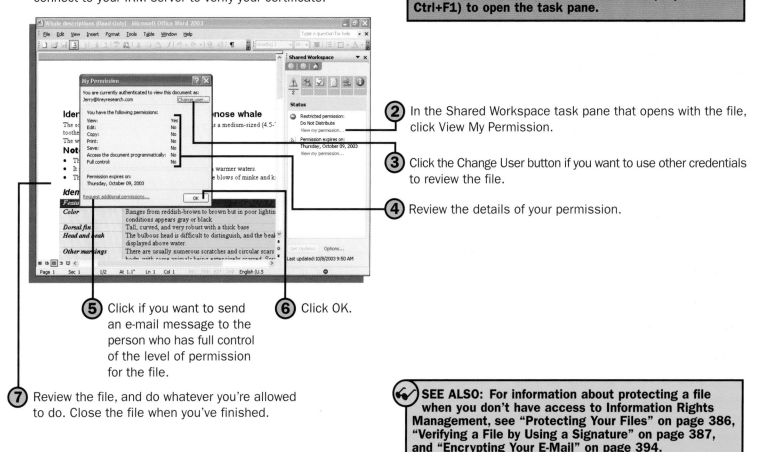

2 In the Shared Workspace task pane that opens with the file, click View My Permission.

3 Click the Change User button if you want to use other credentials to review the file.

4 Review the details of your permission.

5 Click if you want to send an e-mail message to the person who has full control of the level of permission for the file.

6 Click OK.

7 Review the file, and do whatever you're allowed to do. Close the file when you've finished.

SEE ALSO: For information about protecting a file when you don't have access to Information Rights Management, see "Protecting Your Files" on page 386, "Verifying a File by Using a Signature" on page 387, and "Encrypting Your E-Mail" on page 394.

For information about restricted rights and Information Rights Management, see "What Is Information Rights Management?" on page 389.

Limiting E-Mail Snooping

One of the most insidious ways mass mailers and spammers verify that your e-mail address is valid is to include a picture or a sound clip that they hope you'll download from a Web server. When your computer accesses the site that contains the picture or sound clip, your e-mail address is automatically verified. You can guard against this invasion of your privacy by having Outlook selectively prevent automatic downloading of pictures in any e-mail that doesn't come from a known and trusted source.

Set Your Download Options

(1) In Outlook, choose Options from the Tools menu, and, on the Security tab, click the Change Automatic Download Settings button to display the Automatic Picture Download Settings dialog box.

(2) Select this check box to prevent automatic downloading of pictures.

(3) Select this check box to permit automatic downloading of pictures from those you've added to your Safe Senders and Safe Recipients lists.

(4) Select this check box to permit downloads from Web sites that you've added to your Trusted Zone list.

(5) Select this check box to prevent automatic downloading of pictures in a message or file that you're editing, forwarding, or replying to.

(6) Click OK, and then click OK again.

Automatic Picture Download Settings

You can control whether Outlook automatically downloads and displays pictures when you open an HTML e-mail message.

Blocking pictures in e-mail messages can help protect your privacy. Pictures in HTML e-mail can require Outlook to download the pictures from a server. Communicating to an external server in this way can verify to the sender that your e-mail address is valid, possibly making you the target of more junk mailings.

☑ Don't download pictures or other content automatically in HTML e-mail
☑ Permit downloads in e-mail messages from senders and to recipients defined in the Safe Senders and Safe Recipients Lists used by the Junk E-mail filter
☑ Permit downloads from Web sites in this security zone: Trusted Zone
☑ Warn me before downloading content when editing, forwarding, or replying to e-mail

[OK]   [Cancel]

> ⚠ **TIP: If you do want to download and view the pictures that Outlook blocked in an e-mail message, in the message header area, click the message that tells you the pictures were blocked (or right-click any one of the placeholders for the blocked pictures), and choose Download Pictures from the shortcut menu that appears. You can also use this shortcut menu to add to your Safe Senders list the name of the sender of the message or the computer domain from which the message was sent.**

Name Your Trusted Contacts

1 In Outlook, point to Junk E-Mail on the Actions menu, and choose Junk E-Mail Options from the submenu to display the Junk E-Mail Options dialog box.

2 On the Options tab, select the protection level you want.

5 On the Safe Recipients tab, add e-mail addresses and domain names of people or locations you send mail to and expect replies from.

6 On the Blocked Senders tab, add e-mail addresses and domain names of people and locations you don't want to receive mail from.

3 On the Safe Senders tab, click the Add button, and enter the e-mail addresses or domain names from which you receive mail that you can always trust.

7 Click OK.

4 Select this check box if you want to trust any e-mail you receive from anyone in your Contacts list.

> **!** **TIP:** As its name implies, you can use the Junk E-Mail Options dialog box for more than just developing a Safe Senders list. By enabling a high level of junk e-mail protection, Outlook examines your incoming messages for junk e-mail content and places any suspect messages in the Junk E-Mail folder. You should periodically examine the contents of this folder to make sure that no important messages have been mistakenly classified as junk e-mail.

> **!** **TIP:** To quickly add a person to the Safe Senders, Safe Recipients, or Blocked Senders list, right-click a message from that person, point to Junk E-Mail on the shortcut menu, and, from the submenu, choose which list you want to add that person to.

Encrypting Your E-Mail

If you think that an e-mail message is a secure communication limited to the sender and receiver, you're living dangerously! Most e-mail is sent as text that can easily be intercepted and even modified as it travels through the maze of servers on the Internet. To prevent strangers from snooping through your e-mail, you can encrypt your messages using the digital ID key that belongs to the intended recipient, thus ensuring that only that person can decrypt and read the message. The digital ID key is part of a digital ID certificate; the certificate is used to verify that you are who you say you are.

Install and Use the Digital ID

(1) In Outlook, choose Options from the Tools menu, and, on the Security tab, click the Settings button to display the Change Security Settings dialog box.

(2) Type a name for the security setting.

(3) Click Choose, and, in the Select Certificate dialog box, select an existing certificate that you've been issued. Click OK. If you need to use a different certificate for encryption, click Change to display the Select Certificate dialog box, select the certificate to be used for encryption, and click OK.

(5) Click OK.

(4) Select this check box to make sure that anyone who receives your signed message also receives your certificate or certificates.

> **! TIP:** If you don't have your own digital ID, click the Get A Digital ID button on the Security tab of the Options dialog box, and use one of the certificate services listed in the Web page that appears.

(6) Swap digital IDs and certificates with the person with whom you want to exchange encrypted messages. To do so, create an e-mail message, click the Digitally Sign button on the E-Mail toolbar (or on the Standard toolbar if you're not using Word as your e-mail editor), and then send the message to that person. Request that he or she reply and provide a digital ID.

(7) When you receive a reply, right-click your contact's name in the message, and choose Add To Outlook Contacts from the shortcut menu to add that person's address and digital ID to your Contacts list. Request that your contact do the same.

(8) Create another message, click the Encrypt Message button, and send the message to those people whose digital IDs you've stored in your Contacts list. They'll be the only people who can read your messages.

Index

AutoPick feature, 172
AutoPreview feature, 150, 154
AutoReport feature, 196
AutoShapes
  diagrams, 312
  formatting, 319
  inserting, 80, 239, 309, 310–311
AutoSum feature, 120
AutoText feature, 59, 72–73, 158, 381
AutoThumbnail feature, 251, 254
axes, 89, 137, 138, 140–141, 146

B

background colors or pictures
  Calendar Web sites, 266
  diagrams, 312
  e-mail, 160
  Publisher files, 227
  slides, 207
  transparency of, 254, 316
  worksheets, 104
background services, 383
backslash (\), 9
back-to-back printing, 36, 64
banners on Web pages, 244, 248, 255
baseline guides, 236
BCC lines, 153
binding printed documents, 36, 37
black-and-white pictures, 316
blacking out screens for presentations, 221
blank files or forms
  data-access pages, 263
  InfoPath, 276
  Publisher, 225
  side notes, 284
  Web pages, 256, 260
  Word, 8, 260
blank lines before paragraphs, 38
bleeds, 242
blind copies of e-mail, 153

blocking
  e-mail senders, 393
  pictures in e-mail, 392–393
blue down arrows, 127
blue squiggles under words, 24, 370
bold text, 17, 38, 101
bookmarks on Web pages, 252
borders
  conditional formatting, 277
  drawing canvas, 309
  paragraph animation, 17
  paragraph styles, 32, 54
  red outlines in InfoPath, 274
  tables, 49, 68, 70, 258
  Web page thumbnails, 251
  worksheets and cells, 93, 104
bound documents, 36, 37
breaking
  documents into chapters, 78
  lines, 368, 369
  links between text boxes, 231
  pages, 368
brightness, 209, 316, 317
broadcasting slide shows, 222
browsers, 244, 249, 262, 309, 319
bulleted lists
  OneNote, 287
  Word, 32, 33, 48–49, 54, 71
Business Data Import/Export Wizard, 358
Business Manager, 358–360
buttons
  on toolbars. *See* toolbars and toolbar buttons
  on Web pages, 255

C

calculations in Access, 200
calculations in Excel
  addition, 120
  equations, 313
  formulas, 116, 121, 125
  functions, 122–123

operators, 118–119
subtotals, 128
Calendar (Outlook), 164
  appointments, 166
  availability, 167, 171
  e-mail information, 167
  importing or exporting, 339
  meetings, 172–173
  public folder access, 182
  saving as Web pages, 266
  scheduling with, 166–167, 171
  sharing, 168–169
  task assignments, 178
  unshared copies, 169
calendars in InfoPath, 272
cameras, digital, 209, 234, 320
capitalization, 323
captions, 195, 209, 255, 320
caret (^), 118
catalogs, creating, 303
CC field, 152
CDs, copying slide presentations to, 222
cell diagonals in Publisher tables, 233
cell notation and references, 113, 116–117
  AutoFill and, 121
  mixing formats in formulas, 119
  naming cells, 129
  problems in formulas, 124
cells (Excel), 88
  adjusting height and width, 105
  deleting contents, 101
  formatting, 93
  formulas in, 96
  naming, 116, 129
  references. *See* cell notation and references
  selecting, 93
cells (FrontPage), 258
cells (InfoPath), 277
cells (Word), 67, 68, 70
centering text, 38
certificates, 387, 389, 390, 394
chapter divisions in documents, 78
character pairs, 232

converting
  documents to Web pages, 260
  faxes to text documents, 326
  footnotes or endnotes, 86
  handwriting to text, 285, 332
  lists to standard Excel data, 115
  picture color or format, 316, 318
  relative cell references to absolute, 121
  scanned images to text, 325
  text to Word tables, 66
  text to WordArt, 306
copying
  AutoFill feature, 99
  charts, 147
  content in Office files, 18–19
  data, 133, 300–303
  e-mail appointments into Calendar, 167
  formatting in styles, 31, 54
  InfoPath forms, 276
  OneNote information, 288, 289
  read-only documents, 343
  rights-management permissions and,
    389, 390
  slides or presentations, 217, 222, 297
  text, 41, 230, 296, 298–299
  toolbar buttons, 378
  translated text, 324
  Word tables into Excel, 295
  worksheet data, 98–99, 292–295, 304
  worksheet formatting or comments, 99
correcting
  handwriting recognition errors, 332
  speech recognition errors, 329, 330
  spelling. *See* spelling, correcting
  text automatically, 322–323
cover sheets for faxes, 162
cropping
  cells in FrontPage tables, 258
  drawing canvas, 309
  objects, 317, 319
currency symbols, 20, 94, 327
customizing
  AutoCorrect feature, 322–323

databases, 187, 189
forms, 276
interface, 26–27, 373
Office Clipboard, 19
reports, 197
rights-management permissions, 389
slide shows, 213, 219
styles, 32
tables, 191
templates, 56–57
toolbars and menus, 376, 378–381
Web pages and sites, 250, 251, 337, 342
cutting
  content in Office files, 18–19
  data in Excel, 98–99
  text in Word, 41

D

dashed lines, 311
data
  arguments for functions, 123
  binding, 273
  charting, 136–137, 143
  compared with database design, 184
  editing, 96–97
  entering, 90, 192–193
  filtering, 127
  formatting, 101
  highlighting specifics, 132
  importing, 133, 134
  interactive, in Web pages, 261
  Journal activities, 181
  linked to original files, 292–294, 297, 298
  lists in worksheets, 114–115
  merging from forms, 278
  PivotTables, 130–131
  points, 92
  records, 185
  relationships in worksheets, 92
  replacing, 96
  selecting noncontiguous, 136

series. *See* data series
sorting, 126
sources. *See* data sources
data-access pages, 185, 263
data binding, 273
Data Connection Wizard, 263
data points, 92
data records, 185
data series
  charting, 89, 137, 140
  error bars, 145
  order of, 142
  trendlines for, 144
  in worksheets, 102
Data Source Setup Wizard, 276
data sources, 60
  connecting to databases, 263
  mail merging, 62, 302, 303
  online services as, 134
  sorting, 60–61
  updating for charts, 143
  worksheet data as, 304
  XML schemas as, 276
Database Wizard, 188–189
databases, 276, 358. *See also* Access databases
dates
  automatic insertion, 47
  automatic updating, 59
  Date Picker in InfoPath, 272
  ranges on Calendar Web sites, 266
  series of, in worksheets, 102
  task-related, 176
default file locations, 375
defining
  styles, 54–55
  words, 20
deleting
  AutoText entries, 73
  buttons or commands, 378, 380, 381
  data, 143, 263, 285, 339
  e-mail accounts, 151
  fields, 191, 195, 197
  file property information, 386

FrontPage, 6, 244–245
  Accessibility feature, 370
  adding pages to sites, 256
  customizing Web sites, 250
  document-control feature, 250
  double-checking for errors, 268–269
  drawing canvas, 309
  editing Web pages, 248–249, 251
  hotspot hyperlinks, 253
  HTML code in, 267
  hyperlinks, 252
  new Web sites, 8, 246–247
  pictures, 254–255, 308, 310–311, 316–317
  publishing sites, 270
  SharePoint Web sites, 259
  table layout, 258
  Thesaurus feature, 372
  views, 245
  Web components or WebBots, 252, 257
  wizards, 246
  WordArt, 306–307
  wrapping text around pictures, 315
frozen rows or columns in Excel, 111
FTP file transfers, 157, 270
full menus, 376
functions, 122–123, 128

G

GIF files, 251, 254
grammar checking, 24, 158, 366–367
graphics
  alternative text for Web browsers, 309
  AutoShapes. *See* AutoShapes
  backgrounds, 81, 160, 207, 266
  charts as, 294
  Clip Organizer, 320
  ClipArt, 207, 224, 234, 308
  contrast and brightness, 209
  cropping, 317
  diagrams, 312
  drawing, 80–81, 309, 334

  editing, 316–317
  in e-mail, 160, 392–393
  equations as, 313
  file formats, 251, 318
  formatting, 81
  on forms, 195
  frequently used items, 72–73
  hyperlinks on, 253
  importing with Word content, 298
  inserting, 70, 104, 207, 234, 254–255, 314
  optimization, 318
  page banners, 255
  photo albums, 209
  Photo Gallery feature, 255
  placeholders, 226, 234
  positioning in Word, 84–85
  previewing, 314
  in publications, 226, 234
  reducing file size of, 318
  in reports, 197
  rotating, 85
  in slide presentations, 207, 209, 215
  in tables, 70
  thumbnails of, 314
  transparency, 254, 316, 319
  in Web pages, 248, 251, 254–255, 266
  WordArt, 306–307
  in worksheets, 104
  wrapping text around, 27, 81, 84–85, 239, 315
grayed interface items, 13, 319
grayscale pictures, 316
green squiggles under words, 24, 366
gridlines
  in charts, 137
  in FrontPage, 251
  grid and guides in Publisher, 227, 236
  structure of Excel, 92
  in tables, 70
group members. *See* team members
grouping
  data in reports, 196, 197
  mail-merge output, 60

  objects, 235, 238, 311
  ungrouping, 238
guides, page, 236
gutters, 36, 37

H

handouts, 204, 216
handwriting recognition, 284, 285, 332–333
headers, 77
  chapter headings, 78
  e-mail, 159
  pages in OneNote, 283
  publications, 227
  worksheets, 109
headings
  applying, 74–75, 296
  keeping with paragraphs, 368
  keyboard shortcuts, 38
  numbering, 76
  promoting and demoting, 82
  reorganizing documents, 82–83
height
  cells in tables, 70
  charts, 146
  objects, 224, 319
  pictures, 317
  rows in worksheets, 105
Help system, 21, 240, 384
hidden toolbar buttons, 377, 380
hiding
  formulas, 125
  Office Assistant, 21, 384
  rows or columns in worksheets, 103, 347
  slides, 211
  task panes, 14
  tracked changes, 371
  worksheets, 107, 347
highlighting
  data in Excel, 132
  hotspot hyperlinks, 253
Home, returning to in task panes, 14

J

Journal (Outlook), 180
JPG files, 251
junk e-mail options, 393
justified paragraphs, 38

K

kerning, 232
keyboard shortcuts. *See also* quick shortcuts
    AutoCorrect feature, 322
    breaking columns, 368
    field properties in Access, 191
    hyphenation, 365
    macros, 382
    on menus, 12
    moving and editing in Excel, 97
    moving around in Word tables, 66
    moving or copying text, 41
    opening and closing task panes, 14
    opening Help, 21
    running shows in PowerPoint, 220
    saving files, 9
    On Screen Symbol Keyboard, 327
    selecting and formatting in Word, 38
    selecting text, 40
    special characters, 327
    for styles, 54
keys in databases, 185, 190, 202
keywords, 308, 320

L

labels. *See also* mail merge
    mailing, 53
    in worksheets or charts, 109, 131, 137, 138
landscape orientation, 36, 108, 225
languages, 54, 324, 331, 362–363
layers of objects on pages, 81, 238, 254

layers of toolbars, 377
layout grids and guides in Publisher, 227, 236
layout tables, 258, 277
learning speech recognition from documents, 330
left indents, 32
left-aligned text, 38
left-hand pages, 37, 64, 77
Letter Wizard, 50
letterhead, 36, 50
letters, 50–51, 52, 62–63, 64. *See also* mail merge
line breaks, 368, 369
line colors, 311, 319
line spacing, 32, 38
lines
    numbering, 76
    purplish-red dotted, 15
lining up. *See* alignment
link bars, 244
links and linking. *See also* hyperlinks
    Excel data to original file, 292, 293, 294, 304
    opening data to edit, 293
    tables of contents, 79
    text boxes in Publisher, 230–231
    updating for printing, 371
list styles, 48–49
lists
    creating in Word, 33
    Excel lists, 102, 114–115
    OneNote bulleted or numbered lists, 287
    organizing information in, 71
    recent files, 10
    SharePoint Web-site properties, 259
    unnumbered paragraphs in, 33
    Word styles, 32, 48–49, 54
local copies of files, 245, 261, 343
locations for files
    objects, 224
    saving files, 9, 375
    searching, 11

templates, 48, 57
    Web-site files, 246
locations for public folders, 182
logging
    activities in Journal, 180
    Web-site changes, 270
logical tests in Excel, 123, 132

M

macros, 49, 185, 381, 382, 388. *See also* viruses
magnifying view of pages, 228
Mail and Catalog Merge Wizard, 302, 303
mail folders, 152
mail merge, 60–61, 302, 303, 360
Mail Merge Wizard, 61, 302
mailing addresses. *See* addresses
mailing labels, 53. *See also* mail merge
manually taking control
    flowing text in Publisher, 229, 231
    hyphenating words, 365
    sending or receiving e-mail, 153, 154
    updating Web data, 133
mapping Web sites, 269
margins
    cells in FrontPage tables, 258
    guides in publications, 236
    hyphenation and, 365
    markers in Word, 26
    master pages for publications, 227
    objects, 319
    printer issues, 371
    setting up in Word, 36, 37
    text boxes in publications, 229
    worksheets, 108
marking formatting inconsistencies, 370
markup, displaying, 354, 355, 356
master documents, 60
master pages, 227
master-slide formatting, 210
matching formatting for pasted items, 18

navigating
  in databases, 189
  in Excel cells, 90
  in InfoPath, 274
  in Web sites, 245, 256, 262, 264
.NET passports, 170
network permissions, 389
network places, adding, 337
new files, 8–9, 10, 46
next slide, advancing to, 220, 221
next text box, displaying, 231
nonbreaking hyphens, 365, 369
nonbreaking spaces, 369
nonlinear series in Excel, 102
non-Office programs, 19
non-scrolling rows or columns in Excel, 111
notebooks in OneNote, 282
notes
  approaches to OneNote, 281
  classifying with flags, 288
  on Excel worksheets, 95
  formatting in OneNote, 287
  in Outlook, 164–165, 179
  for presentations, 204, 216
  in public folders, 182
  recording audio, 286
  sending from OneNote in e-mail, 290
  typing in OneNote, 283
Notes (Outlook), 164–165, 179
notes masters in PowerPoint, 216
nudging in Publisher, 237
number of copies to print, 23, 64, 242
numbered lists
  creating, 33, 287
  organizing information in, 71
  styles, 32, 48–49, 54
  unnumbered paragraphs in, 33
numbering
  cells consecutively, 102
  footnotes, 86
  headings or lines in documents, 76
  pages, 77, 78, 108
  worksheets, 108

numbers
  formatting, 94
  series of, 102
  spoken, 328

O

objects
  AutoShapes, 310–311
  charts. *See* charts
  Clip Organizer, 320
  ClipArt, 224
  Design Gallery, 235
  diagrams, 312
  editing, 316–317
  equations, 313
  formatting, 319
  importing with Word content, 298
  managing, 320
  pasted into other programs, 294
  picture-frame, 224, 234
  pictures. *See* graphics
  properties in FrontPage, 248
  rearranging on pages, 236–237
  snapping to guides, 236
  sound files, 320
  stacking and grouping, 238
  video files, 320
  on Web pages, 248
  WordArt, 224, 306–307
  wrapping text around. *See* wrapping text
odd-numbered pages, 37, 64, 77
Office
  adding or removing components, 374
  background services, 383
  closing files, 9
  correcting spelling, 24
  creating new files, 8–9
  customizing, 373, 380–381
  digital signatures, 387
  encryption, 394
  exporting to non-Office programs, 19

  finding files, 11
  formatting text, 16–17
  Help system, 21
  Information Rights Management, 389–391
  interface, 5, 7, 373
  interoperability of programs and data, 291
  macros, 382, 388
  menus and toolbars, 12–13, 376–381
  moving or copying content, 18–19
  naming files, 9
  new features, 4
  Office Assistant, 384
  printing files, 22–23
  programs in, 6–7
  researching words and phrases, 20
  saving files, 9
  security, 385
  smart tags, 15
  starting programs, 8
  task panes, 14
Office Assistant, 21, 384
Office Clipboard, 18–19, 41
Office Document Scanning, 325, 326
Office Internet Free/Busy Service, 170, 171
Office Online Web site, 21, 383
Office Picture Manager, 314, 316
Office Tools, 6
On Screen Symbol Keyboard, 327
OneNote, 6, 281, 282
  classifying with flags, 288
  drawing notes, 285
  formatting notes, 287
  inserting pictures, 314
  recording audio in, 286
  sending notes as e-mail, 290
  side notes, 284
  task panes, 14
  transferring information from, 289
  typing notes, 283
Online Broadcast tools, 222
online collaboration about files, 348–349
online e-mail senders, 150
online text effects, 17

running heads, 77, 78, 109, 227
running slide shows, 214, 218, 220, 221, 262

S

safe senders and recipients, designating, 392
saving, 9
  Access reports, 197
  annotations on slide shows, 220
  attachments, 157
  chart designs, 148
  contact information, 174
  data for other programs, 300–303, 304
  default file formats, 375
  default file locations, 375
  to document libraries, 337
  files as Web pages, 260, 261, 262, 264, 266
  forms, 263, 275, 276
  frequently used text or items, 72
  inline discussions in Word documents, 349
  meeting information, 173
  notes, 179, 283
  opening saved files, 10
  preventing with rights management, 390
  read-only documents, 343
  signatures, 161
  smart tags, 15
  templates, 55, 56, 58–59
  Web pages with pictures, 254
  workspaces, 112
scales on charts, 89, 138, 140, 201
scaling. See resizing; scales on charts
scanning pictures or text, 209, 234, 320, 325
schedules, 166–167, 177, 266
schemas, 276, 280
schemes, animation, 212
screen fonts, 371
screens. See monitors
ScreenTips
  displaying, 13, 26, 32, 376
  hyperlinks, 252, 253
  toolbar button names, 247

scripts for presentations, 204, 216
scroll bars, 27
sections in documents, 78, 83
security, 385
  blocking pictures in e-mail, 392–393
  databases, 187
  encrypting e-mail, 394
  file protection, 346, 386
  Information Rights Management, 389, 390–391
  macro protection, 388
  template protection, 56, 276
  workbook protection, 347, 350, 353
selected text
  deleting or editing, 28
  printing, 23, 64
selecting
  cells in Excel, 93, 97, 120
  entire worksheets, 104
  multiple objects, 238
  multiple pictures, 318
  names for distribution lists, 175
  noncontinuous data in Excel, 136
  selection rectangles, 238
  table text, 66
  text, 40, 249, 284
  by vocal command, 331
semicolon (;), 152
sender information
  in letters, 50
  online status, 150, 154
sending
  attachments, 156–157
  e-mail, 152–153
  files as e-mail body content, 159
  files for review, 357
  InfoPath forms in e-mail, 275
  instant messages, 154
  OneNote information as e-mail, 290
  Publisher files as e-mail, 241
servers. See also SharePoint Services
  e-mail accounts, 151
  host servers, 250, 265, 270

  Information Rights Management, 389, 390
  Web server settings, 250
service providers. See Internet service providers; SharePoint Services
services, background, 383
shading. See colors and fill effects
shadows, 307, 311
shared Calendars, 166, 167, 168–169
shared data between programs, 291
  Access data, 300, 301, 302, 303
  Excel data, 292, 293, 294, 304
  presentations, 297
  Word content, 298, 299
shared files. See also SharePoint Services
  controlling changes made, 346, 347
  notes, 179
  OneNote pages, 290
  templates, 56
  workbooks, 345, 350
  working on simultaneously, 343
shared folders, 182, 270
shared Journal activities, 181
shared templates, 56
shared workspaces, 340–341
SharePoint Services, 6, 336
  comparing documents, 344
  copying InfoPath forms from, 276
  discussion boards, 348–349
  information, events, and contacts, 339
  linking to review files, 350
  managing sites, 342
  opening shared files, 338
  receiving updates, 383
  as resource for Web pages, 251
  shared workspaces, 340–341
  sharing files, 290, 337, 343
  templates on Team Web sites, 46
  Web sites, 259
shortcut menus, 12, 13, 24, 379
shortcuts. See keyboard shortcuts; quick shortcuts

Get a **Free**
e-mail newsletter, updates, special offers, links to related books, and more when you
register online!

Register your Microsoft Press® title on our Web site and you'll get a FREE subscription to our e-mail newsletter, *Microsoft Press Book Connections*. You'll find out about newly released and upcoming books and learning tools, online events, software downloads, special offers and coupons for Microsoft Press customers, and information about major Microsoft® product releases. You can also read useful additional information about all the titles we publish, such as detailed book descriptions, tables of contents and indexes, sample chapters, links to related books and book series, author biographies, and reviews by other customers.

Registration is easy. Just visit this Web page and fill in your information:

http://www.microsoft.com/mspress/register

Microsoft®

- -